SIDELINES ™

BEHIND THE SCENES
OF AMERICA'S FAVORITE SPORT

Edited by Richard Kucner

Designed by Steve Beshara

Cadmus

Communications

Corporation

SIDELINES™

BEHIND THE SCENES
OF AMERICA'S FAVORITE SPORT

COPYRIGHT 1992
CADMUS COMMUNICATIONS, INC.

Published by Cadmus Marketing, Inc.
5516 Falmouth Street
Richmond, VA 23262-7367

Licensed by NFL Properties, Inc.

ISBN: 0-962-9648-2-4
Library of Congress Catalog Card Number: 92-074613
Manufactured in the United States of America.
First printing October, 1992.

Developer/Director: Ben Higgs
General Management: Don Remley, Cadmus Marketing, Inc.
Project Management: Don Fish, Tri-Pro, Inc.
Editor: Richard Kucner
Design: Steve Beshara, Beshara Associates, Inc.
Production: Don McClain, Kurt Morton
Editorial Assistant: Leona Sevick

ACKNOWLEDGEMENT

For generous help in the development of this book,
special thanks are due to the following at NFL Properties, Inc.:
John Wiebusch, *Vice President/Editor in Chief*; Tom Richardson, *Publishing Director*;
Jim Perry, *Associate Editor*; Tom Barnidge, *Senior Editor*; Paul Spinelli, *Director-Photo Services*;
John Fawaz, *Fact Checker*; and Kevan Burks, *Library Services Assistant*.

INTRODUCTION

I T'S FUN TO BE A FAN. IT'S ALSO EASY. THERE ARE NO RULES TO FOLLOW, no guidelines. Just have an interest in the game, and a willingness to enjoy.

Most pro football fans share a fascination for the mysteries - the events which occur and the words that are spoken behind those closed doors with the big sign: "Authorized Personnel Only."

Behind those doors, off limits to the fans, teams prepare to win. Games, and championships, usually go to the teams that are best prepared.

Sidelines: Behind The Scenes of America's Favorite Sport, takes you behind those doors. Some of America's leading experts on professional football, sports reporters who have written about the NFL for many years, provide a revealing look behind the scenes.

Each writer takes you where you've never been...

⊘ Inside the minds of the players, revealing their thoughts and actions in the countdown before battle.

⊘ Into the training camps, drawing a stark contrast between today's precisely run, all-business camps and those of bygone eras.

⊘ Into the scout's notebook and the general manager's strategy room, where a club's future may depend on strokes of genius - and strokes of luck.

⊘ Into the world of coaching, where films are scrutinized almost forever in search of secrets, where game plans are written, where a dozen specialists blend their skills to prepare players not simply to play, but to win.

⊘ Inside an NFL playbook, where the secrets are kept. Football is chess on a gridiron, and the playbook is where teams plot their moves and countermoves. The game plan...the audible...the emergency play...all are hidden in the playbook.

⊘ Inside the NFL conditioning room, where specialists push NFL players to the limits of strength and endurance, building the muscle and increasing the speed that spell the difference between victory and defeat.

⊘ Inside the world of the equipment staff and medical personnel who must move four tons of supplies each time their team plays a road game.

⊘ Inside the world of NFL officials, who demand perfection of themselves in a pressure-filled atmosphere of instant decisions.

⊘ Backstage at the Super Bowl, for a fascinating look at what it takes for perfect execution of the greatest entertainment extravaganza in sports.

⊘ Inside the hearts of five former NFL stars who have chosen new paths, providing help to those who need it most.

And that's only half of the book.

Sidelines also focuses on each NFL team in its individual section, recalling the great players and special events.

Each fan's memory bank is a storehouse of treasures - some rarely recalled. But a special photograph, the mention of a name or event, can release the personal joy that comes from, "I remember when..."

It's fun to be a fan.

CADMUS

A Battalion On A Mission

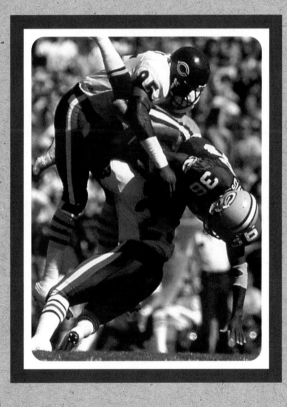

*Professional football games are more than mere contests;
they are special events…only 16 in each season. They demand intensity.
In the countdown to battle, the player's attention is given to one thing
and one thing only: The Game.*

BY DON PIERSON

THE COUNTDOWN BEGINS AT MIDNIGHT SATURDAY. KICKOFF IS JUST HOURS away. The lights are turned out but the mind stays on, churning until sleep overtakes anxiety. In pro football, game day is not taken lightly.

"It really starts early Saturday morning when you're making sure you have everything you need in your bag: what you're going to wear, music, the little things you need to help soothe you a little bit, something to help you sleep, aspirin," says Trace Armstrong, defensive end for the Chicago Bears.

Saturday 12:30 P.M. United Airlines Charter #5067 departs O'Hare Airport.

The team is off the ground now, but hardly up in the air. It is time to get down to business. While the atmosphere remains festive, the purpose borders on somber. Many coaches require players to wear suits and ties to remind them this is no vacation. It's not funny business, either. The late George Halas, founder, owner, and coach of the Bears, once chastised fullback Rick Casares for boarding a plane carrying a hanging bag containing more than one suit - a certain tip-off that Casares was planning to dress up for more than a game. "This is not a two-suit trip," Halas blurted.

In the National Basketball Association, teams play 82 games. Major league baseball teams play 162 games. As the frequency increases, the importance diminishes. National Football League teams play 16 games. Each game is preceded by a week of anticipation and followed by a week of retrospect. Games become more than mere contests; they are events. They demand intensity. The inherent violence of the game requires time to heal the body and the mind. Football is not war. Game day is not D-Day. Touchdown bombs do not explode. Yet the foxhole camaraderie is unmistakable. A football team en route to a game is a battalion on a mission. The plane ride is an airlift.

4 P.M. United Charter arrives Tampa, where Gulf Coast Grayline buses await.

While one truck full of equipment goes directly to the stadium with trainers and equipment men, the players are bused to a hotel. Even for home games, players stay together in a hotel the night before a game. The routine of daily life is incompatible with the extraordinary task at hand. "From Friday after the last full practice, you're just trying to eliminate distractions and start to get into the mindset where there is only one thing: the game," Armstrong says.

Keys arranged on a table in the hotel lobby await the players' arrival. Often, a back entrance and a private check-in are used to avoid the autograph seekers. With few exceptions, every player has a roommate. No wives or girlfriends are allowed to share rooms. Players can make individual arrangements to book separate rooms in the same hotel, but few do.

Trace Armstrong plays defensive end for the Chicago Bears, who selected him in the first round of the 1989 draft after he was a consensus All-America at the University of Florida.

No detail is overlooked. If a player feels ill, he will room separately. If he needs extra pillows, he gets them. The success of the San Francisco 49ers in the 1980s was attributed partly to the meticulous and lavish attention accorded players by owner Eddie DeBartolo, Jr., who chartered wide-body planes and hired a special chef to prepare gourmet meals on every trip. The 49ers consistently produced the best record in the league for winning on the road.

6 P.M. team meeting. Separate meeting rooms for Offense and Defense. Dinner on your own.

"Before the meeting, I'll be looking at my playbook, cramming a little bit because every week there are new plays, new formations, new tendencies we have to study," Bears quarterback Jim Harbaugh says. "We still have the basic same plays, but there will be new plays, different adjustments. There's a lot to learn every single week. I'm making sure I've got it all down. By now, the hay's mainly in the barn, but you still keep glancing at it through the night."

The team meeting lasts 10 minutes before coaches break into separate groups - offense, defense, special teams, quarterbacks. It is at the brief team meeting that coaches often give their best pep talk of the week. The day of a game is too hectic, too crowded, too close for meaningful speeches. The night before is when Bears coach Mike Ditka shines as one of the sport's most eloquent and effective motivators. "His pep talks really come throughout the week," Harbaugh says. "He'll be setting the mood throughout the week. At the end on Saturday night, he'll kind of sum it all up, tell us how we should be thinking, how we should be going into this game, what's at stake. That's when he has a lot of time. You'd think he'd give a pep talk right before the game, but Saturday night is when he sums everything up."

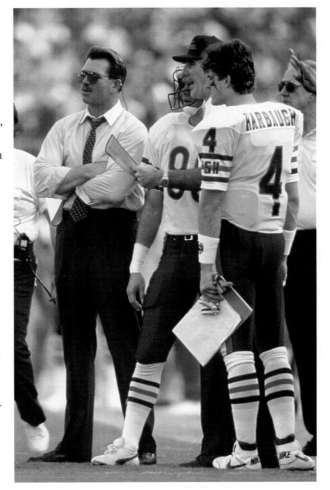

Ditka addresses individuals as well as the entire team. He challenged William (The Refrigerator) Perry before Super Bowl XX against the New England Patriots. Perry was a rookie who was matched against John Hannah, the Patriots' guard who was described by *Sports Illustrated* as the best offensive lineman who ever played. "I challenged William right to his face in front of the whole team," Ditka says, "I said, 'I don't know what your feelings about life are, but if I was you tomorrow, on the first play I'd knock his headgear off. I'd make it a point to knock it off three more times before the game was over.' I said to him, 'I'd let him know who was boss, who the big fat kid on the block was.' I said to him. 'You can do what you want to, Bill, but I'd go out and whip his ass.'"

"It's something Ditka does better than anybody," Armstrong says. "The night before a game, he gives you a little something to think about. That's important. It's something to make you look at yourself and inside yourself. Hopefully, it will make you find a little something to grab onto on game day to turn into something great."

When the players break into smaller groups, coaches remind them of the primary objectives for their particular positions. "Maybe the other team has a great defense, and we have to stress that we have no turnovers. Or maybe they have a great offense, and we have to try to

> The day of a game is too hectic, too crowded, too close for meaningful speeches. The night before is when Bears coach Mike Ditka shines as one of the sport's most eloquent and effective motivators. "His pep talks really come throughout the week," Harbaugh says. "He'll be setting the mood throughout the week. Saturday night is when he sums everything up."

A first-round draft pick from the University of Michigan in 1987, Jim Harbaugh became the Bears' starting quarterback in 1990. An excellent passer, he set club records for pass attempts and completions in 1991.

outscore them," Harbaugh says. "In the quarterback meeting, the three quarterbacks listen to Ditka and Greg Landry, the offensive coordinator. That's when we go over a checklist of about 10 things. Maybe we have audibles that we want to use against certain fronts. We may talk about what cornerback we want to pick on, little things we should be thinking about before we go to bed. You put it all on one sheet of paper - what they're going to do on first downs, what tendencies a defense has on second and third downs, certain plays to run in nickel situations or short yardage or goal line. If there are any trick plays that we put in new that week that may require extra thinking, we'll put it on the sheet. I look at it at night or the next day before I go out on the field."

"You start to get a little nervous. You watch guys and see legs pumping. You see guys playing with their hands. That nervous energy is there."

-Trace Armstrong

The meetings on Saturday night represent the first formal call to arms. The mood changes perceptibly. The wagons are circled. "On Saturdays, we all eat a lot and all sit in a big room and laugh and tell jokes," Armstrong says. "Everybody is kind of excited because the physical preparation is over. We laugh and have fun and try to keep our minds off what is going to happen the next day. Then in the meetings, you go over the game plan and watch film and look for that little key you missed during the week. You start to get a little nervous. You watch guys and see legs pumping. You see guys playing with their hands. That nervous energy is there."

Midnight curfew.

After meetings and dinner, most players retreat to their rooms. Phones are shut off to eliminate all calls - incoming and outgoing. Any emergency call is funneled through the trainer. There is a bed check. There are security guards on the floor to prevent traffic both ways. The legendary curfew-breaking pregame escapades are only a part of pro football lore as it approaches the 21st century, a reminder of simpler times when the game was less lucrative and the stakes less compelling.

Doug Atkins, bigger than life when he defied all rules as a 6-foot 8-inch defensive end with the Bears in the 1950s and 1960s, once woke up half a hotel on a night before a game against the Colts. "Paging Lord Baltimore," Atkins bellowed from a balcony. "Paging Lord Baltimore."

"When you really look at what people make in our game today, there has to be a lot more intelligence used in how they prepare themselves, not only the night before a game but the week before and in the offseason and everything," says Ditka, who was sometimes seen in Atkins's company. "Football to them is a means to an end. Then, you made a good salary and had fun."

Now, players make a better salary and take a modified approach to fun.

"You could not compete today and do the things they used to do," Armstrong says. "The game is so much more physical now. Guys are bigger, stronger, faster. You have a bunch of thoroughbreds out there. The difference between being good and being great in pro football today is a fine line." To help define the line, the Bears went so far as to eliminate junk food and formally educate players on nutrition during the offseason. "Look at this. I'm eating vegetables for lunch," Harbaugh said one day. If such care is taken in the offseason, there is even less reason to get careless the night before a game.

After the Saturday night meetings, players try to turn down the intensity. "I'll go watch college football," Harbaugh says. "I'll hang out with Brad Muster, my roommate, and we'll do a little laughing and joking, trying to relax, cool out, and get your mind off it. But I'll have the playbook sitting there and I'll look at it every once in while."

Movies, cards, or music are welcome diversions for minds that are now zeroed in on football.

"You're relaxing, but your whole focus is on the game," Harbaugh says. "I lose what's going on in my life outside of football."

Life in the NFL is much more than three hours on Sunday afternoons. "People can't appreciate what it's like," says Armstrong. "Because even if we're lucky, we only get to go out on Sunday and do it 16 times a year. When you think about that, you prepare and sacrifice 365 days a year for 16 times. If you have a little hurt or a cold, or something happened at home that maybe is not conducive to great football, there's really a tremendous sense of urgency that you've got to put that behind you. You've got to get through it somehow because this is it. This is one of those 16 times, and you don't want to blow it."

Sunday 8 A.M. wake-up calls. Catholic Mass. Chapel service. 9 A.M. pregame meal. Check out. Pay incidentals. 9:45 A.M. first bus leaves for Tampa Stadium. 10:15 A.M. second bus leaves. 10:45 A.M. last bus leaves.

By 8 A.M. on game day, some players already have left for the stadium. Bears' offensive linemen, led by Tom Thayer, are among the first to leave. "Ideally, by Sunday morning there should be no other thoughts about home life, bills, injuries, nothing," Armstrong says. "All that has to be gone, pushed out of the mind. You've got to have that tunnel vision."

Getting dressed for football is a ritual. "Gladiators," Ditka calls his players.

"I give myself one hour to get dressed," Harbaugh says. "First, I get my ankles taped. I get dressed in the same order. I relax and review my checklist. I go to the bathroom a lot before the game. You still have those jitters. I stretch, put my pants on, stretch more, get my shoulder loosened up. I make sure I get the blood flowing by stretching my rotator cuff using a rubber tube. I'm having fun now. I'm looking forward to going out on the field. It's a fun day. It's not like a lot of high tension. It's what I love to do."

In the Bears' locker room, it is relatively quiet. Music is limited to headphones. Some players meditate. Most keep to themselves. Floyd Little, former running back with the Denver Broncos, said the sound of trainers ripping off adhesive tape was his noisiest recollection.

Dan Hampton, former defensive lineman with the Bears, consumed enough coffee to wake up the dead. He made sure everyone in the room was as ready to play as he was. Mike Singletary, Bears middle linebacker, walks from teammate to teammate with last minute advice, reminding players to check to a different blitz when the offense lines up in the orange formation.

"Hamp didn't care much about the Xs and Os," Armstrong says. "Everybody's different." Walter Payton, the NFL's all-time leading rusher, used to participate in pregame outbursts that rivaled revival meetings for raw emotional response.

Before a 1991 game, a group of Philadelphia Eagles teammates gathered around ailing quarterback Jim McMahon on a training table and laid hands on a battered elbow that had no business on a football field. The result, they say in Philadelphia, was nothing short of a miracle.

"I can tell when we're going to play great, because you sit in the locker room and you just feel this collective energy in the room," Armstrong says. "It's not something you can put your finger on or put a name to, but you can feel it. You can feel the confidence. You can feel the aggression. You can feel we're going to go out and domi-

Defensive captain Mike Singletary takes a studious approach to last-minute preparations.

nate. If you see guys joking and laughing before the game, more often than not, they're doing it because they are not comfortable, not sure if they are ready, and they try and joke and kid themselves into thinking they are ready. But the times when we play our best are when you can almost see that chip on everybody's shoulder. You can feel the raw aggression in the room."

With only 16 games a year, the formula for success would seem simple to master. "But it's tough to get it right every week, where you hit the physical part right and the mental part right. It's tough to put all the pieces together and have it add up the same every week," Armstrong says.

12:05 P.M. special teams on the field. 12:10 P.M. quarterbacks and receivers. 12:15 P.M. everyone on the field.

The countdown is speeding now. As the team assembles, piece by piece, individual parts forming a cohesive unit, players are left with last-minute private thoughts. This is when each athlete wonders whether he is fully prepared to do his best for the greater good of the team. No one wants to fail. "I always go through a process when I ask myself, 'Am I ready?'" Armstrong says. "'Did I do everything right? How do I feel? Do I feel tired? Do I feel good? Boy, I can't tell this week.' You go through the pregame warm-ups and try to gauge how you feel compared to last week. 'Do I feel quick? Maybe I'm not as quick.'"

"It's really draining. There is a lot of introspection to see if you're going to be a great player or just another guy on the field."

"There are weeks when I feel I'm going to do great." Harbaugh says. "Sometimes, I feel like, 'Geez, I don't know if I'm really ready. I can't explain it. Sometimes, I feel the worst, I do the best. Sometimes, when I've felt the best before the game, I've done my worst. They say it's mostly mental, and I don't know why. I've been trying to do a lot more psychological study to try to figure that out. I've been reading a lot about sports psychology and visualization and trying to get myself in the right frame of mind. So many times you hear coaches say football or any sport is 90 percent mental and 10 percent physical. You hear it all the time. Yet, as athletes, all the preparation is physical. If it really is 90 percent mental, we don't practice that way. There's not a lot of psychological practice going on."

1 P.M. kickoff.

Two minutes before players return to the field for the National Anthem, coach Mike Ditka gets one last chance to wield his influence. "Okay, we've got two minutes," he began before Super Bowl XX. "You did all the talking last night. The only thing that I want to say is you made your feelings clear on what has to happen. Everybody said it...Gary, Walter, Dan, Jim, Mike. You know what it is going to take. It is going to take your best effort on every play. Dedicate ourselves to that and we should have no problems. Go out and play Bear football, smart and aggressive. If something bad happens, don't worry. Why? Because we're in this together as a football team and we are going to play it for each other and we're going to win this game for 49, 50, or whatever number we have in this room. We are going to win it for each other. We are going to play it for each other and we're going to pick each other up. That's what it's all about. This is out of love for each other. This is your game. Any other intentions won't be accepted. But you are going to win this game for each other. So let's go out there and play our kind of football. Let's have the Lord's Prayer. Heavenly Father, we are grateful for this opportunity and we thank you for the talents you have given us, the chance to prove that we

"The times when we play our best are when you can almost see that chip on everybody's shoulder. You can feel the raw aggression in the room."

-Trace Armstrong

13

are the very best. Father, we ask that you give us the courage and the commitment to use the talents to the best of our ability so that we may give the glory back to you. Father, we ask that you may protect all the players in the game so that they may play the game free from injury. We pray as always in the name of Jesus Christ your son our Lord. Amen. Let's go."

The huddle at midfield before kickoff is a pep rally for the special teams. Nothing the players or coaches have said or done all week can fully prepare them for what happens next. No film study, no tackling dummies, no blocking sleds, no weight rooms, no practice scrimmages can fully condition the body to accept the collisions that come next. Former Bears lineman Jeff Levy described the game experience as an afternoon spent tumbling uncontrollably inside a hot clothes dryer.

"You see guys taking hits from each other on the sideline," Harbaugh says. "Sometimes, I'll just whack myself a couple of quick times on the helmet. If there is any tension or jitters, you get them out."

Armstrong pays particular attention to the first series of downs. "If you put on a film and watched the 11 guys on defense that first series, more often than not you can see the type of game a guy is going to have will be pretty close to how he plays the first series," he says.

Each game is a test of mental and physical skill, a wrestling match times 11. Individual battles are fought in collective cooperation. "When you get down in your stance, you've got to believe you can make every play, that the other guy cannot block you," Armstrong says. "You try to find that zone where you're not thinking about anything; you're reacting. You don't think, 'Okay, they like to run counter out of red formation.' You see it and right away you know. You get down in your stance and you're waiting for that twitch, that first twitch. Does he twitch to set back for a pass? Does he try to come off the ball? When he twitches, you meet it with a violent reaction. It really is a rush. Football is unique because you have the biggest, strongest, fastest men in the world hitting each other, going after each other in a physical way. To me, it doesn't get any better than that. You talk about great paradigms. When a guy walks out on a football field, normally he's matched up with one other guy and the guy who's going to win is the guy who has two things - the ability God gave him and the amount of determination and fire in his heart. There is nothing more beautiful or noble than that contest. And the great thing about football compared to boxing is you feed off each other's emotions."

> "The way you want to do it is not even think about whether you are going to win or lose. Just think about doing your best, think one play at a time."
>
> JIM HARBAUGH,
> CHICAGO BEARS
> QUARTERBACK

The quarterback often feels a greater sense of responsibility than his teammates. "I go through ups and downs," Harbaugh says. "I'm trying to work on that. I think sometimes you can get in a game and worry too much about what the outcome is going to be. In the first quarter, you're saying to yourself, 'Are we going to win? Are we going to lose?' You're worried about, 'Am I going to lose? Am I going to mess up?' The way you want to do it ideally is not even think about whether you are going to win or lose. You want to think about going out and doing your best, think one play at a time. That's what I want to do more. Just live for the moment. Take each play and have fun."

This is where spectator and participant part. It is virtually impossible for the fan to appreciate what the players endure. Harbaugh says he is only occasionally aware of fan reaction, and then only when he is not on the field. He thinks even spectators who have played the game forget what it's like out there. "I think I'd forget. I think a lot of coaches forget what it's like. Even the guys like Ditka probably forget. You have to put yourself out there or you forget. If I'm watching a golf tournament, I'll forget what it's like. A guy is standing over a shot and flubs one and you say, 'Oh, I can't believe he choked like that.' But anybody can understand what it's like if they're standing over a five-foot putt for 30 bucks. Something happens different to your body. It's that ability to perform under pressure, that courage to still do your job under pressure that separates good players and bad players. Fans don't know what it's like to go to sleep the night before the game and know the next day you could be crippled, break a bone, totally fall on your face, be humiliated out on the field. The guys who are able to put that out of their minds and go out and still have fun, enjoy what they're doing, play well, sink that free throw when the pressure is on; those are the guys who are able to deal with it because when they say choke, your body does tighten. Your breathing gets shorter. It can happen."

It happened to Harbaugh in a 1991 game against the New York Giants on an interception, and Harbaugh surprised reporters when he described what happened as a "choke." The very word gets caught in the throat for most athletes, but Harbaugh had the confidence to admit it happened. "I went to throw the ball and as I was releasing it I could feel my body just tighten," he says. "You get into real problems when you start denying things, saying, 'I never get nervous before a game; I'm always in control.' That's not normal. I don't know anybody like that. What it comes down to is the mental toughness to do your job no matter what the pressure is. Conquering the body gives you a rush. Your body wants to quit sometimes; it wants to give up. Your body tells you to stop, but the thrill is pushing yourself past, saying no to your body. That's why I come and work out every day and it's most enjoyable the days I don't want to work out. The mind can push you past wanting to quit, and then you feel exhilarated.

"What frustrates some athletes is that sometimes a guy can criticize them when he's doing nothing more physical than getting up off the couch and cracking another beer, that someone like that can say you choked, or you're terrible, or you're a piece of garbage."

"What it comes down to is the mental toughness to do your job no matter what the pressure is. Your body tells you to stop, but the thrill is pushing yourself past, saying no to your body."

-Jim Harbaugh

AN REACTION, positive or negative, only adds to the pressure. "It adds to the fun, too," Harbaugh says. "You have to look at it as fun and live for the moment. There are 60,000 people watching. They're all watching me. I'm putting on a show out there. I'm doing something that's fun, that a lot of people would love to be doing. I just have to go out and do my best and not worry, 'Am I going to throw an interception on the next play?' And when we're down by a touchdown with two minutes to go, this is my chance to shine. This is my chance to do something great instead of thinking, 'Oh no, there's only two minutes left, we're going to lose! We're going to lose!' That's what mental toughness is."

Among the many emotions and thoughts racing through a player's mind is what Harbaugh calls "the added element of sheer bodily punishment." In no other sport except boxing is physical pain so unavoidable. Football players who dwell on this don't remain football players for long. Yet players get grim reminders in every contest. "You're really in a very vulnerable position a lot of times. You can be maimed; you can be crippled out there," Harbaugh says, matter of factly.

"There is a sense of imminent danger because a guy can fall on a knee the wrong way and it's over just like that," Armstrong says. "There are so many emotions in a game, there's always a little fear."

Rarely does a player get to watch the game in which he is playing. "It's nice when everything is working the way it's supposed to work and you can go up and watch the offense," Armstrong says. "More often than not, all the pieces don't fit together, so you're always trying to find the missing piece and put it in the puzzle. Steve McMichael and I talk the whole game long about how we're going to mix up rushes and stunts.

"We had times where the defense played great the whole game and it comes down to the last drive and you think back and think, 'God, all the great plays we made, all the things we took away from them don't mean anything if we don't stop them right here.'"

5 P.M. Game over. Team buses depart stadium for airport. 6 P.M. United charter departs Tampa. 7:40 Arrival at Chicago O'Hare Airport.

In professional sports, the game is not over until the last reporter or television crew has left, until all of the day's successes have been described and the mistakes explained. Then the cycle begins anew. "I don't really get that tired," Harbaugh says. "Sometimes, I get real hurt during a game and don't even know it. You've got a lot of adrenaline going. If I stop moving around I usually feel it. If you win, you're better. You stay on an emotional high for a little bit longer."

Sometimes players gather to celebrate victory. More often they go home. "I don't think I've ever gone out after a game and partied since I've been in Chicago," Harbaugh says. "Sometimes I'll go out to dinner. But I just want to get home and get food and lay down."

"You're on an emotional roller coaster because you go from the highs of playing and then it's over and you're just left drained," Armstrong says. "You go out to dinner with your family or friends, and mentally you're somewhere else. You're still thinking about the game, about one or two or three plays you could have made or should have made."

"If we lose, I don't want to talk to anybody; I just want to lay down," Harbaugh says. "When I'm hurt, what feels the best is to lie down to go to sleep, because the whole game I'll replay in my head. If we've won, it's just like lying there in kind of a glow. Your whole body is kind of numb, and you're feeling good. There are some games when I can't go to sleep at night, it hurts so bad. I've had to sleep sitting up. Sometimes I just sit on the couch and watch TV all night because I can't lie down. But it's more fun than sitting on the bench and not doing anything. I went through that, and that was misery."

"You only remember the good things," Armstrong says. "I look at veteran players like Jay Hilgenberg, Keith Van Horne, Mark Bortz, and they are guys who have paid the price to play this game. You look at them after a game and anybody who says guys like that get paid too much is crazy. People don't see the price a guy pays lying on a table after a game on Sunday - got to be helped out to his car, can't get out of bed in the morning. This is like life times 100. The disappointments, the elation, all so concentrated. It's only 16 times."

THE CHOREOGRAPHY OF GAME DAY

The choreography of an NFL team on game day depends on the coach, who has too many players under his command to rely on spontaneity. Getting 11 players on the field for any one play presents enough logistical problems. Seeing that 47 get to the stadium on time requires the skills of a cattle rancher. In some organizations, the game day itinerary is inviolate, passed down from generation to generation.

Then there is Jerry Glanville, iconoclastic coach of the Atlanta Falcons who always manages to find enough time in his schedule to leave a ticket for Elvis. Or James Dean. Or Phantom of the Opera. Or W.C. Fields. The Falcons aren't so much a football team as an entourage. When they blow into a city or a stadium, they want everybody to notice. On one visit to Chicago, Glanville invited the flamboyant Mr. T to address the team.

When he coached the Eagles, former Bears assistant Buddy Ryan signalled his arrival into Chicago by ordering buses from the airport to drive straight to Soldier Field and circle it with horns blowing before delivering the team to its hotel.

Miami coach Don Shula is so meticulous about his game day routine that bus drivers have

Buddy Ryan signalled his return to Chicago by ordering buses to circle Soldier Field with horns blowing.

been told to slow down if there is a chance they could arrive at a stadium earlier than two hours before kickoff. Former Vikings coach Bud Grant never wanted to arrive too early, either. Once, he was fined for arriving late and delaying the kickoff after ignoring warnings about a traffic jam en route to the Pontiac Silverdome.

For Glanville, structure is a threat to the freedoms that keep the Falcons loose. "We do things different and I'll tell you, we don't really care what other people think," Glanville says. Most teams require players to wear individual earphones if they wish to listen to music. The Falcons are bathed in blaring music that drowns out conversation.

Glanville defied protocol by sending every one of his players to midfield for the coin toss before a 1991 playoff game against the Washington Redskins. His action resulted in a rules change during the offseason that limited the coin-toss congregation to no more than six players from each team. Glanville's honorary special teams captains are always invited to say something silly before game time. During game film review, players are encouraged to criticize each other's performances, and any defensive back who avoids a hit must wear a pink shirt to practice.

"It's not just the old regular 9 to 5 around here," Falcons quarterback Chris Miller says. "We do some crazy stuff, but at the same time we're getting the football part of it done."

Shula, who learned pro football from the master of organization, the late Paul Brown, became a creature of habit early in his career and leaves little room for diversity. Only late in his coaching career, for example, did Shula accept modern nutritional advice and permit a choice of pasta at pregame meals to accompany the traditional steak.

The pregame meal provides more than food for Shula's team. It represents a final opportunity to quietly collect thoughts, develop the cohesive mindset necessary to perform together efficiently. No outsiders are allowed. This is all business. NBC commentator Merlin Olsen, a former star player for the Los Angeles Rams, was mistakenly invited into a Dolphins pregame meal by a new employee in the public relations department. Olsen thought nothing of it, because other teams had allowed him to invade their pregame privacy on occasion. Shula waited until Olsen had left, but then firmly reminded everyone that pregame meals were for team members only.

A Little Bit Superstitious

When Bill Parcells coached the New York Giants, winning Super Bowls XXI and XXV, he kept 10 miniature brass elephants, trunks up, facing the doorway of his office. Trunks up?

"To keep the good luck from draining out," Parcells says. "I'm a little bit superstitious."

Most athletes prefer to describe their routines as habit, like putting on the right shoe before the left. Counting the strips of tape on an ankle, as former Bears guard Noah Jackson did, is a quirky habit.

Where is the line drawn between habit and superstition?

Quarterback Mark Rypien of the Washington Redskins wore a 1984 Winter Olympics sweatshirt, unwashed, for 11 straight victories at the beginning of the 1991 season. Every Friday after practice, he ate Buffalo wings. For Super Bowl XXVI, of course, Rypien consumed the entire Buffalo Bills team.

"I wear an old wristband for warm-ups and a new one for games. And I touch the Redskins' insignia with both hands before I go out," Rypien says.

But the question is, when does ordinary routine, like brushing teeth, become abnormal ritual, like always brushing the right incisors after the left bicuspids. Parcells drank coffee every morning on his way to work, but not in a thoughtless manner. At 5:50 A.M., he would stop at one cafe to buy one cup. At 6:20 A.M., he would stop at another cafe to buy two more cups. Same routine every day. Same cafes.

Cornerback Darrell Green of the Redskins ran 100 times diagonally across the auxiliary locker room before each game. After each 10 trips, he stopped to stretch.

During World War II a psychologist found the danger of battle developed ritual forms of preparation in an effort to invite good fortune.

"I think guys have superstitious rituals more to establish routines so they don't have to think about little things, like the route you take to the hotel, or what time you get up, or how you get dressed," says Trace Armstrong of the Bears. "It's so you can focus on one thing: walking out on the field and playing great football. A lot of athletes don't want to break habits because suddenly they have to think about something else, and it's just a distraction."

"We do things different and I'll tell you, I don't really care what other people think."

- Jerry Glanville

Football players try to work themselves into trances on game days. Routines become a form of self-hypnosis. The positive reinforcement of victory ensures the habit for at least another week.

"I try to do things the same all the time," said Bears quarterback Jim Harbaugh. "It keeps you in the same frame of mind, thinking you're prepared. I get dressed in the same order. I make sure I've got my T-shirt exactly where I want it. It has to be the right length, comfortable underneath so I can move my arm. It doesn't sound like it's a big deal, but it's kind of a big deal with me to make sure I have the right clothes on underneath. Once I've got that right, I put my shoulder pads on, put my jersey on, have Brad Muster roll up my sleeves and I'm ready to go."

Most players follow simple routine, such as taping one ankle before another, or having certain trainers doing the taping. Then there are others, performed to extremes.

Willie Alexander, a former defensive back with the Houston Oilers, began preparing for the next game as soon as one ended. "I rinsed my face 15 times at night and 7 in the morning during the week of a game. Then I'd have one cup of coffee. One. Always the same," Alexander told Ron Borges of *The Boston Globe.*

Players follow ritual with great precision. Defensive back Willie Alexander just had a few more rituals than most others.

On Saturdays before home games, Alexander would eat two eggs over easy, five slices of bacon, and four pieces of toast. After the team meeting at the hotel, he would order two beers and one piece of cheesecake. After eating, Alexander showered, wiped off the walls around the tub, folded the used towels, and placed them under the sink. He would repeat the shower ritual in every detail the next morning.

During the pregame warm-ups, Alexander would play catch with only three people. Then he would jog down the field and shake hands with a former equipment manager. When it was time to head back to the dressing room, Alexander would pass only on the right side of the goal posts and take his first step up the stairs with his left foot. Upon returning to the field, he would jog five yards and stretch, apply black grease paint under each eye, and ask a defensive lineman to slap his shoulder three times.

"Sometimes, I'd stop and think, 'This is ridiculous,'" he says. "But I never quit doing it."

The National Football League may never see anything to equal Alexander or Parcells. Parcells said he got his superstitions from his Italian mother. Once, after a truck driver was seen watching practice before two Giants victories, Parcells ordered the man to park his rig outside practice and watch every week.

Another time, after a black cat ran in front of Parcells's car, he backed up the car. "You can erase those cats if you drive across and, where he passed, you back up and then re-drive over," Parcells says. "Then he doesn't count."

As new players and coaches come into the league each year, there is a new supply of superstitions and peculiar habits. In the 1992 draft, for example, the Dallas Cowboys selected Tom Myslinski, a guard from the University of Tennessee. Before each Tennessee game, Myslinski would bang his head on the wall of the shower until it bled. He claimed he adapted the tactic from his days as a weight man in track and field, when he used to psyche himself up by banging the hammer or shot put against his head. "I don't know why I do it," Myslinski says, "because after a game my head hurts."

No practice is too peculiar in the pursuit of victory. ✐

CHAPTER TWO

A Summer Camp For Adults

*It is a special time and special place,
where young men…and some not so young…go in search of fame and fortune.
They have a common goal: a job in the National Football League. For some of them, a professional
football training camp is the first step to stardom.*

BY LARRY FELSER

THERE WAS A TIME, SHORTLY AFTER THE LEATHER-HELMET ERA, WHEN FOOTBALL training camps were one part reform school, one part chain gang, one part Parris Island, and several parts "Animal House." Technology eventually ran down tradition, but the chase covered a multitude of yard markers.

It became evident that training camps had become at least semi-anachronistic in August of 1968 in Santa Rosa, California. That's where the Raiders prepared to defend their American Football League championship. George Blanda, the Raiders' great kicker/quarterback who was destined for the Pro Football Hall of Fame, was easing himself into his psychological comfort zone just three weeks shy of his forty-first birthday. It was Blanda's nineteenth pro camp.

John Rauch, the Raiders' head coach, had hired a new special teams assistant that summer, an apple-cheeked young fellow named Bugsy Engleberg. Bugsy had been a toddler when Blanda was a star quarterback for Paul (Bear) Bryant at the University of Kentucky.

Among the duties of assistant coaches in pro training camps is the taking of bed checks – knocking on the players' doors to determine if everyone is accounted for prior to curfew.

When the 24-year-old Engleberg knocked on the door of the 40-year-old Blanda, the oldest player in football, the crusty veteran opened the door just long enough to tell the coach where he could put his kicking tee.

The NFL was launched into the modern era in the years immediately after World War II, when many soldiers exchanged their duffel bags for shoulder pads. Television, which would make millionaires of their celebrated successors, was little more than a curiosity then. Club owners were about the only people to make a living out of pro football. George Preston

Bobby Layne, shown here with coach Buddy Parker, put the six weeks of training camp to good use...both as preparation for the football season and as opportunity for a little rest and recreation.

Marshall, penurious owner of the Washington Redskins, told all-pro guard Buster Ramsey of the Chicago Cardinals, "There was never an offensive lineman who ever lived that was worth more than three thousand dollars a year!"

So players and coaches supplemented their football income by working at other jobs for six months a year. Buddy Parker, who coached the Cardinals, Detroit Lions, and Pittsburgh Steelers, had to be coaxed back to football each year because he was so successful selling industrial pipe during the offseason. Ernie Stautner, the Steelers' all-pro defensive end, was late to camp each year because he operated a drive-in movie theater near Lake Saranac, New York, and wanted to maximize income from the summer tourist season.

Consequently, training camp was where players would shed rust and extra pounds accumulated from inactive winters and springs. Offseason conditioning sometimes consisted of playing golf with weights strapped to the ankles, or wearing rubber suits under work clothes on construction jobs.

Yet, the early camps were more than fat farms. They were part of the ritual of male bonding; sort of a summer camp for adults.

Bobby Layne, the bon vivant who quarterbacked Detroit to championships, often showed up early at training camp to scout nocturnal headquarters for the players. Six weeks of carousing with Layne put some players in worse condition than they were before camp opened. Consequently, the early arrivals would hide from their field leader when he sought companions.

One year Layne arrived so early in the Lions' camp that only one other player, guard Harley Sewell, had checked in. Layne looked for Sewell, but Sewell, who had made a vow to play the season in the best possible condition, hid from him. Layne looked in the mess hall, opened the door of each room, searched the parking lot, and still couldn't find Sewell. Finally he checked the lavatory, peeking under each stall.

"Harley!" he shouted. "Harley, I know you're in here! C'mon out!"

No answer.

Layne stood still and listened closely. He thought he heard breathing. He kicked in the door of a stall and found Sewell, crouching on a toilet seat. There was no way for Sewell to avoid the hangover he knew he would have the next morning.

Some coaches selected training camp sites the same way movie directors pick locations for horror movies.

In the early days of the New Orleans Saints, players convened each summer in Hattiesburg, Mississippi, one of the hottest and most humid places in the Mississippi delta. Adding to the discomfort was the list of rules rigidly enforced by Saints coach J.D. Roberts, a tough Texan and ex-Marine.

"One thing that drove J.D. crazy was sandals," says Archie Manning, the team's star quarterback. "Two things, actually: sandals and flip-flops. I guess he associated wearing them with being a hippie. He'd go into a rage if anyone wore them into the mess hall. So J.D. instituted the rule that everyone had to wear socks in training camp. He figured that no one would wear sandals or flip-flops over socks."

Roberts also mandated that all meals be eaten in the mess hall and that each player sign in. It was an unpopular rule because the overwhelming consensus among players was that the food was awful.

"One day it was so hot that we couldn't stand it," says Manning. "So just about everyone skipped dinner. We didn't even bother to sign in. We just headed for Pizza Hut.

"The one exception was Julian Fagan, a punter who was my teammate at Ole Miss. Julian was as nice a person and as much a straight arrow as I ever met. He's a minister now, and he didn't drink or have any bad habits back then. Julian showed up in the mess hall, signed in, and ate as usual.

"The next day J.D. gathered us around as soon as we reached the practice field. He was boiling, not at us, but at Fagan. J.D. hated kickers anyway, and he just crawled all over Julian, telling him that when the team violated a rule as a unit, he should have gone along with it, and who did he think he was, anyway?"

The all-time tough training camp may have been that of the 1963 Chargers at Rough Acres Ranch in the southern California desert.

Sid Gillman, the Chargers' general manager and head coach, had suffered through a miserable season in 1962, watching his high-priced talent lose eight of its last nine games to finish with a 4-10 record. Gillman vowed it wouldn't happen again. Before the first game was played, he said, the players would toughen up.

Rough Acres lived up to its name. There was unbearable heat and drought, made worse by the lack of air-conditioning in the players' quarters, and no roof over the communal showers. And there were rattlesnakes - many, many rattlesnakes. Buzzards circled the training site each day.

The closest town of any size was Tecate, Mexico, but the 18-mile journey down rough roads took too long for players to return in time for bed check. Instead, they took their respite in a little beer joint in the nearby town of Boulevard.

That camp marked a milestone in NFL training. Gillman hired Alvin Roy, an expert in physical conditioning, to introduce weight training to the players. When starting wide receiver Don Norton hurt his back lifting weights, he had to make a difficult 60-mile trip to the nearest hospital to get treatment.

Rough Acres worked. The Chargers won 11 games in 1963 and then rocked Boston, 51-10 in the American Football League championship game.

Other coaches have tried less hazardous isolation, usually selecting some bucolic site where they believe players will find it easier to concentrate.

When the Cleveland Browns trained in Hiram, Ohio, Charles Maher, a visiting writer from Los Angeles wrote, "In Hiram the two main recreational activities are jumping on the hose to make the bell ring at the local gas station and watching haircuts at the village barber. The barber's sign reads: 'No one will be admitted once a haircut has begun.'"

Sonny Jurgensen once remarked of the Washington Redskins' summer base in Carlisle, Pennsylvania, "In this town, the Late-Late show starts at 7 P.M."

Sometimes coaches outsmarted themselves in seeking the ultimate in tough camps. In the early 1960s, the Houston Oilers trained at Ellington Air Force Base in Pasadena, Texas. Bobby Brown, the team trainer, says, "Ellington was a perfect setup except for one thing: It didn't have a football field. It had been a navigation school during the war, but then the place was deserted. There were enough broken beer bottles on the field to slice a guy to shreds."

The Oilers hired a cook, an Air Force lifer accustomed to improvisation and avoidance of waste. "I knew we were in trouble when they served us barbecued liver," says Brown.

In 1963, Pop Ivy took over as Oilers coach and shifted the training camp to Colorado College, where he thought the cooler air and high altitude would be more conducive to preparing for football. But that part of Colorado was stricken by its worst drought in 36 years, and there was no fresh water available to water the practice fields.

"Because of the water shortage, they irrigated the fields with sewer water," says Brown. "You can't imagine how terrible it smelled. We had guys up all night trying to find a place to sleep away from the smell. We were constantly inoculating guys against infection. Even minor scratches got infected and wouldn't heal."

Even in the best camps, training methods improved with tortoise-like speed. In the early 1950s, a typical morning workout might begin with brisk repetitions of the hop-straddle-jump exercise, followed by a grueling couple of laps using the infamous "duck waddle." The hop-straddle-jump (also called "jumping jacks") was an ancient calisthenic in which the hands were clapped over the head, then down to the sides as the subject quickly jumped and landed with his feet apart, then with feet together. The "duck waddle" was a torturous exercise in which the subject bent deeply at the knees in an almost-sitting position, grasped his ankles, and maneuvered himself forward like a pintail duck.

A modern physiologist might cringe at those calisthenics. More than a few knee injuries have been traced to the "duck waddle." The kneecap of a Detroit Lions defensive back once slipped out of place between the hop and the jump.

In 1967, weight training still was considered a fad, practiced mostly in San Diego, where coach Sid Gillman introduced it. San Diego's weight training often was ridiculed. "If anyone needs a piano moved at halftime," wrote columnist Steve Weller, "the Chargers are the football team to do it."

Most of Gillman's coaching peers agreed. The consensus in pro football was that weight lifting was likely to make players inflexible, or worse, lead to serious injuries because muscles were too taut. The more sympathetic minority reasoned that lifting weights might help someone who was already a good player. Hank Stram of Kansas City was an exception. In 1968, he hired Alvin Roy to bring his weight training theories to the Chiefs. Two years later, Kansas City won its first Super Bowl. Coincidence? Maybe.

Most coaches preferred the traditional methods of getting ready for the regular season. That meant the players would clobber one another repeatedly.

One treasured ritual was called "the meat grinder," or "the nutcracker." Usually, this meant stationing a center on the offensive side of the ball, flanked by a guard or tackle. Behind them was the quarterback, whose sole duty was to hand off to a ball carrier. On the defensive side were a defensive lineman and linebacker. The defensive players were to fend off the blockers and make the tackle. The offense tried to advance the ball carrier beyond the linebacker.

Once the ball was snapped, mayhem erupted.

Most of the squad members would circle this tableau, offering encouragement or derision.

The usual practice in those days was to conduct a rookie camp for a week or two before the veterans reported. There were always newcomers who would make their reputations among their fellow rookies, the news of which would be lavishly reported in the daily newspapers.

By the time the veterans reported, they could barely wait to test the rookies, who were challenged daily to justify those newspaper reputations.

Some of the best rookies were discouraged and left camp in the middle of the night to escape the shame of a daily whipping by more experienced players. One such story occurred at the 1956 New York Giants' camp in Winooski Park, Vermont. The Giants had drafted a tackle from West Virginia whom they were trying to convert to linebacker. The kid struggled with his new position and the veterans were merciless. Finally, one morning his bed was found empty and his belongings cleared out.

The Giants, who didn't want to lose this prospect, knew he had no transportation and little money. Someone said he had been seen hitchhiking down the highway. Head coach Jim Lee Howell sent one of his assistants out to find the player and talk him into coming back. The assistant coach was a fatherly type named Vince Lombardi. The rookie was Sam Huff. Lombardi talked Huff into returning. Both of them are in the Hall of Fame.

There aren't many kind moments and fatherly talks in training camps, even now. In football's caveman days, it often was a matter of survival of the fittest, or toughest-minded.

Paul Brown, the father of modern pro football, introduced the age of technology to the game in 1946, when he came out of the Navy to found the Cleveland Browns. Brown is remembered as an innovator who began psychological testing for his players, made them diagram plays in notebooks, used game films to the maximum, and made the scouting of future opponents almost a science. Eventually, his rivals adopted most of his methods. One tenet resisted for a long time was his admonition about training: "When a coach doesn't know what else to do, he scrimmages."

Brown's advice was ignored by most of his peers, perhaps because he came into the NFL in 1950 from a "renegade league," the old All-America Football Conference. The Cleveland team, named after Paul Brown, won AAFC championships all four years of the AAFC's existence.

Nearly 20 years later, full-scale scrimmages remained a fact of training-camp life. Often they occurred when a coach was angry. The Buffalo Bills have had a large assortment of peaks and valleys over the last three decades. They played in Super Bowls XXV and XXVI but also finished last in the league four times. Their first experience with the bottom of the football pit began in the training camp of 1968.

The Bills won two and tied one of their first three exhibition games. Then, in a game against the Houston Oilers in Tulsa, Oklahoma, the Bills played dreadfully and were beaten 37-7. Joe Collier, the quiet, gentle head coach, seethed over his team's play. The following Monday he took unprecedented measures, barring the public and press from camp. Then he sent his team out to the most distant field and conducted a game-condition scrimmage.

It was a disaster.

Ron McDole, the team's star defensive end, barreled into the pocket and sacked quarterback Jack Kemp. When players unpiled, they found Kemp with a torn ligament which put him out for the season. A few plays later, Gary McDermott, a rookie halfback who had been the surprise star of camp, suffered a dislocated elbow that ruined his season.

Collier then called an end to the scrimmage, but it was too late. Owner Ralph Wilson was furious and fired Collier after the second game of the season. Collier, one of the finest defensive coaches in NFL history, never got another head-coaching opportunity. Kemp never returned to his previous level of excellence and retired one year later. He ran for the U.S. Congress, was elected, and eventually became Secretary of Housing and Urban Development in the George Bush Administration. McDermott's career ended before it began. He became a secret service agent, assigned to protect the President of the United States.

The Bills? They had a dreadful 1-12-1 season, but ended up with the opportunity to draft O.J. Simpson.

THE SOUND OF SILENCE

The legend of Doug Atkins began in 1953, when the 6-foot 8-inch defensive end came out of the Tennessee mountains to terrorize NFL opponents. His career spanned three teams and

Long-time veterans like Doug Atkins (81), who ended his 17-year career with the New Orleans Saints, have their own pace for preparing for the start of the regular season.

17 years, the last three (1967-69) in New Orleans. Saints fans will never forget him.

Atkins was a tough man who treasured his privacy, especially in training camp when the Saints headquartered in steamy Mississippi. The summer heat there would melt 17 or 18 pounds off a 290-pound man like Doug in a single day's workouts. When he returned to the solitude of his room at night, Atkins demanded peace.

One night in the room above his, loud music blasted forth, disturbing the peace. Atkins pounded on the ceiling. "You better (bleeping) keep that (bleeper) quiet," he roared. The revelers ignored him. Bad move.

Atkins kept a pistol near his bed, hanging from a holster. He didn't hesitate. He picked up the gun and fired a shot through the ceiling.

Doug Atkins treasured his privacy, and he had something to say about the noisy party upstairs. He spoke...and acted...emphatcally.

"There must have been 14 guys in that one room," says Jack Faulkner, an assistant coach with the Saints at that time. "Thank God he missed everyone. When we got to his room, Doug said 'I told those (bleepers) to keep that (bleeper) quiet.'

"No one heard another sound from that upstairs room again for the entire camp."

A Weighty Matter

Because of their great peaks and even deeper valleys, the Buffalo Bills experienced a number of extremes in training-camp methods and results through the years. Long before William (The Refrigerator) Perry played for the Chicago Bears, Buffalo welcomed Birtho Arnold to its first camp in 1960. Birtho, a product of Ohio State, was a defensive tackle of similar-if-softer size, but with far less talent than Perry.

When the first bus pulled up for the first practice, it leaned markedly to one side when Birtho came down the stairwell to waddle out to the field. There were no scales large enough to weigh him in the training room, so coach Buster Ramsey told the trainer to take Arnold to the local feed store. The scale at the store had a limit of 375 pounds. Birtho maxed out. He weighed at least 375.

When a messenger was sent up to Arnold's room to give him the bad news that the coach wanted to see him and that he should bring his playbook, a sure sign he was going to be cut, Birtho couldn't maneuver himself off his bunk. Finally he rolled to one side and fell to the floor. From there he struggled to his feet. That was the last pro football saw of him.

The New Era

Military maneuvers rarely have been planned more meticulously than the modern NFL training camp. Spontaneity went out with spittoons. Weeks before today's player reports to training camp, he receives a mimeographed sheet outlining the day's activities at training camp. There are activities for every single day.

The time that moving vans arrive at the stadium to transport materials to camp is noted; so is each day's schedule. Players know that on July 20 the two-minute drill will be introduced and explained at the evening meeting of August 7. The Big Ben pass, the quarterback kneel, and the pregame warmups will be covered at the evening meeting on August 11. The next morning the player can plan on a talk from the NFL security chief. He will be due at the civic kickoff luncheon at noon on August 29.

Nothing is left to chance. It is all planned, packaged, and aimed at unclogging the player's mind of everything but football.

Who's running for president? Who's leading the American League East? Who's Madonna seeing these days? It's immaterial, even concerning the Material Girl. This is training camp. The focus is on football.

The normal training camp day goes like this:

- Wake up for breakfast. Serving hours and menus are posted well ahead of time.
- Get taped and dressed for morning practice.
- Practice.
- Have lunch at a preposted time from a preposted menu.
- Return to room for rest and maybe a nap.
- Prepare for afternoon practice.
- Practice.
- Eat dinner at a preposted time from a preposted menu.
- Meetings, lasting from 7 P.M. until 9 or 9:30.

After that? Free time until curfew - maybe an hour and a half - assuming you still can move.

Players lose track of time in this routine. Everything runs together. A day becomes a week. The monotony is open-ended. The season is long, someone once said, but training camp is endless.

The only change in tempo occurs when preseason games approach. Then players become more animated, their chatter more frenetic, their antennas raised. As has been said in training camps throughout the years, "We get to bump into somebody other than ourselves."

All-out scrimmages are passé. When Bum Phillips was in charge at Houston, he said, "The Houston Oilers don't have the Houston Oilers on their schedule." It makes sense. Recent league rules mandate that only 80 players can be on a team's active training-camp roster. Years ago the Dallas Cowboys brought 115 players to their camp in search of that one, needle-in-a-haystack free agent who might become a star. It was expensive and, for most teams who tried to emulate the Cowboys, created chaos and turmoil.

With the reduced rosters, it doesn't make sense to have more intramural contact than necessary. It's more beneficial to conduct a controlled scrimmage, with satellite one-on-one and kicking drills against another NFL team from a nearby camp. That was one of the selling points of the Wisconsin-Minnesota "Cheese League," where five NFL teams train within bus-riding distance of one another.

The controlled scrimmages bear little resemblance to an actual game; they are filmed from several angles by the teams. The dissection of the films is the basis for much of the next week's practice. The scrimmages also whet the appetites of football-hungry fans. It is not uncommon to have the action televised back to the home cities.

To an outsider, all those practices, meetings, and film sessions may seem mundane to the point of torture. To football coaches, they are a treasured part of their profession.

After he finished as a player, ex-Cowboys star Calvin Hill analyzed training camps and the role they play in the coaching profession.

Ted Marchibroda, who became head coach of the Colts in 1975 and again in 1992, says a major change is that today's players are allowed frequent water breaks. The philosophy in the 1970s didn't allow players to drink on the field. Now, under the advice of medical personnel, players get as much water as they want.

"One must realize that most coaches are artists," says Hill. "For almost six months of the year, they deal with abstracts, theory. They spend a lot of time performing mechanical and mundane tasks like breaking down film from the previous season, charting tendencies, and unless they coached the Super Bowl winner, analyzing why their team did not win the pinnacle game. And then training camp opens. Imagine Picasso without his beloved paints and brushes for an extended period. The artistic creativeness would not be extinguished by such a separation. In training camp, the artist again has his paints.

"The urge to harvest the ideas would be awesome. So it is with coaches."

As a player, Hill felt differently. "I found it necessary to invent scenarios to get me through camp. I would imagine that the day's practice was the last one, that we were breaking camp tomorrow. That allowed me to approach camp one day at a time."

Camps change. They change slowly, but they change. Ted Marchibroda, like Grover Cleveland in the Presidency, served two terms, non-consecutive, as coach of the Colts. He was a rookie head coach in 1975 in Baltimore, and in 1992 he resumed command in Indianapolis.

"Surprisingly, I didn't change much about our camp regimens over those years," says Marchibroda. "There was one major change: water breaks. As late as the 1970s, we wouldn't allow the players to drink water on the field. They would sneak ice in their helmets or suck on wet towels, but there were no actual water breaks. Now we let them drink as much water as they want under the advice of our medical people.

"I guess the old water discipline was a Vince Lombardi thing: 'You have to be tough.' It was hard to justify, and I'm glad we got away from it."

There is a new breed of coach in the NFL. He demands justification for things that appear to be tradition for the sake of tradition. Bruce Coslet of the New York Jets is one of them. "He'll come to me and tell me he isn't allowing players who report injuries to practice," says long-time Jets trainer Bob Reese of Coslet. "I don't have to persuade him. He doesn't want players on that field if they are not ready to play. He thinks that's foolish."

The old way was to tell injured players "you're not hurt" or "pain is in the mind." The modern coaches understand that forcing or coercing an injured man to play is self-defeating in the long run. They abide by another cliché: "Pain is the means by which your body tells you there is something wrong with it."

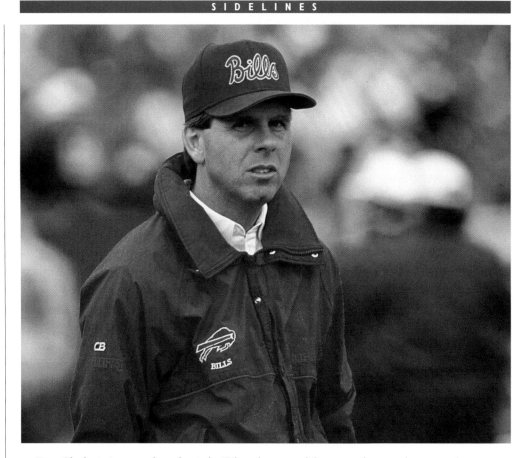

Rusty Jones, Buffalo Bills strength and conditioning coach, emphasizes nutrition education, teaching players which foods are most helpful... or harmful... to their conditioning.

Don Shula isn't a new-breed coach. When he moved from coaching a championship team with the Colts in 1970 to take over the woebegone Dolphins, he actually conducted three or four workouts a day. "We had to," he says. "There was a players' strike that interrupted camp that year, 1974, and we had a lot of catching up to do. We had to work around the intense mid-day heat to do it."

But Shula says he isn't the same coach today. "The game has gotten so sophisticated with situation substitution and offenses that it requires a lot of time to absorb things. It's still a game of conditioning, though, and the team making the fewest mistakes still usually wins. We don't hit nearly as much. We walk through things more often now, but you have to keep doing it over and over. Players learn by rote."

It is the rare, unwise veteran who reports to training camp in poor condition. To help insure against that, most teams conduct year-round, supervised conditioning programs. Bonuses, some reaching six figures, are paid if players participate a certain number of times a week in the supervised workouts.

To assure that all the players know what is expected, minicamps, weekend versions of training camps, are held at the teams' home stadiums each May. Each player's weight, percentage of body fat, shoulder flexibility, arm length, sit and reach, vertical jump, bench press and running times are tested in the minicamps.

Veteran players are assigned a specific weight and percentage of body fat long before they get to the minicamps. Many teams even issue offseason conditioning manuals so the vets know exactly what is expected.

One essential element of the Buffalo Bills' success - four successive AFC Eastern Division titles from 1988-1991 - was Rusty Jones, a former high school coach in New Hampshire, who introduced modern training methods.

Jones taught the Bills about percentage of body fat, individual training programs, offseason conditioning, and testing their limits. He also taught them how to eat.

"The battle we won," he says, "was 70 percent food."

The nutritional battle plan was called "eat the number." Since the time of leather helmets, football players have been big men whose appetites often led them to eat everything but the goal posts. Changing that was not easy. Jones did it by having the Bills enter their daily food intake into a computer, measuring that intake against the nutritional goals that were set for them. Food and nutritional components are treated as important building blocks to optimum physical development.

Gone is the jocks' traditional diet of pizza, fast foods, and a massive intake of red meat. "We gave them more direction in their diets and there is a big improvement in their strength," says Jones.

When the Bills step into the cafeteria line at training camp, they are greeted by a sign bearing the usual menu of food items available for that meal. The difference is that each item is followed by a color or combination of colors. A red mark means, "Stop! There will be no loss of body fat if you eat this." A yellow mark means it is a 50-50 item. Green means, "Go ahead, you'll lose body fat." Mixtures of colors tell the players there is a partial benefit in some food items.

Each player already is guided individually by his personalized nutrition plan. The computer records his age, activity level, and scale weight along with percentage of lean weight and body fat. The body fat is determined by calipers: the "pinch" method.

Body weights are not assigned haphazardly. There is a recommended level of body fat for each position. For a quarterback, it's 10-14 percent. For a linebacker it's 8-10 percent, for a defensive back, constantly on the run during a game, it's less than 7 percent.

The Bills' daily intake is targeted at 60 percent complex carbohydrates and 25 percent fat. The average American eats a diet that has 42 percent fat. Health experts recommend a diet that is 30 percent fat.

Jones, like most strength and conditioning coaches, is a realist. He knows football players will, occasionally, revert to old eating habits. Accommodations are made for those times, although Jones reminds them that a Big Mac with fries and apple pie contains 61 grams of fat and that the day's other meals should be adjusted downward to compensate.

One Bills player had a lifelong addiction to peanut butter-and-jelly sandwiches. Jones took charge of the sandwiches and compromised. "Peanut butter is a great

Marv Levy has brought a variety of changes to the Buffalo training camp. Among the Levy edicts: no hazing of rookies. "There is no room for nonsense like that," says the Bills' coach, whose camps have a reputation for efficiency and time management.

Bum Phillips, whose Houston Oilers were perennial contenders in the 1970s, didn't want all-out scrimmages in his training camp. "The Houston Oilers don't have the Houston Oilers on their schedule," he said.

source of protein, but it's also very high in fat. This player was eating two slices of bread, two tablespoons of jelly and his fat levels at lunch and snack time were too high. We changed it to one tablespoon of peanut butter and two tablespoons of jelly. Much better."

Fred Smerlas, a five-time Pro Bowler at nose tackle who extended his career with hitches in San Francisco and New England after playing 11 years with the Bills, credits Jones with helping him survive so long in the NFL.

"I was 34 years old when I came to the Patriots and I had the lowest percentage of body fat of all the linemen on the team, 11 percent," says Smerlas. "They couldn't believe it. They asked me how I did it. I told them, 'Rusty Jones taught me how to eat, about my body in general and how to condition it.'"

Sound nutrition is a major part of the modern training camp, but there are other important parts. One is the custom-design conditioning program. Gone are the days when wide receivers, running backs, defensive backs, and linebackers were expected to run sprints in roughly the same time.

Players still are timed in sprints, but their best times are recorded, and a conditioning program is designed to push them to their personal limits, not someone else's. A defensive back who runs the 40-yard dash in 4.6 seconds does not have an identical program as a defensive back who is timed in 4.4 seconds.

There is flexibility. In Buffalo's 1992 camp, wide receiver James Lofton was entering his fifteenth pro season at age 36. If there had been any doubt about his credentials for the Hall of Fame, the rebirth of his brilliant career when he joined the Bills in 1989 removed it. Consequently, Lofton charted his own course. His work habits were always excellent. At the end of each season he would return to his Los Angeles home and quickly resume three-times-a-week supervised workouts. His self discipline went unquestioned.

At training camp, if Lofton felt fatigued or was suffering from any injury, he was allowed to adjust his own schedule.

Buffalo head coach Marv Levy adjusts to the individual and his particular situation. "If Marv had been my coach when I played," says his defensive coordinator, 54-year-old Walt Corey, "I might still be playing. I left some seasons in the training camps I went through."

Levy discourages unnecessary contact before the season begins. That is why he wants an offseason conditioning program designed to assure that his players would report to training camp in performance condition. He expects them, with a minimal amount of contact work, to be completely honed by opening day of the regular season.

Levy extends that policy to preseason games. Until the last of those games, his regulars rarely play much more than a quarter. Late in the summer, some play a half or so. In the first game of the 1989 preseason schedule, the Bills' veterans played a couple of series and then retired to the sideline where they took off their pads. Their opponents, the Redskins, played their regulars well into the third quarter.

It is a controversial policy that brought criticism upon Levy, but his way is justified by his Super Bowl appearances.

In the New Era of training camps, experimentation is the hallmark. Some teams force players to do resistance running, dragging small, open parachutes attached to their backs.

In the New York Jets' camp in 1992, linemen grappled and pulled each other in a giant sand box. "The idea is to develop leverage and balance," says trainer Bob Reese. "Like anything else that's new, if we win then it must be a good thing."

Levy's camps have a reputation for efficiency and time management. Every moment seems used for a special purpose. There are no players standing around while a drill is explained to them.

One training camp tradition has all but disappeared: rookie hazing. There once were rookie shows, and mandatory singing by rookies in the food halls. There was a sort of indentured servitude to veterans, especially the stars.

In the Bills' camps of the 1960s, initiation into the pros included rookie haircuts that bordered on butchery. "Now and then I come across my rookie bubble-gum card with me bald, my head forcibly shaved," says O.J. Simpson. "It still makes me cringe."

Levy banned most rookie hazing when he opened his first Buffalo camp in 1987. "There is no room for nonsense like that," he says.

Instead, Levy's camps are used as audition grounds to discover unexpected talent. Rookies get to play, especially in preseason games. No draft choice or free agent ever leaves a Buffalo camp saying he wasn't given a chance.

It paid off for the franchise. The Bills' Super Bowl lineups were dotted with low-round draft choices. Offensive tackle Howard Ballard was an eleventh-round choice. Nose tackle Jeff Wright came in the eighth round, tight end Keith McKeller in the ninth, and defensive lineman Mike Lodish in the tenth. Cornerback Kirby Jackson was a free agent.

There still are vestiges of the star system, however. It is not uncommon to see veterans with perks that reflect their status. One year quarterback Jim Kelly made his way around training camp in his own, personalized golf cart. There was some resentment among his teammates. Now golf carts abound, with even marginal players affixing their uniform numbers on the carts parked outside their dormitories.

It was a major story in Miami when Shula, noted for strict camps, made a startling concession. He allowed veteran married players to return to their homes after the training day was finished.

"Times change," explained Shula. "Most of our married veterans who live in the area are within reasonable distance of camp. As long as they were able to get back here in time for the start of our work, I no longer saw any reason not to allow them to spend nights at home with their families."

Just days into his 1992 training camp, Shula saw plenty of reason to rescind the privilege. Defensive lineman Alfred Oglesby, who had gone home for the night, did not return the next day. When Oglesby did return, he told a harrowing tale of being kidnapped at gunpoint and left in a Florida swamp.

Less than 24 hours later, Oglesby admitted the story was a hoax, something concocted in an attempt to escape Shula's wrath.

The veterans' privilege of living at home during training camp was immediately lifted by the coach. Oglesby was abducted for real, this time by angry teammates. They taped him to a nearby tree, but after a half hour relented and released him.

No matter how many luxuries or concessions are brought to training camps, they still are training camps, a place where careers are ended or disrupted and friendships severed.

"You're playing with a guy forever, then you wake up one morning and he's been released," says David Hill, a former tight end with the Lions and Rams. "He's got his bags packed and he's walking out and you're going to breakfast.

"What do you say? You know that you're looking at yourself one day in the future."

A Different Breed

It is sometimes difficult for kickers to be accepted by their teammates as actual football players, especially during training camp when the kickers are off to one side of the field, practicing their specialty while the rest of the squad labors under sweat-soaked pads.

The Bills have a rich history of landmark happenings involving kickers in training camp. In 1964, they drafted Pete Gogolak, a Hungarian refugee and the first soccer-style placekicker in professional football. Until then, placekicking was a straight-ahead endeavor, as practiced by orthodox-style kickers such as Lou Groza and George Blanda.

Gogolak started with three strikes against him. First was the fact that he approached the ball from the side. Second, he made contact not with his toe, but with his instep. And third, his college experience was acquired at Cornell. An Ivy Leaguer! Skeptics hooted.

At Cornell, Gogolak kicked off and produced long field goals that impressed the Buffalo scouts, but in training camp he seemed to be easing into his first pro job.

"Gogie," warned Harvey Johnson, the scout who signed him, "you gotta get going or you're going to be cut. You gotta show them the sort of things you did at Cornell."

Gogolak was shaken. He didn't understand the concept of being released. "What is this bullyshit?" he asked Johnson. But in his first exhibition game against the New York Jets in New Brunswick, New Jersey, he kicked a 57-yard field goal. It was unofficial because it came in preseason, but no straight-ahead kicker ever had kicked one that far in any game. Football would never be the same again.

In 1982, the Bills thought they had reached the end of a six-year search for a dependable kicker when they drafted South African Gary Anderson of Syracuse. What did the Bills in was democracy. Coach Chuck Knox threw the job open in training camp, a dangerous practice when dealing with kickers. Nick Mike-Mayer kicked well. Anderson, pressing, did poorly. On cutdown day, Anderson went and Mike-Mayer stayed.

The next day, Anderson was signed by the Pittsburgh Steelers. He became the Steelers' all-time leading scorer, went to two Pro Bowls, was voted the team's most valuable player one year and is among the most accurate field goal kickers in NFL history.

The Bills cut Mike-Mayer early that season and went searching for kickers once again. ✐

CHAPTER THREE

The Day That Fortunes Rise...and Fall

The NFL's Draft Day is the most fascinating offseason event in sports.
Dynasties are built, but teams that misfire pay the price. Success depends
on good planning, good scouting, and good luck.

BY VITO STELLINO

T O UNDERSTAND HOW UNPREDICTABLE AND FASCINATING THE NFL DRAFT can be, consider Paul Brown's plight in 1957.

The late founding father of the Cleveland Browns needed a quarterback. Brown was searching for a replacement for Hall of Famer Otto Graham, who had retired after taking the Browns to 10 straight championship games from 1946-1955 in the All-America Football Conference and the NFL.

Brown, who owned the sixth pick, thought he had a good chance to draft a blue-chipper because there were three star quarterbacks available: Paul Hornung of Notre Dame, John Brodie of Stanford, and Len Dawson of Purdue.

The Packers opened the draft by taking Hornung, and the Rams took running back Jon Arnett. When the San Francisco 49ers selected Brodie third and the Packers, who had the fourth pick, took tight end Ron Kramer, Brown was just one pick away from Dawson.

That's when his hopes were dashed. Pittsburgh selected Dawson.

Brown pounded the table in frustration.

"Cleveland was at the table right near us," remembers Ed Kiely, a Steelers executive, "and Brown knocked some books off the table with his fist."

There were no more first-round quarterbacks in the draft, so he settled on a Syracuse running back with his first-round pick.

The running back's name: Jim Brown.

He may have been the best running back of all time.

Brown played in the NFL nine years and set an all-time rushing record of 12,312 yards before retiring. Although three runners later surpassed Brown's yardage total, he's the only one among them who averaged more than five yards per carry throughout his career. His mark of 5.2 may never be topped.

Dawson also arrived at the Hall of Fame, but only after flopping in Pittsburgh. Given a second chance with the Kansas City Chiefs of the AFL, he later made it big.

It's important to be both smart and lucky in the draft. The Cleveland Browns drafted Jim Brown, perhaps the best running back of all time, only because the quarterback they wanted was no longer available.

The tale of how Paul Brown had to "settle" for one of the game's best running backs explains why the draft is the most interesting offseason event in sports.

The draft offers the joy of victory and the agony of defeat, but it can take years to determine whether a team drafted well. Dynasties are built in the draft, but teams that misfire pay the price in the won-lost column.

There's another fascinating "almost" to the Steelers' selection of Dawson over Brown. Pittsburgh had a chance to put Johnny Unitas and Jim Brown, the best quarterback and running back of their time, in the same backfield.

Pittsburgh selected Unitas on the ninth round of the 1955 draft, but cut him. The Steelers were set at quarterback with Jim Finks, now president of the New Orleans Saints, and Ted Marchibroda, now coach of the Indianapolis Colts. Unitas became a Hall of Famer for the Baltimore Colts. Two years later, the Steelers bypassed Jim Brown. A chance to build a dynasty was lost.

A decade and a half later, the Steelers rectified the mistake when they put Terry Bradshaw and Franco Harris in the same backfield.

They won a coin flip with the Chicago Bears for

the first pick in the 1970 draft, with which they selected Bradshaw. Two years later, the Steelers took Harris with the thirteenth pick in the first round, but only after deliberating.

Coach Chuck Noll liked Robert Newhouse, who went on to have a good, but not outstanding career, with the Dallas Cowboys. Pittsburgh scouts, though, convinced Noll to take Harris, who was bigger than Newhouse.

With Bradshaw and Harris playing major roles, Pittsburgh, which had never won a championship, won four Super Bowl titles in six years. Bradshaw and Harris both landed in the Pro Football Hall of Fame.

Pittsburgh was not the only team to nearly bypass the final piece of a championship puzzle.

The Miami Dolphins, who went to three straight Super Bowls in the 1970s and won Super Bowls VII and VIII with Bob Griese at quarterback, came close to bypassing Griese in the 1967 draft.

Chief scout Joe Thomas wanted to take Griese, but Dolphins owner Joe Robbie argued it would be a public relations disaster for the only pro football team in Florida to pass up Steve Spurrier, the University of Florida's Heisman Trophy winner.

But San Francisco, which had the third pick, took Spurrier. Miami, which picked fourth, then grabbed Griese.

Spurrier, who has been a successful coach, never excelled in the NFL as he did in college, while Griese went on to the Pro Football Hall of Fame.

In the same draft, the Minnesota Vikings had three of the first 15 picks. With the second and eighth picks in the first round, they took a pair of Michigan State stars, Clint Jones and Gene Washington.

With their third choice, they took Notre Dame defensive lineman Alan Page, who had nine Pro Bowl seasons in 12 years with Minnesota and was elected to the Hall of Fame.

"We weren't too smart," says Vikings assistant general manager Jerry Reichow. "We had three picks, and he's the third one we take."

Teams often disguise their true intentions in the draft; they never want to tip off their strategy.

George Young, general manager of the New York Giants, says a monsignor approached him in church one year and asked whom the Giants were going to draft.

"I can't tell you," Young said.

The monsignor replied, "George, I'm a priest. You can trust me."

"I told him that when it comes to the draft, I don't trust anyone," says Young.

The Giants' GM remembers sweating out the 1981 draft, when he had the second pick. New Orleans coach Bum Phillips had the first choice, and he told Heisman Trophy winner George Rogers of South Carolina that he would be their selection. Phillips had built his running game around Earl Campbell when he coached the Houston Oilers, and he planned to do the same with Rogers in New Orleans.

Young wanted North Carolina linebacker Lawrence Taylor with the second pick, but he didn't know whether Phillips was bluffing about Rogers.

Young's stomach turned flips when Phillips invited Taylor to New Orleans the weekend before the draft. Inasmuch as NFL officials usually invite the number one pick to New York for an appearance at draft headquarters, the Giants checked all the major hotels in New York until they found out that Taylor had returned to college in North Carolina.

The Saints drafted Rogers and the Giants grabbed Taylor, who went to 10 straight Pro Bowls and spearheaded a pair of Super Bowl championship teams. Rogers didn't appear in a

The Pittsburgh Steelers faced a tough decision – whether to draft Franco Harris or Robert Newhouse. They opted for Harris, and he became a vital factor in four Super Bowl victories in six years.

Super Bowl until he was traded to Washington near the end of his career.

Looking back on that experience, Young says, "You have to maintain a good, level attitude about the draft or you wind up a mental case."

Good luck can be as important as good drafting.

For example, the Philadelphia Eagles were in the market for a wide receiver in 1982 and rated Perry Tuttle of Clemson slightly above North Carolina State's Mike Quick because he had more speed.

Lawrence Taylor, the second player chosen in the 1981 draft, was a great pick for the New York Giants. But the Giants didn't know until the last minute whether he would be available.

The Eagles, picking twentieth in the first round, were happy when Tuttle was still available after the Giants selected Butch Woolfolk with the eighteenth pick. But the Eagles were stunned when Buffalo made a trade with Denver to get the nineteenth pick and grabbed Tuttle.

The Bills knew the Eagles wanted Tuttle because Eagles coach Dick Vermeil had let that information slip. The Eagles then "settled" for Quick and got the last laugh. Tuttle survived only three NFL seasons; Quick was a five-time Pro Bowl selection.

Kansas City Chiefs president Carl Peterson, then an Eagles scout, says, "We lucked out. Sometimes your best laid plans are askewed."

There are times when teams are happy they don't have to make a decision.

In the 1983 draft, Bobby Beathard, then general manager of the Washington Redskins, was happy he had the last pick. That's because in the twenty-eighth position, he didn't have to explain why he didn't pick Dan Marino, who was still around when Miami drafted twenty-seventh.

The scouts had overemphasized Marino's subpar senior season at Pittsburgh. Five quarterbacks - John Elway, Todd Blackledge, Jim Kelly, Tony Eason, and Ken O'Brien - were chosen ahead of Marino.

Beathard, with the final pick in the first round, selected Darrell Green, who became a Pro Bowl cornerback on a Super Bowl championship team.

Every team in the league had a chance to draft Joe Montana in 1979. Because of questions about his size and arm strength, 81 players were selected before the 49ers chose Montana in the third round. The Rams, Dolphins, and Bills each selected five players before he was finally chosen.

The Bears' quarterbacks were a young Vince Evans, an old Mike Phipps, and a middle-aged Bob Avellini, but they bypassed Montana with their first four picks.

Jim Finks, then the Bears' president, explained: "We have a young quarterback, an experienced quarterback, and a quarterback who got us into the playoffs."

Bill Tobin, the Bears' director of player personnel, says, "I've never been able to live it down because of how it unfolded. But who knows if Montana would have had the career here that he had in San Francisco. That's true of any player."

A player's success can hinge on being in the right place at the right time. When Montana went to San Francisco, he fit perfectly with coach Bill Walsh's passing offense.

Actually, Walsh had his eye on Phil Simms, but the Giants grabbed Simms with the seventh overall selection.

Simms and Montana met in an especially dramatic showdown in the twelfth game of the 1990 season when both were quarterbacking teams with 10-1 records. Montana and the 49ers won a defensive duel, 7-3.

Interestingly, another quarterback was selected ahead of Simms and Montana in the 1979 draft. That was Jack Thompson, taken with the third pick by the Cincinnati Bengals; he never matched his college reputation.

If the draft is nerve-racking for teams, it is equally so for players. Not only do top players wonder where they'll start their careers, they know they'll lose money if they are selected later in the draft.

Cris Collinsworth, a former wide receiver for the Cincinnati Bengals who was taken on the second round in 1981, says, "It's an emotional roller coaster. You move around the country with every pick. Here goes Philly. Okay. Philly would be okay. Then, it's on to L.A. Not bad. You pack your bags and move every 30 seconds."

Collinsworth was bypassed on the first round by the Bengals in favor of wide receiver David Verser of Kansas. Collinsworth turned out to be the better player.

Todd Christensen, a former tight end for the Raiders, remembers being selected by the Dallas Cowboys at the end of the second round.

"The longer that phone didn't ring, the more money I was losing. It's like watching the stock market drop. You put a grand on pork bellies and watch it go down," he says.

Christensen was cut by the Cowboys as a running back, but he was a five-time Pro Bowl selection with the Raiders as a tight end.

The draft was less sophisticated in earlier times.

Art Donovan remembers getting a letter in 1950 from the Baltimore Colts.

"They said they had taken me in the third round. They included a contract for $4,500 and asked me to sign it and report to training camp that summer," Donovan recalls.

"Well, I thought I should get more money, so I sent it back to them and told them I wanted more. I never heard from them again."

When summer came, Donovan decided to show up at training camp.

"When I got there, I asked why they hadn't written me back. They told me that since I said I didn't like their offer, they thought I wasn't interested. They told me they didn't care whether I signed or not," he says.

Donovan signed, played 11 years, and was elected to the Hall of Fame.

Noll had a similar experience in 1953 when he heard about the draft as a senior at Dayton.

"Somebody told me I was drafted and I said I couldn't be, I haven't had a physical yet. I thought they were going to send me to Korea," Noll says.

He hadn't been drafted by Uncle Sam, but by the Cleveland Browns.

"I had no contact with pro scouts. I had no thought about professional football," he says.

Noll had planned to be a school teacher. The starting salary for teachers was $2,500. The Browns offered $5,000.

"I went for the money," Noll says with a smile.

Noll was a messenger guard for the Browns before becoming head coach with the Steelers and winning four Super Bowls.

The draft is such an extravaganza now that it may be hard to believe that it started as a

modest affair on Feb. 8, 1936, the same year the Heisman Trophy was first awarded. The first Heisman winner also was the first player drafted: Jay Berwanger, a halfback at the University of Chicago.

Berwanger was so underwhelmed with the honor that he passed up a pro football career to enter the business world.

The first draft, held at the Ritz Carlton Hotel in Philadelphia, was a nine-round affair. The Eagles chose Berwanger with the first pick and, after failing to sign him, traded his rights to Chicago. He also turned down the Bears.

Berwanger's decision didn't cause much of a stir in those days. The NFL was what the late Art Rooney, the founder of the Steelers, called a "hop, skip, and jump from semipro ball."

There were no scouting combines, mock drafts, or sense of anticipation in those days. The

When the Pittsburgh Steelers selected Joe Greene on the first round in 1969, a Pittsburgh newspaper referred to him as "Joe Who?" Today, potential first round picks are household names by draft day.

teams simply announced the names of players they had drafted when it was over.

No one dreamed that the draft would become the NFL's biggest non-game day of the year.

The NFL draft has been held in November, December, January, February, March, April, and May. In 1960, when the NFL was fighting the AFL for players, it held a secret draft to get a jump on signing players.

Teams have traditionally picked in inverse order of their won-lost records, allowing weaker teams to pick earlier.

But from 1947 to 1958, there was another wrinkle: a bonus pick. That selection, to be used to begin the draft, was awarded in a random draw. The club that won the bonus pick forfeited its normal first-round selection. The system was abolished in 1958 after every team had received a bonus pick.

The draft took on added importance with the arrival of the AFL in 1960. Suddenly, there was competition for players. Teams wanted to know if players would sign with them before expending a draft pick.

It was also the year that Clint Murchinson hired Tex Schramm as president of the new Dallas Cowboys, an expansion team.

Schramm had been an executive with the Los Angeles Rams in the 1950s when they were one of the first teams to emphasize the draft. Schramm hired Gil Brandt to run his draft, and gave him a big budget.

Brandt scoured the country for players. He remembers visiting Montana State in 1962. "I was the second pro scout that ever visited the place," he says. "It was a big deal at the school."

The Cowboys were the first team to use computers to compile and grade scouting information. When the Cowboys started winning in 1966, their success in the draft forced other franchises to try to match them. The club that did it best was Pittsburgh, which made a commitment to the draft in 1969 when Chuck Noll was hired as head coach.

Noll's first draft pick was defensive lineman Joe Greene of North Texas State. A Pittsburgh newspaper referred to him in a headline as "Joe Who?"

Greene was the fourth player picked in the draft, yet virtually unknown to NFL fans. Today many players are known more for their draft status than for their accomplishments in college. Quentin Coryatt got more attention for being the second pick in the 1992 draft than for his performance at Texas A&M.

By the mid-1970s, when Pittsburgh and Dallas played a pair of Super Bowls with teams built almost exclusively through the draft, all teams were putting more emphasis on the draft.

But it was an unusual ramification of the 1977 bargaining agreement between the players and the owners - and the rise of cable TV - that made the draft a true spectacle. In the 1977 agreement, the draft was pushed back to late April so that players whose contracts had expired could have time to test the market.

The postponement of the draft to April allowed more time for evaluating talent. It wasn't long before the emergence of the scouting combine meetings at which more than 450 prospects were flown into Indianapolis for extensive pre-draft tests.

A later draft meant more newspaper stories about the draft. It meant time for sportswriters to prepare mock drafts. Never again would the fourth player be called "Joe Who?" The fourth player would be a household name.

The April draft also fueled the rise of "draftniks" who prepared and marketed their own draft reports, which helped to hype the draft.

In 1980, ESPN, a new all-sports cable channel, seeking to fill air time, began televising the draft. As the cable audience grew, the interest grew. In 1988, the draft was switched from Tuesday to Sunday to reach a larger audience.

The draft is now much more than simply a way for the NFL to distribute players coming out of college.

It has become an event with a life of its own.

THE BEST DRAFT CLASSES

Judging a draft class is like rating a vintage wine.

It can take several years to determine how good it is.

But three drafts that have stood the test of time - 1957, 1981, and 1983 - were especially outstanding.

1957

Even though scouting was not as sophisticated as it would be in later years, NFL teams hit the jackpot in this draft.

Four of the first eight players in the 12-man first round made the Hall of Fame and the four others were solid players.

Paul Hornung

Here's how that draft started:

1. *Green Bay Packers* - **RB Paul Hornung**
2. *Los Angeles Rams* - **RB Jon Arnett**
3. *San Francisco* - **QB John Brodie**
4. *Green Bay* - **TE Ron Kramer**
5. *Pittsburgh* - **QB Len Dawson**
6. *Cleveland* - **RB Jim Brown**
7. *Philadelphia* - **RB Clarence Peaks**
8. *Baltimore* - **OL Jim Parker**

Of that group, Hornung, Dawson, Brown, and Parker were all selected for the Hall of Fame and played on championship teams. Dawson was cut by the Steelers and didn't become a star until he hooked on with the Kansas City Chiefs in the early days of the AFL.

The other four players also became valuable performers. Brodie was a standout quarterback with the 49ers, and Arnett was a dazzling runner with the Rams. Kramer was one of the best tight ends with the Packers and Lions, while Peaks was a dependable running back for the Eagles.

Making the 1957 draft more amazing is the fact that teams used primitive scouting methods and had limited contact with the prospects.

As George Young, general manager of the New York Giants, says, "Scouts and coaches would look at magazines and read newspapers and decide who they wanted."

The key was that all eight players were from major schools, so it was easy for NFL teams to find them. Dawson, Parker, Kramer, and Peaks played in the Big Ten, Arnett and Brodie in the Pacific 8 (forerunner to the Pacific 10), Hornung at Notre Dame, and Brown at Syracuse.

They were can't-miss players in college who turned out to be can't-miss players in the pros.

A year earlier, Pittsburgh made Gary Glick, a defensive back from Colorado A&M, the first pick in the 1956 draft. A year later, Rice quarterback King Hill was the first player picked by the Chicago Cardinals in 1958. Neither excelled in pro football.

1981

The 1981 draft was a dream-come-true for scouts. Seven of the first eight players selected that year became the star performers they were supposed to, and at least two seem destined for the Hall of Fame.

This is how the round started:

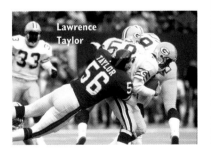

Lawrence Taylor

1. *New Orleans* - **RB George Rogers**
2. *New York Giants* - **LB Lawrence Taylor**
3. *New York Jets* - **RB Freeman McNeil**
4. *Seattle* - **DB Kenny Easley**
5. *St. Louis* - **LB E.J. Junior**
6. *Green Bay* - **QB Rich Campbell**
7. *Tampa Bay* - **LB Hugh Green**
8. *San Francisco* - **DB Ronnie Lott**

Of those, only Campbell was a major disappointment; the seven others each played in at least two Pro Bowls. Taylor and Lott seemed destined to be enshrined in Canton. If top-rated players panned out that well every year, scouts wouldn't get ulcers.

1983

The 1983 draft is considered the draft to end all drafts.

The first six players all proved to be standouts:

John Elway

1. *Baltimore* - **QB John Elway**
2. *Los Angeles Rams* - **RB Eric Dickerson**
3. *Seattle* - **RB Curt Warner**
4. *Denver* - **OL Chris Hinton**
5. *San Diego* - **LB Billy Ray Smith**
6. *Chicago* - **OL Jim (Jimbo) Covert**

Elway and Hinton switched teams in one of the most celebrated trades of the decade, but both became Pro Bowl players. Dickerson, who set the single season rushing record, and Warner were two of the best running backs of their time. Smith was a good linebacker, and Covert has been an outstanding offensive lineman.

But what made this draft so special was its depth. Houston took offensive lineman Bruce Matthews with the ninth pick, the Giants selected safety Terry Kinard with the tenth, Buffalo grabbed quarterback Jim Kelly with the fourteenth choice, New England took quarterback Tony Eason with the fifteenth, Chicago got wide receiver Willie Gault with the eighteenth, Minnesota selected safety Joey Browner with the nineteenth pick, San Diego took running back Gary Anderson with the twentieth and cornerback Gill Byrd with the twenty-second, and the Jets selected quarterback Ken O'Brien with the twenty-fourth.

The round even ended with a bang. Miami got quarterback Dan Marino with the twenty-seventh pick, and Washington took cornerback Darrell Green with the last selection.

Four of the six quarterbacks selected in the first round - Elway, Kelly, Eason, and Marino - started seven of eight Super Bowls for the AFC between 1984 and 1992. The only frustration for the Class of 1983 is that they were 0-7 against Joe Montana, Phil Simms, Doug Williams, Jeff Hostetler, and Mark Rypien.

The 1983 draft remains the standard by which all drafts are measured.

BEST DRAFTS

What's the secret to winning four Super Bowls?

It helps to have good coaching and a good organization, but the most important ingredient may be the ability to find blue-chip players in the draft.

The only two teams to win four Super Bowls - the Pittsburgh Steelers in the 1970s and the San Francisco 49ers in the 1980s - showed a deft touch in the draft to mold their championship teams.

Both teams drafted well for a number of years before putting together one super draft that enabled each to build a dynasty.

The Steelers' 1974 draft may have been the best of all time. A good team became a great team and won four Super Bowls in the next six seasons.

For the 49ers, the key was the 1986 draft. A roster that had won two earlier Super Bowls was aging and needed new talent. The talent unearthed in 1986 set the stage for two more championship seasons in 1988 and 1989.

The contrasting styles of the two teams showed how successful teams can have different philosophies. The Steelers weren't wheeler-dealers. They simply waited their turn in each round. The 49ers traded their first-round pick and dealt with six different teams in acquiring eight Super Bowl starters.

Here's how they did it:

Steelers

The Steelers had drafted five future Hall of Famers in a four-year span from 1969-1972 to set the stage for the 1974 draft. They selected Joe Greene in 1969, Terry Bradshaw and Mel Blount in 1970, Jack Ham in 1971, and Franco Harris in 1972. In addition to Ham, they got important depth in 1971, selecting future starters Frank Lewis, Gerry (Moon) Mullins, Dwight White, Larry Brown, Ernie Holmes, and Mike Wagner.

In 1974, Pittsburgh had only four selections in the first five rounds after trading away a third-round pick. The four players selected with those four picks:

- Lynn Swann
- Jack Lambert
- John Stallworth
- Mike Webster

In addition, the Steelers signed Donnie Shell as a free agent.

Lambert is already in the Hall of Fame, Webster seems destined to join him, and the three others will get consideration.

When they were selected, they weren't household names.

Art Rooney, Jr., then head of the scouting department, says coach Chuck Noll considered drafting Stallworth on the first round even though he was from a small school, Alabama A&M. The Steelers were concerned about Swann's speed.

The Pittsburgh Steelers scored one of the all-time great drafting coups when they got both Lynn Swann and John Stallworth in the 1974 draft. They became one of the greatest wide receiver combinations of all time.

But when Swann posted a quick time in the 40-yard dash, he became the logical first-round pick. He had played in big-time competition at Southern California.

The Steelers didn't consider Stallworth in the second round because they had taken a wide receiver with their first pick. But Lambert, out of unheralded Kent State, was no sure thing.

Rooney says they debated taking some other player, whose name he no longer remembers, but settled on Lambert because of his special teams potential.

"Woody Widenhofer (linebackers coach) said, 'This guy can make a helluva contribution on the special teams while he learns the system,'" Rooney says.

Lambert got a chance to start at middle linebacker when veterans staged a strike during training camp. He didn't budge when the veterans came back.

Lambert didn't have a classic linebacker's build - he was 6 feet 4 inches tall and weighed 207 pounds - and he lacked experience in a big-time program.

Dick Steinberg, New York Jets' president, says, "He was a stiff guy, skinny as a rail, but he made tackles all over the field."

The Steelers didn't have a pick in the third round, but were astonished when Stallworth was available. He had been tried at defensive back at the Senior Bowl and dazzled nobody. When he was still there on the fourth round, the Steelers grabbed him. Stallworth paired with Swann to form one of the best wide receiver duos of all time.

Webster, standing just 6 feet 1 inch, lasted until the fifth round because of his size, but Noll liked agile linemen he could help develop.

"Noll did a lot of good things with the scouts. He defined what he was looking for," Rooney says.

The Steelers took a chance on Shell, a free agent from South Carolina State, after the draft. He was a special teams dynamo on Pittsburgh's first two Super Bowl teams and became a hard hitting safety on the second two.

In Super Bowl XIV, six years after the 1974 draft, when the Steelers won their fourth Super Bowl, Swann, Lambert, Webster, and Shell all were in the starting lineup.

49ers

The 49ers had drafted well enough since Bill Walsh took over in 1979 to win a pair of Super Bowls. They selected Joe Montana on the third round and Dwight Clark on the tenth in 1979. They added Keena Turner in 1980, plus three fine defensive backs, Ronnie Lott, Eric Wright, and Carlton Williamson, in 1981. The 49ers selected Roger Craig in the second round in 1983 and traded a second-round pick to New England in 1985 to move up in the first round to get Jerry Rice.

Walsh, though, had opponents scratching their heads early in the 1986 draft. Instead of picking players, he kept trading down.

He swapped the eighteenth pick in the first round for the Dallas Cowboys' fifth-round pick and their first-round pick, in the twenty-seventh position. He then took a second-and third-round - pick from Buffalo for the twenty-seventh pick on the first round and a tenth-round choice.

Walsh then traded the Bills' second-round pick for the Lions' second-and third-round picks.

Club owner Eddie DeBartolo, listening to the draft-room talk on a speaker phone from his office in Youngstown, Ohio, said, "When are we going to pick somebody?"

There was method to Walsh's madness. The first-round players he liked - John L. Williams (selected by Seattle), Ronnie Harmon (picked by Buffalo) and Gerald Robinson (selected by Minnesota) - would be gone before he could draft. He thought he could trade down and get the players he wanted.

Walsh finally selected defensive end Larry Roberts, on the second round, traded his other second-round pick to Washington for a first-round pick in 1987 and a tenth-round pick. He then traded backup quarterback Matt Cavanaugh to the Philadelphia Eagles for a third-round choice and a second-round pick in 1987.

He then had four third-round choices and swapped one to the Rams for two fourths and backup quarterback Jeff Kemp.

He wound up with six picks on the third and fourth rounds and picked a Super Bowl starter with every one of them: fullback Tom Rathman, cornerback Tim McKyer, wide receiver John Taylor, defensive end Charles Haley, offensive lineman Steve Wallace, and defensive end Kevin Fagan. In addition, he took cornerback Don Griffin on the eighth round.

When Walsh got his third Super Bowl victory in Super Bowl XXIII, McKyer and Griffin were the starting cornerbacks, Fagan and Roberts were the defensive ends, Taylor started at wide receiver, Wallace at left tackle, Haley at outside linebacker, and Rathman at fullback.

The 49ers acquired eight Super Bowl starters from one draft, while picking just one player in the first two rounds.

When the 49ers won their fourth Super Bowl in 1989 under George Seifert, who succeeded Walsh, five of those players - Taylor, Rathman, Fagan, Haley, and Griffin - still started and the three others were reserves.

During the 1986 draft, Walsh swung trades with the Cowboys, Bills, Lions, Redskins, Eagles, and Rams.

"Bill wasn't afraid to do things," 49ers vice president John McVay says. "He liked to wheel and deal. Some clubs are afraid to make trades. Once Bill made them, he didn't look back."

DeBartolo says, "We rebuilt this team while it was aging and that's almost unheard of in pro football."

That's why the 49ers' 1986 draft is in a class of its own. ✍

CHAPTER FOUR

"What's He Got Inside His Heart?"

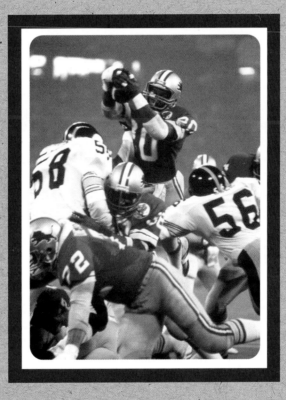

*The scout measures height, weight, speed, and athletic ability. In the end, though,
he's judging people, and the ultimate question is: "What's he got inside his heart?"
A team's success or failure can depend on the scout's ability to judge.*

BY VITO STELLINO

EARNING TO JUDGE PEOPLE IS THE REAL TRICK FOR NFL COLLEGE SCOUTS.

Obviously, scouts evaluate players for football skills. They research height, weight, speed, and overall athletic ability.

In the end, though, they're judging people.

That's why scouting is an inexact science. The goal is to find out so much more about a player than just how much athletic talent he has.

"Does this kid really love playing football?" asks Bobby Beathard, general manager of the San Diego Chargers who earlier built the Washington Redskins into a Super Bowl team with shrewd scouting and drafting. "If there weren't any money involved, would he still be out there playing football? What's he got inside his heart? Does he have the desire to win? What sacrifices will he make to be a winner?"

Those are the questions Beathard likes to ask about the college players he scouts.

"It's a problem to find out which kid has that burning desire and knows the price he has to pay to be a good football player," Beathard says. "Some guys are motivated and some aren't. It's a world of achievers and underachievers."

Because there are virtually no secrets in the draft, the key to the job is evaluating information. That's the essence of the art of scouting.

In the 1960s and early 1970s, the Dallas Cowboys and Pittsburgh Steelers had a jump on their rivals because they were more thorough in their scouting.

Art Rooney, Jr., who headed the Steelers' personnel department when they drafted the future Hall of Famers who would go on to win four Super Bowls, recalls, "Wherever I went, the Cowboys already had been there."

Today, nearly all the teams get there. For those that don't, the top 450 or so prospects are brought into Indianapolis each February to be evaluated by scouts from all 28 teams.

"It's not a matter of collecting the information, it's interpreting it," Rooney says.

Carl Peterson, president of the Kansas City Chiefs, says, "It's not easy. It's humans trying to evaluate humans."

> "I've always believed you go with the numbers. You don't deviate. If you start grabbing and making rash decisions you can make mistakes."
>
> - Carl Peterson, president of the Kansas City Chiefs

"We're dealing with equals for the most part," says George Young, general manager of the New York Giants. "You want to know what makes a guy more successful than the other equals, whatever that edge is. Maybe it's self-motivation. Some guys are winners and some guys are losers. The edge might be that one guy is a little smarter, a little better under pressure. In a word, it's intangibles."

Peterson cites former running back Wilbert Montgomery as an illustration of a player who had those intangibles. Peterson was a scout for the Eagles when they drafted Montgomery in the sixth round in 1977 - even though he was a medical risk because of a calcium deposit in his thigh.

"Because of what was inside Wilbert, there was no way he could fail to make our team. The two things you can't measure are character and desire, what really burns in a guy," Peterson says.

Montgomery was the workhorse in the Eagles' running attack when they played in Super Bowl XV.

Dick Steinberg, the president of the New York Jets, says the team likes to evaluate each player by five major criteria:

- Character
- Athletic ability
- Competitiveness
- Mental capacity
- Strength

In the character department, Steinberg says scouts try to find out if a player is reliable, loyal, stable, unselfish, and has a positive attitude. They want to know if he can handle the pressure of performing in the spotlight.

"Everything players do is dissected and magnified by the media. If a guy drops a pass, it's going to be on the halftime show, the wrap-up show, and every show until next Sunday," Steinberg says.

Athletic ability is probably the easiest to judge. Steinberg says most mistakes are made in assessing competitiveness.

"You're looking for tough, aggressive, motivated guys who rise to the occasion and produce in games. You don't want guys who just run around and waste a lot of energy," he says.

Mental ability means more than intelligence. Scouts want players who have football instincts and quick reactions.

"Some guys are instinctive," says Peterson. "When the ball is snapped, the linebacker knows where the ball is going. He's gone."

Scouts believe a player can improve his strength. "We can't make a guy a better athlete, but if he has all the other things and the frame to get bigger, we can get him stronger," Steinberg says.

A difficult item to judge is how a player will make the transition from the college game.

"Sometimes, a college player won't play against a pro caliber player his whole senior year," says Charlie Casserly, general manager of the Washington Redskins.

The key for a scout is consistency. Some scouts may downgrade players for lack of height or some other peculiarity, but if he always grades them by the same criteria, his grades are meaningful.

"We're all biased," says Jack Butler, veteran head of the BLESTO scouting combine. "I may be biased towards tough guys. Other scouts might be biased towards quick guys. Others might be biased towards size, speed, or intelligence."

Duke Babb, head of the National Scouting Combine, says, "When we send our people out, I don't want them to come back and tell me what other people thought. I want to know what they thought. Each scout builds his own credibility. Some are liberal graders and some are hard graders. That's your credibility. People pick up your reports and know you're a hard grader. We want them to be consistent."

Butler says a good scout has to be "organized and self-disciplined. He has to want to do it, to hustle, to make the stops, and talk to the coaches. The longer you do it, the better you get."

Butler has had success hiring high school football coaches - particularly from Western Pennsylvania - in their early thirties.

"They have to do everything in high school from sweeping the floor to looking at film to teaching and planning for their classes. These guys are organized and they know football," Butler says.

"A good scout is someone who is conscientious to detail and realizes it takes long days and short nights when the curtain comes up," says Babb. "They've got to be willing to do the detail work it requires."

"It's a tedious, time-consuming job," says Peterson. "There are a lot of miles to travel, a lot of bad hotels, a lot of airports, and a lot of rental cars. You've got to have a love for it. You've got to really enjoy the players and the game."

For combine scouts, the job starts in the spring when they start visiting schools to evaluate the upcoming crop of seniors.

When the draft is over, combine scouts have a week-long meeting in May with scouts from individual teams to give them a rundown on all prospects.

The team scouts then go back and start requesting film of the prospects and map out a schedule for the fall. An NFL team typically has five or six scouts. They divide the country

"All that stuff has to be taken in the right context. You can neglect how a player actually played football, and fall in love with his exotic workouts. You can forget what's really important."

- Dick Steinberg, president of the New York Jets

45

into areas, but they also crosscheck in order to get more than one opinion on a player.

When a scout arrives at a school, he watches film of the prospects and, with luck, a practice. He also interviews as many people as possible in the college football program to learn about the athlete. One bad report won't outweigh several positive ones, because a player could have a personality clash with a trainer or an assistant coach.

The scouts meet around Thanksgiving to go over their reports again and rate players prior to the postseason games.

The scouts assemble at the Blue-Gray game on Christmas Day in Montgomery, Alabama, the Senior Bowl in Mobile, Alabama, and at the East-West game in Palo Alto, California, in January. Players tend to treat the Hula Bowl in Honolulu and the Japan Bowl in Tokyo as vacations, so scouts don't put as much stock in those games.

The Senior Bowl, played the week before the Super Bowl, serves as a convention for scouts. In addition, many teams have their coaches present. Coaches' actual involvement in evaluations and drafting varies from team to team.

The head coach is in control of the draft on some teams. Former 49ers coach Bill Walsh is a prime example of a successful coach who did well in the drafting room.

Don Shula of the Miami Dolphins, Jimmy Johnson of the Dallas Cowboys and Bill Belichick of the Cleveland Browns also oversee their drafts.

Other teams put the general manager in charge of the draft but allow input from coaches and send them to scout top players in the offseason. The Redskins, Giants, and Chiefs are among successful teams who do it that way.

Although Peterson and his personnel director, Lynn Stiles, run the Kansas City draft, Peterson wants coaches to look at the leading prospects.

"When you put coaches on the road, they come back with a renewed appreciation for scouts," Peterson says. "I like to have my coaches write out what qualities they're looking for at a position. I also believe in having the scouts in training camp going to team meetings. If you have that communication, you mesh together as a team."

When coaches are involved in the process, there's less likelihood that scouts and coaches will blame one another for a draft choice who doesn't pan out.

Peterson won't take a player the coaches like if the scouts don't. But if the scouts like a player and a coach has reservations, Peterson might ignore the player or select him only in a lower round.

"When there's a big difference of opinion, I'll get off a guy. You want players that the coaches and scouts agree on," Peterson says.

Some general managers believe coaches shouldn't be involved in the draft. They think coaches should coach, and scouts should scout, and never the twain shall meet.

Jim Finks, president of the New Orleans Saints, believes in that philosophy.

"We don't send coaches out," he says. "If a coach likes a player, he's going to root for him and give him every benefit of the doubt."

He says scouts tend to compare college players with the successful players in the team's program.

"We might say, 'This guy compares very favorably with Jim Dombrowski when he was coming out of college.' It's a way of comparing players," he says.

There's really no right or wrong way. There are just different approaches.

A player's stock can go up or down in postseason games. A player from a smaller school who hasn't had a chance to play against big-time competition has a perfect opportunity to make a good impression.

After the postseason games, the next big event is the annual combine meeting at Indianapolis, to which 450 prospects are invited for physicals and workouts.

This is a chance for the scouts to get an up-close-and-personal look at the top players, but the danger is that scouts can become too impressed by workouts. Some players do agility drills better than they play football.

"You can get fooled by those drills," says Butler. "You can see a guy go through those drills like Grant went through Richmond. A good athlete can have a great workout, but he doesn't play the game that well."

Says Steinberg, "The important thing is how he plays football, not how high he jumps. All that stuff has to be taken in the right context. You can neglect how a player actually played football in the fall and fall in love with his exotic workouts. You can forget what's really important."

After the Indianapolis meeting, scouts spend two months going back to the colleges for individual workouts. Some teams send their coaches out at this time. It's the time when they look at juniors who have decided to skip their final season of eligibility. The scouts usually don't look closely at juniors until they declare they're coming out of college.

After the annual league meetings end in mid-March, the teams get to the serious business of putting together their final draft board. This is when heated arguments can take place. The arguments can be healthy, though.

"You want a guy to fight to the end," says Ernie Accorsi, former vice president for football operations for the Cleveland Browns. The best scouts have the courage of their convictions even when they're in the minority.

One factor that every team must ponder is how a player drafted on the first round will react to his financial windfall.

A player drafted at the top of the round can get a contract worth more than $2 million a year, while late first rounders average about $700,000 per year.

"Some players never make the adjustment to getting more money than they ever thought they'd see. They lose their drive and motivation," Steinberg says.

"There's that immediate gratification problem," says Beathard. "It's amazing what happens to some kids between the draft and the start of training camp. They get the car and all the money and they forget how they got there."

"Sometimes a guy isn't motivated when he walks in and signs a big bonus and knows that we'll keep him for at least a couple of years because he was drafted on the first round," Peterson says.

The stakes are high when so much money is involved.

"There was a time when you made a mistake with a high-round pick, you'd only lose the value of that pick. The money wasn't that big. Now when you make a mistake, you've lost a lot of money," Steinberg says.

Once a team finalizes its draft board - its pecking order of talent - the waiting starts.

"That's when you have strategy sessions," says Accorsi. "Who do you really want? Who do you think you can get? Do you have to move to get him? Do you want to trade down? Do you want to trade up? You talk to clubs. What you shouldn't be doing the last ten days is evaluating players."

STEINBERG SAYS, "You've got to have a plan and stick to it. There's always a guy like (linebacker) Chris Spielman (a second-round choice of the Detroit Lions in 1988 who's a six-footer and doesn't have great speed) who goes against the mold. But if you keep picking guys who aren't big enough and aren't fast enough and get away from your standards trying to find another Spielman, you make a lot of mistakes. If you have a consistent method of evaluating players, you do better than if you go off the top of your head."

Wide receiver Tom Waddle is another example. He wasn't drafted in 1989 because he was too slow, but he latched on as a free agent with the Chicago Bears. In 1991, he had 55 receptions. Just because Waddle made it, though, there won't be a demand for slow receivers. Waddle is the exception to the rule.

Another priority is to get the right "value" for a player. There's no reason to spend a first-round pick on a player who will be available later.

But teams sometimes have to make adjustments because of their draft position. For example, Young's first selection after being named general manager of the Giants in 1979 was

"Some players never make the adjustment to getting more money than they ever thought they'd see. They lose their drive and motivation."

- Dick Steinberg, president of New York Jets

47

quarterback Phil Simms with the seventh pick in the draft, even though Simms was considered a late first-rounder at best.

"I needed a quarterback and I didn't have a late first-round pick," Young says, explaining how he picked the quarterback who became a Super Bowl MVP.

At the start of a round, teams write the names of four or five players they're interested in for that round.

"We might say, `We'll take this guy first because he's an offensive lineman and we need one' if they're all rated about the same," Steinberg says. "But we won't dip down to the next group if he's gone. We take the guy who makes the most sense."

Steinberg's draft room is business-like on draft day. "Sometimes, there's a little cheering or some anxiety if the one guy we really wanted is gone and we have to go to a lower level," he says. "But it's basically pretty calm unless we're trying to make a deal to move up."

The oldest cliche in football is that scouts draft the "best available athlete."

Most personnel people try not to draft a player by his position if there's one rated higher at another position. But teams sometimes give in to the temptation if they're desperate for help at a specific position.

"I've always believed you go with the numbers," Peterson says. "You don't deviate. If you start grabbing and making rash decisions you can make mistakes."

The most difficult drafting position is the last third of the round.

"You've got to hope you get lucky and some guys fall through the cracks and you get a true first-rounder at the end of the first round or a true second-rounder at the end of the second round," Peterson says. "You can wind up with a third-rounder near the end of the second round."

Giants GM George Young earned a reputation as a draftmaster by building a powerhouse in New York. Among his key picks: quarterback Phil Simms and linebacker Lawrence Taylor.

"Whether your order is right or wrong, you're crazy to change it after you've had all that time to work on it," Steinberg says. "You take them the way you've got them. We've all got mistakes on our boards. You've got to get lucky and hope that one of your mistakes isn't the highest rated guy when it's your turn to draft. Nobody is infallible."

When the draft is completed, scouts turn the players over to the coaches and hope they live up to expectations.

"You'd like your first-round choice to become a starter and play for you for 10 years," Peterson says.

Regardless of how the draft turns out, the scouts don't have time to look back.

They've got to start preparing for the next one.

SUPERSCOUTS

Bucko Kilroy remembers the long drives across Oklahoma and Texas, on to California, and up the West Coast in the 1950s before the days of Super Bowls or super highways.

"I was the first pro scout ever to hit Arizona State University in 1957," Kilroy says.

"We knew where the people were in those days," he says. "We had an advantage. Not many people were doing it."

Kilroy, vice president of the New England Patriots, is the senior scout in the NFL. In 1992, he celebrated his fiftieth season in the NFL as a player, assistant coach, or scout.

He remembers going to the Senior Bowl in the 1950s when there were only a dozen NFL scouts in attendance, including Paul Brown, the founder of the Cleveland Browns. Now hundreds attend.

A rookie in 1943, Kilroy played 13 years for the Philadelphia Eagles, including championship teams in 1948 and 1949. He doubled as an assistant coach and scout for the Eagles before becoming a full-time scout.

He drafted quarterback Sonny Jurgensen on the fourth round in 1957 and, after moving to the Redskins, traded Norm Snead for him in 1964. The same year, Kilroy drafted another future Hall of Famer, Arizona State wide receiver Charley Taylor. The Jurgensen-Taylor combo was one of the best ever.

In 1955, after the Pittsburgh Steelers cut Johnny Unitas, Kilroy recommended the Eagles pick him up. The coach, Jim Trimble, didn't think Unitas could beat out Adrian Burk and Bobby Thomason because he couldn't beat out backup Ted Marchibroda in Pittsburgh. Signed by Baltimore, Unitas had a Hall of Fame career.

Kilroy became a superscout for the Dallas Cowboys in 1965, when they were one of the first teams to emphasize the draft, and he joined the Patriots in 1971. Pro Bowl players John Hannah, Mike Haynes, and Russ Francis were among his selections at New England.

Kilroy says one of the biggest changes since he started has been the size of the players.

"Back in 1979-1980, we might rate a 6 foot 4 inch, 265-pound defensive lineman an eight or a nine. Today he'd be a four or a five," he says.

At positions such as wide receiver, though, there has been little change. There still are speed receivers and those with less speed but great hands. Kilroy says that Steve Largent, who rarely dropped a pass, was the Raymond Berry of his day. Berry was a Hall of Famer in Baltimore from 1955-1967, and Largent retired from the Seattle Seahawks in 1989 as the NFL's all-time leading receiver.

Kilroy still enjoys evaluating prospects.

"I think it's a lot of fun; it's very, very challenging," he says.

Those words are echoed by Bobby Beathard, general manager of the San Diego Chargers, who earned a reputation of being one of the best scouts in the league while building the Washington Redskins into a Super Bowl team.

"I still like to go out," Beathard says, "I get antsy if I'm at home too long. I want to get out on the road. Seeing the players in person is a big part of it. What's neat is that it's something new every year."

Beathard's not a corporate type. He almost never wears ties, and he likes to jog and surf, but he has an eye for talent.

He says the job has become more complicated in this era of big money. "There's always been a football part and a people part, but now the people part plays a much bigger role. It's a big problem to explain to a kid who thinks he's working hard that he's not," he says.

The increased number of scouts has changed things on college campuses.

"There used to be a more relaxed atmosphere. You might even go out and get something to eat with the (college) coach and talk about his players. Now it's not unusual to see twelve scouts on one day, and people get into each other's way," Beathard says.

Beathard, who played quarterback at Cal Poly - San Luis Obispo, wasn't good enough to make it as a player in the pros. He started scouting on a part-time basis with the Kansas City Chiefs in 1963 and worked briefly in the AFL office in 1966 before taking a full-time job with the Chiefs. He moved on to Atlanta and Miami before becoming the Redskins' general manager in 1979.

He made his mark in Washington by finding talented players among free agents and late-round draft picks such as Joe Jacoby, Monte Coleman, Darryl Grant, Clint Didier, and Neal Olkewicz.

Bucko Kilroy, vice president of the New England Patriots, is the senior scout in the NFL. He was a trail-blazer, the first scout to arrive on many campuses. His team benefited by selecting numerous little-known, but highly talented players.

Beathard says a player who has athletic limitations can compensate with determination.

"I remember [tight end] Donnie Warren [a fourth-round pick in 1979] wasn't that big, but he had a burning desire to do well," he says.

Beathard is willing to take a chance on a player.

"I think in my job, people who do well are those who stick their necks out. If you're afraid of failure, it's tough to succeed in anything," he says.

Although Beathard had success with underrated guys, he says he has learned not to expect players to change. If they don't work hard in college, they're not likely to work hard in the NFL.

"A guy's not likely to turn it around," he says. "If he's not a winner [in college], he's not likely to turn out to be a winner."

And Beathard has one of the better track records in picking winners.

No Detail Overlooked

The event that reflects the intensity of college scouting is the annual combine scouting meeting in Indianapolis each February. That's when the top 450 college prospects - only 336 are drafted - are invited for a weekend of in-depth scrutiny.

All 28 teams have scouts in attendance; most teams also bring coaches to study the players.

Although the workouts last four days, the players are brought in by position, so each spends only two days in Indianapolis.

The first day, each player receives a thorough physical examination. On the second day, he is put through drills without pads. The drills are videotaped. Players work out by position.

The concept of assembling the top players was first implemented in Tampa, Florida, in 1982, when 150 players were brought in for physicals. That eliminated the need for each team to give each player a separate physical.

The teams then decided that as long as the players were on hand, they would time them in the 40-yard dash. One thing led to another, and now players undergo a series of agility drills and get a chance to demonstrate their football skills.

The meeting site was changed each year until the combines made centrally located Indianapolis the permanent site in 1987. Because the Hoosier Dome is enclosed, the scouts don't have to worry about the weather.

The meeting is run by National Invitational Camp, Inc., a branch of National Football Scouting, Inc., one of the two scouting combines. The other combine is BLESTO. Both combines, as well as the individual teams, help decide which players are invited.

The meeting is the only scouting event in which all 28 teams share information. The rest of the year, the combines share information only with teams in their group.

National has 12 members; BLESTO has 10. Six teams (the Raiders, 49ers, Chiefs, Browns, Broncos, and Buccaneers) don't belong to any combine. They scout independently and don't share information.

The National Combine, run by Duke Babb, a former NFL player, services the Falcons, Bengals, Packers, Oilers, Rams, Patriots, Saints, Jets, Eagles, Cardinals, Chargers, and Seahawks.

The BLESTO combine dates back to the early 1960s, when it was called LESTO, an acronym derived from the team names of the original members - the Lions, Eagles and Steelers. When the Bears came in, the name was changed to BLESTO.

When the Vikings became the fifth team, it was called BLESTO V, but since has reverted simply to BLESTO. Other teams subscribing to the service are the Cowboys, Colts, Bills, Dolphins, and Redskins. ⊘

Coaching Can Make All The Difference

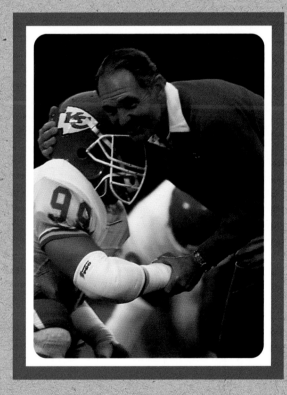

*They are professional football's brains behind the brawn, the specialists
who teach their prized pupils how to play to win. Assistant coaches are the men
who develop the game plans, who search for secrets in the game films, who understand
the true meaning of team effort.*

BY RICK GOSSELIN

T HE GREEN BAY PACKERS WON THEIR FIRST NATIONAL FOOTBALL LEAGUE championship under Vince Lombardi in 1961. They did it with 36 players and five coaches.

Thirty years later, the Washington Redskins won the NFL crown. They did it with 11 more players and 10 more coaches than the Lombardi Packers.

Lombardi coached his offensive unit in those days and Phil Bengtson was in charge of the defense. Bill Austin coached the offensive line and Red Cochran the backs. Norb Hecker handled the defensive backfield of the Packers. That was it. No strength coach. No tight ends coach. No running game coordinator. It was basic coaching for basic football.

The 1991 Redskins had two coaches for the offensive line (Jim Hanifan and Warren Simmons), two for the receivers (Jack Burns and Charley Taylor), one for the running backs (Don Breaux), and a passing game coordinator (Rod Dowhower). On defense they had an assistant head coach (Richie Petitbon), a defensive coordinator (Larry Peccatiello), and coaches for the line (LaVern Torgeson), secondary (Emmitt Thomas), and quality control (Bobby DePaul). They also had a special teams coach (Wayne Sevier), two strength coaches (Dan Riley and Steve Wetzel), and, of course, head coach Joe Gibbs to oversee the operation.

The Redskins cut down to 14 coaches for the 1992 season, the same number employed by five other teams. The New England Patriots have coaches for inside and outside linebackers, and the Cleveland Browns have a quarterbacks coach. The Raiders have a tight ends coach, the Dallas Cowboys a kickers coach and the San Diego Chargers a running-game coordinator and passing-game coordinator. As the game becomes more and more specialized, the coaching becomes more specialized.

"In my opinion, it hasn't gone far enough," says Raymond Berry, who has played and coached in the NFL. "It's a matter of protecting your investment. When you have that much money tied up in a player, it's absolute nonsense not to surround the guy with a supporting staff. It makes great economic sense to have specialists around who are able to lengthen his career and make him more productive when he is playing."

Berry coached the New England Patriots to an AFC championship in 1985 and has been an assistant on staffs at Dallas, Detroit, Cleveland, and Denver. But he was a believer in coaching long before he started drawing a paycheck as one.

Berry arrived in the Baltimore Colts' camp in 1955 as a skinny, twentieth-round draft pick from SMU. He caught 13 passes as a rookie and 37 more in the next year. Nothing special, and certainly not Hall of Fame material. Like Lombardi, Baltimore coach Weeb Ewbank operated with a staff of four assistants.

"Weeb had two men who helped him on offense," Berry says. "But they had no professional football experience and had not played receiver. Their job was to teach you the basic system, grade you, and make sure you knew your assignments. If you were supposed to go down ten yards and hook, they made sure you went ten and hooked. There was no other coaching. There was no finesse, no real knowledge of the game."

But that changed in 1957 when Ewbank hired Bob Shaw to coach his receivers. Shaw had been an NFL receiver, having played with the Los Angeles Rams in the late 1940s and the Chicago Cardinals in 1950.

"Weeb basically hired him to work with me," Berry says. "In two years he revolutionized my whole career. He had a great grasp of the game. He was a tremendous teacher and taught me a new concept of running pass routes."

In those days a pass receiver would run straight at the defensive back and try to make his cut at the last second, hoping to momentarily freeze his man. But Shaw instructed Berry to run at the defender's inside shoulder one time and outside shoulder the next.

"That forced the defensive back to move laterally, which got him leaning and turning his legs," Berry explains. "Out of that concept I developed a whole repertoire of fakes. I didn't

Bob Shaw

In an era when coaching staffs were small, the Colts hired Bob Shaw, an experienced receiver, to teach Raymond Berry the fine points of running pass routes.

have the speed to outrun people. But the knowledge of how to develop multiple fakes saved me and added years to my career. It took people a long time to catch up with some of the things I was doing."

Berry improved to 47 catches under Shaw's tutelage in 1957 and tripled his touchdown count to six. That propelled him to stardom. From 1957-59, Berry led the NFL in receiving. He finished his career in 1967 as the game's all-time leading receiver with 631 catches for 9,275 yards and 68 touchdowns. Berry was inducted into the Pro Football Hall of Fame in 1973.

"The value of a skilled teacher who knows the position can add a world of dimensions to a young player who doesn't understand much about the fine points," says Berry. "A little coaching can make all the difference in the world."

Today, the NFL gives its players a lot of coaching. Back in the 1950s and 1960s, players went to camp in July, worked themselves into shape, played the season and then went home in January for the offseason, but there is no such offseason in today's NFL. Offseason weight programs run for 15 to 19 weeks. In most cases the players are paid to participate. That's why so many teams employ two strength coaches. A well-conditioned athlete is less likely to suffer an injury.

"The instruction and teaching in that area is every bit as important as what we do on the field," Kansas City head coach Marty Schottenheimer says.

Teams are allowed to have 80 players under contract in the offseason, so the roster size almost doubles during the winter and spring. Even during the season, the 47-player roster understates the team's payroll.

"If someone showed up at any NFL team the first of November and counted noses, there'd be an average of 65 guys there," Berry says. "You'd have 47, plus 8 to 12 players on injured reserve. The rest would be the taxi squad."

Minicamps and quarterback

Hall of Fame wide receiver Raymond Berry, later a coach in the NFL, says a top-flight staff of assistants makes economic sense: "It's a matter of protecting your investment...it's absolute nonsense not to surround the (player) with a supporting staff."

schools also abound in the offseason. Coaches find themselves doling out as much instruction on the field in April and May as they do in October and November. Many teams fine-tune their offenses and defenses before they ever check into training camp.

Another recent NFL trend incorporates assistant coaches in the scouting process. Some teams send entire staffs to the Senior Bowl practices in January and to the NFL scouting combine tests in February. Some send their coaches to work out prospects on an individual basis in March as teams finalize their preparations for the draft.

But for the overwhelming majority of NFL coaches, long hours always have been the rule rather than the exception.

"I broke in as a graduate assistant," Dallas offensive line coach Tony Wise says. "You got the mail, brewed coffee, picked up the doughnuts. You were at everyone's beck and call. I knew what the head coach's favorite lunch-time order was and got his car washed. That was before you ever got to coach. So we all knew what we were getting into."

LOYALTY IS JOB 1

Jimmy Johnson knew it was time to start looking.

Johnson had been college football's most successful coach during a four-year stretch at the University of Miami, winning 41 games and going to four consecutive New Year's Day bowls. In his fourth year (1987), he guided the Hurricanes to a 12-0 record and a national championship.

At age 43 and in need of a new challenge, Johnson began exploring his next stop - the NFL. So that summer he visited the training camp of the Los Angeles Rams and sought out John Robinson, who had won national titles in college before moving into the NFL. Johnson wanted to know the differences between the pro and college games and if any hidden pitfalls were in his path.

"One of the things he emphasized to me was that it's important to hire people that are loyal to you, people you are comfortable with and confident in," Johnson says. "In his opinion, you should sacrifice professional experience in order to have people you know. That just confirmed my convictions."

Dallas Cowboys coach Jimmy Johnson places a premium on loyalty. It's essential, he says, to have "guys locking together and fighting through adversity."

Less than a year later, Johnson's former college teammate Jerry Jones bought the Dallas Cowboys and invited Johnson on board as head coach. Because he had no NFL experience himself, Johnson was urged to surround himself with coaches familiar with the pro game, but he didn't listen. Johnson hired seven coaches from his staff at the University of Miami, none of whom had pro experience.

"I knew those coaches very well," Johnson says. "They came up the ladder. I knew their loyalty. I knew their work ethic. I knew how they got along with each other. By the same token, they all knew what to expect from me. So there wouldn't be any surprises."

Johnson brought along Dave Wannstedt as his defensive coordinator, Butch Davis and Tony Wise as his line coaches, Joe Brodsky as his running backs coach, Hubbard Alexander as his receivers coach, Dave Campo as a defensive assistant, and Steve Hoffman as his kicking coach.

Wannstedt, Wise, Davis, and Campo all had been graduate assistants at the University of Pittsburgh when Johnson was defensive coordinator there in the mid-1970s. Johnson gave Wannstedt, Wise, and Davis their first coaching jobs when he became head coach at Oklahoma State in 1979. They were more than his coaches; they were his friends.

"The attitude of the staff was important to me because I knew it would carry over to the players," Johnson says. "You can eliminate a lot of negative talk that way. Everything they say about each other, about me, about the direction we're headed, is positive."

The attitude of his staff proved to be contagious. After a 1-15 start under Johnson, the Cowboys improved by leaps and bounds to 7-9 in his second year and 11-5 in his third.

"I don't think you can put a dollar sign on the value of staff chemistry," Wannstedt says. "When you get a bunch of coaches believing in the same things, working for the same goals and doing everything possible to eliminate the jealousies and egos, good things happen.

"Everyone knows that when success comes we're all going to share in it. That carries over to the players and I think it speeds things along."

Bobby Ross followed Johnson's lead when he made the same jump from college to the NFL in 1992. Ross, who won a national championship at Georgia Tech in 1990, brought four of his college assistants with him when he became head coach of the San Diego Chargers.

Miami Dolphins head coach Don Shula produced instant loyalty and trust on his staff by hiring two of his sons, David in 1982 and Mike in 1991. David was 23 when he was hired and Mike 26. David left to become Johnson's offensive coordinator with the Cowboys in 1989 and later became the head coach of the Cincinnati Bengals. New Orleans Saints head coach Jim Mora added his son Jimmy to his staff in 1992, and Bum Phillips employed his son Wade during his two head coaching stops at Houston and New Orleans.

David Shula, who joined his father's staff in Miami at age 23, learned the business so well he earned the head coaching job with the Cincinnati Bengals 10 years later.

Detroit Lions head coach Wayne Fontes hired his brother Lenny in 1990. When Lenny died of a heart attack in 1992, Wayne replaced him on the staff with another brother, John. Marty Schottenheimer hired his brother Kurt to coach special teams at Cleveland in 1987 and brought him along to Kansas City when he became head coach there in 1989.

"I don't even think of Kurt as my brother, certainly not professionally," Schottenheimer says. "In a high profile business like ours, any relative you hire needs to be better than he might otherwise have to be. Had he not been, it would have been a mistake to hire him.

"But I felt that the things Kurt could bring to the staff were far better than what others who were available could bring. It was with that in mind that I selected him."

Bill Cowher, Schottenheimer's former defensive coordinator, was at the other end of the spectrum. When he became head coach of the Pittsburgh Steelers in 1992, he had no ties with the assistants. Cowher had never worked a day with any of his 10 new assistant coaches, but chemistry still was important to him.

"When you hire a staff, you look for a blend of people," Cowher says. "That's what I was trying to get here - some coaches who have been in this league a long time, some young coaches, some college coaches. There's a little bit of everything on this staff. I feel good about the guys I was able to hire. But time will be the measure of our chemistry."

Johnson did hire some professional experience on his first NFL staff, bringing in David Shula to coordinate the offense and retaining Alan Lowry and Dick Nolan from Tom Landry's staff. Nolan coached the defensive backfield and Lowry the special teams, but all three departed after the 1990 season. Johnson released Lowry and Nolan, and Shula left for the Bengals. Their departures gave Johnson the opportunity to hire more friends and friends of friends.

Johnson brought in Joe Avezzano to coach special teams; they had coached together at Iowa State in 1969. As strength coach he hired Mike Woicik, who had coached with him at Syracuse in 1984. He hired Norv Turner as his offensive coordinator. Turner had coached with Wannstedt at Southern California in 1983-84. Johnson also hired Robert Ford, who served a coaching internship with the Cowboys at their 1990 training camp, to coach the tight ends. Finally, he added Bob Slowik to his defensive staff. Slowik went to the same Pittsburgh high school as Wannstedt, and they had remained close.

Johnson tightens those bonds of friendship in the offseason with a staff vacation. He started the tradition at Oklahoma State in 1980 and has taken his staff on a holiday 11 times in the last 13 years. Johnson foots the bill - travel, lodging and meals - for his assistant coaches and their wives. He took them to the Bahamas in 1992.

"It helps build a unity on the staff," Johnson says. "When you have a relationship like that, you don't have finger-pointing when you get into the tough times. Instead, you've got guys locking together and fighting through adversity."

THE SECRETS IN THE FILM ROOM

The blocking scheme raised a few eyebrows the first time it was spotted by Bill Cowher and other defensive coaches of the Kansas City Chiefs. The next time they saw it, Cowher and the other coaches almost jumped out of their seats.

NFL coaching staffs use film study as the basis for their game preparations. Most staffs watch 23-25 hours of film each week, searching for weaknesses and probing for holes in an opponent's makeup.

On this particular Tuesday in 1990, the Chiefs struck gold. While preparing for a game against the Seahawks, Kansas City's defensive staff was studying Seattle's third-down-and-long yardage tendencies. All third-down-and-long plays from Seattle's previous three games had been loaded onto one reel of tape by Chiefs film director Mike Dennis for analysis by Cowher, the defensive coordinator, plus line coach Tom Pratt and backfield coach Tony Dungy.

The Kansas City staff watched play after play as Seattle's three-wide receiver offensive set sparred with the four-man pass-rush fronts of its opponents. But the first red flag went up when one team stayed in its base 3-4 alignment against the Seahawks for a play. Instead of substituting an extra lineman to rush the passer, the opponent blitzed an outside linebacker. It produced a sack.

"The first time you see it," says Dungy, himself a former defensive coordinator, "you say, 'Is this something that just happens once? Is this a freak thing...a mistake?' If you only see it once, you don't know. But then you see it again and your eyes light up. You figure maybe you can get one shot out of this."

The Chiefs saw it again later in the reel. Then a third time. When the defense stayed in the 3-4 alignment, the Seahawks blocked the nose tackle with the center, the defensive ends with the tackles, and kept the guards in to block for the two inside linebackers. That left fullback John L. Williams to handle the

"The first time you see it, you say, 'Is this a freak thing...a mistake?' But then you see it again and your eyes light up. You figure maybe you can get one shot out of this."
- Tony Dungy

blitzing outside linebacker.

In Kansas City's standard third-down package, the Chiefs would line up their blitzing line-backer extraordinaire, Derrick Thomas, in a three-point stance at end - and he would have to overcome the blocking of a much larger man to reach the quarterback. But by keeping Thomas in an upright position off the line against Seattle, the Chiefs would be able to create a favorable matchup for him against a much smaller blocker. Instead of a 290-pound offensive tackle standing between Thomas and the quarterback, there would be a 230-pound fullback.

It was such an obvious mismatch and the Chiefs knew they would get only one chance at it. Having been hit once, the Seahawks would surely make an adjustment to help Williams.

"We knew we had to pick our shot, wait for the right time, and then spring it on them," Dungy says.

The first time Cowher called that alignment on game day, Thomas sacked quarterback Dave Krieg. Cowher came back with it a short time later to see how the Seahawks had adjusted to it. They hadn't, and Thomas sacked Krieg again. So Cowher continued to call that same defense in long-yardage situations, and the Seahawks never did solve it. Thomas racked up an NFL-record seven sacks that day. Ironically, Thomas had Krieg in his grasp for an eighth sack in the closing seconds of the game, but Krieg wrestled free and fired the winning touch-down pass in a 17-16 victory over the Chiefs.

"The public sees that Derrick Thomas got a sack," Dungy says. "But as a coach, your satis-faction comes from the fact that you set it up. The player still has to execute - Derrick had to go out there and beat the guy - but you have a good feeling because you know you put your player in a position to succeed. You gave your player an edge."

Defensive staffs study tapes of what the opponent does in various yardage situations on all three downs. At the same time, in another office, the club's offensive staff analyzes the down-and-distance tendencies of the opponent's defense. In yet another office, the club's special teams coach studies how the opposition protects and covers kicks. All are looking for an edge.

"It gets harder to find all the time," Buffalo special teams coach Bruce DeHaven says. "Over the last five years there have been four or five times when we've made a big play because of something we've seen on tape. When you do see something, you almost jump out of your chair. It's exciting."

The heavy film work comes Tuesday, which is traditionally a day off for NFL players. That frees the coaches to spend eight to ten hours with their VCRs, then formulate a game plan. On Tuesday, many coaches do not leave the office until midnight.

The staff implements the game plan on Wednesday. They review how the players respond in practice that day, then make adjustments in the game plan for Thursday's practice. Friday's practice is spent polishing the plan; a light walk-through on Saturday serves as the final review.

Film study can be a revelation. Not only the opposition's flaws can be uncovered. Your own team's flaws can be exposed as well. Dungy saw it happen to his team when he was a member of the Pittsburgh coaching staff in 1979 that prepared the Steelers for Super Bowl XIII against the Dallas Cowboys. The Steelers pinpointed a pass play the Cowboys liked to use in short-yardage situations. They practiced and practiced against it without much success the week preceding the game - and that was against the scout team. Dungy and the defensive coaches knew the play would be executed faster and more efficiently with Cowboys quarterback Roger Staubach taking the snap.

"We got to a point where we could cover it in practice - when we knew it was coming," Dungy says. "But in a game situation, we didn't feel comfortable with it. We knew it was going to be tough to handle."

The play called for the Cowboys to send in their blocking unit, removing the wide receivers in favor of extra tight ends and fullbacks. The Steelers would counter by replacing some defensive backs with linemen and linebackers. It was a play-action pass with Staubach faking a hand-off and then firing quickly to the tight end crossing the middle.

"In theory, we had a linebacker responsible for coverage," Dungy says. "But play-action happened so fast that the guy responsible for picking up the tight end could never see him. He would step up just for a second to take a look, and the tight end would be by him.

"In those situations you just do the best you can. At that point in the season, it's tough to revise your rules to take care of one thing. If you start changing for one thing, you might screw up four or five other things."

Sure enough, with the Steelers leading 21-14 late in the third quarter, the Cowboys found themselves in a third-and-three situation deep in Pittsburgh territory. After the short-yardage offenses and defenses were dispatched, Staubach took the snap and faked a handoff to Scott Laidlaw. Staubach dropped back and fired a pass to tight end Jackie Smith, who was alone in the middle of the end zone.

"Just like we saw it in practice," Dungy says. "I was on the sidelines at the time and I thought it was a touchdown."

Film study told the Steelers they'd have trouble stopping the pass from Staubach to Smith. They were right. But Smith dropped the ball. It helps to be lucky.

Jackie
Smith

It wasn't. Smith dropped the ball - one of the most notorious drops in Super Bowl history. The Cowboys settled for a field goal and the four-point difference proved to be decisive. The Steelers prevailed, 35-31.

"You know you've got some holes and you hope you can stay out of those situations," Dungy says. "It becomes a chess match."

UPSTAIRS/DOWNSTAIRS

Tony Dungy missed the halftime elevator at Mile High Stadium.

As the secondary coach of the Kansas City Chiefs, he spent the first half of the game against the Denver Broncos in the press box, and now he needed to get to the locker room at halftime to help out with defensive adjustments. Halftimes last only 12 minutes in the NFL, and Dungy knew the wait for the elevator would take about three minutes. Too long. So he decided to hoof it, which entailed walking down a flight of stairs, through the stands and onto the field.

"You figure you know the way," Dungy says, "but then you run into all that traffic [of fans] and you're going against the flow."

Dungy never made it to the locker room; he got lost. He wasn't the first assistant, nor will he be the last to do so. Dave Wannstedt got lost at the University of Michigan when he was the defensive coordinator at Miami. Working his way through a crowd of 106,000 was more of a challenge than he had anticipated.

"I got down there as the halftime was ending," says Wannstedt, now defensive coordinator of the Dallas Cowboys. "I went right into the training room and got a drink of water and my wind for the trip back."

Splitting coaching staffs on game day - some coaches upstairs in the press box and others downstairs on the field - is a way of life in the NFL.

The offensive and defensive line coaches are usually on the field, where they can have direct dealings with their players. Line play is a game of emotion, and emotion can best be conveyed though eye-to-eye contact. Placement of the remaining staff is determined by the location of the offensive and defensive coordinators. Some are on the field with the head coach and others prefer to be upstairs, communicating by headphones.

If the offensive coordinator is downstairs, he needs dependable and educated eyes in the press box to keep him informed of pass coverages, quirks in the defensive scheme, and basic information such as down and distance. So a coach at a skill position, either running backs or receivers, operates by headphones out of the press box. The same is true for the defensive coordinator. If he is on the field, he needs a set of eyes upstairs to keep him abreast of the situational substitutions, types of pass routes being run, and the basics. That is usually the defensive backfield coach.

There are both advantages and disadvantages. The obvious advantage to being upstairs is the vantage point. The coordinator can see everything on the field and on both sidelines. He can see substitutions before they are made and breakdowns as they develop. He can make snap judgments based on what he sees.

A press box seat also eliminates the distractions.

"When you're trying to walk on the sideline, people step on your phone cord," says Dungy, the defensive coordinator of the Minnesota Vikings. "A runner might come running out of bounds and knock you over - knock your papers everywhere. Or it might start raining. It's more of a constant, controlled environment upstairs. It's a much better atmosphere to think."

The coordinator on the sidelines has his game plan in hand or in his back pocket, generally encased in plastic to protect it from the elements. Upstairs, the coordinator can have his game plan and much, much more.

"You can lay out all your statistics, computer reports, field charts, down-and-distance charts, tendency charts," Wannstedt says. "In the heat of battle, I can turn to that. It's all at my fingertips. Collectively, you get a chance to gather your thoughts."

One drawback to the press box locale is travel time at the end of the half. Because time is at a premium, the coaches often try to leave the press box before the half ends. An early departure proved to be a nightmare for Pittsburgh's press box staff in the 1984 AFC Championship Game in Miami against the Dolphins. With the Steelers in possession of the ball in the final minute, the defensive coaches headed downstairs.

"I assumed we were going to run out the clock," says Dungy, who was then defensive coordinator for the Steelers. "But when we got off the elevator, I heard screaming, so I started running. By the time I got on the field, the Dolphins were sending their goal-line unit in, and they scored on the next play." Mark Malone had thrown an interception, which forced the coaches on the field to make the defensive calls.

Another disadvantage for the upstairs coordinator is the extra link in the chain. After he calls the alignment, it must be relayed to the players on the field by another coach on the sideline. The more links, the longer it takes to convey the call, and the greater the chance for error.

The major drawback for an upstairs coordinator is the absence of direct contact with the players. Instructions to a player must be delivered by a third party, or the player must speak by phone with his boss upstairs. The coordinators on the sideline, however, can talk to any player at any time. He can grab the player coming off the field or between plays.

"I feel I'm more in touch with the players," Buffalo's downstairs defensive coordinator Walt Corey says. "If I have to chew them out, well, that would be hard to do over the phone, one player at a time. On the field I can gather them and talk to the whole group. Also, they can see me. When they come off the field, they can see my face and know what I'm thinking."

The sideline coordinator also has a better feel for the action. He can sense the intensity on the sideline and the emotion on the field. He is better prepared to make the "gut" call than the coordinator upstairs observing the action from afar.

"You get a good feel for the flow of the game," says Kansas City offensive coordinator Joe Pendry, who operates from the sideline. "Sometimes you can feel when you're getting your butt kicked. You might be trying to pound the ball...but you're not getting any movement. Or you might get a feel down there that you are kicking someone's butt when it might not look like it from the press box.

"You get a feel for the tempo and it can influence your play-calling. I like being down there on the field closer to the action."

EVERY MAN A SPECIALIST

Their areas of coaching responsibility differ, but not their styles.

Ernie Zampese handles the offense, Floyd Peters the defense, and Frank Gansz the special teams on NFL staffs, but they coach in the same way - in the attack mode. The ability to convey their philosophy to their players has lifted them to the top of their professions.

Zampese is the offensive coordinator of the Los Angeles Rams, Peters the defensive coordinator of the Tampa Bay Buccaneers, and Gansz the special-teams coordinator of the Detroit

> "I don't want guys to play special teams. I want guys to play special teams with a passion. I want guys who feel the same way about special teams as I do."
>
> - Frank Gansz

Lions. They all believe in forcing the action. That forces mistakes by the opposition, and mistakes open doors.

The roots of Gansz's coaching philosophy can be traced to a 1969 game at the Naval Academy, where he was defensive coordinator of the freshman team. Gansz watched that afternoon as the Plebes blocked or deflected five punts, paving the way for an easy victory. He can't remember the score or the opponent, but he does recall that footballs were bouncing all over the field on fourth downs.

"It was really something," Gansz says. "The other team could hardly get a punt off. It got to a point where they were afraid to punt. Every time they dropped back to kick, we got instant field position and instant momentum. I realized then the impact of special teams. They create tempo. You can win games with your special teams."

Gansz arrived in the NFL as a special-teams coach with the San Francisco 49ers in 1976. He also coached the kicking games at Cincinnati, Philadelphia, and Kansas City for two stints before becoming head coach of the Chiefs in 1987.

Gansz had his greatest success with the Chiefs, and the blocked kick became his calling card. In the 1982 strike season, Kansas City blocked seven kicks in nine games. In his second tour of duty with the Chiefs in 1986, they blocked or deflected 12 kicks. He also coached the ultimate special-teams game in the regular-season finale.

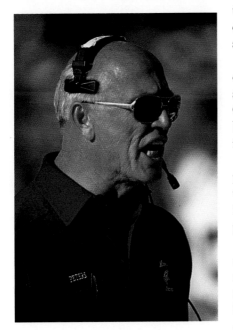

Needing a victory on the road at Pittsburgh to clinch a playoff berth, Gansz's special teams supplied all the points in a 24-19 victory. The Chiefs scored touchdowns on a kickoff return, a blocked punt and a blocked field goal plus a 47-yard field goal.

Gansz had a losing record as a head coach, dropping 22 of 31 games with the Chiefs, but he was welcomed as a special-teams coach with the Lions in 1989. Two seasons later, Detroit led the NFL in performance by special teams.

Gansz works hard on the mental and physical aspects of the kicking game. He stresses fundamentals and execution, telling his players that nothing frustrates the enemy more than the inability to break them down. He is an excellent motivator, often quoting Churchill, MacArthur, or Patton during his meetings with players. He likes what he does, and that is clear to the players.

Floyd Peters, a long-time assistant coach, has been a master at developing great defensive lines. His lines set club sack records at Detroit, St. Louis and Minnesota and led the NFL in sacks three times.

"I don't want guys to play special teams," Gansz says. "I want guys to play special teams with a passion. I want guys who feel the same way about special teams as I do."

Peters formulated his defensive philosophy in the 1975-76 seasons. He coached the defensive lines of the Giants in 1975 and the 49ers in 1976.

The 1975 season was a struggle - Peters tried to forge a respectable unit with players that were either too old, too young, or playing out of position. So he stunted his players, moved them around, and prevented them from becoming sitting ducks for offensive linemen. Peters got surprising productivity from that group. When he went to the 49ers in 1976, he inherited an enormously talented line that included Cedrick Hardman, Tommy Hart, and Cleveland Elam.

"I thought, if we made backup players and guys out of position a threat at New York, what can we do with these guys?" Peters says. "I decided we weren't going to sit there and catch blocks from these big 300-pound linemen. We were going to go after them and wear them down. Then in the fourth quarter we'd eat them alive."

Peters made the defensive line and the pass rush the focal point, and the 49ers responded with a club-record and NFL-leading 61 sacks. Peters has kept up the attack ever since. In his next three coaching stops, at Detroit, St. Louis and Minnesota, each team set single-season sack records during his tenure. His defenses have led the NFL in sacks three times and the NFC on two other occasions.

"Floyd doesn't ask any player in the scheme to do something he can't do," says linebacker Jesse Solomon, who played for Peters at both Minnesota and Tampa. "He creates ways for every player to have success. Every player on our defense is a potential Pro Bowler. He does it with a lot of stunts and maneuvers."

The key element in Peters's scheme is the four-man line, which limits double-team blocking by the offense. And Peters prefers speed over size by his linemen because speed gets to the quarterback. That leads to fumbles and interceptions.

"Great defenses have great defensive linemen," Peters says. "They affect the timing of a quarterback. If you can make him have a bad day or throw some bad strikes, you've got a chance in any game."

But that doesn't mean his defense is one-dimensional. When Peters was with the Vikings, they once went 38 consecutive games without allowing a 100-yard rushing day. The Lions also led the NFL in run defense under Peters.

Zampese developed his offensive philosophy in 1979 out of fear. Don Coryell hired him as the receivers coach of the San Diego Chargers - even though all of Zampese's coaching experience had been on the other side of the ball as a defensive backfield coach.

"It scared me to death," Zampese says. "I didn't know what I was going to do. So I attempted to teach what the other offensive coaches were talking about."

Zampese listened and learned from Coryell, the architect of the NFL's most explosive passing offense. He also learned from Joe Gibbs, who was the offensive coordinator of the Chargers then, and from Jim Hanifan, who was the offensive line coach. Both Gibbs and Hanifan went on to become head coaches in the NFL in the 1980s.

ZAMPESE ABSORBED the Air Coryell system for four years. He became so well versed in that system that Coryell promoted him to offensive coordinator in 1983, and the Chargers led the NFL in both passing and offense that year. In the next eight seasons with the Chargers and Rams, Zampese's offense finished in the NFL's top five on five occasions.

Zampese has put his stamp on the offense with situational substitutions and matchups. That's where his defensive background really comes in handy.

"Ernie is a great evaluator of people - what a guy does best, what he doesn't do well, who to use where," says Norv Turner, a Zampese protege and now offensive coordinator of the Cowboys. "He's also a great evaluator of defensive personnel. He's really good at matching the right guy with the right defender.

"It's a plus for anyone to coach on the defensive side of the ball. He has a real feel for what the defense is trying to do. Having watched defensive players so long, he's used to looking at them for strengths and weaknesses. He'll match guys up and give your team the best chance to make plays."

Zampese coaches a ball-control passing scheme: Throw the ball quickly to receivers and let them do the work. The tight ends, running backs, and everyone is involved. Lionel James became the first running back in NFL history to post a 1,000-yard receiving season under Zampese in 1985. The offense is geared to matchups and attacking defensive weaknesses.

Zampese thrives in his role. Unlike many of his peers, he has no aspirations of becoming a head coach.

"I like being an assistant," Zampese says. "I like setting game plans for different types of defenses. I like calling plays. I like being in the press box, completely removed from the emotion of the game. It's almost like a chess match up there." ⌀

Where The Secrets Are Kept

*Playbooks vary in size from 400 pages to more than 1,000.
It is between the covers of those books that teams conceal their battle plans;
it is on those pages that players find the information that enables them
to pass their Sunday exams.*

BY KEVIN LAMB

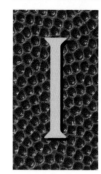

IF ALL THE NFL'S PLAYBOOKS WERE LAID SIDE BY SIDE, YOU'D HAVE A HARD TIME telling them apart. They're not identical, certainly, but the similarities are strong. And that may come as a surprise. The way some coaches talk about protecting a playbook's security, you'd think a player would have to put his fingerprint on a sensor pad just to unlock it.

The standard heavy fine for losing a playbook is intended to protect against carelessness more than espionage. If a guy can't remember where he put his playbook, how can he remember the plays? A well-known football phrase– "Coach wants to see you. And bring your playbook."–rarely is heard any more. When a player is released and an airline ticket home is issued, the playbook is collected with the helmet and hip pads.

Coaches reveal their true feelings about the value of playbook secrets the week before the season opener. If a coach wanted to learn the contents of an opponent's playbook, this is when he could do so. The opponent just released 11 players in the final roster cutdown, and one of those players probably is as good as the worst one on the coach's own team. The coach could learn all about the opponent's playbook by signing such a player. But such player signings are rare.

The differences in NFL playbooks aren't in the plays. Except for the teams with a specialized offense or defense, like the Run-and-Shoot, most playbooks have very similar plays. They represent a common body of knowledge because all coaches fish from the same video pool of game tapes. No secret lasts longer than the first game it helps to win.

The real difference between teams is in game plans, the weekly abridged versions of playbooks that a team intends to use on Sunday. A coach's challenge is to adapt that knowledge to his own players and a specific opponent, not just week to week, but possession to possession.

The best coaches also adapt year to year. When fashions change seasonally in NFL trends, the best coaches tailor their playbooks before the fans start demanding, "Why can't we have one of those? Everyone else does."

Playbooks differ most in terminology. Teams use code words that allow them to reduce 11 players' assignments to less than a dozen syllables. The Redskins' famous counter trey is the Raiders' counter gap and the Bears' counter trap.

Another difference is in emphasis. Even if most teams have the same plays, they don't use them the same way. One team might use a play six or eight times a game, another might use it twice a month. One team might use a play from 10 different formations, another might use it from only one. All teams have plays with three tight ends, for example, and plays with three wide receivers and one back. The Chiefs and the Giants, however use three tight ends more than most other teams, and Washington and Buffalo use three wide receivers more often.

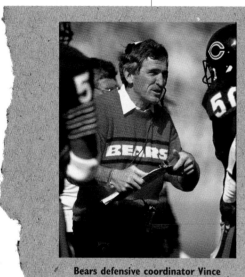

Bears defensive coordinator Vince Tobin uses a playbook of more than 1,000 pages. "I believe in having a very thorough playbook."

Playbook sizes vary from merely thick to weight-room-apparatus proportions. Some are barely 400 pages, and others are more than 1,000.

"At one time, there were coaches who didn't hand out their playbooks because they were worried about all their secrets getting out," says Vince Tobin, Chicago's defensive coordinator. The playbooks were just for coaches. The coaches let the players know what they needed to know, one week at a time, in game plans prepared for specific opponents.

Former Cleveland Browns and Cincinnati Bengals coach Paul Brown gave his players playbooks, but they contained few diagrams. Brown was concerned about letting information slip into the wrong huddle, but he had another reason for leaving the drawings out. He wanted the players to draw up the plays themselves. Each player had his own spiral notebook to go with the playbook.

When a coach explained a play on the chalkboard, the players drew it in their notebooks. They drew the entire play. An offensive guard had to know not only whom he blocked on a pass play, but also all the pass routes. Brown and the assistant coaches checked the notebooks carefully. Years later, when he was owner of the Cincinnati Bengals and hired Sam Wyche as coach in 1984, Brown said, "I always kept the playbooks of players who for one reason or another seemed to stand out in my mind. Sam's was one I kept. Even when he was a free-agent quarterback on that 1968 team, he had everything in excellent order."

Washington coach Joe Gibbs operates much the same way. His coaches convey the most important information on erasable chalkboards, not indelible playbooks.

Tobin is at the other extreme: Chicago's defense uses a playbook of about 1,000 pages. Tobin is one of the few coordinators or head coaches who doesn't collect playbooks at the end of training camp.

"I believe in having a very, very thorough playbook, to the extent that the player should be able to pick it up and study it and really understand what you're trying to teach," Tobin says. "A lot of times, coaches aren't around when the players are studying. If they have a question, I'd like them to be able to go to the playbook and get the answer."

Whatever their size, playbooks look much the same, like three-ring binders that students take to school. Binders make it easier to add or delete pages, something coaches do every year. Playbooks, after all, must be works in progress as long as NFL strategy is changing.

"When one team does something, other people pick it up," says Ted Plumb, who coaches the Phoenix receivers. "You go, 'Hey, we have trouble stopping that. Why don't we do it?'"

Even as coaches scoff at the gimmickry of the Run-and-Shoot, they're not too proud to borrow bits and pieces of it. Other teams were using four wide receivers before the Lions brought the Run-and-Shoot to the NFL, but not on first down. Now they do. The Run-and-Shoot also has bred some specific plays that are being inserted into playbooks every offseason.

One is the quick screen over the middle. Screen passes had fallen out of favor in many NFL offenses, even though they're effective antidotes to hard-charging defenses. The problem is that standard screens aren't effective against man-to-man coverage, which defenses use when they have an aggressive pass rush.

The old, four-second screen, with the quarterback holding the ball and backpedaling from pass rushers, waits for defenders in zone coverage to scatter away from the receiver and his entourage of blockers. But the same play gives a man-to-man defender the chance to recognize and collar his receiver before blockers can interfere.

"Our play's probably a little bit better against man-to-man," says June Jones, the Atlanta offensive coordinator who has spent much of the last 20 years in Run-and-Shoot offenses. The quarterback sprints toward the sideline instead of dropping back, and throws the ball in less than two seconds. The back catches the ball a yard or two behind where the guard and tackle lined up, instead of in the flat. So he catches the ball quickly in a congested area, where it's easy for a lineman to get in a man-to-man defender's way without being flagged for an illegal block or basketball-style pick.

"The screen is coming back again," says Cincinnati defensive coordinator Ron Lynn. "One, because some of the pass rushers are doing a great job and this slows them down, and also because now they run the picks off it."

The naked bootleg is another popular play out of the Run-and-Shoot playbook, although its popularity stems from Washington's counter trey. It appears to be a handoff to the single back, but the quarterback keeps the ball and sprints away from the flow of the play. He can run, or he can pass.

The purpose is to slow the pursuit of a run defense, just as a screen is to put speed bumps in front of the pass rush. Both the counter trey and the Run-and-Shoot runs are vulnerable to being chased down from behind. When the quarterback keeps the ball, he flies right past an oncoming linebacker who's chasing the running back.

The counter trey is in every playbook. It's an old play. Sid Gillman says he had it in his playbooks when he coached the Rams in the 1950s.

It probably was in every playbook before January, 1988, when Redskins back Timmy Smith rode it for 204 yards rushing and a Super Bowl record, but that was when most of the league began using it regularly. Nothing gets a coach to blow the dust off a playbook page faster than a Super Bowl record by some guy whose previous career highlight was a couple of short runs on kick returns.

Successful innovations aren't always copied. Tom Landry's flex defense was successful; Dallas stopped the run effectively for years, but the only other head coach to use the flex was Dick Nolan, who had been a Landry assistant. At one point in the late 1980s, Landry had five former offensive assistants coaching NFL teams, and none of them put even a footnote from Landry's flex into his own defensive playbook. "I never understood it well enough," Chicago coach Mike Ditka says.

Coaches aren't just copying other teams' good ideas when they update their playbooks between seasons. They're also trying to combat the good plays that gave them problems in the previous year. They can't always wait until the offseason for that sort of brainstorming, either.

In 1981, Lawrence Taylor was a rookie linebacker who turned opposing coaches prematurely gray and rendered pass-blocking schemes outdated. Taylor wasn't the first linebacker who was too good for backs to block, but he was the first who actually rushed the passer most of the time. When the Giants made the playoffs, their first appearance in 18 years, it was clear the traditional pass-blocking matchup of backs on linebackers made no sense against Taylor.

So the 49ers tried something different. They took a guard, 265-pound John Ayers, and pulled him outside to meet Taylor on the way to the quarterback. That idea led to what's called sliding the line, the prevailing way to block Taylor, Pat Swilling, Derrick Thomas, and all the other pass-rushing outside linebackers on 3-4 defenses. Instead of moving the guard all the way to the outside, teams slide the tackle over to the linebacker and the guard over to the defensive end.

Washington's Gibbs came up with a more extreme solution. He put a big tight end in front of Taylor, who usually lined up on the weak side with no one across from him. In case Taylor moved to the other side, Gibbs put a big tight end over there, too. Taylor was the problem that inspired the one-back offense.

"We spend a lot of time on our playbooks every year in the offseason," Tobin says. "If there are things that can be taught better, we rewrite them. If there are things we're not using, we take them out. If there are things we started using during the year that weren't in the playbook, we get them in."

Counting the rewritten teaching phrases, Tobin estimates he replaces a third of his playbook every year. That

Timmy Smith's great success in Super Bowl XXII caused coaches everywhere to reconsider the merits of a very basic play.

Teams make major changes in the playbook from year to year, sometimes changing as much as one third of the book.

might be more than most, but other teams make changes, too. Maybe the coaches found a better way to adjust to a certain offensive formation. Perhaps they saw new formations that they hadn't accounted for in the playbook. Maybe they discovered some skills in a young player of which they hadn't taken advantage.

That's the other way playbooks change. Offensive coaches, for example, can't simply respond to the new problems other defenses have created or the new solutions other offenses have found. They also adapt to their own personnel. After the Eagles drafted Keith Jackson, a big tight end capable of finding holes in pass coverage and catching 80 passes a year, they broadened their package routes, where the tight end runs to an area instead of a specific spot.

There's very little that's new in football, says Bill Walsh, who is recognized as one of the game's brilliant offensive planners.

Within that area, he can take whatever steps he needs to get open, or uncovered.

"There are new ideas that come up, but most of them have been seen at some point in the history of football," says Bill Walsh, the former 49ers' coach who was the most widely renowned innovator of the 1980s. "Some of the most effective plays utilized now originated in the 1950s. So much of what I learned and evolved into, I learned in the 1950s and 1960s and I'm sure the 1970s. It's a broad base from which we draw."

The best innovators recognize which forgotten treasures to take off the shelf. They adapt pro football's encyclopedic history to current conditions and to the things in their playbooks that they already do well. They use a play before other teams figure out how to beat it and return it to the archives again. Innovation isn't so much creating as it is anticipating and remembering.

"You look to history, as we do in so many areas," Walsh says, "and you utilize it. Then you're willing to adapt to present circumstances."

George Halas did exactly that in 1961. The Bears' coach had been in pro football 40 years by then, and he dusted off an old, out-of-date playbook, took some pages from it and used them to engineer the most shocking rout of the season.

That was the year coach Red Hickey made the Shotgun San Francisco's basic offensive formation and blew holes in NFL defenses. The 49ers won four of their first five games by 35-3, 49-0, 35-0 and 38-24 scores, losing only to the eventual champion Packers. The Bears were the 49ers' sixth opponent, and Halas noticed that the Shotgun had a strong resemblance to the old Single-Wing, with extra receivers but the same long center snap. So he went back to his old defenses against the Single-Wing.

Those defenses used a lineman across from every offensive lineman, where contemporary defenses left some space between the center and the middle linebacker. The center, with that long snap, was vulnerable again. Halas moved middle linebacker Bill George up to the line and had him crash through before the center could react. Chicago beat San Francisco 31-0.

THE GAME PLAN

A game plan rarely uses material that isn't in the playbook. It's sort of the Cliff's Notes of NFL football: just the stuff the players need to know to pass their Sunday exam.

Playbooks are organized by the type of play; game plans are organized by situation, especially on defense. Both the offensive and defensive units prepare game plans according to what they expect the opponent to do in specific situations. The coaches watch the opponent on at least three game tapes - and often as many as six. They feed the information into computers and determine the other team's tendencies. Then they use the parts of their own playbook that they feel can best attack what they have uncovered.

Defenses can be fairly sure of what to expect. Offenses know defenses are going to react to them. Houston coach Jack Pardee says it's harder for Run-and-Shoot coaches to make a game plan because there aren't enough Run-and-Shoot teams against which to watch opposing defenses. A defense won't play a Run-and-Shoot the same way on second-and-short that it would play a two-back offense.

A defensive game plan typically has three headings: (1) situation; (2) opponent tendencies; (3) our response. The situations come in three categories, each acting as a filter to narrow down the opponent's likely play selection. The lists could go from 3-30 pages, depending on how many diagrams the coaches use.

First is field position. Then comes down and distance. On third down, for example, an offense tends to use different plays depending on first-down distance: (a) 10 or more yards; (b) 6-9 yards; (c) 3-5 yards, or (d) less than 3 yards. The last consideration is personnel and formation. Formations don't tip off plays as much as they used to, because so many plays are being run from different formations, but there still are things a team can't do from certain formations. That's why defensive players are always jabbering at each other before the snap, making sure everyone knows the formation.

Offenses keep their game plans more similar to their playbooks. They have separate sections for runs, play-action passes, passes, and trick plays, but offenses also have situational sections for short yardage and goal line, inside the defense's 20, and the two-minute drill. They list defensive tendencies, but in a separate section, and they incorporate the fronts, coverages and blitzes the defense uses most.

By game day, the game plans have been reduced to clipboard-sized cards that the coaches carry on the field. They are lists of plays - lots of lists - and each situation has a separate list.

One time, it dawned on 49ers coach Bill Walsh that he didn't have a distinct category for desperation plays to win a game. He had a two-minute list, but what about 20 seconds? Or two seconds? That was all the time he had in 1987, after the Bengals tried to run out the clock on fourth down and left San Francisco the ball on the Cincinnati 26.

IG BEN plays were in vogue in last-chance situations. Three receivers would line up on one side and run down field in a cluster, hoping one would come up with the quarterback's pass. The 49ers noticed that Cincinnati, like most teams, defended the lone receiver on the other side with man-to-man coverage. They put Jerry Rice on the other side. He caught the winning pass.

Offensive game plans have a foundation of several plays the team uses every week. Gillman called them his "dirty dozen," and coaches fill out the list with plays specific to the opponent.

An offensive game plan has 15 to 20 running plays, some with only subtle distinctions. In addition to basic runs, there are a couple of draws, two or three runs from the Nickel defense, two or three more for short yardage, and at least one reverse or other trick.

"If we coaches are guilty of anything, most of us are guilty of putting in too many plays," says Ted Plumb, receivers coach for the Cardinals.

Walsh's game plans sometimes included more than 100 pass plays, twice the norm. The 49ers didn't even practice their basic, every week plays - they didn't have time. There were too many new ones and too many playbook modifications designed for each week's opponent. Walsh sometimes came in on Friday night with a dozen new plays, had the 49ers practice them on Saturday, and called them on Sunday. Joe Montana was a good enough quarterback to make them work.

All coaches make adjustments to plays between the playbook and the game plan. When Bill Belichick was defensive coordinator of the Giants, he coached against the Redskins 17 times, and watched them block for the counter trey 17 different ways.

With blocking changes and formation changes, Redskins line coach Jim Hanifan says, "You're cutting down the defenders' recognition time. You're banking on the fact that at a certain point in time, they're not going to make the proper adjustment, and boom, all of a sudden, a big play."

"If you take that simple play and run it from 15 looks, you don't need any more offense," says Sid Gillman. He's not guessing. The Redskins proved it when they ran the counter trey 27 times in Timmy Smith's Super Bowl. The backs only had 36 carries that day.

Game plans for preseason games aren't really game plans. A coach often limits his play list to certain sections of the playbook - the one-back offense, for example. When Ted Marchibroda was Baltimore's coach, he had notoriously short play lists and poor records in the preseason, but the Colts were ready for season openers with plays the opponents hadn't seen. In preseason games, former Colts line coach Whitey Dovell said, "All I want to do is find out if these guys can knock somebody on his ass."

But when the games count, game plans need contingency plans for contingency plans. "You have to be ready for everything," Tobin says, which is why a defense might limit its fronts game-to-game but carries virtually the whole playbook of coverages.

The coach who says he scrapped his game plan at halftime is less apt to be a resourceful genius than a guy who didn't adequately prepare his players. Inevitably, individual assignments will need revision as the game goes on. "The game comes down to who adjusts the best," Plumb says, "but you try not to use plays that you haven't practiced all week."

Football games are lost by surprised players. The purpose of playbooks and game plans is to make sure those players are on the other side of the ball.

COOL UNDER PRESSURE

With 70,000 fans screaming and the 45-second clock racing toward zero, the quarterback has to make an important decision.

If he sees danger in the defense and realizes the play he called in the huddle won't work, he needs to replace the ill-fated play with something that will work.

With all the calm of a guy pumping gas in the self-serve lane, the quarterback calls an audible.

Football fans love audibles. They create an aura of mystery and suspense, a chess match on the gridiron. They snip the puppet strings from the quarterback to the coach. It's an act of independence.

Or is it?

Most audibles are carefully planned. Throughout the week, the coaches tell the quarterback, "If this is the play and that is the defense, use this other play instead. Call this audible." It's in the script, not really some bold ad lib.

That's not to say that any fan from the stands could sit through a week's worth of meetings and call the right audibles on Sunday. It's not easy to recognize a defense before the snap, determine the need for an audible, and say the right words at the line, all in the time it takes to unbuckle a chin strap. But it's not usually heroic initiative, either.

George Halas added the audible to pro football in the mid-1940s, after other teams started figuring out how to stop his T-formation offense with the newfangled man in motion. Sid Luckman, Halas's quarterback at the time, says his basic audibles were to: (1) run away from an overshifted defense, (2) pass away from double coverage, and (3) throw a quick out or slant-in against a blitz. Quarterbacks have been calling the same audibles for nearly 50 years.

They've called them less often in the past 10 years. Sight adjustments have eliminated some of the need for audibles. A quarterback and a receiver, without exchanging a word, adjust to what they see. They see a blitz coming, and they both know the receiver changes his route to a slant-in.

Sight adjustments have wider applications than audibles, too. They can be made after the snap. Maybe the cornerback lines up a yard in front of the wide receiver, in bump-and-run position, and the deep pass from the huddle looks inviting. But if the defender drops off just before the snap, the receiver can change his route to a comeback and still get open in front of the corner.

The Run-and-Shoot offense demands sight adjustments. Mouse Davis, the former Detroit offensive coordinator and the Edison of the Run-and-Shoot, says he has only a few basic pass patterns in his playbook. But the plays change according to the coverage, and when they change, every receiver has to make a change. "Our routes are a little more dependent on one another than just being individual adjustments," Davis says.

At the other extreme, Indianapolis coach Ted Marchibroda uses virtually no sight adjustments, because they entail risk. If a quarterback and receiver see different things, they'll make different adjustments. And from Marchibroda's standpoint, they're unnecessary. It's a big field. Eleven defenders can't possibly cover it all. He'd rather have his quarterback see where the defenders are going and use a play that sends the ball where they're not.

So what did Marchibroda install as Buffalo's offensive coordinator in 1990? An offense composed almost entirely of audibles.

Buffalo's plays were simpler than most other teams' plays, so the Bills could communicate without a huddle. Wide receiver James Lofton even called the offense conservative.

Buffalo quarterback Jim Kelly was well programmed to make the right choice. If they do this, call that. He never had more than 8-10 plays to choose from in any situation, and the list shrank further after the defense lined up.

Kelly, however, chose the plays. He didn't have coaches whispering in his ear, signalling by hand, or sending messengers. "He lines up and he calls what he sees," Marchibroda says. And the Bills went to two Super Bowls while other coaches gasped at the heresy of giving a quarterback the keys to the offense.

There's no real risk that a good quarterback with that responsibility will crash the offense. Kelly had his best seasons in 1990 and in 1991, when operating under Marchibroda's system. His passer ratings were 15 and 11 points higher than his previous best.

The other brand of no-huddle offense, the one Sam Wyche introduced in Cincinnati and took with him to Tampa Bay, doesn't use audibles. The quarterback calls the play at the line of scrimmage, but only after the coaches signal it in. Wyche describes it as huddling at the line of scrimmage instead of seven yards back. He wants to wear the defense down emotionally more than physically, making defenders wonder if this will be the down when the offense snaps it quickly. He also wants to keep the defense from substituting without giving up the play selection.

Wyche's way strains the limits of terminology. His quarterback has to convey as much information at the line as other quarterbacks do in the huddle. The plays aren't simplified, as they are in true audibles. Wyche's quarterback has to use codes that are elaborate enough to keep the eavesdropping defense from understanding them.

Since starting the system in 1985, Wyche says, the terminology has been refined to the point where only "a short phrase" will describe a play and formation in detail. The other words the quarterback hollers are merely to confuse the defense. Those other words might be names of animals, cartoon characters, colors, numbers, and perhaps even bird calls that make no sense to anyone but the offense.

Somewhere in between the audible and the huddle call is a hybrid called "check-with-me" that has expanded its horizons greatly in recent years. Hall of Fame quarterback Luckman used check-with-mes, too, but until recently, they meant only one thing: The quarterback called the play in the huddle, but he didn't call the direction until he got to the line and saw where the

Sid Gillman has been one of pro football's primary authors of playbook chapters. He is a master of offense, one of the game's great innovators.

defense had fewer people. Then the quarterback's teammates learned whether the play went left or right.

A more recent usage of check-with-me occurs when the offense has a play that will work against almost any defense, with the exception, perhaps, of the 46, in which an eighth man is near the line of scrimmage. The quarterback puts mental asterisks by some plays on the game plan and calls alternates that the offense will use if he gives the word at the line of scrimmage.

The alternate might be no more than a change in blocking schemes, or it could be an entirely different play. It might be a trap instead of a toss. It might even be a pass instead of a toss. The quarterback makes the call - but he's only following orders.

INSTANT QUARTERBACK

Johnny Unitas had his fractured kneecap in a splint and Gary Cuozzo had his separated shoulder in a sling, so Tom Matte had the game plan around his wrist.

It fit nicely - the game plan wasn't very long. A coach tends to simplify things when his team is in the playoffs and his quarterback is really a halfback.

Matte hadn't taken a snap in five years, not since he was a senior at Ohio State, running off-tackle and throwing occasional passes. But Matte was the closest thing the Baltimore Colts had to a quarterback in 1965 after Unitas and Cuozzo were injured for the last regular-season game.

Don Shula was the Colts' coach, and he devised a simplified game plan that Matte could grasp and execute. Shula added some quarterback running plays that weren't suitable for Unitas and Cuozzo, and he excluded all but the shortest and simplest pass plays. He pared the usual dinner menu of play selections down to luncheon size, and he had Matte wear the essentials of it on a card in his wristband.

Matte called it his "ready-reference list" and his "crib sheet." It told him the things a stand-in quarterback needed to know for calling plays in the huddle and lining the players up in the right spots.

When the Colts beat the Rams to finish the regular season, they earned a tie with the Packers for the Western Conference championship, a tie to be broken in a memorable game at Green Bay on December 26, 1965. Shula tried to activate either taxi squad quarterback George Haffner or veteran Ed Brown, who had signed with the Colts to back up Matte in the last game. However, either move required unanimous approval of all NFL teams, and the Packers refused. Matte would wear his wristband once again, his arm sore from so much throwing in practice and an ulcer raging.

The Colts almost pulled it off. They led 10-0 at halftime. The defense knocked Packers quarterback Bart Starr out of the game, scored a defensive touchdown and made a goal-line stand. The Packers needed a 22-yard field goal at the end to take the game into overtime. On that disputed field goal - Don Chandler's kick was so close to the upright plane that the league doubled the height of uprights from then on - the Packers tied the game. Chandler made another field goal to win it 13-10 in overtime.

Matte ran 17 times, more than any other Colt, for 57 yards against the Packers. He completed 5 of 12 passes for 40 yards without an interception. The completions all went to halfback Lenny Moore and tight end John Mackey.

"Coach Shula talked about rising to the occasion," Matte said. "I just wish I could have risen a little higher. But I guess everyone already knows I'm no Unitas." ⌀

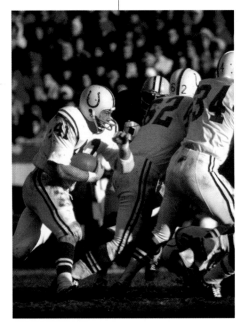

Tom Matte - "The Instant Quarterback"

Built To Play Professional Football

They are not built like normal men. They are built to play professional football. Molded. Sculpted. Defined. Refined. That is today's NFL player. He undergoes a demanding regimen of conditioning and strength training to prepare himself for success.

BY CLARE FARNSWORTH

SOMEWHERE BETWEEN LES BINGAMAN AND BO JACKSON, TRAINING AND conditioning in the National Football League made a hairpin turn.

The game has changed because the men who play it have changed.

"Players today are genetic freaks," says Frank Raines, a former national-class sprinter who is strength and conditioning coach for the Seattle Seahawks.

Raines means that as a compliment, and he need look no further than the Seahawks' weight room for the bodies to confirm his claim. In one corner, sliding additional weights onto a barbell, is Bill Hitchcock, a 6 foot 6 inch, 305-pound tackle who has 11 percent body fat. He also owns a black belt in karate. Over by the windows, effortlessly gliding on a treadmill, is Chris Warren, a 6 foot 2 inch, 226-pound running back who can cover 40 yards in 4.38 seconds. In the center of the room, pounding out sit-ups on an incline track, is John L. Williams, a 5 foot 11 inch, 231-pound fullback whose sloping shoulders, long arms, and thick thighs mask his combination of speed and power.

"Freaks," says Raines, shaking his head and shrugging his shoulders. "These guys are not built like normal men. These guys are built to play professional football."

Built. Molded. Sculpted. Defined. Refined. That's today's NFL player.

"We're dealing with a different type of player because we provide just about every amenity available to help them be better football players," says Tom Flores, president and coach of the Seahawks. Flores has been in professional football since 1960 as a quarterback, assistant coach, head coach, and administrator.

Today's training and conditioning methods are dramatically different from the era when 335-pound Les Bingaman played for the Detroit Lions.

Trying to find similarities between present training techniques and facilities and those used in earlier decades is like comparing the bodies of Bingaman, a 335-pound guard for the Detroit Lions during the 1950s, and Jackson, the two-sport phenomenon whose body was perfectly sculpted.

Tom Catlin was there during the 1950s. Weight rooms were not. An All-America center from the University of Oklahoma, he was selected in the fourth round of the 1953 draft by the Baltimore Colts. Catlin, now assistant head coach of the Seahawks, was traded to Cleveland the following season and played in three NFL title games with the Browns.

"I never used any weights," Catlin says. "For one thing, there wasn't a weight room when I got to the Browns. It hadn't surfaced at that time. Maybe some people were lifting weights, but I never saw them. And I know I wasn't doing it."

The NFL was comprised of 12 teams in the 1950s, each playing 12 regular-season games with 33-man rosters. In Cleveland, where coach Paul Brown helped transform the game, Catlin and his teammates practiced twice a day during training camp, but only for 45 to 55 minutes.

"I was a backup center," says Catlin, who also was a linebacker and defensive signal-caller on the Browns' 1954 championship team. "Just to get running in, I'd snap the ball and run down the field about 30 yards and then run back. That was conditioning in those days."

The 1960s brought the arrival of the eight-team American Football League, but no new interest in conditioning and training. Flores was there, a quarterback for the Oakland Raiders then. Chuck Allen was a linebacker for the San Diego Chargers.

"Did we have a weight room? Are you kidding?" Flores says. "Guys would show up for training camp tremendously out of shape. We had six preseason games and a long training camp, so basically guys played themselves into shape once they reported."

Offseason training at the team's facilities? Sorry. It didn't exist. A young quarterback like Flores, trying to earn passing marks in a fledgling league, had to do conditioning work on his own.

"I used to run at a local high school and beg people to come and work out with me," Flores recalls. "I'd talk little kids into running routes for me. They couldn't catch the passes, but at least I had a target in the general area of where the ball should be thrown."

The Chargers trained at Rough Acres, a ranch in Boulevard, California. There were no weights when Allen arrived in 1961 after being a two-way standout at the University of Washington.

"We were pretty much on our own," says Allen, now vice president of football operations for the Seattle Seahawks. "That meant a lot of guys went their own way when it came to training, and their way didn't necessarily lead to the gym."

Two years later, however, Alvin Roy joined the club as strength coach and brought weight training with him. The Chargers, a 4-10 team in 1962, went 11-3 in 1963, the first of seven straight winning seasons.

"That wasn't a coincidence," Allen says. "What Alvin Roy did greatly helped the San Diego Chargers."

Even if it wasn't greatly accepted by everyone.

"Let's just say some of the players weren't that enthusiastic," Allen says. "You have to remember, some of these guys never had been in a gym, and definitely never had lifted weights. Then we had everybody lifting the same amount of weight, or trying to. The defensive backs and wide receivers were right in there with the offensive linemen and the defensive linemen. As you can imagine, it created a few problems at first."

The 1970s brought the NFL-AFL merger, the Super Bowl, and a new breed of athlete. It was a time of blending the old with the new - leagues, teams, players, and training techniques. Reggie McKenzie, a member of the Buffalo Bills offensive line known as The Electric Company because it turned on "The Juice" (O.J. Simpson), remembers well.

"When I first got to Buffalo in 1972," says McKenzie, "the locker room was behind the Regency Hotel in downtown Buffalo, the trainer had one whirlpool, and the weight room consisted of a universal gym. One universal gym. That was it."

McKenzie, now sales and marketing director for the Seahawks, was accustomed to more. As an All-America guard at the University of Michigan, he had played for head coach Bo Schembechler and line coach Larry Smith.

"I was conditioned that you come to camp in shape," McKenzie says.

What he found in Buffalo were holdover players from the AFL who did not share his sentiments.

"There were still old-school guys, guys from the AFL, and they still used training camp to get into shape," McKenzie says. "You just ran and did what you could. Some guys were so out of shape all they could do was throw up. There was always a lot of throwing up."

Rusty Tillman, now the Seahawks' defensive coordinator, was a linebacker in Washington, where Redskins coach and innovator George Allen was building a weight room and hiring a strength coach in 1971.

"It wasn't emphasized as much then as it is now," Tillman says. "A lot of players just didn't want to do it. George let that go. But for anybody that wanted help, we had a guy there and not just during the season."

Today, every NFL team has a strength and conditioning coach. At the Seahawks' year-round training complex in the Seattle suburb of Kirkland, Raines reigns over a state-of-the-art weight room that is crammed with 36 machines in 2,200 square feet. It includes everything from the traditional weight bench with barbells and stationary bikes to stairmasters, Nautilus machines, and a six-speaker stereo system.

The room was smaller when the Seahawks built their headquarters in 1986. It was

"This game is no longer bigger is better. Now it's bigger, faster, quicker, and more agile is better. Today, strength is not just how much you can lift. Strength is speed. Strength is quickness. That's what wins, and winning is what counts,"

- Frank Raines

"When I first got to Buffalo in 1972, the trainer had one whirlpool, and the weight room consisted of a universal gym. One universal gym. That was it."

- Reggie McKenzie

Today's sophisticated training equipment enables a player to continue conditioning the rest of his body before he can start rehabilitating the injured part.

expanded and re-equipped in 1990 after Raines was hired.

Free weights remain a staple of the Raines program, but he also likes the Hammer machines because they put less stress on joints. That allows an injured player to continue conditioning the rest of his body before he can start rehabilitating the damaged area, and also lets all players continue to lift for strength during the season.

"It's easy to lift 400 pounds during the offseason," Raines says. "I say, try it during the season when your body is being pounded and beaten on. That's when you need strength."

Players lift during the offseason to build a strength base, and during the season to maintain it. That's made easier by the introduction of new machines and methods.

While these new machines are impressive, it takes something more old-fashioned to make them work: Sweat.

"That's the bottom line," says Tom Zupancic, strength and conditioning coach for the Indianapolis Colts. "You can have a whole room filled with machines and free weights, but it's people that make it work. You have to get in there and after it. We don't allow players who just want to be spectators. You have to come in there and get a little sweaty."

A 185-pound wide receiver does not follow the same workout as a 300-pound lineman, right? Wrong. "I don't tailor workouts," Raines says. "I treat them all the same." Adds Zupancic, "If you strip off an offensive lineman's helmet, pads, and skin, you've got the same thing as a wide receiver."

Who started this revolution? That depends on who you ask. Flores and Chuck Allen credit Roy, who introduced conditioning in San Diego. Tillman says George Allen, in the early 1970s, had as much to do with it as anybody. Raines remembers the concept really taking off in the early 1980s after Tom Williams developed a system that incorporated speed training, diet, and weight training.

The introduction of year-round training and conditioning has done as much to reshape the game as any rule change or coaching innovation.

Not surprisingly, McKenzie sees these changes in training and conditioning as they relate to a running play.

"When I was in college, the hole was here and the scheme was to set up to make sure it was here," he says. "Now, blocking schemes call for three or four holes, with the fourth hole being a cutback line. Over a period of time, the sport has changed and so has the way we prepare to play it."

Or, as Raines puts it, "This game is no longer bigger is better. Now it's bigger, faster, quicker, and more agile is better.

"Today, strength is not just how much you can lift. Strength is speed. Strength is quickness. That's what wins, and winning is what counts."

HOME, SWEAT HOME

Tom Zupancic is a thick-necked, thick-chested, thick-legged barrel of a man. A finalist in the 1984 Olympic wrestling trials, Zupancic also is a powerlifter who can bench press 600 pounds.

Frank Raines is rail thin, with a cheetah-like sleekness that makes him look fast even when he's standing still. Raines qualified for the 1984 Olympic trials in the 200-meter dash and has personal bests of 19.8 seconds in that race and 10.3 seconds at 100 meters.

Two distinct body types, but just the types of bodies that NFL teams have selected to rule their weight rooms and oversee the conditioning of today's players.

All NFL teams have strength and conditioning coaches, but only one, Doug Wilkerson of the Raiders, has played in the league.

"The National Football League usually promotes and recruits from within," says Chuck Allen, who is an example.

The Seattle
Seahawks' weight-
room covers 2,200
square feet and fea-
tures 36 state-of-the
art bodybuilding
machines. The
Seahawks, like other
NFL teams, recom-
mend a year-round
strength and condi-
tioning program for
their players.

"But when teams started looking for strength and conditioning coaches, the expertise just
wasn't there with former players, so they had to look outside," he says.

Every team joined the search in the early 1980s. Many teams went to the colleges to recruit
the coaches who were shaping players there.

But some teams took their searches elsewhere. Chicago's Clyde Emrich was a weightlifter.
The New York Jets' Greg Mackrides was an Olympic wrestler. Others were trainers or
owned gyms.

"Everybody has their own style, their own needs," Allen says.

The first generation of strength and conditioning coaches is producing the next. The

Redskins' Dan Riley has sent two proteges to the West Coast - John Dunn in San Diego and Raines.

"Dan and I shared a lot," Raines says. "He was really instrumental in getting me into the league and finding a team for me to go to. He is probably the most intelligent man I have known. He knows virtually everything about anatomy. I owe a lot to him for bringing me in and showing me the ins and outs of conditioning and strength training."

Raines entered the league in 1984, as a part-time assistant with the Redskins. He became a full-time assistant in 1988 after Dunn left. Raines left two years later to join the Seahawks.

As an outsider looking in, Raines's view was skewed by his track background.

"I saw that if guys could learn how to run and develop their form, they could break on the ball better, run routes better, etcetera," Raines says. "I saw a need, but I didn't think there would be this big of a change."

Before joining the Colts' staff in 1984, Zupancic owned a gym in Indianapolis. He grew up a gym rat - not basketball or even boxing, but weightlifting.

"I started in grade school at a place called Hoffmeister's in downtown Indianapolis," Zupancic recalls. "My dad would drop me off on his way to work and pick me up on the way home. It was probably one of the oldest gyms in the United States, so it had a definite dungeon-like feel to it."

Palatial best describes Zupancic's new gym, a 3,000 square-foot weight room in the Indianapolis Colts' training complex. It is well lighted and brightly painted, with mirrored walls. Then there's the music - as much a part of any modern weight room as the weights - and the louder, the better. It comes from a 600-watt system that "will blast you right out of the room," Zupancic says.

The locker room is the players' home away from home. The weight room has become a special place within that home.

"What we ask the players to do in here, what we expect them to do in here, is not easy," Zupancic says. "We've tried to create an atmosphere that is both inviting and motivating."

Raines runs a similar program in Seattle. Players' workouts are charted throughout the year. Each player is constantly challenged to do more.

"Nobody likes to work to their maximum, and you'd be surprised at how much it changes when the coach is around, pushing the player," says Raines. "My job is to break through the wall of doubt in the player's mind."

For Raines, that not only means pushing, but prodding, provoking, screaming, yelling, and whatever else might get the players' attention.

Raines occasionally arrives for stretching exercises before practice with a towel draped from his head a la Lawrence of Arabia. He emerges from the locker room to conduct the post-prac-tice running in war paint and with strips of tape on the legs of his sweatpants - one strip for every sprint they will run. In the weight room, he stands on machines and waves towels to motivate players through a workout.

"I want them so mean, so ticked off that they can't wait to tee off on somebody," Raines says. Even if that somebody is him.

"When Frank first got here, there were more than a few guys who felt like taking a swing at him in the weight room," offensive tackle Andy Heck says. "But Frank works our bodies and our minds. He is excited about his job, and he gets excited about us lifting weights. That enthusiasm is contagious."

"You want the weight room to be the players' room," Raines says. "It should be a fun place, somewhere to work hard, but it should also be a place for camaraderie. This is where you build spirit between players.

"The room should be a recreational-type thing. Sure, they have to come in and do it, but it should be, 'Hey, I'm in here because it's going to prolong my career and it's going to help us win games.' Those are the attitudes I want to instill." ⌀

Pro Football's Roadmasters

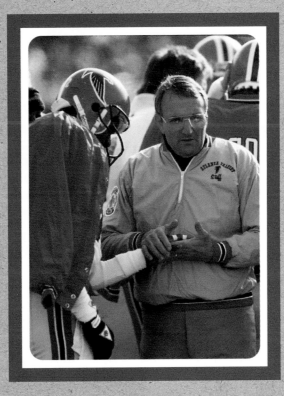

*Packing more than three tons of supplies and equipment,
professional football teams go on the road, preparing for everyday needs and
unexpected emergencies. Life on the road is never easy, and attention to detail
can mean the difference between victory and defeat.*

BY LEN PASQUARELLI

I N THE THIRD CENTURY B.C., LEGENDARY CARTHAGINIAN MILITARY GENIUS Hannibal loaded 40 mighty African elephants with provisions and weapons and, in a daring offensive aimed at laying waste to Rome and claiming victory in the second Punic War, set out across the Alps. Nearly 2,300 years later, Whitey Zimmerman says that, compared to the mammoth mobilization efforts that he undertakes at least 10 times annually, Hannibal may have gotten off easy.

The only equipment manager in the Atlanta Falcons' history, Zimmerman has been stowing steamer trunks filled with football equipment and medical supplies for three decades. And there have been times, he concedes, when he'd gladly have accepted an invitation to try to coax a herd of elephants through a treacherous mountain pass. That chore might have been less difficult than keeping tabs on three tons of shoulder pads, helmets, jerseys, pants, braces, and bandages that accompany the Falcons to every road game.

"Hey, that Hannibal guy only had to go over the mountains," says Zimmerman, who started his service-with-a-smile career as a batboy for the St. Louis Browns baseball club. "When we go on the road, the way the game's played now, we're just about loading the damn mountains themselves. Back in the old days a guy'd come in and toss his duffel bag onto the bus or the train and that would be it. Now, it's like packing up for a cruise around the world, there's so much stuff that has to go along. You name it, we take it."

If Hannibal's failed attempts earned him eternal hero's status, Zimmerman's lifetime of tending to the needs of professional athletes has gotten him steady paychecks, but few plaudits. While his tenure with the Falcons equals that of owner Rankin Smith, Sr., only those who work closely with the club realize the important role he fills. Not until a player reaches into his locker on the road and discovers that he forgot to pack his hip pads - only to find that Zimmerman found them on the floor of the team's Suwanee, Georgia, practice facility and at the last minute tossed them into his own briefcase - is the equipment manager fully appreciated.

While his primary task is purchasing and maintaining the hundreds of thousands of dollars worth of equipment and supplies required for a season, Zimmerman is like a mother hen and a father confessor to the Atlanta players. He is equal parts guardian angel and babysitter, and he's definitely at his best when the club goes on the road. At that point, he becomes like Hannibal - a general of sorts - the master of mobilization, packing up an inventory of incredible diversity.

Like their colleagues around the league, Zimmerman and his long-time assistant, Horace Daniel, are a silent and anonymous rear guard. They perform the tasks that few people see or even know about.

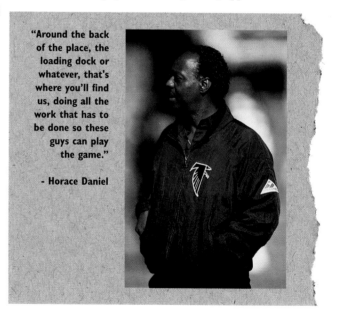

"Around the back of the place, the loading dock or whatever, that's where you'll find us, doing all the work that has to be done so these guys can play the game."

- Horace Daniel

"You come on the road with us and go into the hotel lobby and there's all the kids with their autograph books, yelling for the players," says Daniel, who, like Zimmerman, shares a critical attention to detail. "Then you walk around to the back of the place, the loading dock or whatever...that's where you'll find us, doing all the work that has to be done so these guys can play the game. Don't get me wrong, I'd actually rather be doing that than being hounded by a bunch of fans. But I know for a fact that the common fan who turns on a football game on Sunday afternoon, and pops open a beer and puts his feet up, has no idea what it took to get the visiting team there. There's a helluva lot of stuff that goes on behind the scenes that nobody sees."

"Be prepared." It's not only the motto of the Boy Scouts, but also of NFL equipment managers.

Pittsburgh Steelers equipment man Tony Parisi, a 28-year veteran with the NFL says: "When Mick Jagger gets to an arena, he wants everything to be just so, right? Well, (Steelers quarterback) Bubby Brister's the same way. These guys have enough on their minds without having to worry about whether their flak jacket's been packed or not. You want to be totally prepared so that they're prepared."

Today, the preparation takes much more planning and more personnel than it did a decade ago. As the game has grown in sophistication, so has the planning. The list of people involved with getting an NFL team ready for the road isn't as long as the team's 47-player roster, but it's close. For most clubs, it involves at least one person from every department, and preparations begin as soon as the league announces its schedule, usually in mid-April.

Most of the details involving the moving of equipment - and determining what should be moved - are handled by the equipment manager, the trainer, and their assistants. All clubs travel with staff physicians, and some, like the Falcons, bring along a chiropractor. Increased amounts of protective equipment have added to the tonnage, but it's the medical supplies that have most dramatically increased the number of boxes, cases, and trunks that follow a team.

"You count on the (home) team for things like x-ray equipment and stretchers and things like that, which have become standard amenities," says Philadelphia Eagles trainer Otho Davis. "But you still don't want to be standing on your own sideline and find you're without something that might be needed for an injury."

By Zimmerman's calculations, the Falcons pack about 3 1/2 tons of equipment for a trip. Parisi figures the Steelers haul about four tons. Houston's Gordon Batty estimates that the Oilers haul the same amount in a combination of soft equipment bags identified by each player's jersey number, and hard, steel chests.

Leave a bag or a trunk behind, and the consequences can mean begging, borrowing, or stealing from the camp of the enemy. That's something no equipment manager or trainer wants to do, despite the tight bond their professional brotherhood seems to inspire.

"The main thing is coordination among the different departments, because you don't want someone making arrangements that have already been taken care of," says Indianapolis Colts director of operations Pete Ward, the man responsible for booking hotel rooms and chartering flights. "After you've been doing this for a while, you develop a mental checklist. But that list gets longer every year."

The inventory runs from the ridiculous, to the sublime, to the esoteric - like Atlanta's "valuables box," which is among the first chests to be loaded. Because not all locker rooms have facilities to safeguard the players' possessions, the Falcons bring their own. The valuables box, a large, black steel chest, is separated into numbered compartments. Before the game, players are responsible for storing their watches and rings in the compartment that corresponds to their uniform number. Daniel is then responsible for bolting the box securely.

"It's just about the first thing we put in that locker room and the last thing we take out," says Daniel. "It's heavy, but we need it. It's just part of the planning. Not many people would think, 'Hell, where do they put all that gold (jewelry) during a game?' See, it's details, details, always little details that drive you nuts on this job."

Most NFL teams charge the public relations department with coordinating details directly involved with travel - buses from the home training site to the airport; round-trip charter flights; buses from the airport to the hotel; rooms for coaches, players, management personnel, and guests; a road practice site; meals; meeting rooms equipped with video equipment.

Usually assistant public relations directors are involved in soliciting bids from hotels.

Decisions about where to stay are sometimes based on proximity to the airport or stadium more than on cost. Occasionally, a head coach requests a specific hotel.

Or in some cases, he rules one out. When the Falcons stayed at a posh Phoenix area resort in 1991 before a game against the Cardinals, Atlanta coach Jerry Glanville found the place too sprawling. Glanville didn't blame his club's upset loss on the accommodations, but he made it clear he wasn't thrilled by the night-before-the-game freedom the place afforded his players. The Falcons will stay elsewhere on their next visit to the Valley of the Sun.

Such incidents are rare. Except for fans loitering in the lobby and badgering players for autographs, the advance planning of people like Zimmerman usually keeps distractions to a minimum.

And because most football trips are for one night only, the chances of problems are minimal.

"You're in, you're out. And if you've done your homework and done it well, it goes smoothly," says Zimmerman, who arrives at the road site one or two nights before the game. With a public relations staffer having made travel arrangements, Zimmerman's task is to ready the visiting team's locker room for the Falcons' arrival.

Because Glanville insists on practicing at game sites on Saturday (the Falcons bus directly from the airport to the stadium, checking into their hotel following a one-hour workout), Zimmerman makes certain that players have clean, dry practice clothes and their choice of cleats for that week's playing surface.

After practice, he stows the dirty clothes, lays out the uniforms for Sunday, checks with trainer Jerry Rhea for last-minute needs, and takes an early dinner before getting to bed no later than 10 P.M. Five or six hours before game time, he's at work again.

"I guess guys like me bitch a little about having to take care of these guys like they're babies," says Zimmerman. "But when we win the battle on Sunday, you feel like you've contributed by making things as close to home conditions as you can. You've overcome that mountain of having to win on the road."

A Tight Schedule

Join the NFL and see the world, right? Not quite. If it's adventure, souvenir-hunting, and casual strolls through exotic shops of faraway ports you seek, the NFL is not the place for you. So says former Pittsburgh Steelers defensive tackle Joe Greene.

"There's probably this perception among the public that when we're on the road, we have all kinds of free time to go out and have fun," says Greene, a Dolphins defensive line coach. "Man, nothing could be further from the truth. I mean, I can't tell you how many road trips I made in my career where I never even left the hotel. Mostly what you do is flop yourself on the bed, stare at four walls and think about the game."

The manner of travel in the NFL has progressed from the barnstorming days when teams crossed the country by train, to today's one-day trips by jet, but the agenda for away games has been altered very little. NFL players rarely have even a half-day to themselves.

By league rule, teams must arrive in the host city the day before game time. From the moment of arrival, the schedule is planned. The players' time belongs to the club. While head coaches' day-before preparations vary, the pattern rarely strays from the norm.

Land. Walkthrough practice, usually with emphasis on special teams. Hotel check-in. Meetings with coaches. Team dinner. An hour or two of free time. Team meeting. Curfew.

"It's a game of discipline, and the regimentation of the system - what happens the day before a game - reflects that," says Atlanta Falcons offensive tackle Mike Kenn, a 15-year veteran. "The fact is, you're there to play a football game, not to go sightseeing. And in his own way, every coach has a way of reminding you of that."

Wives of NFL players rarely travel with their husbands. Life on the road is a Spartan existence built on a tight schedule.

If their hotels rate four stars, the players rarely realize it - unless, perhaps, by the quality of the room service.

"You want a typical road trip?" asks Indianapolis Colts quarterback Jack Trudeau. "It's meet. Dinner. Meet. Room service. Maybe a TV movie. Go to sleep. Breakfast. Game. Crawl back on the plane. Get home at midnight. Have your wife or kids say, 'Did you bring me anything?' Shake your head [no] and go to bed again.

"I can think of a lot more glamorous existences."

Over a two-season span (1990-91), one Atlanta Falcons player calculated that, on the Saturday nights before away games, the players averaged two hours of free time before their final team meeting. And, the player added, even stepping out of his room to walk to the lobby for a newspaper had become a chore because of a crowd of autograph seekers.

"There's a hundred people waiting down there hoping Deion (Sanders) will come through, and you can't even squeeze past to get to the gift shop sometimes," says Falcons guard Bill Fralic. "Forget trying to sneak into the bar for a quick beer. You're better off holing up and hoping there's a good college game on TV."

Even cab drivers realize that they're more apt to get rich from the presence of a baseball team than a football club.

"You line up when you know the baseball guys are here," says Pittsburgh cabby Tony Sciulli, whose regular post is outside a downtown hotel. "Football? Those bums never go nowhere."

THE LONG, LONG ROAD

It was not the longest road trip in NFL history. It just seemed that way.

On the morning of November 7, 1981, the Pittsburgh Steelers departed for a game to be played the next afternoon in Seattle. By the time the Steelers returned by charter flight to the Greater Pittsburgh Airport three days later, they had lost not only a game, but also a quarterback and a shot at the season's NFL playoffs.

"It was a gruesome experience, that's the best way to sum it up," says former Steelers linebacker Jack Lambert. "It was more than just the game, which was bad for all of us. It was the events that surrounded it, everything goofy that happened. It was probably the most discom-

"Back in the old days a guy'd come in and toss his duffel bag onto the bus. Now, it's like packing up for a cruise around the world. You name it, we take it."

- Whitey Zimmerman

bobulated, and also the most [ticked] off that I ever saw Chuck Noll. He was a coach gone berserk because things had gone so poorly. Let's put it this way: We all remember it as the road trip to hell."

The events of the game were bad enough for the Steelers, who entered the contest with a 5-4 record and were playing inconsistently. The club had lost its first two games of the season, rallied to win four straight, then alternated defeats and victories over the next three weeks. That Sunday afternoon in the Kingdome was a microcosm of the 1981 season for the Steelers.

Leading 21-3 in the second quarter, Pittsburgh saw Seattle mount a comeback, but even earlier the game had been weird. Example: Steelers third-string quarterback Mark Malone, forced to play a few snaps at wide receiver because of injuries to other players, caught a club-record 90-yard touchdown pass. Later, on the strength of two 1-yard touchdown plunges by Theotis Brown, the Seahawks assumed a 24-21 lead late in the fourth quarter. As if embarrassed, the Steelers fought back. But on third-and-goal from the Seattle 1-yard line, Steelers fullback Sidney Thornton was stopped for no gain. Electing to settle for the tie and a subsequent overtime period, Noll sent kicker David Trout onto the field for a 22-yard chip-shot field goal. Trout promptly shanked the kick wide right.

The jubilant Seahawks ran out the clock. Steelers players, including Thornton and Franco Harris, sought out Pittsburgh newspaper reporters to complain about Noll's decision to opt for the field goal.

"What that said to me," said Harris, "was, well, we're not the Steelers anymore. It meant that we were afraid we couldn't bang the ball in against somebody like Seattle. The season pretty much went down the toilet from that point on."

So did the trip. Forced to stay in Seattle because a thick fog prevented the club's charter flight from taking off, Noll spent the night in his hotel room plotting lineup changes. Quarterback Terry Bradshaw's season performance had been spotty and Noll decided that in the next week's game he would start Cliff Stoudt. What he didn't know was that at that moment, Stoudt was in a country-western bar, impressing the locals by banging on a mechanical punching bag. On his fourth or fifth shot at the bag, Stoudt fractured his hand.

Noll was furious when he received news of Stoudt's injury. "I thought he was going to just waive me and leave me (in Seattle) to die," Stoudt says. "That's the kind of look he had on his face. It was that 'Great Stoneface' of his, only the stone was turning every shade of red."

With fog still enveloping the city, the team was forced to stay in Seattle another night. The coaching staff, of course, imposed a strict curfew.

"Not as if anyone would have dared leave their room anyway, especially after what happened to Cliff," says defensive tackle Joe Greene.

The next morning, with the fog still heavy, the Steelers boarded their charter and waited for the shroud to lift. Two hours into the vigil, Noll decided he'd had enough. He marched to the cockpit and confronted the captain, who attempted to explain the treacherous situation. Noll would have none of it.

"All I can remember," says Lambert, "was hearing Chuck tell the captain, 'Let's go. We're getting out of here.' Hell, at that point, Chuck, who flew his own airplane, probably would have taken the controls had the guy ignored him.

"Sure enough, we took off. I swear, we were climbing through fog for what seemed to be five minutes. When we finally broke through, a few guys cheered. But not many. Everybody knew Chuck was angry. Everybody knew it was a road trip we'd never live down and we'd never forget." ◯

Linebacker Jack Lambert describes the Steelers' 1981 trip to Seattle as "a gruesome experience." Almost everything that could go wrong, did.

No Ordinary Spectators

*They look alike. They dress alike. They are even encouraged to act alike.
In the center of the furious action that is NFL football, officials are expected
to see all and know all, and to be nothing less than perfect. That is what
they demand of themselves.*

BY CLARK JUDGE

I T'S OCTOBER 23, 1960, AND JIM TUNNEY WALKS INTO THE LOS ANGELES Coliseum. He has witnessed only three professional football games, but today he can't wait to watch the Chicago Bears and the Los Angeles Rams.

Tunney is no ordinary spectator. He is part of an officiating crew working a National Football League game. As field judge, it is his job to get the visiting team's captain for the coin toss 30 minutes before kickoff.

Walking out of the cavernous tunnel that leads to the playing field, Tunney approaches Chicago head coach George Halas.

"Hello, coach," Tunney says politely. "My name is..."

"Jim Tunney," Halas interjects.

"Yes sir," Tunney says.

"Occidental College," growls Halas.

"Yes sir," says Tunney.

"You played football, baseball, and basketball."

Tunney nods.

"You were Athlete of the Year your senior year."

Tunney is speechless.

"Jimmy," says Halas, "I've been in this game a long, long time, and I know a lot about it. If there's anything I can do to help you be a success in this league, you let me know."

Tunney thanks Halas and walks away.

"The guy had me cold," Tunney recalls, three decades later. "I knew what he was doing. He was putting me in his back pocket...I thought, 'Wow, what am I doing here? Do I really deserve to be here? Am I in over my head?' But I said, 'You know something? I belong here.'"

George (Papa Bear) Halas, who coached in the NFL 40 years, frequently offered his help - and opinions - to the officials.

Tunney eventually graduated to referee and served 31 years as one of the game's most recognizable faces. He worked three Super Bowls. He called the famed "Fog Bowl," a 1988 playoff game between Philadelphia and Chicago, during which visibility was so limited that Tunney announced down and distance to thousands of spectators in Chicago and millions of television viewers who tried to watch the second half.

In August, 1992, more than a year after his retirement from the National Football League, Tunney was in New Orleans to accept an award when he was stopped by a passerby.

"Say, aren't you..."

"Nick Buoniconti?" Tunney said, grinning.

"Naw," the stranger said. "You're that official. You're...Tunney."

That incident is not, pardon the expression, the rule with NFL officials, who live in a world of such uniformity, conformity, and regularity they often appear to have been cloned.

They look alike. They dress alike. They are even encouraged to act alike.

During the season, they won't talk for public consumption. They seldom show emotion. They can't root for teams. They can't root for players. They appear as drab and colorless as their black-and-white uniforms, known not by their names, but by their numbers.

"It seems like we're robots or automatons," says Tunney.

But the human touch is there, and it is there in people such as back judge Paul Baetz. Famed robot R2-D2 never experienced the chill that shook Baetz at Super Bowl XXIII in Miami, Baetz's first NFL Championship Game. When he learned of his selection, determined by a complex grading system, Baetz was so overwhelmed he telephoned his father, a retired high-school official in New Jersey, to deliver the news and extend an invitation.

"The greatest situation I ever had," says Baetz, "was working two Super Bowls. That meant that, for one day, I was the best at what I did out of everyone in the whole world. Nobody can take that away from me.

"My dad loved the game, and when I got my first Super Bowl I called him up and said, 'Would you like to go?' He said, 'I don't think so. There are too many people, and I don't enjoy crowds.' 'Well,' I said, 'you're going to go because I'm working the game.' So I brought him and my son to the game. For me, to look up and see two people I love was just priceless. All the money in the world couldn't pay for that experience."

It was the last time Paul Sr. watched his son officiate. He died of cancer the following October.

Officials are you. Officials are me. They work during the week. They go to church on Sundays. They have families. They read the sports pages. They watch TV. They laugh. They cry. They make mistakes. They even admit to them.

"They are human," says Detroit assistant coach Dan Henning.

Yet, they work a game that allows them little contact with insiders and even less with those on the outside. When Tunney traveled to games, and strangers asked what he did for a living, he would respond, "professional speaking." Officiating seldom was mentioned.

"Not if I could help it," he says. "I would try to avoid discussing it because you never know who you're talking to."

From the beginning of the season, officials are forbidden to talk to reporters. If they're approached, they're to walk away. The only exception is after a game when interviewed by a "pool reporter," a member of the media designated by each team. Pool reporters are allowed to visit the officials' locker room, but only when accompanied by NFL personnel, and only to inquire about controversial plays.

"Basically," says Jerry Seeman, the league's director of officiating, "we don't want people bothering them and asking them questions. We want them focused on the game and not potentially distracted."

Contact with players or coaches, especially prolonged conversations, is discouraged. Though officials sometimes stay at the same hotels as clubs, they try to avoid socializing with anyone outside their crew. The reasons are obvious.

Sometimes, an official's only display of personality is in his signalling of plays. "You are not a robot out there. But an official who referees a game must behave like he's on cruise control."

- Jerry Seeman

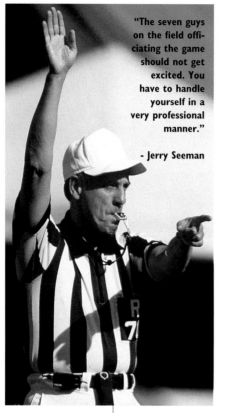

"The seven guys on the field officiating the game should not get excited. You have to handle yourself in a very professional manner."

- Jerry Seeman

"Let's say I talk to John Elway one night for fifteen minutes," says Tunney, "and some 49ers fan sees me and says, 'Uh-huh, look at that.' Then the next day, we get into the ball game, John throws a ball away, and I don't call intentional grounding. That same fan says, 'He probably was talking to him about a play just like that.'

"In this business, you've really got to be like Caesar's wife: above reproach. You've got to behave in such a way there's no way anyone can question your integrity. It's not good enough to say, hey, I'm an honest guy. That doesn't make it. The most paranoid people in the world, besides politicians, are football coaches. They always think the other guy is going to get some kind of advantage."

For that reason, Tunney says, when he spoke to one head coach before a game, he spoke to the other, and usually for the same amount of time. And when he talked to players, he clasped his hands behind his back, thereby discouraging physical contact that observers could construe as favoritism. If a player he knew grabbed Tunney by the arm, Tunney would simply pull away.

"I'd say, 'Don't touch me,'" says Tunney. "It's not that I'm sensitive, it's just that people don't understand. It's like preventive maintenance for a car, but it's called preventive officiating. You do things to keep problems at a minimum."

Sometimes, an official's only display of personality is in his signaling of plays. Referee Pat Haggerty double-pumps his arms to signal touchdowns. Former referee Tommy Bell would pound his right fist into his left palm to signal first downs, a practice since copied by referee Fred Silva. Among NFL officials, that passes for flamboyance.

"You are not a robot out there," says Seeman. "But an official who referees a game must behave like he's on cruise control. There may be coaches who get excited and players who get excited, but the seven guys on the field officiating the game should not get excited. There are a lot of things going on out there, and you have to handle yourself in a very professional manner."

THE SEASON STARTS IN MARCH

For NFL officials, the season doesn't start in August. It starts in March.

By that time, the staff is in place - 107 officials, including 15 seven-man crews and two "swing men." The league office mails each official two open-book exams of 75 questions each, encouraging officials to discuss problems and solutions with each other. It also sends out paperwork for physicals, including stress tests, that must be completed by the middle of May.

In April, the league sends out a 200-item review of unusual play situations, as well as rules changes approved at league meetings the month before.

In May, the NFL sends each official a videotape of calls he made the previous season, along with a video of calls by others at this position.

"If you don't understand the rules or the philosophy," says Seeman, "you're not going to be a good official. If I were to write a book about officiating and there were ten chapters, the first nine would be preparing for the game, and the tenth would be working it. If we take care of the first nine, the tenth will take care of itself."

In July, Seeman holds two four-day clinics - one on the East Coast and one on the West Coast. At the clinics, officials take written and physical examinations.

The second day of this exhausting schedule begins at 6 A.M. with drug testing, and ends at 9:30 P.M. with individual position meetings. In between, there are three 15-minute breaks - one each in the morning, afternoon, and evening - and a rigorous 33-question penalty-enforcement exam.

By the end of July, officials are on practice fields, working at training camps. They stay only three days, but the work is important. This is the first time they put into practice the study of the previous months.

Officials are nothing if not diligent. When umpire Bob Wagner and line judge Tom Barnes were at the San Diego Chargers' 1992 training camp in La Jolla, California, they spent a free afternoon at the beach curled up with an NFL casebook of approved rulings.

"I don't think we're normal," says Barnes. "Here we are, out in San Diego, we go to the beach and what do we do? Bring along an approved ruling book to ask each other questions. When we asked each other questions, people thought we were nuts."

In August, officials are working preseason games.

In September, they're working the 16-game regular season schedule.

"The official must be the ultimate professional," says Seeman. "That's a demand I have on them."

NEITHER RAIN NOR SNOW

Saturday morning. Alarms across the country rattle early as nearly 100 NFL officials hurry off to work. Neither rain nor snow...

"You know something?" says Baetz. "I think the average fan believes we show up a half-hour before the game, work the game, then go out and have a few beers afterwards."

For NFL officials, there is no rest. They work Mondays through Fridays at 9-to-5 jobs, then put on their coats and ties on the weekend to work in faraway places.

If they have a Monday night game, they leave Sunday and, generally, don't return until Tuesday morning.

"It bothers me when people refer to it as part-time officiating," says umpire Gordon Wells. "Heck, in the time it takes me to leave home Saturday and return again Sunday, it's a 40-hour week. It's definitely a full-time job."

Travel arrangements are made by and paid for by the league, usually three to four weeks in advance. Officials fly first class during the season, coach during preseason. The dress code requires coats and ties - or turtlenecks in cold weather - when traveling to and from games, and sport coats on airplanes.

Officials are paid a per diem that covers the costs of a hotel room, meals, and ground transportation. In 1992, that figure was $155 for the first night and $135 for the second.

The referee, or crew chief, is supposed to check in by noon the day before a Sunday game, while others should be there no later than 3 P.M. That itinerary is subject to change, depending on kickoff time and weather conditions. Crews working Monday night games are required to be in the host city by Sunday.

Each member of the seven-man crew has a pregame task. One secures two rental cars; another makes dinner and breakfast reservations; another acts as treasurer, in charge of financial matters; yet another picks up a VCR delivered by the home team to hotel security, as well as videotapes mailed by Seeman.

At 3 P.M. the group convenes and reviews two videotapes, one of their previous game and one of an estimated 50-60 plays from across the league.

All NFL officials attend clinics, which include instruction and rigorous examinations.

Often, they break for dinner and return later.

"I probably led the league in room service," says Tunney. "I would say, 'Listen, why don't we just order room service and keep going. The food will come here, and it'll take us 20 minutes to eat. If we go out, it will take us an hour-and-a-half.' I had a lot of club sandwiches and salads the night before a game."

The next morning, after church service and breakfast, they meet again, for about one hour to review a three-page rules exam given out the Sunday before and completed during the week. Everything is done together.

Says Wells, "My wife is always asked, 'Do you travel with your husband?' And she'll say, 'Not often. What's the fun sitting around a hotel? They're always working.'"

About three hours before game time, officials board two rental cars and head for the stadium. They should arrive no later than two hours and 15 minutes before kickoff. Pulling into a prearranged gate, they are met by the head of security and escorted to their locker rooms.

Work officially has begun.

DETAILS, DETAILS, DETAILS

Nobody is sure how the custom started or why it is repeated, but when officials walk to their locker room, some of them will drop off their bags, then troop, en masse, into the empty stadium.

"It's almost like a ritual," says Tunney. "They go out in the rain. They go out in the snow. If they don't, it's like they believe they might have a bad day."

In the dressing room, some officials kick back and relax. The line judge is not one of them. He immediately leaves for the TV truck outside to set his coordinate times. When he returns, he synchronizes watches with his colleagues. Pro football's on-time machine is about to take off.

11:15 A.M. - The umpire walks into team dressing rooms. He meets with trainers and picks up "cast cards," pieces of paper indicating injured players and their protective equipment. The line judge prepares to sit down with the electronic clock operator to cover the mechanics of timing. The task that befalls the least experienced member of the crew: he must wet a towel and wipe off 24 shiny, new footballs (36 if the weather is bad) delivered by the home team. Later, each ball is checked for air pressure - no more than 13 pounds apiece.

11:45 A.M. - The referee meets the public relations directors of both teams, who notify him of inactive players and emergency quarterbacks for the game. When finished, the P.R. directors return to their teams' locker rooms with two officials each in tow - usually the line judge and back judge to the home team, the side judge and head linesman to the visitors. They synchronize watches with the head coach and are told the names of his captains. The referee, meanwhile, is in the officials' locker room with the TV production staff, discussing the day's scheduling, including the 18 prescribed commercial breaks. In the same room, the field judge confers with the 45-second clock operator.

Whew.

"The locker room," says Tunney, "can look like Grand Central Station."

12:25 P.M. - Officials are ready for on-the-field inspections. Usually, they leave without incident, though there was that time in Chicago when line judge Jack Fette discovered he had forgotten to pack his game pants. A crew member loaned him gray sweatpants, which Fette wore inside out.

Although officials don't solicit opinions from players, they often hear them, anyway.

"Hey, Little Bo Peep!" a fan yelled as Fette walked into Soldier Field. "Lost your sheep?"

Fette was not amused. Eventually, the Bears produced a pair of defensive tackle William Perry's pants, removing the stripes that ran to the bottom, and gave them to Fette.

12:30 P.M. - Officials are on the field, checking for any abnormalities in players' equipment or irregularities in the arrangement of the field. Sometimes a goal post is out of alignment. Occasionally, a field is marked improperly. Rarely, a band is out of place.

Honest.

One year, officials had to move the band in Atlanta because it was too close to the field.

"They were about three yards outside the end zone," back judge Jim Poole says. "You got the feeling a guy flying out of the end zone could have wound up in the middle of the band. We moved them...they didn't like it."

The head linesman is off with the chain gang, the referee checks his mike, the umpire delivers 12 balls to the sideline (12 per half) and the entire group is fair game for inquisitive coaches.

It was at such a time that Kansas City head coach Marty Schottenheimer alerted Tunney to an end-around the Chiefs planned to use. Schottenheimer didn't want Tunney's crew getting in the way.

"When will I know you're going to use it?" Tunney asked.

"The quarterback will tell you before the play," Schottenheimer said.

He did. There were no casualties.

All officials are on the prowl for equipment improprieties, weaving among players to check protective coverings against cast cards and to inspect equipment. If irregularities are detected, players are told to make the necessary changes. If they don't, coaches are alerted.

"I make it a point as I'm walking around to check every kicker's shoes," says Wells.

ASHINGTON KICKER Mark Moseley, with the Redskins from 1974-1986, was a favorite target of umpires. Dallas officials claimed Moseley wore a lead inner sole in his kicking shoe, and the Cowboys would demand that officials inspect it.

They did. But they found no lead. Moseley had six to seven pairs of socks on top of a heavy tape job.

"Hell," says trainer Keoki Kamau, who worked with the Redskins before moving to San Diego in 1989, "he had nothing in his shoe. It was all socks and tape. But with all that it seemed like his foot weighed 30 pounds."

Hank Ilesic was not a placekicker. He was a punter for San Diego in 1989. Prior to his first game, Ilesic, who joined the team out of the Canadian Football League, was told by officials that his Canadian-made kicking shoe was illegal. The problem: its tongue covered the laces.

Ilesic returned to the locker room, where equipment manager Sid Brooks sawed off the tongue to expose the laces. When Ilesic jogged onto the field moments before kickoff, he again was told the shoe was illegal. The trouble this time was the alteration: league rules forbid the doctoring of shoes.

"It was a Catch-22 situation," says Henning, then head coach of the Chargers. "He couldn't wear it with; he couldn't wear it without."

Accompanied by officials, Brooks hurried back to his dressing room office and telephoned Art McNally, then the league's supervisor of officials, for a ruling. McNally declared the shoe illegal.

Slick jerseys are another concern for field inspectors. Sometimes linemen spray uniforms with a slippery substance, often polyurethene, to keep opponents from holding on. Detection is tricky and usually not made until someone complains.

"But the guy on defense won't blow the whistle on the guy on offense," says Henning, "because he has coated his own uniform."

12:40-45 P.M. - Officials and players return to locker rooms. The home team has delivered programs and rosters earlier for each official. Team captains' jersey numbers are noted, and scribbled on white cards carried in shirt or pants pockets. The cards, which officials use to note fouls and time outs, are turned in afterward for the referee's postgame report. The same two officials, who visited coaches an hour before, return to see them. This time, they mention they'll be back to signal two minutes to introductions.

12:50 P.M. - Officials return. Two minutes to introductions.

12:52 P.M. - Locker room doors thrown open. Teams take the field.

12:54 P.M. - Teams introduced. Officials take the field. The referee goes to the TV coordinator on the sidelines to indicate three minutes remain until coin toss.

12:57 P.M. - Team captains escorted to center of field for coin toss with referee.

1:00 P.M. - Show time. The National Anthem. Boisterous fans. Nervous energy. Wagner, the umpire, is edgy.

"There's nothing greater for me," he says, "than that moment when we sing the Star-Spangled Banner in the middle of the stadium, surrounded by 70,000 people, knowing we're going to kick off a football game here pretty quick. I just love to belt out that song with everybody else. I may be corny, but I love it."

1:01 P.M. - Kickoff.

There always is the danger, albeit remote, of getting too excited for a game. Tunney recalls working with an inexperienced side judge who was so nervous he signaled the two-minute warning two minutes before the end of the third quarter.

It happens.

"Obviously," says Baetz, "we're all human beings, and there are errors in judgment at times. Of course, if there are too many errors, they get rid of you."

Officials are in constant communication with each other, players, and coaches. Talk among themselves is not noticeable to spectators. Talk with coaches is. Coaches and players often holler at officials, but officials never holler back. If they have something to say, they first shoo away outsiders and huddle among themselves.

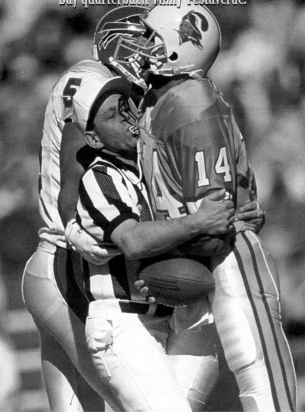

Caution: Officiating in the NFL can be hazardous to your health. Referee Jerry Markbreit has a close encounter with Tampa Bay quarterback Vinny Testaverde.

"Everybody tries to help everybody else," says Wagner. "You really have a responsibility to communicate what's taking place out there. The main thing is to make an accurate call." Case in point: September 17, 1989. New Orleans at Green Bay. The Packers, down 24-7 at the half, rally to trail only 34-28, with less than two minutes to play. It's fourth-and-17. Quarterback Don Majkowski drops back to pass, spots receiver Jeff Query along the sidelines and connects on a 23-yard strike.

At first, side judge Doyle Jackson rules Query out of bounds. But after conferring with the line judge - in this case, Barnes - the call is reversed. Two plays later, Green Bay scores. Final score: Packers 35, New Orleans 34.

"From where I was standing," Barnes said later, "I could see the guy definitely had both feet in. What do you do? You can't let it go. So, I ran up to him and said, 'Are you 1,000 percent sure?' and he said, 'No, I'm not.' We changed the call on the field."

A sideline replay later confirmed that Query was in bounds.

That didn't satisfy New Orleans. Losing coaches seldom go quietly into the night. They yell at officials. They curse at them. They shake their fists at them.

Officials understand. They anticipate that kind of behavior. They even expect it. As one official says, "They can yell at me all they want. But question my integrity, and they better watch out."

The same goes for players.

"They just want their fair advantage," says Poole. "We had an instance in 1991 when a linebacker got so emotional his veins were popping out of his head. I mean, he was just screaming at the ref. So the referee straightens up and says, 'Do you know you're screaming?' And the player steps back and says, 'Well, it's an emotional game.'"

No one is more emotional than coaches and players. No one is more detached than officials.

"The one set of people out there who has to maintain its equilibrium at all times is the officials," says McNally.

And the coaches?

"Every coach is mad when he is losing," says Tunney. "And I don't blame him."

Norm Van Brocklin's Minnesota Vikings were losing to Baltimore one day in the 1960s when McNally, then a field judge, mistakenly dropped a flag after a Colts defender tipped a punt, then ran into the punter.

"But, Art, I tipped the ball," the player pleaded.

"I know you did," said McNally, picking up the flag. "Don't worry about it. It won't be a foul."

After the Colts ripped off a big return, McNally informed the Vikings' head coach of his mistake. Van Brocklin had his back to McNally when the official first approached. He turned to face him only as McNally drew closer.

"Norm had that great knack of waiting for the crowd to die down to hit you full blast," says McNally. "He ripped into me and called me every name in the book. I thought, 'I'm not going to warn him or penalize him because I kicked the play. When he was finally out of breath, I turned to him and said, 'Anything else?' He was exasperated. He didn't know what to say."

NFL officials always put a priority on working together and getting the call right.

Tunney recalls a similar experience. It happened that October day in 1960, when he worked his first pro game. It was the third quarter, and Chicago had the ball. A pitchout sprang a back outside and, for a moment, he was wide open. Then along came linebacker Les Richter to make the tackle. The ball carrier wiggled to cut. He slipped. Then, he fell.

Tunney, who had worked scores of high school and college games in which a downed runner meant the end of a play, immediately blew his whistle. Richter pulled up. Untouched, the runner climbed to his feet and raced to the end zone, permissible in the NFL.

Trouble.

"When I blew the play dead," Tunney recalls, "I had Halas dropping at me from twelve feet out of the air. The vessels in his neck were like the Alaska pipeline. He was screaming and hollering because I'd just taken a touchdown away from him. I said, 'Mr. Halas, if you'd just calm down a minute there's something I'd like to say: I kicked it. It was my fault.'

"Later, he told me there was nothing I could've said to alleviate the situation. 'But,' he said, 'when you admitted your mistake you disarmed me.'"

Sometimes players and coaches disarm each other when taking on officials. At Super Bowl XXVI, one of the Buffalo Bills spent much of the second half chewing out Baetz until quarterback Jim Kelly intervened.

"Get outta here," Kelly told his teammate. "The guy's doing the best job he can do."

When Baetz worked a Bills' midseason victory over Chicago, Bears defensive end Richard Dent had been on his case. According to Baetz, head coach Mike Ditka was right behind to tell his player to zip up and sit down.

"You've got to know coaches and players are going to get excited," says Poole. "You can't take anything that's said personally."

Officials put coaches in one of two categories: those who try to soften them up with exaggerated expressions of gratitude, and those who beg for make-up calls by reminding officials of earlier games in which they believe the officials missed calls that cost them.

The San Diego Chargers have kept computer files on every official since the late 1980s. The idea, reportedly hatched by the equipment manager, Brooks, was to provide the Chargers with what they believe is an edge in the battle with officials.

"We know everything about them," says Kamau, the trainer. "We know their wives' names, where they went to school, the street they live on, and we definitely know how many years they have been in the league."

Brooks and Kamau study crews for upcoming games, pocket useful information about them on computer printouts and hand-sized cards, then stand at the ready when coaches jaw with officials.

"On a particular call," says Kamau, "we might say, 'Bob, that's a bad call and you know it. By the way, how's Patty, your wife?' Maybe you get to an individual and one way or another sway him."

"When you've been around a long time, you understand all that stuff," says Poole. "Most of the officials I know couldn't care less."

As the game winds on, officials are scrutinized by millions of viewers, scores of reporters, a battery of TV cameras and one gigantic stadium screen, all awaiting the slightest slip or hesitation. It is a no-win situation. If officials perform flawlessly, they remain faceless, nameless, anonymous to the outside world. If they fumble a call, they're held to public ridicule and become punch lines to a bad joke.

Question: What's black and white and makes you red all over?

Answer: NFL officials.

"The biggest change in officials I saw over the years," says Tunney, "was the scrutiny. More and more TV analysts are prodded by producers or directors who want more controversy. The result is that officials have been put in a fishbowl more than ever."

The result is that officials aren't permitted human error.

"It's one of the few jobs," says Wagner, "where you don't want recognition."

"AFTER FURTHER REVIEW"

With those words, the NFL in 1986 introduced its newest and most controversial official: instant replay.

The union of men and machine was supposed to minimize mistakes that could influence the outcome of games. To some extent, it worked. But it also tried the patience of players, coaches, and fans, and finally, frustrated owners in 1992 decided to suspend its use for a year.

The problem was the mechanics of operation. Too often the video review took more than the allotted two minutes. In a 1991 game between Kansas City and San Diego play stopped for eight minutes before a ruling was complete.

Some coaches charged replay took the game away from officials on the field and made them indecisive. Some said it interrupted the game's flow and affected momentum. Some even claimed it was unjust because regional telecasts had fewer cameras - and thus fewer views of controversial plays - than nationally televised games.

But replay served a useful purpose. It proved officials remarkably accurate when separating fact and fiction on difficult calls. In six years, replay was used to review 2,967 calls. Only 376 (13 percent) were reversed.

"With instant replay," says Detroit assistant coach Dan Henning, "it was obvious these guys were doing a good job. When you have five or six different views of a play and it takes eight minutes to settle - and even then it's unclear - then you know they have a very, very difficult job."

Or as back judge Jim Poole puts it: "Replay showed we do a pretty good job of calling things right."

Officials are sensitive to charges that replay compromised their abilities to make quick and correct decisions. Almost to a man, they rebutted those accusations and voiced support for its return. Officials also insisted replay did not affect the way they did business. They still called them as they saw them.

"It never changed my perception of a game at all," says Gordon Wells. "If I made an honest error that might cost someone the game, I'd rather go through the review then than on Monday morning."

Referee Jim Tunney, who officiated 31 years in the NFL before retiring after the 1990 season, says officials first rebelled at the idea of replay as an aid because they believed it might usurp their authority. Only when they realized it was there to help, he says, did they embrace it.

"We're not going to be perfect, but we're always going to be excellent. And in order to be excellent, we're going to try to be perfect."

- Jerry Seeman

Back judge Paul Baetz realized it when he blew a critical call, and replay was there to correct his mistake. It was December 14, 1986, in a game between the Los Angeles Rams and Miami.

The Rams trailed 21-7 in the third quarter when quarterback Jim Everett launched an apparent touchdown to wide receiver Henry Ellard. But Baetz, who saw the catch, ruled that Ellard didn't have both feet in bounds. His decision: incomplete pass.

Upon further review, however, the play was overruled. Replays showed Ellard touched down with both feet before going out of bounds. The catch was good. Final decision: six points.

"It was a very, very big play," says Baetz, "because both teams had a chance for the playoffs, and if my decision stood, the Rams still would have been down by two touchdowns and they could've blamed me for their loss (37-31 in overtime). That made me a believer in replay."

Instant replay proved officials remarkably accurate. In six years, replay was used to review 2,967 difficult calls. Only 376 were reversed.

When the system was in effect, each crew had a replay official, with experience working college or NFL games, and each crew was responsible for checking equipment linking its eighth member - who sat in a press-level booth - to officials on the field. Typically, that was done as part of the pregame routine.

Replay review was limited to plays of possession or touching - such as fumbles, catches or interceptions - and most plays governed by the sidelines, goal line, end lines and line of scrimmage. Calls were overturned only when the replay official had incontrovertible visual evidence warranting a change.

"I am convinced officials were not tentative because of replay," says Art McNally, former supervisor of officials. "You don't have time to be tentative. You see a call, and you call it now."

As replay proved, officials almost always call it right.

"We're not going to be perfect," says Seeman, "but we're always going to be excellent. And in order to be excellent we're going to try to be perfect."

JOB APPLICANTS

Every year, the National Football League's New York headquarters handles hundreds of inquiries from aspiring officials, and every year the casting call looks the same.

Dozens of qualified applicants, handfuls of frustrated football fans.

"I've had women who called," says Art McNally, the league's supervisor of officials from 1973 to 1990, "and they'll say, 'My husband loves football. I think it would be nice for him to be an official.' But, essentially, she wants to get an application for him because he loves to watch TV.

"She thinks he'd be good for football because he knows so much about the game. What he doesn't know, of course, is anything about officiating."

At that point, McNally would quote the league's requirement for candidates, including a minimum of 10 years' experience. The response was predictable.

"You'd never hear from them again," he says.

To be an NFL official, getting there is half the fun. The league requires interested persons to work games for at least a decade, though it can and will waive that requirement for ex-NFL players. It also demands applicants have experience as players or coaches, work major college conferences, and submit schedules for the past two years as well as for the upcoming season.

And that's just the beginning.

"You can tell me all sorts of things about what you've done," says McNally, "but when you show me the schedule you've been working, we have an indication right away how well you've progressed.

"If you tell me you've been working 10 years and that next week you've got a junior high game and two varsity high school games coming up the rest of the year, it's a waste of time.

"But if you tell me you're in the Pac-10 or some other major college conference and you show me the schedule, we know we're on to someone who has enough experience and has progressed well enough that we could bring him into the league."

When the season begins, Jerry Seeman, who succeeded McNally in 1991 as the league's director of officials, assigns an estimated 40 observers, or talent scouts, to observe officials on Saturdays. They file evaluations with the league office, sometimes without the knowledge of their subjects.

"Normally," says Seeman, "we follow officials three years, but they don't know when we're around at games."

The league reaches out and touches as many as it can. When a potential candidate is scouted, his entire crew is evaluated, and the results are passed on to New York. The NFL compiles voluminous files on every official in every major college conference.

"We developed a system where I'd say we try to scout 110 to 120 officials during the year," says McNally, "but, in reality, the scout or observer will give a report on the six other officials at the game. So, coming out of it, you're dealing with something like 600 people you had a chance to see in a given year."

At the end of the season, Seeman and a group of experienced and trusted assistants review candidates and produce a group of finalists that, in 1992, was shrunk to 12.

Normally, McNally says, the league has a turnover of about six officials annually. In 1991 there were nine. In 1992 there were four.

Finalists are brought to New York and interviewed for approximately three hours each. In the meantime, the league's security office pores over applicants' backgrounds, delving into areas such as financial and professional security, personal references, and psychological examinations.

"What really makes a good official," says Seeman, "is someone who can be decisive in a professional manner, a person who isn't on an emotional roller coaster. The official must be the ultimate professional. He must be dedicated and understand the game."

He must be lucky, too.

Line judge Tom Barnes was.

Barnes, who lives in St. Paul, Minnesota, always wanted to return to a game he quit playing because of a bad knee. One day, his brother-in-law, a high school official, gave him the chance. He called and asked Barnes to help work a game that night.

Barnes agreed.

He drove for 2 1/2 hours to tiny Finlayson, Minnesota, a town of several hundred, worked the sidelines as part of a three-man crew, and enjoyed every moment. Barnes was hooked.

It wasn't long before he joined the Officials Association in St. Paul and got weekend assignments working junior varsity games on Fridays and high school games on Saturdays.

Several years passed before he heard from a small college officiating crew, anxious to replace a colleague who had hurt his knee. Once again, Barnes stepped in.

The following year, when the Minnesota Intercollegiate Athletic Conference expanded from four to five officials per crew, Barnes was hired. He worked Friday nights at home and Saturdays in far-flung locations.

"I told my wife, 'You know, I'm going to try for the Big 10 because it's going to be the same amount of time,'" says Barnes, "so I applied."

Within two years, the conference expanded from six to seven officials per crew, and Barnes made it again. This time, he stayed four years before moving on to the NFL. Now he's a permanent fixture.

"It's all in the luck and the timing," says Barnes. "I owe my brother-in-law everything. And he never lets me forget it." ✐

To be an NFL official requires at least 10 years officiating experience, including a background of working in a major collegiate conference.

CHAPTER TEN

Super Show At The Super Bowl

*Super Bowl Sunday has become an unofficial national holiday, a celebration of America.
Besides being the biggest event in the world of sports, the Super Bowl has become
The Entertainment Extravaganza of the Year…every year. Those who plan
and produce it are well aware of the great expectations.*

BY JIM DONALDSON

HE CARS WERE LINED UP IN THE CONCOURSE UNDERNEATH THE LOUISIANA Superdome, engines idling.

There were 17 antique Buick convertibles, one for each former Super Bowl MVP. In just a few minutes, the guests of honor would be introduced to the crowd awaiting Super Bowl XX.

Bart Starr and Joe Montana...Lynn Swann and Fred Biletnikoff...Joe Namath and Terry Bradshaw...Jake Scott and Chuck Howley...Roger Staubach and Jim Plunkett...John Riggins and Marcus Allen...each perched above the rear seat of a vintage auto. They were lined up in the order of their Super Bowl heroics, ready to roll.

The parade was to kick off a pregame show that would celebrate the twentieth anniversary of the Super Bowl. As each MVP was driven onto the field, his Super Bowl highlights would be shown on screens at each end of the stadium while a popular song from that year played over the loudspeaker system.

Everything had been planned not just to the minute, but to the second.

Suddenly, five minutes before the show was to start, producer Bob Best got a call on a walkie-talkie from an assistant stationed on the concourse.

"I'm standing here with the fire marshal," the assistant said. "He insists all the cars be turned off. He wants them all out of the building."

None of Best's alternatives seemed good. It was too late to wrangle with the fire marshal. It was much too late to change the show.

"I told the person on the walkie-talkie to tell the drivers to pull out on cue," Best says. "I told him that if the fire marshal wanted to come up and arrest me, he could, but we were going on with the show."

The show must go on. Especially when it's the Super Bowl.

Nothing can stop the Super Bowl. And nothing can top the Super Bowl.

Many years ago, the Super Bowl became much more than a game deciding the championship of the National Football League. It now is an international event, televised to almost 60 countries around the world.

Super Bowl Sunday has become virtually a national holiday - a celebration of America, a mid-winter Fourth of July.

More Americans watch the Super Bowl on television than any other sports event. All 10 of the highest-rated sports events in TV history are Super Bowls. Of the 10 most-watched programs, nine were Super Bowls. Only the final episode of M*A*S*H, which ranks third, managed to break the Super Bowl's hold on the top spots.

In the summer of 1969, seemingly all America watched as Neil Armstrong became the first man to walk on the moon. Just 18 months later, even more Americans watched as the Baltimore Colts beat Dallas 16-13 in Super Bowl V.

"I can remember," says Don Weiss, director of planning for the NFL, "Pete Rozelle remarked the next day the ratings for Super Bowl V were higher than when men walked on the moon. That's when we realized the Super Bowl has become a much bigger event, going far beyond merely sport and evolving into a spectacle." The business of sports has become show business. And the Super Bowl has become the Show of Shows.

There is never a guarantee of how well-played the

The producer of several Super Bowl pregame extravaganzas, Bob Best has experience in dealing with precise timing. Every event is on an exact timetable planned not just to the minute, but to the second.

BOB BEST

Super Bowl halftime shows have developed a tradition of being spectacular entertainment events. The challenge is to make each one better than those that preceded. The Super Bowl XXVI production was among the best.

championship game will be. But the show...the show is always Super.

It was January, 1991, and the United States was on the verge of war. In response to Iraq's invasion of Kuwait, American troops and planes were stationed in Saudi Arabia, Naval forces were gathered in the Persian Gulf. Days were filled with tension. Reserve units were being called to active duty, and Americans wondered each morning whether that day would be the day of U.S. involvement in combat.

In Tampa, where Super Bowl XXV was to be played on January 27, security was tight at the stadium because of concerns about terrorism. Barriers were erected to prevent cars from getting near the stadium. A fence was built around the perimeter of the stadium, and no one was allowed inside without a ticket. Before entering the stadium fans had to pass through metal detectors, as at an airport gate.

It was in that atmosphere that Whitney Houston sang the Star-Spangled Banner.

"It was just an amazing atmosphere that existed in there," says Best. "I don't know that I'll ever again experience anything like that in my life."

To those in the stadium, Whitney Houston's rendition of the National Anthem was an unforgettable experience.

The Super Bowl pregame show always has a patriotic theme. It is not coincidence that the colors of the NFL logo are red, white, and blue.

"The anthem is a tradition at American sporting events," says Best. "The NFL has determined that they'd like to do the most possible. The anthem is patriotic, so the pregame show should be patriotic, too."

The NFL had long been planning to make its Silver Anniversary Super Bowl something truly spectacular.

"It's a patriotic ceremony every year," says Best. "Because it was the twenty-fifth anniversary game, we were trying to make things as special as possible. We wanted to find somebody to sing the anthem who was a superstar. Whitney certainly qualified. She was extremely popular."

She also was delighted to do it.

"Her father is her manager," says Best. "He's a great guy. He was pumped up about it. He told us, 'You're going to get a patriotic, conservative, emotional rendition of the anthem. You're going to get a powerful thing.' That's exactly what we got."

Because precise timing is required in the pregame show, the anthem was prerecorded.

"We always - always, always, always - have a prerecorded version of the anthem," says Best. "We do it to protect against the unexpected. If an artist who has spent four or five months putting the production together wakes up the morning of the game and can't talk, it's not like we can just run anyone in from the sidelines to do it."

There also was the matter of the jets. As the anthem ended, fighter planes were to fly over the stadium.

"Whenever we have a jet flyover," says Best, "the coordination is absolutely incredible. To synchronize the anthem, the jet flyover, and television requirements is a highly pressurized scenario. We can't miss by even a few seconds. We have to be right on the money.

"If someone's doing the anthem live, they're singing not only to thousands of people in the stadium, but also to 130 million people watching on television. A live performance easily can vary by four or five seconds from one time to another."

Obviously, it wouldn't do for the closing bars of the anthem to be drowned out by the roar of jet engines.

"We felt it was critical at that time to give the people of the United States a positive diversion from the war," Best says. "We wanted to stir up the crowd in the stadium. It would have been awful if there were any missed cues during the anthem. That's why it was vital to prerecord. Whitney Houston was against the notion in the beginning, but she finally understood the logic in doing it."

An airborne visitor was one of the highlights at Super Bowl I. The show has evolved into an entertainment spectacular done on an epic scale that would have impressed even Cecil B. DeMille.

The arrangement of the anthem was done by her music director, Rickey Minor, and a colleague, John Clayton. It was very deliberate, very slow, and it heightened the drama and intensified the emotion.

As her voice rang over the field that afternoon, tears rolled down the cheeks of fans throughout the stadium.

Powerful emotions welled up and crested when, as the song ended, the roar of jets merged with the roar of the crowd.

"It's tough to beat flyovers," says Best. "They really affect people. At an event like that, people's patriotism really comes out during the ceremony. As the anthem builds to a crescendo, when you have that big noise at the end, it really gets people fired up."

It also had a terrific effect on American servicemen and women in the Gulf region who were able to watch the game on television.

"I deal with the Pentagon quite a bit, because the military usually is involved in our production in some way," Best says. "The thing that made me happiest of all was that everyone I talked with at the Pentagon told me how much they liked it. They said that everyone in the Gulf region that they'd communicated with was very appreciative. When I heard that, I didn't really care if anyone else liked it or not. Those troops were risking their lives and, if it meant a lot to them, that was wonderful."

The Super Bowl halftime show is an entertainment spectacular done on an epic scale that would have impressed even Cecil B. DeMille.

Since the Super Bowl is no ordinary game, an extraordinary halftime show is only fitting.

So, there have been rock stars and the Rockettes, magicians and musicians, 100 motorcycles and 88 grand pianos, Disney characters and Peanuts characters, astronauts, ice skaters and jazzercisors, classic cars and the world's largest juke box, fireworks and marching bands.

Nor is all the action always on the field. Several times, fans have been asked to participate by performing card stunts. And, for Super Bowl XXIII, fans at home were able to get into the act by using 3-D glasses obtained with a purchase of Diet Coke.

The show that year, entitled "BeBop Bamboozled," featured music of the fifties and sixties, recalling the era of drive-in movies, poodle skirts, tail-fin cars, and soda fountains.

To maximize the 3-D effect, NBC director John Gonzalez painstakingly choreographed the halftime show, preplanning every shot and camera angle to coordinate with the music.

Such attention to detail is typical of the Super Bowl telecast.

"It has almost become a cliché in television sports to say that you're going to cover the Super Bowl just like any other football game," says Sandy Grossman, director of six Super Bowl broadcasts for CBS. "But you wind up using twice the equipment and personnel. It honestly is not just another game. It's a very special day."

And it has to be broadcast in a very special way.

"It's difficult," says Grossman, "because you're not only catering to the die-hard fan who's been building up to the game all season, but you've also got the peripheral fan who watches to be part of the event. Consequently, you have to show a lot of different aspects of the game."

There is almost as much pressure on people televising the game as on those who are playing in it.

"The NFL is the only major professional sports league that has a one-game championship," Grossman says. "All the other sports play a championship series, so if one broadcast doesn't go particularly well, you have other chances.

"But the Super Bowl is different. You have one shot at the highest-rated television program ever. Every part of the broadcast is that much more important, because so many people are focused on it. The pressure is tremendous. But it's the job we all strive for."

It's not as if the Super Bowl is all work and no play, however.

The week preceding the game is a week of celebration in the Super Bowl city. It's as if every corporate entity associated with the event finds reason to throw a party. The biggest and best-known of these, over the game's first 24 years, was the Commissioner's party, staged in lavish surroundings every Friday prior to the game.

It was nearing midnight at this event one year, and anyone who still could move after four hours of oysters on the half-shell, baby back ribs, sushi, smoked ham, Florida stone crabs, coconut cream pie, and double-trouble chocolate brownies was rocking and rolling to the fifties sounds of Captain Cardiac and The Coronaries.

The crowded dance floor looked like a high school hop when, suddenly, Bruce Willis, co-starring at the time with Cybill Shepherd in the television show "Moonlighting," made his way through the jitterbugging couples.

Seeing a celebrity at the party was not unusual. But Willis didn't merely show up and blend in with the crowd. He jumped up on stage, grabbed a microphone, and began to sing with the band. Flashing an impish smile, Willis pushed his sunglasses to the back of his head and launched into a rollicking rendition of "Roll over, Beethoven," as people cheered and danced.

The Commissioner's party was canceled prior to Super Bowl XXV, at a time when American soldiers were stationed in the Persian Gulf and partying seemed inappropriate. It was formally discontinued a year later. Wiser heads decided that the celebration had outgrown itself.

But no one who attended the earlier affairs is apt to forget what they were like. So in demand were the invitations, it was almost easier to get tickets for the game.

What the Super Bowl is to the average football game, the Super Bowl party was to the standard soiree. It was not just a big bash - more than 3,000 in attendance - but a big production. It was a larger-than-life extravaganza that Robin Leach would have loved.

The party has been held aboard the Queen Mary and in a movie lot at Universal Studios, in convention centers and in airplane hangars. In each case, the party's theme was related to the city where the Super Bowl was being held. In Miami, in 1989, it was "Salsa and Spice." The following year, it was "La Fete New Orleans." When Willis wowed the crowd in Los Angeles in 1987, it was "Hooray for Hollywood" which was staged on Lot Z at Universal Studios. The party was on an AstroTurf carpet under 160,000 square feet of tent - the equivalent of three football fields - and was typical of the grand scale of Super Bowl parties.

Upon arrival, guests boarded a tram for a tour of Universal Studios, which included a close-up look at the Great White shark from "Jaws," a brush with King Kong, a drive down the dusty street of an Old West town, and past the house where Norman Bates lived in "Psycho."

Returning to the party, guests were greeted by members of the Tri Delta sorority of UCLA, wearing white tuxedos and top hats, ready to escort them into the tent through a replica of Mann's Chinese Theater.

The combination program/menu/map given to the guests explained that they were about to enter "the Hollywood of another era... an era of romance, adventure, and, most of all, glamour."

Sooner or later, everybody went to Rick's Cafe in the Hall of Romance. There, the music was played not by Sam, but by Johnny Knapp and his Casablanca Quintet.

Attendance at Super Bowl games often has provided fans with an opportunity to be part of the show. Several times, fans have been asked to participate by performing card stunts.

Les Brown and his Band of Renown were in the Hall of Adventure, where the film classic "20,000 Leagues Under the Sea" provided the backdrop for a sumptuous seafood buffet and sushi was served in the "Teahouse of the August Moon." The Goodyear blimp wouldn't fit under the tent, but a facsimile of the hot-air balloon from "Around the World in 80 Days" floated overhead.

In the Hall of Kong, the Rhythm Kings played the music of Manhattan from the 1920s, '30s and '40s, while guests dined at an all-American grill. Desserts were in The Fifties section, where Willis went wild.

The menu in Miami in '89 was as extensive as Joe Gibbs' playbook.

In "Little Havana," there were Cuban sandwiches, plantain chips, guava banana shakes, and dancing to the hot rhythms of two Latin American bands. In "The Everglades," where the Joe

Dragon Calypso Band provided entertainment, there were hot and cold tapas, including Spanish ham and figs and grilled chistora. There were whole roasted pigs and boiled spiny lobsters on "Fort Lauderdale Beach," along with beach music by Captain Harry and the Surf Riders.

Barbecued Peking duck with Mandarin crepes was available along "Ocean Drive," while in "The Keys" there were stone crabs, conch fritters, and Paella Valenciana.

"We tried to make it a fun event," says Susan McCann Minogue, who coordinated the Super Bowl parties in her role as assistant director of special events for the NFL.

Where the Super Bowl is concerned, the pursuit of fun knows no bounds.

"Like everything else at the Super Bowl," Best says, "the shows are getting bigger every year. We're always swimming upstream."

Best nearly found himself upstream without a paddle the year he decided to use the lunar module as the finale to his pregame show for Super Bowl XXIII.

Because the game was in Florida, the idea was to pay tribute to NASA and the Kennedy Space Center at Cape Canaveral. Eight astronauts, representing the four phases of America's space program - Mercury, Gemini, Apollo, and Space Shuttle - were scheduled to appear, along with space vehicles and hardware, including the lunar rover.

Best had seen the module in "Moonraker," a James Bond movie, and said, "I've got to have it. How can I end the show with anything but that?"

But what he ended up with was a moon-size headache.

"I forget all the problems, but every time we talked to the company who owned it, and the one guy in the U.S. who could run it, there was a new problem. They'd need a special kind of propane. They'd need a golf cart. They'd need a particular pipe. They'd need green plywood. They'd need liquid nitrogen. Every time, I'd ask, 'Is this it?' They'd say, 'Oh, yes, yes.'

"Then, the morning of the game, the operator had what I guess you might call stage fright. I didn't know this, but he had crashed in his previous attempt. He had plummeted to the ground and broken some bones. So I didn't blame him for being nervous. But I wished he'd told me about it two months before - I would have found something else to end the show.

"I talked to him. We decided he wouldn't get real high. He finally took off okay, and ended up going higher than we had planned. It was spectacular - the crowd loved it. But if I could have figured out another way to do it, I would have."

SUPER SHOWCASE

Joe Namath guaranteeing a victory by the Jets over the Colts in Super Bowl III. Budweiser beating Bud Light in Bud Bowl I.

Joe Montana and Jerry Rice teaming up to topple the Bengals in Super Bowl XXIII. Michael Jordan and Bugs Bunny combining as "Hare Jordan" and trouncing four guys in a pickup basketball game.

Whitney Houston singing the National Anthem at Super Bowl XXV. Ray Charles singing "You got the right one baby. Uh-huh," in a Pepsi commercial televised during the same game.

They are among the most memorable of Super Bowl moments.

Each year, more than 100 million people around the world see the Super Bowl on television. They watch not only the game, but also the commercials. Often, the commercials are memorable.

"There's no other showcase like it on television," says Doug Seay, a senior vice-president at Hal Riney & Partners, a New York advertising agency. "To be able to reach half the country all at once is a truly remarkable feat."

"There's no other single advertising vehicle in which you can reach so many people so fast," says Bob Wolf, North American CEO for Chiat/Day/Mojo, an international advertising agency based in Venice, California.

"It's more than a game," Wolf says. "It's a media event. You can add up the numbers and say,

One of the entertainment highlights of Super Bowl XX was the presentation of the Most Valuable Players of the preceding championship games.

'Well, heck, I could be on two professional games and two college games and reach the same number of people for a better price.' But it ain't the same. There's a mental receptiveness you get, an excitement, an expectation like no other game."

As a result, another competition has emerged on Super Sunday - a Super Bowl of commercials, in which advertisers and their agencies battle to see whose spot is best. The Super Bowl telecast has become the preeminent showcase for advertising creativity.

The turning point came in 1984. That was the year the Super Bowl also became the Ad Bowl, a creative test where new campaigns are launched and companies vie to produce the most memorable commercial.

The breakthrough was a futuristic spot developed by Chiat/Day for Apple computers to introduce a new line of Macintosh computers.

Filmed by British director Ridley Scott, the commercial had its roots in George Orwell's novel *1984*. In keeping with that theme, the 60-second spot featured a woman in colorful jogging clothes eluding uniformly-clad guards and freeing a pale troop of blue-suited drones by hurling a sledgehammer through a screen filled with the face of a "Big Brother" figure.

The intent was to urge people to think for themselves, to resist Big Brother-imposed conformity. Apple wanted to convey that something was coming that would change the way people thought about the company and its products.

Malcolm MacDougall, at the time a creative director for a New York City advertising agency, called the commercial "the most courageous thing an advertiser has done in this country in a long time. It's the only commercial that has ever appeared on the Super Bowl that got people in bar rooms talking about a commercial instead of the game."

That has been the goal of advertisers ever since.

Among others receiving major attention were Pepsi, with Ray Charles and the "Uh-huh" slogan, and Anheuser-Busch, whose annual Bud Bowl has become a popular part of Super Sunday. The Bud Bowl, which made its debut in 1989, was presented amid major fanfare.

The 1989 Bud Bowl commercial cost $1 million to produce, and the attention to detail was evident.

Broadcast Arts, which created the animation in its New York studio, built a 70-foot scale model of St. Louis's Busch Stadium. The players were beer bottles, and the fans were 11,000 beer cans. The long-neck linemen wore protective collars. The coach of the Bud Light team wore the type of hound's tooth hat Paul (Bear) Bryant made famous in his coaching days at Alabama. Spuds MacKenzie, the original party animal, sat in the owner's box surrounded by three beautiful women wearing sequined gowns. And then there were all those can "fans" doing The Wave.

Although less than five seconds of the commercial were devoted to The Wave, the filming took 18 hours, with an animator rearranging the cans through 120 frames.

"After twelve hours," recalls Steve Oakes, president of Broadcast Arts, "the animator tripped into them."

For a moment, it seemed like a disaster.

"Fortunately," Oakes says, "he had a videotape and was able to recreate their positions."

The spot produced dramatic results - a 17 percent rise in sales - which prompted Anheuser-Busch to continue the Bud Bowl in succeeding years.

But not all sequels are successful.

Apple followed its landmark 1984 ad with one depicting blindfolded men in business suits, marching in lockstep and singing "Hi-ho, Hi-ho, it's off to work we go," following each other, lemming-like, off a cliff and into the sea.

The commercial was preceded by a print ad campaign in which Apple warned Super Bowl viewers: "If you go to the bathroom during the fourth quarter, you'll be sorry."

As it turned out, Apple was sorry. The lemming spot was a lemon, and Apple stopped advertising during the Super Bowl telecasts.

Back in 1967, it cost $42,500 for 30 seconds of air time during Super Bowl I. Because of the assumed superiority of the NFL over the AFL, the championship game was expected to be a mismatch that wouldn't generate exceptional interest.

The TV ad rate remained the same for Super Bowl III. But, after Joe Namath and the Jets stunned the Colts, the perception of the game changed dramatically.

The following year, CBS charged $100,000 for 30 seconds, and prices have continued to soar. The first "million-dollar minute" came in 1985 and, for Super Bowl XXVI, CBS was asking $850,000 for 30 seconds.

Media buyers say that, despite the high price tag of the Super Bowl's commercial time, the unmatched popularity of the game and its high composition of male viewers - particularly in the 18-45 age group - still make it a good value for many big advertisers.

"There's no better window than the Super Bowl," says media buyer Paul Schulman. "Commercials are as much of an event now as the game itself."

THE NFL EXPERIENCE

The man in the business suit lined up to attempt a field goal from the 15-yard line.

He took off his jacket, then loosened his tie. He bent down to take off his loafers and kick barefoot but, looking at the crowd around him, he smiled self-consciously, then stood up again.

Taking a few steps backward, the man glanced at the uprights. Focusing for a moment on the ball on the tee, he quickly stepped forward with his left foot and kicked with his right.

The kick was good.

But his right shoe went wide left, landing high in the netting behind the goal-posts as the crowd laughed and cheered.

Elsewhere in the Minneapolis Convention Center, people were testing their arm strength and accuracy at the NFL Quarterback Challenge. Or comparing their time in the 40-yard dash to the NFL's fastest man - Redskins cornerback Darrell Green. Or seeing how many of their fingers they could slip into a replica of William (Refrigerator) Perry's size-32 Super Bowl ring.

It was all part of the NFL Experience, an indoor football theme park that made its debut at

Super Bowl XXVI.

NFL President Neil Austrian called the NFL Experience an "indoor fan spectacle - a true fan's delight." And it certainly was that.

Lots of people wanted to try to kick the ball through the uprights, and the Quarterback Challenge also was popular. But fewer fans were willing to test their speed in the 40 by racing against an advancing path of flashing lights that simulated the speed of Green, who runs the 40 in 4.35 seconds.

It was fun to boot the ball toward the goal-posts and to throw passes against an electric target that calculated how far the ball would have gone. But trying to beat Green's time seemed like racing against the speed of light.

For fans who preferred strolling to sprinting, there was plenty to see at a more leisurely pace.

Most people never have the opportunity to go inside an NFL locker room, but one was on display at NFL Experience. Fans found that NFL players enjoy few frills: each player has a cubicle smaller than most closets, often cluttered with enough pairs of shoes to conjure up thoughts of Imelda Marcos.

Next to the locker room was the stadium tunnel, like those that players run through to get to the field. For those who wondered what it is like to stand in the tunnel just moments before kickoff, hearing the roar of the crowd, the NFL Experience provided everything except the butterflies in the stomach.

A myriad of exhibits included in The NFL Experience gave fans a glimpse of many behind-the-scenes aspects of NFL football.

With recorded voices shouting "Come on now! Let's go! Everybody out there!" it was difficult to refrain from dashing out of the tunnel, hollering and yelling, ready to run downfield on the opening kickoff.

Among the exhibits in the "Measure Up to the Pros" section were plaster molds of players' arms and legs. Fans could place their own limbs in the molds, and make their own comparisons.

As one woman stood with her leg inside a cast of Kansas City running back Christian Okoye, a 6-foot 1-inch, 260-pounder, she was asked how she'd feel about being married to someone that big.

"No way!" she said quickly, as her friends laughed.

Among the highlights of the NFL Experience was the NFL Films Theater, featuring an eight-screen format with Surroundsound and showing a videotape depicting the sights and sounds of an NFL game.

At the Wilson Football Factory, fans could see how a football is made while, at the CBS Broadcast Booth, they could try sportscasting.

Many fans posed for pictures behind cardboard cutouts of their favorite team's uniform and some had their photos made into football cards.

Kids were able to burn off energy at a playground with hundreds of foam-rubber footballs. And for people who had worked up an appetite, there was a food court with favorites from stadiums around the league.

There also was plenty of shopping. Fans flocked to buy NFL merchandise and special Super Bowl apparel at a 15,000-square foot store operated by Foot Locker. And there also was an extensive card and memorabilia show, with NFL players on hand to sign autographs free of charge. And, on the way home, fans could dream about having a bedroom like the one at NFL Experience, decorated in the colors of their favorite team and filled with dozens of NFL-licensed products, including sheets, curtains, and furniture.

The NFL Experience got off to a spectacular start, immediately establishing itself as another "must see" in Super Bowl week. ⌀

Making A Difference

When their days as NFL headliners are over, they go to a variety of occupations. Some become businessmen, others go to the TV booth. Some become doctors, others are lawyers. The following are profiles of five former NFL stars, each of whom selected a special path for himself…a mission to help those who need it most.

BY MARY KAY CABOT

R ETIREMENT AGE FOR MOST AMERICANS IS THE MID-60S. BUT FOR THE PROFES-
sional football player, retirement comes much earlier. It is a rare player who
is still active past his fortieth birthday.

Because they are still young men when they leave pro football, each of
them is faced with the question: "What do I do with the rest of my life?"

Each man finds his own answer; the paths they choose are as varied as
the individuals themselves. Some become businessmen, others are
coaches. Some are farmers, others salesmen. Some become educators,
others are entertainers.

The following are profiles of five former NFL stars who have chosen to
give special meaning to the phrase, "giving back to the community."

REVEREND JOE

Joe Ehrmann was certain he had all the answers in 1978. A talented defensive tackle for
the Baltimore Colts, he was a member of the famed Sack Pack that had set a club record with
59 quarterback sacks in 1975. He had a ribald sense of humor and could drink like a fraternity
brother on spring break.

Ehrmann was the life of every party. In fact, he was the host of every party. "I held all the
poker games and the Halloween parties at my house," he recalls.

Ehrmann's days were filled with football. His nights were filled with parties.

Despite his life in the fast lane, Ehrmann invited his 18-year-old brother, Billy, to live with
him in Baltimore to escape the tough street life they had known in Buffalo. "We came from a
broken home," Joe says. "Billy was my only brother. We were very close."

A ball boy with the Colts, Billy was 10 years younger than Joe. "I taught him all the values
I had learned - if you want to be somebody, you have to make it in sports," Ehrmann says.

Billy never got the chance. One day at the Colts' training camp, the team trainer noticed
black and blue marks on Billy's
chest. Billy was diagnosed with
terminal cancer. He went home to
Joe's house in Baltimore and, after
five months of suffering, died a
painful death.

Joe Ehrmann was
an outstanding
defensive tackle, a
vital member of
the Baltimore
Colts' famed
"Sack Pack."

"At his funeral, I was standing
next to that open grave, that
casket," Joe says. "Many of the players and coaches and hundreds of
other people were at this funeral for
an 18-year old kid.

"After the last 'Amen' was said
and everybody walked away, I asked
myself, 'What is the purpose of
life?' Here I was, 28 years old and in
my seventh year in the NFL, and I
had no idea."

Ehrmann's quest for answers led
him to the Colts' team chaplain,
and from there, to Westminster Theological Seminary in Philadelphia. He became a student
at the seminary during offseasons from football.

Joe underwent a conversion to Christianity that was not easily understood or accepted by
some of his Colts' compatriots. To them, he was still Joe, the party guy.

"Reverend Joe" and the kids of Baltimore's inner city. A mutual love affair.

"I think it was very difficult for a lot of them," he says. "Some didn't want to accept it. Others were skeptical. I was a kind of caricature of the born-again jock. But I was only in Baltimore another year before I went to play for the Detroit Lions, where I didn't have the history." A new purpose in Ehrmann's life emerged while he studied at Westminster. While growing up on the mean streets, he had always been aware of the disparity between the haves and the have nots. "I had seen the lack of opportunities for poor people and the growing sense of hopelessness," he says. "I knew this was where I wanted to be, working to help people find a sense of hope."

From that burning desire evolved The Door - a Christian ministry in Baltimore's inner city. Ehrmann founded the ministry in 1986 to meet the needs of poor families. There, this 6-foot 6-inch, 260-pound giant of a man is affectionately known to the kids as "Reverend Joe." The Door is a place where the indigent can find food, shelter, and clothing, where a young girl can get pregnancy counseling, where latchkey kids can hang out after school, where moms and dads can learn parenting skills, and where boys and girls can learn about arts and athletics.

"I want this ministry to provide people with one-stop shopping," Joe says of The Door, "sort of a little mall, so that if an inner-city family comes in, they'll all be taken care of right there. The problem with services in this city is that a family has to go nine different directions to get them. It means they have to get on the bus, take the kids...it just doesn't work."

A program of which Ehrmann is especially proud is STOMP (Summer Teen Occupational Mentoring Program), in which 10 high-risk youngsters are given a chance to learn vocational skills, thanks in large part to a donation of power tools by Black and Decker.

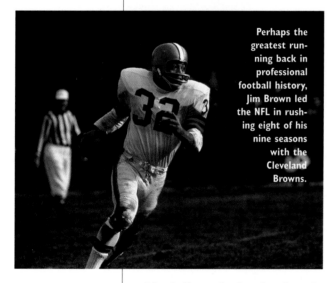

Perhaps the greatest running back in professional football history, Jim Brown led the NFL in rushing eight of his nine seasons with the Cleveland Browns.

"That's a real significant program because if we're ever going to reach the inner-city male, it's got to come through some economic viability," he says.

Since 1986, The Door has gone from a staff of one to seventeen. "We've had tremendous growth," he says. The Door plans to host national conventions for cities wishing to implement similar programs.

"I'm thrilled with where we are and where we're going," Ehrmann says. "We don't have all the answers, but we're asking a lot of the right questions."

Ehrmann, who lives in the inner-city with his wife Paula and their three children, says the lessons he learned both on the streets and on the football field have been important.

"The thing that impacted me most in twelve years of football was the fact that forty-five men could come together for one purpose and set aside personal goals. That's the challenge facing the church and society - how we can learn to come together to glorify God. I want The Door to be a catalyst in making that happen."

Ehrmann says the Los Angeles riots in the spring of 1992 were just a symptom of the nation's inner-city woes. "I don't think there's a city in this country that's not ready to explode," he says. "The L.A. riots just made it more visible to people who don't want to talk about such things.

"But as far as I'm concerned, there's nothing I'd rather be doing."

"WE KNOW HOW TO REACH PEOPLE"

After Jim Brown had proven to himself - and perhaps to the rest of the world - that he was the greatest running back of all-time, he traded in his Cleveland Browns playbook for a movie script.

Applying the same zeal to the big screen that he had to the gridiron, Brown was soon established as a Hollywood star.

Brown was sure to be wherever the action was. He hung out at the hot nightspots, hobnobbing with the likes of Frank Sinatra and Dean Martin.

He starred in dozens of movies, including "The Dirty Dozen," "The Slaughter," "The Split," "Black Gun," and "One Hundred Rifles." He was romantically linked with numerous Hollywood beauties. His nights were punctuated by loud parties, many of them chronicled in his controversial best-seller, "Out of Bounds." By day, the pool at his luxurious Hollywood home was often lined with sunbathers.

Today, Brown is still where the action is. But now, it's a different kind of action.

As founder and president of the Amer-I-Can program, Brown has devoted his life to helping gang members and ex-convicts turn their lives around.

"The basic philosophy is that gang members and ex-cons must learn life-management skills and how to use them," Brown says. "When they learn those skills, it brings their self-esteem up. The young people I deal with are left out of the system, so they become an alternative negative corporation out there. Turn them around and they can make a tremendous impact in a positive way."

The Amer-I-Can program, begun in Los Angeles, has branched out to other cities: Cleveland, San Francisco, New York, and Portland, Oregon.

"We're grassroots," Brown says. "Our gang members and ex-convicts speak the language, so they know how to reach people. They're also teaching the authorities how to better do their jobs."

Jim Brown, a superstar first in professional football and later in the movies, finds his work with the gangs of Los Angeles to be the most rewarding experience of his life.

In Portland, for instance, ex-gang members have briefed the police force on the ins and outs of street life - the language, the rules and the attire, among other things. In Los Angeles, ex-cons work with educators in the department of corrections.

During the Los Angeles riots in 1992, members of the Amer-I-Can program were instrumental in helping to quell the violence.

"We set up a lot of meetings during the riots between gang members and police," Brown says. "All of our people went out and did a lot of good work during that time. We had hundreds of ex-gang members with us."

Later that summer, Brown showed up at the Cleveland Browns' training camp with his chief of staff, a former member of the Crips gang from the notorious Watts section of Los Angeles. "Do you know who this is?" Brown asked, as if he were about to introduce Michael Jordan.

A young man, 24, was decked out in a double-breasted designer suit with a one-carat diamond stud in his left ear.

"This is the man who helped set up the truce between the Crips and the Bloods," Brown said, patting him on the back. "The killing is almost down to nothing. We've had thousands out there celebrating together instead of killing each other."

The man to whom Brown referred was David Sherrills, who several years earlier, along with his younger brother, James, had approached Brown about helping them do something about gang warfare. Brown had always had an interest in what he describes as the disenfranchised African-American male.

"I've always been interested in working with the young, troubled black males," he says. "Law enforcement hasn't been doing the job. There are overcrowded prisons and there's a tremendous homicide rate. I'm interested in saving lives and creating job opportunities. It's a long haul getting rid of these negative activities. It's never-ending."

Brown soon discovered that treading into gang-infested territory required more courage than running headlong at Giants linebacker Sam Huff. "I gained the respect (of gang members) not by strength, but by submission," Brown says. "I wasn't afraid of them, and they weren't afraid of me. They knew they could speak the truth.

"They know this isn't an eight-week program. This is for life."

Funding for the Amer-I-Can program has come from contracts with states and cities and from private donors such as Browns president Art Modell and coach Bill Belichick.

"We have a service, and we sell it," Brown says. "There's no question, we're the best gang-intervention program in the country."

Brown says he has found the work more rewarding than football or movies.

"I don't want any more film work," Brown says. "Movies are in the past. I will no longer sit in a trailer and watch the world go by."

MOTIVATED TO GIVE

When Seattle Seahawks wide receiver Steve Largent announced his retirement from football in 1989, former NFL commissioner Pete Rozelle commented, "It took only seven months to find my successor, but it will be years before anyone with the character, human decency, and on-the-field skills will be found to replace Steve Largent."

Earlier that year, Largent had been honored as the NFL's Man of the Year for putting as much time and effort into community service as he did into rewriting the NFL's pass-receiving records during his 14-year pro football career. Largent set NFL all-time records for receptions, reception yardage, and touchdown catches.

"When you're not good enough for playing honors," Largent said jokingly, "they give you humanitarian ones."

Largent's community involvement has been anything but a joke. When his football career ended, he was able to give even more of himself.

"I think life is about giving," Largent says. "Somehow it's tainted when you're only giving because you feel like somebody gave you something. I think a person who's motivated

Steve Largent set NFL records for receptions, reception yardage and touchdown catches. Acquired as a free agent on waivers as a rookie, Largent played for the Seattle Seahawks 13 seasons before retiring in 1989.

correctly just gives out of the goodness of his heart. It's just a part of his life. I look at my life and see all of the things by God's grace that I've received. And I'm more motivated to give. The Bible says 'To whom much is given, much is required.' And as a professional athlete, I feel I've been given much."

Some of Largent's post football projects have included fund raising for the Ronald McDonald House for families of hospitalized children in his hometown of Tulsa, Oklahoma, and The Little Lighthouse, a free school for handicapped children. He also has raised thousands of dollars for Seattle's Children's Hospital.

But much of Largent's work has centered around a Christian ministry called Focus On The Family, based in Colorado Springs, Colorado. A supporter of the ministry since 1982, Largent is now a part-time staff member, traveling around the country to speak about the importance of the family.

"My message deals primarily with how essential my own family has been in my life and how easy it is to become distracted from maintaining that set of priorities that places your family so high," he says. "I think back through my NFL career...there were a lot of highs and a lot of lows, and if it were not for my family, I wouldn't have been able to deal as well with all the ups and downs."

Largent, who lives in Tulsa with wife Terry and their four children, was attracted to Focus On The Family because of what he describes as his dysfunctional background.

He was six years old when his parents divorced and his mother was left with four small boys. Steve, the oldest, saw his father only a couple of times following the divorce, until he was in college.

"We do as much as we can together, as a family. We pray together, we play together, and we camp together. We're real involved in our kids' lives."

-Steve and Terry Largent

"I can remember some of the struggles my mom went through and I remember thinking, 'I never want my family to be like this,'" he says. "It made me very motivated to make sure my family didn't become one of the statistics of our country - the disintegrating family.

"My wife, my children and I try to do as much as we can together, as a family. We pray together, we play together, and we camp out together. We're real involved in our kids' lives."

The Largents received the ultimate test of their strong Christian faith when their youngest son, Kramer, was born in 1985 with spina bifida, a spinal defect that can cause paralysis and impair other bodily functions.

"[At first] it was devastating to me and I didn't have a positive attitude about it at all," Largent says. "All that came to my mind were the things he'd never be able to do. But he's been a great blessing to us. He's taught us what it means to be compassionate and how much we need to help each other. He's a great kid."

Kramer's illness has led to Steve's involvement with the Spina Bifida Foundation and the United Way. He also makes phone calls to hospitalized children, including those who are terminally ill.

"It used to be very hard for me until Kramer was born," he says. "It doesn't take much time, but when I get comments back about how much [a call] meant to them, it's humbling and gratifying. You suffer for the parents and you grieve for them, because I've been there."

Largent says professional athletes have no choice but to be role models for kids.

"The only decision we have to make is whether we're going to be a good one or a bad one," he says. "My feeling has always been that in the scheme of things, with just a little bit of my time, because of the platform God has given me as a professional athlete, I can have a tremendous impact."

BEHIND PRISON WALLS

Bill Glass, former all-pro defensive end for the Cleveland Browns, retired from professional football in 1968. After 11 years of bashing in heads in the NFL, he wanted to start mending hearts. He didn't anticipate that his journey would take him into damp, dark prisons, where he would meet hardened criminals.

When Glass established his city-wide ministry in Dallas, his plan was to reach out to people like himself, upstanding citizens with plenty of amenities but not enough amens.

But a higher power apparently had different plans.

The warden of a prison in Marion, Ohio - former Browns player Pete Perini - invited Glass to share his faith with the inmates, robbers, rapists, and murderers. "I hated the idea," Glass says. "I totally resisted it. I had a bad experience visiting a prison when I was in college and vowed I would never go back. It was a hellhole."

But a board member from Glass's Evangelical Association appealed to his conscience. He said, "It seems to me that if you really believe the Lord can transform a person's life, why not try it in a really tough place, the prisons."

Glass still despised the notion, but yielded to the urging of his board members. "I can see now from the better vantage point of twenty years that God was dragging me, kicking and screaming, into His perfect will," Glass says. "But that's the way it is with God. One way or another, He always gets His way."

Glass assembled an all-star lineup of athletes to accompany him on his first "Weekend of Champions." The game plan was simple. First, they'd share their faith. Then, they'd demonstrate their athletic skills. The 750 assembled inmates represented a truly captive audience, but the last thing they wanted was a bunch of do-gooders talking about God.

The hecklers started in immediately, and Glass, scheduled to speak last, began looking for

Bill Glass was accustomed to battling fierce competition when he starred for the Browns, but he encountered the toughest resistance behind prison walls.

an exit. "But there was no way out," he says. "I had to go through with it."

Glass decided to drop the "God Squad" routine, and began telling stories of his stellar seven-year career with the Browns, his run-ins with the Bart Starrs of the NFL. Hallelujah! He captured their attention. "I was amazed at how they listened, particularly considering that they hadn't really listened to the others," he says. "Amazingly, forty inmates stayed for the counseling that first time out."

The next day, the athletes conducted sports clinics for an enthusiastic crowd. "The wise-cracking subsided," Glass recalls. "The crowds were huge and the response was fantastic. Soon, prison officials from all over the country were calling us and we had more invitations than we could take." Today, 20 years later, the Bill Glass Prison Ministries have visited more than 500 prisons. Each year, they reach out to 115 facilities. The Bill Glass Team works closely with nearly 5,000 committed counselors throughout the U.S. and Australia.

Athletes and coaches who have participated include Roger Staubach, the late Pete Maravich, former

Cowboys coach Tom Landry, and Bears linebacker Mike Singletary.

Glass has authored 10 books, including "Free at Last," "Expect to Win," and "How to Win When the Roof Caves In." He has also produced three television specials, including the Emmy-nominated "Bill Glass Prison Special."

"Bill Glass has made a life-changing impact on many people, in and out of prisons," says Landry. "I have personally traveled with him to prisons and met with inmates whose lives have been changed by this Christian ministry."

One of those was "Nick the Greek," an armed robber from the Ohio State Penitentiary in Mansfield, Ohio, who wrote, "I can't find no words in Greek or English to describe how beautiful I feel inside since the crusade. People were scared of me because of the evil I did. People don't fear me now. I have a new gang. This is the gang that spreads love and His word."

Glass says he hears hundreds of such stories each year. "The Bible is full of impossible conversions. And the longer I work in the prisons, the less surprised I am to see God work His miracles. I'm thankful He specializes in lost causes."

In retrospect, Glass laughs at how he initially fought the concept of prison ministry.

"Thank God we don't always get our prayers answered the way we request them, because if I had, I would have missed the thrill of a lifetime," he writes in "Free at Last." "I gradually became aware that I'm on the firing line. I'm on the first team. I'm shooting the tube.

"Now, I'm committed to telling them and others who will listen to this worn-out football player that only when you turn your life over to Him will you be totally free. That's the good news I want to share with people on both sides of the iron bars."

Now, There is Hope

Nick Buoniconti enjoyed the kind of life most guys only dream about. He was smart, handsome, and talented. He had a loving wife and three great kids. He was a professional football star for the Miami Dolphins, a linebacker on two Super Bowl championship teams, with eight Pro Bowl appearances on his resume.

Then, in 1985, Buoniconti had to face a nightmare.

Tragedy struck.

While visiting friends in New Jersey, Nick and his wife Terry learned that their son, Marc, a linebacker for The Citadel, had suffered a broken neck during a football game. He was paralyzed from the neck down. There was even a possibility that Marc might not live through the night.

Nick Buoniconti, a leader in the Miami Dolphins "No-Name Defense," was selected to play in the Pro Bowl eight times.

"The first forty-eight hours he was barely hanging on," says Buoniconti. "When you see your son on life-support with a respirator breathing for him, and he's fighting for his life, it's a hell of a jolt.

"Once Marc's condition was finally stabilized, I kind of did an introspection. You look into your heart and your soul and you say, 'What is my priority in my life?' It was plain to me and my family that we were going to refocus our lives, and the most important thing was Marc. Whatever it would take for him to have a better life - a more productive life - we were going to do."

After learning that there was little research being done in the field of spinal cord injuries, Buoniconti joined with Dr. Barth Green from the University of Miami to found the Miami Project to Cure Paralysis.

"From almost no research labs and a skeletal crew working on spinal cord injuries, we've grown to twenty-five labs and more than seventy researchers all over the world," Buoniconti says. "We've raised millions of dollars and ninety-five percent of that money has come from private funds."

Buoniconti organized fund-raisers such as the annual "Great Sports Legends" dinner at the

Marc Buoniconti, paralyzed as the result of a college football injury, has become the inspiration for the Miami Project to Cure Paralysis.

Waldorf-Astoria Hotel in New York City, which raises about $1 million each year. Athletes who have been honored include Yogi Berra, Hank Aaron, Bart Starr, Jimmy Connors, Joe DiMaggio, and O.J. Simpson.

With that type of support, the Miami Project soon began to show results. In 1991, it produced a major breakthrough in spinal cord research. "Five years ago, there was no hope for anyone in a wheelchair," Buoniconti says. "Now there is phenomenal hope. About a year ago, they discovered that the adult central nervous system can be regenerated in experiments. The work that's been going on from there is progressing rapidly. The doctors tell me that within five years they'll be doing clinical work in humans and they think they'll be restoring some functioning, so I'm very excited. It destroyed a lot of myths and refocused a lot of research that some people were dismissing."

To devote more time to the Project, Buoniconti retired as chief operating officer of U.S. Tobacco in 1989 and took a less demanding but similar position with a relatively new pharmaceutical company, Columbia Labs. He also co-hosts a weekly show on HBO, "Inside the NFL." But most of his waking hours are spent on the Project.

"The Miami Project is more than an avocation," he says. "It's a dedication and a commitment and whatever time it takes, I give. We schedule things so it doesn't interfere with my work at Columbia. We meet weekends, we meet nights. Whatever it takes, I do. I travel, I raise money. Wherever I have to go, I just try to tie it in."

Marc, who graduated from Miami with a degree in psychology, also works full-time for the Project.

"He's very active in fund-raising," says Buoniconti. "He can't shake hands because he can't lift his arms, but he smiles a lot and he acknowledges and thanks a lot of people. He lives with us, but he's a very independent kid."

Buoniconti says his son has been a great inspiration to other disabled people.

"The great thing about Marc is that he never complains about being a quadriplegic. He never looks back, and he never says 'Why me?' He just goes forward. He deals with this disability as if it doesn't exist, although he knows it does exist, because every time he gets up in the morning, he knows that his arms and legs don't move. He's reminded of it all the time. But he deals with it and he doesn't complain, and he makes everybody's life a lot easier."

Neither Nick nor Marc doubt their efforts will one day lead to a cure for paralysis.

"Marc may not ever get out of a wheelchair," says Nick. "But we wouldn't be doing this if we didn't think it would help someone someday.

"I know what Marc goes through because I see him every day. I know he dreams of walking, and until that day happens, we won't give up."

Buoniconti says the Project has meant more to him than his Super Bowl victories, his Dolphins team MVP award in 1973, and his eight Pro Bowl appearances.

"Hopefully, my legacy in life will not be my accomplishments on the football field," he says. "Hopefully, the legacy I leave will be that I made a major contribution to helping find a cure for paralysis. I'm not a scientist, but we've raised about fifteen to eighteen million dollars and I'm responsible for a lot of that. I think I have the ability to continue to raise the funds to find a cure. Until that happens, we won't give up." ∅

The Teams of the NFL

Each NFL team holds a unique place in pro football history,
and each has its heroes, its special events. The following pages profile each team,
recalling some of its most memorable days and its greatest players.

BY RICHARD KUCNER

Atlanta FALCONS

YEAR	WINS	LOSSES	TIES	RECORD	PLACE	COACH
1966				3-11	7th	Norb Hecker
1967				1-12-1	4th	Norb Hecker
1968				2-12	4th	N. Hecker, N. Van Brocklin [1]
1969				6-8	3rd	Norm Van Brocklin
1970				4-8-2	3rd	Norm Van Brocklin
1971				7-6-1	3rd	Norm Van Brocklin
1972				7-7	2nd	Norm Van Brocklin
1973				9-5	2nd	Norm Van Brocklin
1974				3-11	4th	N. Van Brocklin, M. Campbell [2]
1975				4-10	3rd	Marion Campbell
1976				4-10	3rd	M. Campbell, P. Peppler [3]
1977				7-7	2nd	Leeman Bennett
1978				9-7	2nd	Leeman Bennett
1979				6-10	3rd	Leeman Bennett
1980				12-4	1st	Leeman Bennett
1981				7-9	2nd	Leeman Bennett
1982				5-4	5th	Leeman Bennett
1983				7-9	4th	Dan Henning
1984				4-12	4th	Dan Henning
1985				4-12	4th	Dan Henning
1986				7-8-1	3rd	Dan Henning
1987				3-12	4th	Marion Campbell
1988				5-11	4th	Marion Campbell
1989				3-13	4th	M. Campbell, J. Hanifan [4]
1990				5-11	4th	Jerry Glanville
1991				10-6	2nd	Jerry Glanville

1 — Norb Hecker (3 games), Norm Van Brocklin (11 games)
2 — Norm Van Brocklin (8 games), Marion Campbell (6 games)
3 — Marion Campbell (5 games), Pat Peppler (9 games)
4 — Marion Campbell (12 games), Jim Hanifan (4 games)

he competition was fierce; the stakes high. It was the Battle of Atlanta. The National Football League and the American Football League were at war in the early 1960s, and their focus was on the South. Both leagues wanted to expand, and each coveted the city of Atlanta.

The NFL timetable called for expansion in 1967, but when the AFL set its sights on Georgia, NFL Commissioner Pete Rozelle accelerated the schedule and awarded a franchise to Atlanta in 1965.

Only 14 NFL franchises existed at the time, and there were eager bidders throughout the nation. But Rozelle recognized that Georgians

Home, Sweet Georgia Dome

When the Atlanta Falcons began play in 1992, they had the newest home in the NFL - the 70,500-seat Georgia Dome. The first game played in the Dome was on August 23, 1992, a preseason game against the Philadelphia Eagles. The first regular season game was against the New York Jets on September 6, 1992.

The Georgia Dome is the sixth indoor home field in the NFL. The first was the Houston Astrodome; others include the New Orleans Superdome, Seattle Kingdome, Pontiac Silverdome, and Hubert H. Humphrey Metrodome.

The Georgia Dome is the world's first cable-supported dome; its teflon-coated fiberglass roof is held together with five miles of bridge cable. Other domed stadiums have either solid roofs or air-supported roofs.

1965

ATLANTA FALCONS

Turning Points

NFL awards Atlanta franchise to Rankin Smith. "Name the team" contest winner: Falcons. 45,000 season tickets sold within seven weeks.

would make a franchise in Atlanta something special. He was right.

Football-hungry fans stood in long lines for the chance to buy tickets for a team that didn't yet exist, and Atlanta rewrote the NFL record book for season-ticket sales by an expansion franchise with 45,000 in less than seven weeks.

Atlantans distinguished themselves from the outset, and then bettered their own records. Season-ticket sales were halted at 55,144 in 1982, and new levels of attendance were in the offing with the 1992 opening of the 70,000-seat Georgia Dome.

It has taken patience and perseverance to be a Falcons' fan over the years. In the first 25 years of the team's existence, Atlanta won a total of one playoff game, a one-point victory that required a miracle finish. In its first

Big Bart

The first player taken in the 1975 draft, Steve Bartkowski became the Falcons' starting quarterback as a rookie and didn't surrender the role for a decade.

He completed 1,870 passes for 23,468 yards and 154 touchdowns. A two-time Pro Bowler, Bartkowski had his best year in 1980, when he led Atlanta to a 12-4 record and threw for 31 touchdowns.

ALFRED & ALFRED

The Falcons enjoyed their most productive passing attack with 3,700 yards in 1981, and two guys named Alfred played major roles in the success.

Atlanta's bookend wide receivers were Alfred Jackson and Alfred Jenkins, small (175-pound) men who made big plays. Jenkins, the Falcons' all-time leading receiver (359 catches, 6,257 yards and 40 touchdowns) accounted for 70 catches and 1,358 yards in 1981, while Jackson contributed 37 catches and 604 yards.

1966

After nine defeats, Falcons win 27-16 over Giants. Team wins three of last five, posts 3-11 first-year record.

1968

Falcons draft defensive end Claude Humphrey, who ranks among league's best for next decade.

25 years, Atlanta never posted back-to-back winning seasons.

Until Jerry Glanville arrived as coach to alter the face of Falcons' football and spur Atlanta to the 1991 playoffs, the team had finished in last place in seven of the previous eight years. Of the seven head coaches who preceded Glanville, only Leeman Bennett managed a winning record (47-44).

With rare exception, when it hasn't been one thing, it's been another. When the Falcons' defense was the best in the league, the offense couldn't score much. And when the offense was racking up points, so was the opposition. In the years when the Falcons managed to get it together, the perennially powerful 49ers and Rams, NFC Western Division rivals, were a little bit better.

Not that there haven't been some great players and special moments in Falcons' history.

The NFL welcomed Atlanta by awarding it the first pick in the 1966 draft. The Falcons chose Tommy Nobis, who for 11 years was one of the best linebackers in the business. Nobis

Same Note - 18 Years

No other player gave the Falcons as much as Jeff Van Note…in more ways than one. A superb center, he anchored the Atlanta line for 18 years, playing in a club record 246 games before retiring after the 1986 season. His six Pro Bowl appearances tie Claude Humphrey for most by a Falcon.

One Step Forward, Two Steps Back

Dave Hampton's plight symbolized the trials and tribulations of the Falcons' early years. Hampton joined the Falcons in 1972 and immediately became the number one running back. In the last game of that year, he briefly became Atlanta's first 1,000-yard rusher, when he reached the cherished goal late in the game against Kansas City. He was ceremoniously presented the ball, and then the game resumed. But on his next carry, Hampton was thrown for a 6-yard loss, reducing his total to 994. He got only one more carry, a 1-yard gain, and finished the season at 995. The next year, Hampton's season ended at 997 yards. He didn't reach 1,000 again until the final game of the 1975 season, when he hit 1,002 with two minutes left to play. Taking no chances, coach Marion Campbell took Hampton out of the game, and the Falcons finally had the first 1,000 yard rusher in their tenth season.

SENIOR JUNIOR

Many of the 42 players Atlanta got in the expansion draft of 1966 were here-today, gone-tomorrow types, but running back Junior Coffey came to stay. Junior became the senior member of the expansion class by lasting through the sixth game of the 1969 season, after which he was traded to the New York Giants. He was the leading rusher in Atlanta's first two seasons, running for 722 yards each year.

1975

Tackle George Kunz is traded to Baltimore for two draft choices, with which Falcons acquire quarterback Steve Bartkowski and linebacker Fulton Kuykendall, both long-time standouts.

Norm Van Brocklin

1977

Leeman Bennett becomes Falcons' fifth head coach; "Grits Blitz" defense yields only 129 points - NFL best for 14-game season.

was a superstar, but he was an exception. Few others performed at a superstar level for extended periods. In Atlanta's first 17 years, 15 different players were cited as the team's player of the year. Besides Nobis, the only player honored twice was running back Dave Hampton.

Nothing ever has come quickly or easily for the Falcons. Their first winning season came after five years of frustration, and then it took a fantastic finish to make it happen. A last-minute pass from Bob Berry to Ken Burrow in the season finale gave Atlanta a 24-20 victory over New Orleans for a 7-6-1 record in 1971.

The 1973 Falcons opened the season in explosive fashion, a 62-7 rout of the Saints. But fans were jolted back to reality the next week, when the Falcons were shut out by Los Angeles 31-0...and the following week, when they again failed to score a touchdown in a 31-6 loss. But the Falcons regrouped and rallied, and seemingly were on the verge of their first playoff berth with an 8-3 record before they lost two of their final three games to fall out of the postseason picture.

Heroes - The Hard Way

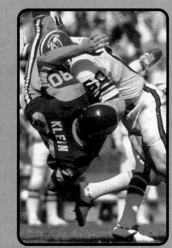

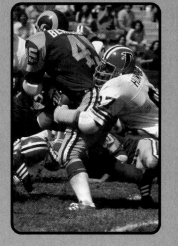

Tommy Nobis and Claude Humphrey - heroes the hard way.

In the early years of an expansion team's existence, the defense is likely to spend too much time on the field. And foes design their attack to avoid certain players.

When opponents mapped their strategy against Atlanta in the first decade, the Falcons' defenders they wanted to avoid were Nobis and Humphrey. But that was easier said than done.

Nobis was a linebacker, Humphrey a defensive end. They had few peers.

Nobis, an All-America at Texas and the first pick in the 1966 draft, instantly lived up to his billing. In the Falcons' first year, he was credited with 173 tackles and 121 assists in the 14-game season. On average, he was involved in 21 stops per game. He played in the Pro Bowl as a rookie and was all-pro by his second season. Nobis played in five Pro Bowl games before retiring after the 1976 season.

The only Atlanta defender in more Pro Bowls was Humphrey, who arrived in 1968 as a first-round draft choice out of Tennessee State. A demon against both the pass and the run, he made six Pro Bowl appearances. He finished his Falcons career in 1978.

Grits Blitz, Y'all

The Atlanta defense was something special in 1977. Known as "The Grits Blitz," the Falcons held opponents to only 129 points, the fewest in a 14-game season and the fewest allowed by any NFL team in 31 years.

Amazingly, none of the Atlanta starters was accorded all-pro honors and only two - end Claude Humphrey and cornerback Rolland Lawrence - were invited to the Pro Bowl.

Despite the spectacular work of the defense, the Falcons, at 7-7, didn't have a winning season.

1978

Falcons qualify for play-offs for first time. Beat Eagles 14-13 then lose divisional playoff 27-20 to eventual NFC champion Cowboys.

1980

Quarterback Steve Bartkowski, running back William Andrews and wide receiver Wallace Francis rewrite team record book, spark Falcons to 12-4 record, NFC Western Division title.

Leeman Bennett

1982

Season ticket sales are cut off at 55,144 mark.

When the Falcons finally made the playoffs as a wild card in 1978, Steve Bartkowski had to throw touchdown passes of 20 and 37 yards in the final five minutes to rally Atlanta to a 14-13 victory over the Eagles. It was to be the Falcons' only postseason victory in the franchise's first 25 years.

There was a 12-4 record and an NFC West title in 1980, followed by high expectations for 1981. Bartkowski, William Andrews, and Alfred Jenkins starred in a high-powered offense that led the NFC in scoring with 426 points. But the once-feared defense fell apart, giving up 355. Go figure.

The stunning collapse of 1981 started the darkest era in Falcons' history - nine losing seasons in ten years.

High Flying Falcon

Gerald Riggs was the ninth player taken in the 1982 draft amid huge expectations. Then he arrived in Atlanta and sat. And sat. For two years, he sat and watched as William Andrews continued to roll up 1,000-yard rushing seasons. Riggs, meanwhile, got only 299 yards as a rookie, 437 his second year.

But Andrews suffered a serious knee injury in the 1984 training camp, and Riggs immediately established himself as number one. He ran for a club record 202 yards in the season opener and 1,486 for the year.

Before leaving Atlanta after the 1988 season, Riggs rewrote the club rushing record: 6,631 yards and 48 touchdowns.

At Least It Didn't Wear Out

It takes time for most young quarterbacks to prove themselves, but Chris Miller, the Falcons' first-round draft pick in 1987, proved the durability of his arm as early as 1989. On Christmas Eve, Miller launched 66 passes, just two short of Norm Van Brocklin's NFL record. He completed 37. The Falcons lost 31-24 to Detroit.

1984
A changing of infantry forces. When knee injury sidelines all-time rushing leader William Andrews, Gerald Riggs gains 202 yards in opener, 1,486 for season

1987
Falcons draft quarterback Chris Miller in first round.

Michael Haynes

1989
Falcons draft defensive back Deion (Prime Time) Sanders in first round. Atlanta will never be the same again.

When Jerry Glanville arrived in 1990, he took over a team that had finished last in its division in six of the previous seven years. Atlanta was last again in 1990, but several of the losses were by narrow margins.

By 1991, Glanville had instituted his "Black Wave" defense and "Red Gun" offense, and the Falcons soared to a 10-6 record, recording the second-highest victory total in club history. There were new heroes - Deion Sanders and Jessie Tuggle on defense, Chris Miller, Andre Rison, and Michael Haynes on offense. There also was a new excitement as Falcons fans anticipated the 1992 opening of a new domed stadium.

After so many years of unfulfilled promise, of so many untimely collapses, Atlantans could be positive of at least one thing: win or lose, the Georgia Dome would assure there would never again be a soggy Sunday for the Falcons in Atlanta. ⌀

Bill Fralic

Mike Kenn

BIG
FOOTSTEPS
TO FOLLOW

When the Falcons chose Stanford tackle Bob Whitfield in the 1992 draft, he was the fifth offensive lineman they had taken in the first round. Four of the previous five earned Pro Bowl honors, including tackles George Kunz (1969) and Mike Kenn (1978), and guard Bill Fralic (1985). Tackle Warren Bryant (1977) was the only first-round offensive line pick who didn't make it to the Pro Bowl.

1990

Coach Jerry Glanville, "The Man in Black," comes to town. Despite 5-11 record, there's hope because six losses were by total of 25 points.

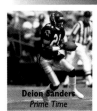

Deion Sanders
Prime Time

1991

Jerry Glanville

Falcons post 10-6 record, second-best in 26-year history. Second-place finish highest in 10 years.

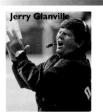

1992

Dome, sweet home. Falcons move into 70,500 seat Georgia Dome.

YEAR	▰ WINS ▰ LOSSES ☐ TIES	RECORD	PLACE	COACH
American League Football				
1960		5-8-1	3rd	Buster Ramsey
1961		6-8	4th	Buster Ramsey
1962		7-6-1	3rd	Lou Saban
1963		7-6-1	2nd	Lou Saban
1964		12-2	1st	Lou Saban
1965		10-3-1	1st	Lou Saban
1966		9-4-1	1st	Joe Collier
1967		4-10	3rd	Joe Collier
1968		1-12-1	5th	J. Collier, H. Johnson [1]
1969		4-10	4th	John Rauch
National League Football				
1970		3-10-1	4th	John Rauch
1971		1-13	5th	Harvey Johnson
1972		4-9-1	4th	Lou Saban
1973		9-5	2nd	Lou Saban
1974		9-5	2nd	Lou Saban
1975		8-6	3rd	Lou Saban
1976		2-12	5th	L. Saban, J. Ringo [2]
1977		3-11	5th	Jim Ringo
1978		5-11	4th	Chuck Knox
1979		7-9	4th	Chuck Knox
1980		11-5	1st	Chuck Knox
1981		10-6	3rd	Chuck Knox
1982		4-5	9th	Chuck Knox
1983		8-8	3rd	Kay Stephenson
1984		2-14	5th	Kay Stephenson
1985		2-14	5th	K. Stephenson, H. Bullough [3]
1986		4-12	4th	H. Bullough, M. Levy [4]
1987		7-8	4th	Marv Levy
1988		12-4	1st	Marv Levy
1989		9-7	1st	Marv Levy
1990		13-3	1st	Marv Levy
1991		13-3	1st	Marv Levy

1 — Joe Collier (2 games), Harvey Johnson (12 games)
2 — Lou Saban (5 games), Jim Ringo (9 games)
3 — Kay Stephenson (4 games), Hank Bullough (12 games)
4 — Hank Bullough (9 games), Marv Levy (7 games)

During a four-year period, 1972 through 1975, O.J. Simpson was the king of pro football. He won AFC player of the year honors three times in four seasons. Within six years, he won four NFL rushing titles. Marvelous performances by a great athlete. He was in a class by himself.

And yet, when his career ended, fans were left to wonder just how good Simpson might have been if circumstances had been a little different.

Simpson was a superstar at the University of Southern California - a Heisman Trophy winner and two-time All-America. He was the obvious choice to be chosen first in the 1969 NFL draft.

But the first pick belonged to the Buffalo Bills, and Simpson had made it known that he did not want to play in Buffalo. He was,

You've Come A Long Way, Buffalo

When Ralph C. Wilson, Jr., a Detroit resident, was awarded a franchise in the new American Football League, he wanted to establish his team in Miami and play home games in the Orange Bowl.

But he had difficulty getting a lease, so he had to look elsewhere. Wilson decided on Buffalo, with its antiquated, 22,000-seat War Memorial Stadium. That was more than adequate at the time; the Bills averaged fewer than 16,000 per game in 1960.

Eventually, the Bills got a new home, 80,000-seat Rich Stadium, which has been packed consistently in recent years.

1959

BUFFALO BILLS

Turning Points

Ralph C. Wilson Jr., is granted American Football League franchise in Buffalo. Team is named Bills, after former AAFC team.

after all, a Californian, and it's a long, long way from the West Coast to Buffalo - in more ways than one.

It was more than a matter of geography or lifestyle. The Bills were a terrible team. It was because they owned the worst record (1-12-1) in the league in 1968, that they had the number-one draft pick.

The Bills viewed Simpson as the cornerstone around whom they could build a contending team.

Buffalo drafted Simpson, and after protracted negotiations he finally signed. But during the 1969 season, Bills fans must have wondered what all the fuss had been about. O.J. could have been initials for Ordinary Joe. Simpson gained 697 yards, averaging fewer than 4 yards per carry. He ran for only 2 touchdowns, and his longest gain in 181 carries was 32 yards. Where was the star that had been advertised?

There were extenuating circumstances. The new running back had great ability, but the

O.J. - 2,003

When O.J. Simpson ran for 2,003 yards in 1973, it marked the first 2,000-yard season in pro football history.

Date	Opponent	Carries	Yards
9/16	at New England	29	250
9/23	at San Diego	22	103
9/30	N.Y. Jets	24	123
10/7	Philadelphia	27	171
10/14	Baltimore	22	166
10/21	at Miami	14	55
10/29	Kansas City	39	157
11/4	at New Orleans	20	79
11/11	Cincinnati	20	99
11/18	Miami	20	120
11/25	at Baltimore	15	124
12/2	at Atlanta	24	137
12/9	New England	22	219
12/16	at N.Y. Jets	34	200
Totals		332	2,003

Simpson's total has been exceeded once, by Eric Dickerson of the Rams in 1984. Simpson gained his yards in a 14-game schedule, averaging 143.1 yards per game. Dickerson gained 2,105 yards over 16 games, averaging 131.6 per game.

Wall of Fame

The Buffalo Bills' ultimate honor to former players is membership in the team's Wall of Fame, displaying their names on the upper deck facade at Rich Stadium.

Through 1991, only four players had been awarded the honor: running back O.J. Simpson, quarterback Jack Kemp, defensive tackle Tom Sestak, and guard Billy Shaw.

1962

Bills make three key additions: head coach Lou Saban, quarterback Jack Kemp, fullback Carlton (Cookie) Gilchrist.

Lou Saban

1964

Powerhouse Bills have 12-2 record, best in league; win AFL Championship Game 20-7 over San Diego.

1965

Buffalo, 10-3-1, makes it two in row with victory over Chargers in title game 23-0.

old offensive line didn't. The blocking was poor. And head coach John Rauch, newly arrived from Oakland, emphasized a passing game.

If the fans expected Simpson to ignite the Bills, they were badly disappointed. Buffalo won only four games in Simpson's rookie season, three in 1970, and only one in 1971.

Simpson missed half of the 1970 season because of a knee injury, and struggled for yardage in 1971, when the Bills' offensive line consisted of five rookies.

Simpson's yardage totals didn't reflect his obvious talent. After three years in Buffalo, he had gained only 1,927 yards and the Bills had compiled a record of 8-33-1.

Simpson's fortunes changed in 1972, when Lou Saban became head coach and brought in a new philosophy - rebuild the offensive line and get the ball to Simpson.

O.J. responded. He rolled for 1,251 yards and Buffalo won four games, equaling its victory total of the two previous years. It was a hint of things to come.

In 1973, Simpson did what no one had done before - he rushed for more than 2,000 yards.

Shifting Speeds

The helmet worn by the Bills in 1960 was silver, with blue numbers on the side. In its second season, Buffalo had a new look - a white helmet with a red, upright buffalo. It was only after O.J. Simpson rushed for an NFL-record 2,003 yards in 1973 that the Bills decided to put a bit of zip into the design.

Hot Hands in a Cold Town

Buffalo is known for its snowy winter days, and Rich Stadium can resemble a wind tunnel in November and December. Upstate New York is hardly the easiest place for a pass catcher to excel.

But that didn't deter wide receiver Andre Reed. He came to Buffalo as a fourth-round draft pick from Kutztown (Pennsylvania) State in 1985 and caught 48 passes in his rookie season. It was the only one of his first seven seasons in which he had fewer than 50 receptions. The 6-foot 2-inch wide receiver caught 81 passes in 1991, bringing his career total to a club record 469. It was the sixth consecutive season he led the Bills in receptions.

$100 Well Spent

Before Jack Kemp was a congressman from the state of New York, he was a star quarterback for the Buffalo Bills. Before that, he played for San Diego. Chargers fans remember Kemp as the one who got away and returned to haunt them.

Kemp quarterbacked the Chargers to division championships in 1960 and 1961. But when Kemp was injured the next season, San Diego coach Sid Gillman tried to sneak him through waivers. The Bills claimed Kemp for $100.

He was their quarterback for the next eight years, taking the Bills to American Football League championships in 1964 and 1965. The team he defeated in each of those championship games was the Chargers.

Joe Ferguson

1966
Saban shocks Buffalo, quits championship Bills for college coaching job at University of Maryland.

Joe DeLamielleure

1969
Buffalo takes O.J. Simpson with first pick in draft.

1972
Wandering Lou Saban returns as head coach, vows to make better use of Simpson's skills.

With 200 yards in the season finale, a nationally televised game against the Jets at New York's Shea Stadium, he carried the ball 34 times on a muddy field to finish with 2,003 yards.

Mobbed by reporters after the game, Simpson heaped praise on The Electric Company, the offensive line that made The Juice go.

O.J. remembered the years of frustration and futility in running behind anemic blocking, and he had lavish praise for the unit that included center Mike Montler, guards Reggie McKenzie and Joe DeLamielleure, and tackles Donnie Green and Dave Foley.

The Bills were 9-5 that year and again in 1974, when Simpson gained 1,125 yards. He followed with seasons of 1,817 and 1,503 yards before another knee injury brought him down in 1977 after only 126 carries and 557 yards. In 1978, he was traded to San Francisco, where he played unremarkably for two seasons before retiring.

His career totals: 2,404 carries for 11,236 yards, a yardage figure that had been exceeded previously by only Jim Brown. And yet, the question persists: How good might O.J. have been if:

Tom Terrific

Tom Sestak epitomized what Buffalo Bills' fans wanted their players to be. Rough and tough, Sestak was a dominating 270-pound defensive tackle.

Sestak, who had played at McNeese (Louisiana) State, was bypassed until the seventeenth round of the 1962 draft. He quickly became Buffalo's best defensive player for most of the team's first decade. Injuries forced him into retirement after the 1968 season. He later was selected to the All-Time AFL team.

Sestak is the only defensive player honored on Buffalo's Wall of Fame.

The First of His Kind

From the moment that a kicker's toe first met an NFL football, pro football kickers had used the same straight-on approach.

And then Pete Gogolak came along.

Gogolak was the first of the soccer-style kickers (known then as "sidewinders"), drafted by the Bills in the twelfth round in 1964.

An Englishman who had attended Cornell University, Gogolak kicked a 57-yard field goal in the Bills' first preseason game in 1964, helping to assure himself of a job. From that day, the NFL had a new way of looking at kickers.

1973

O.J. Simpson becomes pro football's first runner with more than 2,000 yards in season - 2,003.

Reggie McKenzie

1976

Saban quits at midseason, Bills plunge to 2-12 record.

1978

Chuck Knox becomes head coach, O.J. Simpson is traded to 49ers.

⊘ He had spent his entire career under a coach with the same offensive philosophy as Saban?

⊘ He had played more seasons behind a superb blocking unit such as The Electric Company?

⊘ He had not sustained two serious knee injuries?

⊘ He had played on more talented teams?

During Simpson's nine years in Buffalo, the Bills had only three winning seasons and one trip to the playoffs. In the six other years, Buffalo failed to win more than four games. His career was a reminder that one player, no matter how outstanding, cannot carry a team in the NFL.

Nine years after Simpson's career in Buffalo ended, quarterback Jim Kelly's began. A refugee from the United States Football League, Kelly quickly ascended to NFL superstar status.

Jim Kelly

Bruce Smith
First pick in 1985
NFL draft

1980	1983	1985
Bills win first division title in 14 years, post 11-5 record.	Knox quits, takes head coaching job with Seattle Seahawks.	Bills get first pick in draft, take defensive lineman Bruce Smith from Virginia Tech.

Chuck Knox

Just as the Bills had won only four games in Simpson's first year, they won only four in Kelly's inaugural campaign. But Kelly's circumstances were different from Simpson's. Kelly's Bills had other highly talented players on offense and some of the league's best defensive players.

The combination vaulted Buffalo into first place in the AFC East. Beginning with the 1988 season, the Bills finished first in their division four consecutive years, matching the number of first place finishes the franchise had in its previous 28 years.

After the 1990 season, when they set a club record with 13 regular-season victories, the Bills made their first Super Bowl appearance - a 20-14 loss to the New York Giants in Super Bowl XXV.

One year later, the Bills were back again, only to lose Super Bowl XXVI 37-24 to the Washington Redskins. ✐

The Cookie Man

The Bills' tradition of excellent running backs has included O.J. Simpson, Joe Cribbs, Greg Bell, and Thurman Thomas, but the man who started it all was Carlton (Cookie) Gilchrist.

A powerful fullback who came from the Canadian Football League in 1962, Gilchrist was the first runner in the AFL to rush for more than 1,000 yards in a season, gaining 1,096 as a rookie.

Gilchrist, who never played college football, ran for 979 yards in 1963 and 981 in 1964, then was traded to Denver after a salary dispute.

Buffalo's Best Punter

Paul Maguire is best known today as a football analyst on network telecasts, but Buffalo fans remember him from the early days of the AFL, when he was an outstanding punter.

Maguire played linebacker and punted for the Bills from 1964-1970. His career average of 42.1 yards per punt is the club's all-time best.

1986

Quarterback Jim Kelly, refugee from USFL, arrives in Buffalo; Marv Levy named head coach after nine games.

1991

Bills have club-record fourth consecutive division title, but lose second consecutive Super Bowl.

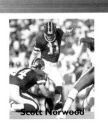

Scott Norwood

Chicago BEARS

YEAR ■ Wins ■ Losses □ Ties	RECORD	PLACE	COACH
Decatur Staleys			
1920	10-1-2	2nd	George Halas
Chicago Staleys			
1921	9-1-1	1st	George Halas
Chicago Bears			
1922	9-3	2nd	George Halas
1923	9-2-1	2nd	George Halas
1924	6-1-4	2nd	George Halas
1925	9-5-3	7th	George Halas
1926	12-1-3	2nd	George Halas
1927	9-3-2	3rd	George Halas
1928	7-5-1	5th	George Halas
1929	4-9-2	9th	George Halas
1930	9-4-1	3rd	Ralph Jones
1931	8-5	3rd	Ralph Jones
1932	6-1-6	1st	Ralph Jones
1933	10-2-1	1st	George Halas
1934	13-0	1st	George Halas
1935	6-4-2	3rd	George Halas
1936	9-3	2nd	George Halas
1937	9-1-1	1st	George Halas
1938	6-5	3rd	George Halas
1939	8-3	2nd	George Halas
1940	8-3	1st	George Halas
1941	10-1	1st	George Halas
1942	11-0	1st	G. Halas, Anderson & Johnsos [1]
1943	8-1-1	1st	H. Anderson & L. Johnsos [2]
1944	6-3-1	2nd	H. Anderson & L. Johnsos [2]
1945	3-7	4th	H. Anderson & L. Johnsos [2]
1946	8-2-1	1st	George Halas
1947	8-4	2nd	George Halas
1948	10-2	2nd	George Halas
1949	9-3	2nd	George Halas
1950	9-3	2nd	George Halas
1951	7-5	4th	George Halas
1952	5-7	5th	George Halas
1953	3-8-1	4th	George Halas
1954	8-4	2nd	George Halas
1955	8-4	2nd	George Halas
1956	9-2-1	1st	John Driscoll
1957	5-7	5th	John Driscoll
1958	8-4	2nd	George Halas
1959	8-4	2nd	George Halas
1960	5-6-1	5th	George Halas
1961	8-6	3rd	George Halas
1962	9-5	3rd	George Halas
1963	11-1-2	1st	George Halas
1964	5-9	6th	George Halas
1965	9-5	3rd	George Halas
1966	5-7-2	5th	George Halas
1967	7-6-1	2nd	George Halas
1968	7-7	2nd	Jim Dooley
1969	1-13	4th	Jim Dooley
1970	6-8	3rd	Jim Dooley
1971	6-8	3rd	Jim Dooley
1972	4-9-1	4th	Abe Gibron
1973	3-11	4th	Abe Gibron
1974	4-10	4th	Abe Gibron
1975	4-10	3rd	Jack Pardee
1976	7-7	2nd	Jack Pardee
1977	9-5	2nd	Jack Pardee
1978	7-9	4th	Neill Armstrong
1979	10-6	2nd	Neill Armstrong
1980	7-9	3rd	Neill Armstrong
1981	6-10	5th	Neill Armstrong
1982	3-6	12th	Mike Ditka
1983	8-8	3rd	Mike Ditka
1984	10-6	1st	Mike Ditka
1985	15-1	1st	Mike Ditka
1986	14-2	1st	Mike Ditka
1987	11-4	1st	Mike Ditka
1988	12-4	1st	Mike Ditka
1989	6-10	4th	Mike Ditka
1990	11-5	1st	Mike Ditka
1991	11-5	2nd	Mike Ditka

1 — George Halas (6 games), Hunk Anderson & Luke Johnsos (co-coaches) (5 games)

2 — Hunk Anderson & Luke Johnsos (co-coaches)

George Halas was head coach of the Chicago Bears for 40 years - in four 10-year stints.

He always selected his own replacement, and even though his first three successors had winning records, Halas eventually reappointed himself to the position.

But when he retired after the 1967 season, he was 72, and he knew his coaching days were over; it was time to confine himself to the front office. The Bears had four

When most teams were using the Single Wing offense, the Chicago Bears perfected the T-formation, and they showcased the offense in the 1940 NFL Championship Game, a 73-0 demolition of the Washington Redskins. The Bears' 11 touchdowns were scored by 10 different players.

Washington came into the game with a 9-2 record, but the Redskins were baffled by the Chicago attack, which rolled up 519 yards in total offense, including 381 rushing.

Bears quarterback Sid Luckman threw only 6 passes, completing 4 for 102 yards. Chicago's top rushers were fullback Bill Osmanski, who carried 10 times for 107 yards, and Harry Clark, who had 75 yards on 7 carries.

1920

CHICAGO BEARS

Turning Points

A.E. Staley hires George Halas to work in his manufacturing plant and to start football team; Decatur Staleys have 10-1-2 record, 10 shutouts.

different coaches from 1968-1981; but each left with a losing record.

When Halas made the fifth selection - Mike Ditka - he said, "Ditka has a style, and he gets his players to play that style. He knows what a Bear is all about."

"He knows what a Bear is all about."

The Bears' founder died less than two years after appointing Ditka, but he knew he had left the job in good hands. When Halas passed away on October 31, 1983, the Bears had played 18 games under Ditka and had won only six. But Halas knew.

"He knows what a Bear is all about."

Halas was right about Ditka. Entering the 1992 season, Ditka had a record of 107-57, a record worthy of Papa Bear himself. The Bears had won 10 or more games seven times in eight years (1984-1991) and had earned six division championships.

Halas was there at the NFL's beginnings. He was at the meetings that started the American Professional Football Association, which became the National Football League. He was in the league that maiden season of 1920 as a 25-year old player and coach of the Decatur Staleys, who became the Chicago Staleys, who became the Chicago Bears.

BRONKO

Bronko Nagurski has been the legend by which fullbacks have been measured for more than 60 years.

A powerful 225-pounder, Nagurski played in the era of leather helmets and minimal padding. He ran roughshod through the league from 1930-37, then became a professional wrestler because the pay was better. He returned to the Bears for the 1943 season, then went back to wrestling.

Dick Butkus
*Hall of Fame
Middle Linebacker*

A Different Style At Quarterback

It was in 1972, after Gale Sayers's retirement and before Walter Payton's arrival, that the Bears had a most unusual rushing leader - quarterback Bobby Douglass.

A strong runner, Douglass carried 141 times for 968 yards and 8 touchdowns. The left-handed passer had almost twice as many carries as completions - he hit on 75 of 198 passing attempts for 1,246 yards. Douglass was Chicago's starting quarterback for three seasons, from 1971-73.

1921
Halas moves club to Chicago, it is known as Chicago Staleys.

1922
Halas changes team name to Chicago Bears.

1925
Headed by rookie running back Red Grange, Bears take 17-game postseason barnstorming tour; crowds exceed 70,000 at New York and Los Angeles.

Willie Galimore

A Great Defender

Doug Atkins symbolized the big, bad Monsters of the Midway as well as any player in club history.
A 6-foot 8-inch, 280-pound defensive end, Atkins played for the Bears from 1955-1966. A powerful pass rusher, he played in the Pro Bowl eight times in nine years (1958-1966).

Halas was iron-willed, a tough guy, and he fashioned his team after himself. The Halas Bears were always the roughest, toughest, team in the league. And, usually, one of the best. His career coaching record was 325-151-31, with six NFL championships.

The Halas Bears had a consistency...tough, aggressive, and punishing on defense...and careful to control the ball with a great runner on offense.

Ditka's Bears are also tough, aggressive, and punishing on defense...careful to control the ball with a great runner on offense. Through the period 1980-1990, the Bears were number one in the league in rushing offense and rushing defense. That's the Halas - and Ditka - style.

"He knows what a Bear is all about."

A Bear is about a great linebacker, a devastating hitter who sends fear through the opposition. Clyde (Bulldog) Turner, and then George Connor, Bill George, Joe Fortunato, Dick Butkus, and most recently, Mike Singletary.

A Bear is about a running back who continually has fans turning to each other and saying, "Wow, did you see that last run?" Harold (Red) Grange was followed by Bronko Nagurski, then Beattie Feathers, George McAfee, Rick Casares, Gale Sayers, Walter Payton, and most recently, Neal Anderson.

Red Grange

C. C. Pyle

THE GALLOPING GHOST

Harold (Red) Grange, better known as "The Galloping Ghost" when he was an All-America at the University of Illinois, was promised a percentage of the gate by George Halas to go on a 17-game barnstorming tour with the Bears after the 1925 season.

Crowds of more than 70,000 packed the Polo Grounds in New York and the Coliseum in Los Angeles. The tour provided pro football with its largest public exposure, drawing more than 400,000, and earned Grange and his manager, C.C. Pyle, $100,000 each.

The next year, Grange and his manager started the American Football League. Grange returned to Chicago in 1929 and played for the Bears until retiring in 1934.

A Crowded Hall

The Chicago Bears have more representatives in the Pro Football Hall of Fame than any other team - 26 in all, 22 of whom gained stardom while with the team.
Three Bears - founder/coach George Halas, and running backs Harold (Red) Grange and Bronko Nagurski, were charter members in 1963.
Since then, quarterbacks George Blanda and Sid Luckman, running backs John (Paddy) Driscoll, George McAfee, and Gale Sayers, center George Trafton, center/linebacker Clyde (Bulldog) Turner, guard Danny Fortmann, tackles Ed Healey, Stan Jones, Roy (Link) Lyman, George Musso, and Joe Stydahar, ends Mike Ditka and Bill Hewitt, defensive end Doug Atkins, and linebackers Dick Butkus, George Connor, and Bill George, have been added.
Hall of Famers Guy Chamberlin, Walt Kiesling, Alan Page, and Bobby Layne, more closely associated with other teams, also played for the Bears.

Gale Sayers

1930	1932	1934
Bears sign fullback Bronko Nagurski.	Bears beat Portsmouth Spartans 9-0 in playoff game to win NFL championship; repeat as champions next season with 23-21 victory over Giants in first scheduled NFL Championship Game.	Bears' Beattie Feathers becomes first NFL player to rush for 1,000 yards in season.

The Pro Football Hall of Fame could open a separate wing to honor the Bears. In fact, the Hall already houses more players and coaches who gained stardom with the Bears (22) than representatives from any other team. Halas is there. So is Ditka. And so are Grange, Nagurski, McAfee, Sayers, Turner, George, and Butkus. More are on their way.

It seems the Bears are always blessed with excellence at linebacker and running back, and there have been enforcers on the defensive line - Doug Atkins, Ed Sprinkle, Dan Hampton, Richard Dent.

The Bears came to be known as the Monsters of the Midway in the 1940s. It is an image, and a style, that has remained. Even in years when their won-lost record was mediocre, the Bears had a hard-hitting, physically punishing team.

In the 1940s, defenses hadn't evolved into today's 4-3 or 3-4 alignments. The search-and-destroy style linebackers didn't exist yet, and Chicago's strength was in its defensive line...greats such as Danny Fortmann and George Musso were standouts both on offense and defense. Thus, the Monsters of the Midway.

Turner, an exceptionally quick 235-pounder, was perhaps football's best linebacker in the 1940s and also played center. But Bill George is credited with being pro football's first middle

THE AMAZING MR. PAYTON

Not only was Walter Payton the most productive running back in pro football history, he also was the most durable.

Payton played 13 years, from 1975-1987, and missed only one of the 191 games Chicago played. A nine-time Pro Bowl player, Payton was the Bears' leading rusher 12 consecutive years, giving way to Neal Anderson in 1987. He topped the 1,000-yard mark an NFL-record eight times.

Payton's major NFL records: 3,838 attempts, 16,726 yards, 110 rushing touchdowns.

1939	1940		1946
Chicago drafts Columbia tailback Sid Luckman and turns him into quarterback.	Bears beat Washington 73-0 in NFL championship game, go on to win three league titles in four years.	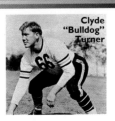 Clyde "Bulldog" Turner	With Halas back as full-time coach after returning from Navy, Bears win fourth NFL championship in 1940s.

linebacker. He joined the Bears in 1952 as a middle guard in the five-man line, but began dropping off the line regularly in 1954. Connor (1948-1955) and Fortunato (1955-1966) were outside linebackers.

George's last season with the Bears was Butkus's rookie year, and the transition from one all-time great in the middle to another was smooth. Butkus played most of his seasons (1965-1973) on teams with losing records, and although the team was mediocre, Butkus personified the Monsters of the Midway image. A ferocious hitter with speed to patrol from sideline to sideline, Butkus was the middle linebacker on the all-pro squads of both the 1960s and 1970s as selected by the Hall of Fame.

Seven seasons passed after Butkus was forced into retirement by knee injuries until Singletary's entry as a rookie starter at middle linebacker in 1981. Singletary became the Bears' defensive captain in 1983 and played in nine consecutive Pro Bowls, beginning that season.

Defenders like Turner, Connor, George, Butkus, and Singletary symbolize the ferocity of the Bears, and explosive runners like Sayers, Payton, and Anderson exemplify the club's excellence on offense.

Nagurski, a powerful fullback, relied more on strength than on finesse or speed. But

Papa Bear
George Halas

George Halas with
Sid Luckman

The Bears' Great Quarterback

The greatest quarterback in Chicago Bears history was Sid Luckman, the club's field leader from 1939-1950.

Luckman, a first-round draft choice from Columbia, is the Bears' all-time leader in pass attempts (1,744), completions (904), yards (14,686) and touchdown passes (137). Luckman led the Bears' T-formation attack that won four NFL titles, including the 73-0 victory over Washington in the 1940 championship game.

His best season was 1943, when he passed for 2,194 yards and 28 touchdowns, including 7 touchdown passes in a game against the New York Giants.

1954

Middle guard Bill George becomes first NFL middle linebacker.

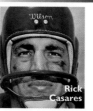

Rick
Casares

1963

Assistant coach George Allen installs zone coverage in Bears' defense; Bears win NFL championship 14-10 over Giants; title is club's eighth, and sixth under Halas.

1965

Bears draft Kansas halfback Gale Sayers and Illinois linebacker Dick Butkus in first round.

1967

George Halas, 72, retires as head coach.

McAfee was a spectacular broken-field runner (his average of 12.78 yards on punt returns is an NFL record). Feathers had a career average of 5.8 yards a carry. Casares, like Nagurski, was a hard-charging fullback.

Sayers was a first-round draft pick in 1965. A scintillating talent, he scored 22 touchdowns his rookie season and led the NFL in rushing in 1966 and 1969. His career was cut short in 1970 by a knee injury. He ran for 4,956 yards and averaged 5 yards per carry during his career; at 34 he was the youngest ever inducted into the Hall of Fame.

Payton enjoyed a 13-year career and rewrote the record book. His 3,838 carries, 16,726 yards and 110 rushing touchdowns are all NFL records, and he holds three other league marks. Payton played in nine Pro Bowl games before retiring in 1987.

Anderson became a starter in 1987, his second year, and had rushed for 4,938 yards entering the 1992 season. He was selected to every Pro Bowl from 1988-1991.

The Bears were dominant under Halas, who coached them to seven first-place finishes and six NFL Championships. Ditka's teams have been division champions six times, and his Bears won Super Bowl XX, 46-10 over New England. ✐

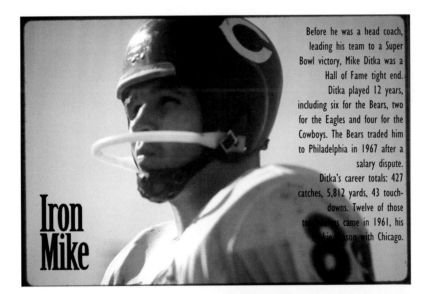

Iron Mike

Before he was a head coach, leading his team to a Super Bowl victory, Mike Ditka was a Hall of Fame tight end. Ditka played 12 years, including six for the Bears, two for the Eagles and four for the Cowboys. The Bears traded him to Philadelphia in 1967 after a salary dispute. Ditka's career totals: 427 catches, 5,812 yards, 43 touchdowns. Twelve of those touchdowns came in 1961, his rookie season with Chicago.

THE FRIDGE

William (Refrigerator) Perry, a massive defensive tackle, gained notoriety in the Super Bowl year of 1985 as an occasional ball carrier.

Coach Mike Ditka called on the 300-something pounder for 5 carries; he had a 3-yard gain, a 2-yard gain, and three 1-yarders, and scored twice. He also caught a 4-yard touchdown pass.

Perry carried once in Super Bowl XX, scoring a touchdown on a 1-yard plunge. He also was sacked for a 1-yard loss.

Perry's last rushing attempt came in 1990, when the Green Bay Packers stopped him for a 1-yard loss.

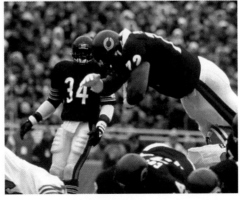

1975	1982		1985
Running back Walter Payton out of Jackson State is Bears' first draft pick.	Mike Ditka becomes Bears head coach.		Bears win 18 of 19 games, win Super Bowl XX 46-10 over New England.

Mike Singletary

Cincinnati
BENGALS

YEAR	■ WINS	▨ LOSSES	▢ TIES	RECORD	PLACE	COACH
American Football League						
1968				3-11	5th	Paul Brown
1969				4-9-1	5th	Paul Brown
National Football League						
1970				8-6	1st	Paul Brown
1971				4-10	4th	Paul Brown
1972				8-6	3rd	Paul Brown
1973				10-4	1st	Paul Brown
1974				7-7	2nd	Paul Brown
1975				11-3	2nd	Paul Brown
1976				10-4	2nd	Bill Johnson
1977				8-6	3rd	Bill Johnson
1978				4-12	4th	B. Johnson, H. Rice [1]
1979				4-12	4th	Homer Rice
1980				6-10	4th	Forrest Gregg
1981				12-4	1st	Forrest Gregg
1982				7-2	3rd	Forrest Gregg
1983				7-9	3rd	Forrest Gregg
1984				8-8	2nd	Sam Wyche
1985				7-9	2nd	Sam Wyche
1986				10-6	2nd	Sam Wyche
1987				4-11	4th	Sam Wyche
1988				12-4	1st	Sam Wyche
1989				8-8	4th	Sam Wyche
1990				9-7	1st	Sam Wyche
1991				3-13	4th	Sam Wyche

1 — Bill Johnson (5 games), Homer Rice (11 games)

Paul Brown didn't have anything left to prove. He already had:

- Coached Ohio State to a national collegiate championship.
- Led the Cleveland Browns to 16 winning seasons in 17 years.
- Won four championships in the All-America Football Conference and three more in the NFL.
- Established himself as one of the great innovators in football history.
- Earned induction into the Pro Football Hall of Fame.

He was secure financially as he neared his sixtieth birthday; clearly, it was a time to relax.

A Cat of a Different Color

When Paul Brown was hired to coach Cleveland's entry in the All-America Football Conference, he rejected the nickname Panthers because that had been the name of a Cleveland team in the old American Football League of the 1920s. After Brown vetoed Panthers, the Cleveland team was named the Browns.

When Cincinnati was awarded an AFL franchise in 1967, the name Bengals was suggested because that had been the nickname of Cincinnati's AFL team in the early 1940s. This time, Brown didn't object.

1967

CINCINNATI BENGALS

Turning Points

Cincinnati group led by Paul Brown is awarded American Football League expansion franchise for 1968 season. Team is named Bengals.

But Paul Brown couldn't relax. He had tremendous energy and drive, a remarkable will to win, and a need to continue proving himself. Those traits had made him a coaching legend. Those same traits enabled him to acquire an expansion franchise for Cincinnati in 1968 and, in the club's third season, win a divisional championship - an unequalled feat.

Brown was an intense competitor, and he felt he had some unfinished business when he left the NFL in 1962. Replaced at Cleveland by Blanton Collier, he hadn't left on his own terms.

In 1967 Brown headed a group that petitioned for an American Football League expansion franchise. A year later, the Cincinnati Bengals were born.

Brown had experience in starting up a pro football team. More than two decades earlier, he was the first coach of the Browns in the AAFC. His team won the championship all four years of the league's existence, posting a 47-4-3 record. But the Browns had started life in the AAFC with an important advantage.

Paul Brown

Cincy's Do-It-All Man

When Cincinnati traded fullback Pete Johnson to San Diego in 1984, Bengals fans knew the team was giving up its all-time leading rusher. They didn't realize the player they were acquiring, James Brooks, would replace him at the top of the club's record book.

Brooks gave the Bengals eight outstanding seasons as a multipurpose running back, accounting for almost 10,000 yards from scrimmage. The 5 foot 10 inch 180-pounder rushed for a club record 6,447 yards and caught 290 passes for 3,012 yards.

1968	**1969**	**1970**
With Brown as head coach and John Stofa as quarterback, Bengals post 3-11 record.	Rookie quarterback Greg Cook throws 5 touchdown passes in first two games, leads AFL passers in 4-9-1 season.	Cincinnati's 8-6 record wins AFC Central title; Bengals first expansion team to win division title in third year.

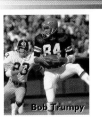

Bob Trumpy

Number 54 Was Number 1

Bob Johnson, a center from Tennessee, was the first player drafted by the Bengals. He played for Cincinnati 12 years and was considered one of the best offensive linemen in the league. His number 54 is the only one ever retired by the Bengals.

Brown's military assignment during World War II included coaching the Great Lakes Naval Station football team. When the war ended, he had a ready supply of outstanding players who joined him in Cleveland, including future Hall of Fame running back Marion Motley. Brown signed two other future Hall of Famers, quarterback Otto Graham, who had played at the Naval Pre-Flight center, and guard Bill Willis, who had played for Brown at Ohio State.

When he began to assemble the Bengals, Brown had no such mother lode of talent. He had to stock his roster from an expansion pool - players left unprotected by existing teams - and from the annual draft of collegiate players.

The Bengals began in typical fashion for an expansion team. They were 3-11 the first year (1968), 4-9-1 the second, and lost six of the first seven games in their third season.

But then the Cincinnati defense produced an unexpected turnaround. After yielding 20 or more points in each of their first seven games, the Bengals began to play defense the way

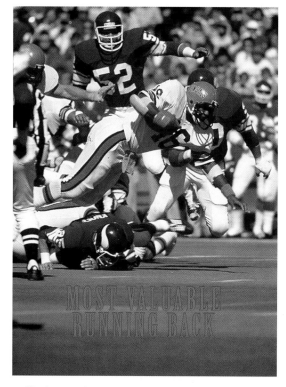

Fullback Pete Johnson may have been the most valuable running back in Bengals history. Not only did he have a productive seven-year career with the Bengals, but the player for whom he was traded, James Brooks, set the club rushing record.

Taken on the second round of the 1977 draft, Johnson led the team in rushing each of his seven years in Cincinnati, rolling up what was then a club record 5,421 yards.

Cincinnati traded Johnson to San Diego in 1978. Brooks eventually overtook Johnson, rushing for 6,393 yards.

When the Bengals scouted Penn State defensive tackle Mike Reid, they were so impressed that they made him their first pick in the 1970 draft. They should have done a little more in-depth scouting.

Reid was, indeed, an outstanding football player. But he was also an outstanding pianist, and after only five years with the Bengals, he retired from pro football to become a professional musician. His 1991 record, "Walk On Faith," was his first number one on the country music charts.

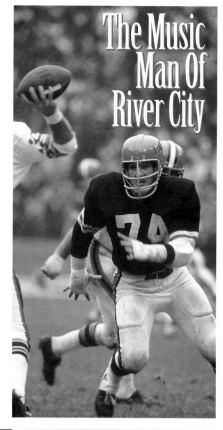

The Music Man Of River City

1971	1973	1975
Bengals draft quarterback Ken Anderson.	Draft provides offensive firepower: wide receiver Isaac Curtis, running backs Boobie Clark and Lenvil Elliott; Bengals post 10-4 record, win division.	After leading Bengals to 11-3 record, Paul Brown retires as coach; retains general manager position.

Bill Bergey

Brown diagrammed it. They held four opponents to 10 or fewer points, won six of the last seven games, produced an 8-6 record and won the AFC Central Division championship. In second place, with a 7-7 record, were the Cleveland Browns.

No other NFL expansion team had won a divisional title so quickly.

Brown led the Bengals to three playoff berths in his eight years as coach and experienced only three losing seasons. The Bengals were 0-3 in playoff games under Brown. He retired in 1975 with a 55-59-1 record, after enjoying an 11-3 season, the best of his reign.

Paul Brown left pro football coaching with more than an outstanding record and a long list of championships. He played a major role in the development of modern football and was a leading force in the evolution of coaching techniques and strategies.

Brown was a tough and demanding coach. A former high school teacher, he used many of his classroom techniques for coaching football players.

Tower of Strength

When Sam Wyche was coaching the Bengals, he referred to Anthony Munoz as "the greatest offensive tackle the game has known." He may have been right.

Munoz was a unanimous choice on the NFL's team of the 1980s, and missed selection for the Pro Bowl only in his rookie season.

A 6-foot 6-inch, 285-pound powerhouse, Munoz was a first-round pick from Southern California in 1980. For more than a decade, he was the epitome of what a pro football offensive lineman should be.

Tiger Stripes

For more than a decade, the Bengals wore brown jerseys and orange helmets…a uniform bearing some resemblance to that of the Cleveland Browns, coach Paul Brown's former employer.

But in 1981 the Bengals made a bold change to a uniform that resembled no other in pro football - a helmet covered with orange-and-black tiger stripes, and jerseys and pants trimmed with tiger stripes.

37

Tom Casanova

1980	**1981**	**1983**
Forrest Gregg becomes head coach, Anthony Munoz is Bengals' first draft choice.	With new-look: tiger stripes on helmets and uniforms, Bengals go 12-4, beat Buffalo and San Diego in playoffs, lose Super Bowl XVI to 49ers 26-21.	After two winning seasons, Bengals slump to 7-9; Gregg is replaced by Sam Wyche.

A Shooting Star

The Bengals began in 1968 with John Stofa at quarterback, acquired at the cost of two draft choices sent to Miami. But in the 1969 draft, they drafted hometown hero Greg Cook, star quarterback from the University of Cincinnati. Cook, a first-round pick, led the AFC in passing as a rookie, throwing for 1,854 yards and 15 touchdowns. But he suffered an arm injury and threw only three more passes for the Bengals after that season.

"My policy is to stress fast thinking and clean living to build greater athletes," he said.

He attempted to measure his players' aptitude for "fast thinking" by giving them intelligence tests. He required each player to fill in a notebook with the team's plays rather than distributing the plays already drawn. He used game films to grade his players.

Measure intelligence...teach...grade...all concepts familiar to the educator, but new to football.

An expert in plotting a passing attack, Brown enjoyed developing an offense and then devising a defense that could stop it. He then countered his own countermoves.

Brown's offense demanded an accurate passer, and in Cincinnati he developed one of the best. Ken Anderson had pinpoint accuracy, setting an NFL record for completion percentage

Record-Setting Quarterback

There were doubts about Ken Anderson when the Bengals took him in the third round of the 1971 draft. He had been a collegiate standout at Augustana, a small school that faced no big-time competition.

Anderson quickly erased all doubts. He spent part of his rookie season on the sidelines, then took the starting job from Virgil Carter, who had led Cincinnati to a division title the previous season.

Anderson kept the starting job for the next 13 years, leading Cincinnati into the playoffs four times. The Bengals' best season with Anderson at the helm was 1981, when they had a 12-4 record and played in Super Bowl XVI, losing 26-21 to the 49ers.

The Cincinnati quarterback was named the NFL's most valuable player by the *Associated Press, Pro Football Writers,* and the Maxwell Club in 1981, and the next season set a league record for completion percentage (70.55). Anderson retired in 1986. During his 16-year career, he completed 2,654 passes for 32,838 yards and 197 touchdowns.

Isaac Curtis

1984

Bengals trade for running back James Brooks.

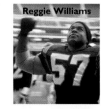

Reggie Williams

1985

A changing of the guard: Isaac Curtis retires, Eddie Brown is number-one draft choice.

(70.55) in 1982.

A trademark of Brown's teams was the messenger system in which guards who alternated on every down delivered plays to the huddle. Brown believed the head coach should call plays and a precision passer should execute the commands. Anderson was the right man for the job.

A third-round draft pick out of tiny Augustana College in 1971, Anderson replaced Virgil Carter as the Bengals' starter by the end of his rookie season. He fit perfectly into Brown's system and was the AFC's leading passer four times in his career.

Paul Brown resigned as head coach after the 1975 season, but maintained his position as general manager until his death in 1991, at age 82. ✐

Boomer:
THE END OF A SEARCH

Ken Anderson was an excellent quarterback, but the Bengals realized that in time he would have to be replaced.

Cincinnati spent premium-round draft picks in search of another quarterback – John Boryla in the fourth round in 1974, ... in the third round in 1975, Jack ... round in 1979 - but ... didn't find their man until 1984.

... took Norman (Boomer) ... the University of Maryland in the second round.

Esiason played sparingly as a rookie, then took the starting job in his second season. In 1988, the left-hander was named the NFL's most valuable player by the *Associated Press* and the *Pro Football Writers* and took the Bengals to Super Bowl XXIII.

Little Big Foot

Jim Breech, at 5-feet 6-inches and 161 pounds, is one of the smallest players in pro football history, but few have ever loomed larger in NFL scoring records. After the 1991 season, Breech had scored in 181 consecutive games, 30 games more than second-place Fred Cox.

Breech, signed as a free agent in 1980 after being released by the Lions and Raiders, was eleventh on the all-time NFL scoring list with 1,158 points after 1991.

1988

Bengals rally from 4-11 record previous year to 12-4 season; beat Seattle, Buffalo in play-offs, lose Super Bowl XXIII to 49ers 20-16.

Chris Collinsworth

1992

Head coaching change: Wyche out, Dave Shula in.

Year	Record	Place	Coach
All-America Football Conference			
1946	12-2	1st	Paul Brown
1947	12-1-1	1st	Paul Brown
1948	14-0	1st	Paul Brown
1949	9-1-2	1st	Paul Brown
National Football League			
1950	10-2	1st	Paul Brown
1951	11-1	1st	Paul Brown
1952	8-4	1st	Paul Brown
1953	11-1	1st	Paul Brown
1954	9-3	1st	Paul Brown
1955	9-2-1	1st	Paul Brown
1956	5-7	4th	Paul Brown
1957	9-2-1	1st	Paul Brown
1958	9-3	2nd	Paul Brown
1959	7-5	2nd	Paul Brown
1960	8-3-1	2nd	Paul Brown
1961	8-5-1	3rd	Paul Brown
1962	7-6-1	3rd	Paul Brown
1963	10-4	2nd	Blanton Collier
1964	10-3-1	1st	Blanton Collier
1965	11-3	1st	Blanton Collier
1966	9-5	2nd	Blanton Collier
1967	9-5	1st	Blanton Collier
1968	10-4	1st	Blanton Collier
1969	10-3-1	1st	Blanton Collier
1970	7-7	2nd	Blanton Collier
1971	9-5	1st	Nick Skorich
1972	10-4	2nd	Nick Skorich
1973	7-5-2	3rd	Nick Skorich
1974	4-10	4th	Nick Skorich
1975	3-11	4th	Forrest Gregg
1976	9-5	3rd	Forrest Gregg
1977	6-8	4th	F. Gregg, D. Modzelewski [1]
1978	8-8	3rd	Sam Rutigliano
1979	9-7	3rd	Sam Rutigliano
1980	11-5	1st	Sam Rutigliano
1981	5-11	4th	Sam Rutigliano
1982	4-5	8th	Sam Rutigliano
1983	9-7	2nd	Sam Rutigliano
1984	5-11	3rd	Rutigliano, Schottenheimer [2]
1985	8-8	1st	Marty Schottenheimer
1986	12-4	1st	Marty Schottenheimer
1987	10-5	1st	Marty Schottenheimer
1988	10-6	2nd	Marty Schottenheimer
1989	9-6-1	1st	Bud Carson
1990	3-13	4th	B. Carson, J. Shofner [3]
1991	6-10	3rd	Bill Belichick

1 — Forrest Gregg (13 games), Dick Modzelewski (1 game)
2 — Sam Rutigliano (8 games), Marty Schottenheimer (8 games)
3 — Bud Carson (9 games), Jim Shofner (7 games)

The greatest of all time... No other phrase sparks lively discussions among pro football fans as effectively as: "The greatest of all time was..."

Who will be remembered as the best quarterback of all time? Joe Montana? John Unitas? Fran Tarkenton? Bart Starr? Roger Staubach?

Who was the greatest runner? O.J. Simpson? Walter Payton? Gale Sayers? Or Earl Campbell?

Was there a better coach than Vince Lombardi? What about

Thank Goodness FOR EASY NAMES

The most popular nickname in the 1946 name-the-team contest was "Panthers" - 36 entrants selected it - but coach Paul Brown rejected that choice. Panthers had been the name of a Cleveland team in a failed league two decades earlier.

Among other entries, "Brown Bombers" was a frequent suggestion, in honor of the nickname by which popular heavyweight boxing champion Joe Louis was identified. When that was shortened to "Browns," the nickname served the dual purpose of also acknowledging the club's head coach. No telling what would have happened if the coach had been named Wojciechowicz or Conzelman.

Brown picked the team colors...brown with orange trim.

1946

CLEVELAND BROWNS

Turning Points

Cleveland gets franchise in new All-America Football Conference. Arthur McBride is owner, Paul Brown coach, Otto Graham quarterback, Marion Motley running back.

George Halas? Don Shula? Bill Walsh? Chuck Noll?

How about tight end? Has anyone been better than Mike Ditka? How about John Mackey? Or Kellen Winslow?

Fans' opinions about "the greatest of all time" are influenced by the era in which they began watching NFL games, and the teams they followed most closely.

Fans of the Cleveland Browns can nominate candidates in several categories - running back Jim Brown, quarterback Otto Graham, tight end Ozzie Newsome, and coach Paul Brown - and offer impressive evidence to back their claims.

Consider the running backs.

Has anyone been the equal of Jim Brown? He had power, speed, quickness, durability, and numbers...incredible numbers.

Jim Brown's numbers tell quite a story. He played in the NFL nine years and led the league in rushing eight times. He gained more than 1,000 yards seven times in nine years, at a time when the regular season consisted of only 12 or 14 games instead of today's 16.

Brown broke in with a smash, rushing for 237 yards in his ninth game. He was NFL rookie of the year and player of the year. In his second season, it took him only eight games to break the NFL record for yards and touchdowns in a full season.

Who Was That Man?

Jim Brown left an indelible impression in the memories of NFL fans: a powerful running back racing around the corner, ball tucked tightly against the "32" on his jersey.

But it wasn't always that way. Brown wore 45 in his first appearance for the Browns. The number 32 had already been assigned to Jack Bayuk. But after one exhibition game, Bayuk was released, and Brown claimed the number.

Mike McCormack

1948
AAFC champs two previous years, Browns achieve ultimate - perfect season, 15-0.

1950
After four-year AAFC record of 47-4-3 and four championships, Browns join NFL; win conference or league title in each of first six seasons in NFL.

1955
Otto Graham retires, ending career with two touchdown passes, two touchdown runs in 38-14 NFL Championship Game victory.

There was little mystery about the Browns' offense when Brown played. The only question was whether he would run right, left, or up the middle. Stopping him was something else. Defenses were stacked against him. Opponents consistently tried to gang-tackle him. Still, he racked up yardage and made his team a winner.

The Browns had three first-place finishes, four seconds, and two thirds during Jim Brown's nine-year career (1957-1965). And then he quit. Only 30 years old, in good health, with no reason to doubt that he could continue as the game's dominant ground gainer for several more years, he quit football to become a movie actor.

When Brown retired, he had run for 12,312 yards and 106 touchdowns. Some of his NFL records have been broken by players with longer careers, but one continues to stand: No other back finished his career with a better average-per-carry (5.2 yards on 2,359 attempts).

Statistics are only one yardstick used to measure quarterbacks. More than any other player on the field, a quarterback is held accountable for winning and losing. And by that criteria, few have been as good as Otto Graham.

Other quarterbacks passed for more yardage than Graham, but his winning percentage was phenomenal. The Browns finished

The AAFC's Best

Before there was Jim Brown, there was Marion Motley, the best runner in the four-year history of the All-America Football Conference. A powerhouse who ran in a unique crouch, Motley would explode upward out of his crouch when hit, scattering would-be tacklers. The 6-foot 1-inch, 238-pounder had played for Paul Brown at the Great Lakes Naval Training Center during World War II, and followed Brown to the Cleveland Browns of the newly created AAFC. Motley's combined statistics for the AAFC (four years) and NFL (five years) were 4,720 yards and a 5.7 yard average. In NFL games, he gained 1,696 yards, averaging 5.0 yards per carry.

Kosar
TURNS IT AROUND

Bernie Kosar made a difference. The Browns were weak in 1984, losing 11 of 16 games. But then they drafted Bernie Kosar from the University of Miami in the 1985 Supplemental Draft, and the kid led the team to first-place finishes in the AFC Central the next three seasons. Although his quarterbacking mechanics were unorthodox - he passed with a three-quarters arm motion - Kosar got the job done as the Browns posted a three-year record of 30-17.

1956

Dante Lavelli

Mac Speedie

Minus Graham, Browns have first losing season in history, only losing season of Paul Brown's 17-year head coaching tenure.

1957

Cleveland drafts Jim Brown, who becomes rookie of year. Brown leads league in rushing and Browns vault from fourth to first.

1961

Art Modell buys Browns, becomes one of NFL's most respected owners.

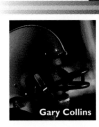

Gary Collins

in first place every year during Graham's 10-year career. They won the league championship game seven times in ten tries.

The Browns had a sophisticated passing attack - the most advanced of its time - and Graham had a superb crew of receivers, led by Dante Lavelli and Mac Speedie.

When Graham retired in 1955, he had completed 1,464 passes for 23,584 yards and 174 touchdowns. He led the league in passing twice, and made all-league nine times in ten years, including four times in the All-America Football Conference (AAFC) and five times in the NFL.

Ten years. Ten first-place finishes. Seven league championships. Nine times all-league. It's a record of success that's unlikely to be duplicated.

In spite of that, Graham's talents sometimes weren't appreciated as much as those of other quarterbacks. The reason: He was part of a team that overwhelmed the opposition. And that's to the credit of Paul Brown.

Hired as the team's first coach in 1946, Brown assembled a club that was almost unbeatable. Indeed, during the four-year life of the AAFC, the Browns compiled a record of 47-4-3.

When the AAFC folded after the 1949 season, the Browns were absorbed into the NFL. They quickly proved they were more than a good team in a weak league. The Browns won 21

Brian's Time

Brian Sipe was the Browns' starting quarterback for eight of his ten years in Cleveland, long enough to completely rewrite club passing records.

Sipe is Cleveland's all-time passing leader in attempts (3,439), completions (1,944), yards (23,713), touchdowns (154), and interceptions (149). He was named NFL MVP by the Associated Press and the Pro Football Writers Association in 1980. He left the Browns after the 1983 season to join the United States Football League.

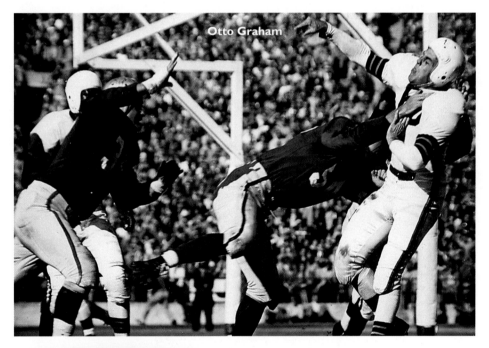

Otto Graham

Leroy Kelly

The Post-Brown Era

When Jim Brown was ending his career, Leroy Kelly was just getting started. Kelly's rookie year at Cleveland was 1964, Brown's last year was 1965. When Brown left, he knew he was leaving the ball in good hands.

Kelly was Cleveland's workhorse in the post-Brown era. He led the NFL in rushing in 1967 and 1968, gaining more than 1,200 yards each season.

In his 10-year career with the Browns, Kelly produced 7,274 rushing yards, second only to Jim Brown.

1963	**1965**	**1970**
Paul Brown is replaced as head coach.	Jim Brown wins eighth NFL rushing title in ninth season, the last of his career.	Browns shift to American Football Conference as part of NFL-AFL merger agreement.

Michael Dean Perry

Big, BIG Deal

The Browns combined with the Colts to make the biggest player trade in NFL history, a 15-man swap on March 26, 1953. Cleveland obtained five players - tackle Mike McCormack, guard Herschel Forester, defensive tackle Don Colo, linebacker Tom Catlin and defensive back John Petitbon. The Colts got 10 players - defensive backs Don Shula, Bert Rechichar, and Carl Taseff, wide receiver Gern Nagler, quarterback Harry Agganis, tackles Dick Batten and Stu Sheets, and guards Art Spinney, Ed Sharkey, and Elmer Willhoite.

of 24 regular-season games in their first two seasons in the NFL and finished first in the division or conference in each of their first six years.

Brown was the genius who made it happen. He was blessed with gifted players such as Jim Brown, Otto Graham, Mac Speedie, Dante Lavelli, Marion Motley, Bill Willis, Dub Jones, Bobby Mitchell, Mike McCormack, Lou Groza, and many more, but it was the coaching genius of Paul Brown that enabled the team to be so dominant.

When Paul Brown's team had Graham, Speedie, and Lavelli, he orchestrated an aerial circus like pro football had never seen. When Graham was gone and Jim Brown arrived, the Browns became an awesome infantry.

Paul Brown raised professional football to a new level as a thinking man's game. He was the first to retain assistant coaches on a year-round basis, to use classroom teaching techniques extensively for his players, and to develop sophisticated spread-formation passing attacks. Clearly, he was a man ahead of his time, setting new standards in his profession.

Brown coached the Browns for 17 seasons. In 16 of those years, the team had a winning

If One Don't Get You...

Cleveland's leading ground gainer every year between 1974 and 1983 was a Pruitt. Greg Pruitt, from Oklahoma, carried the load from 1974-78. Then Mike Pruitt, from Purdue, took over. Greg gained more than 1,000 yards three years, Mike topped the 1,000 mark four times. No, the Pruitts were not related.

Mike Pruitt

Playing It By The Numbers

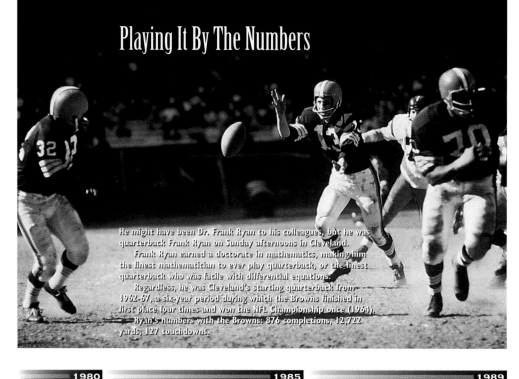

He might have been Dr. Frank Ryan to his colleagues, but he was quarterback Frank Ryan on Sunday afternoons in Cleveland.

Frank Ryan earned a doctorate in mathematics, making him the finest mathematician to ever play quarterback, or the finest quarterback who was facile with differential equations.

Regardless, he was Cleveland's starting quarterback from 1962-67, a six-year period during which the Browns finished in first place four times and won the NFL Championship once (1964). Ryan's numbers with the Browns: 876 completions, 12,722 yards, 127 touchdowns.

1980	1985	1989
Browns win AFC Central for first time in nine years; Brian Sipe is named MVP by PFWA and Associated Press.	Browns draft Bernie Kosar. Marty Schottenheimer, coaching first full season, leads team to first of three consecutive first-place finishes.	Schottenheimer and Browns part ways in dispute over coaching staff.

Ozzie Newsome

record. After starting his career with 10 first place finishes, he had one first, three seconds, two thirds and one fourth-place finish in his final seven years at Cleveland. The tough-minded coach was strict and demanding, and he clashed with some of his players, including superstar Jim Brown. Owner Art Modell put an end to the clashes by replacing the coach after the 1962 season.

Paul Brown's career record at Cleveland was 167-53-8. His teams won four AAFC championships and three NFL titles.

Tight end Ozzie Newsome played for the Browns from 1978 through 1990, long after the Paul Brown era. In fact, Newsome played for four different head coaches in 13 years. But no matter who the coach, Newsome caught passes - 662 receptions for 7,980 yards. By way of comparison, second on Cleveland's all-time reception list is Gary Collins, with 331 catches - exactly half of Newsome's total. When Newsome retired, he was fourth on the NFL's all-time list of pass catchers, first among tight ends.

Has there been a better tight end? Not if they are measured by the number of receptions. ⊘

The Toe

No one played more seasons (21, including 17 in the NFL and four in the AAFC) in a Cleveland Browns uniform than Lou (The Toe) Groza. Nobody scored more points (1,608) or kicked more field goals (234), either.

But Groza did more than kick. He was an offensive tackle who earned all-pro honors five times. He was inducted into the Pro Football Hall of Fame in 1974.

Kardiac Kids

It wasn't whether they won or lost, it was how they played the game. The 1979 and 1980 Browns loved to keep fans in suspense. In 1979, 12 of the team's 16 games were in doubt until the final minute. Three of the games were decided in overtime.

The next year, 13 of 16 games were decided by a touchdown or less. Cleveland's record those two years was 20-12, the Browns winning an AFC Central Division championship in 1980. But the Kardiac Kids' exciting stint ended in typical fashion - a nail-biting 14-12 loss in a divisional playoff game. Oakland's Mike Davis made an end zone interception of a Brian Sipe pass that would have provided the go-ahead touchdown with 41 seconds left.

The next year, the Browns collapsed to 5-11.

1990

Browns have 3-13 record, setting club record for losses and most points allowed in a season.

Matthews

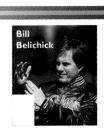

Bill Belichick

1991

Bill Belichick becomes Browns' eighth head coach.

Dallas COWBOYS

YEAR	WINS	LOSSES	TIES	RECORD	PLACE	COACH
1960				0-11-1	7th	Tom Landry
1961				4-9-1	6th	Tom Landry
1962				5-8-1	5th	Tom Landry
1963				4-10	5th	Tom Landry
1964				5-8-1	5th	Tom Landry
1965				7-7	2nd	Tom Landry
1966				10-3-1	1st	Tom Landry
1967				9-5	1st	Tom Landry
1968				12-2	1st	Tom Landry
1969				11-2-1	1st	Tom Landry
1970				10-4	1st	Tom Landry
1971				11-3	1st	Tom Landry
1972				10-4	2nd	Tom Landry
1973				10-4	1st	Tom Landry
1974				8-6	3rd	Tom Landry
1975				10-4	2nd	Tom Landry
1976				11-3	1st	Tom Landry
1977				12-2	1st	Tom Landry
1978				12-4	1st	Tom Landry
1979				11-5	1st	Tom Landry
1980				12-4	2nd	Tom Landry
1981				12-4	1st	Tom Landry
1982				6-3	2nd	Tom Landry
1983				12-4	2nd	Tom Landry
1984				9-7	4th	Tom Landry
1985				10-6	1st	Tom Landry
1986				7-9	3rd	Tom Landry
1987				7-8	2nd	Tom Landry
1988				3-13	5th	Tom Landry
1989				1-15	5th	Jimmy Johnson
1990				7-9	4th	Jimmy Johnson
1991				11-5	2nd	Jimmy Johnson

America's Team. The Dallas Cowboys were the NFL's dividing line for two decades, inspiring either love or loathing from pro football fans everywhere.

The Cowboys were not a team to be watched with indifference. Millions admired them for their cool precision and machine-line success; millions of others resented them for the confidence that allowed them to claim the title of America's Team.

While other teams rose and fell, the Dallas Cowboys won...and won...and won, stringing together 20 consecutive winning seasons.

No other team in professional football history had such success. And no other team was better suited for its time.

Dallas RANGERS?

When Clint Murchison, Jr., was awarded an NFL franchise in January, 1960, he announced that the team would be called the Rangers.

Within two months, however, he had a change of heart and the team had a change of name. When they began play on September 24, 1960, they were the Dallas Cowboys.

1960

DALLAS COWBOYS
Turning Points

Dallas gets NFL franchise; Clint Murchison, Jr., is owner, Tom Landry head coach, Tex Schramm general manager. Team goes 0-11-1.

In an era when most teams were still scribbling with pencil on paper, the Dallas Cowboys were the Computer Team for the Computer Age. They drafted by computer, coached by computer, and called plays by computer.

And it worked. During the 20 years from 1966 to 1985, the Cowboys finished in first or second place 18 times, winning 13 division titles and appearing in five Super Bowls. Dallas was the organization that drew the blueprint and set the pace in professional football.

Success in the NFL typically is cyclical. This year's winning record translates to a late selection in next year's draft - after competitors have picked over the most obvious prizes in the talent pool. It's a cycle almost impossible to avoid. Few teams can resist it for long.

But Dallas resisted. If the top prospects from the top schools were already taken when the Cowboys' turn came up, the vaunted Dallas computer would uncover talented prospects from small schools, places like Elizabeth City State (Jethro Pugh), Florida A&M (Bob Hayes), Fort Valley State (Rayfield Wright), Hawaii (Larry Cole), Tennessee State (Ed "Too Tall" Jones), Amherst (Jean Fugett), East Texas State (Harvey Martin), Langston (Thomas Henderson), Virginia Union (Herb Scott), and California-Riverside (Butch Johnson).

Like other teams, the Cowboys had injuries and assorted other problems. But unlike most

CTHE DALLAS
Cheerleaders
National Favorites

The Coach

It's a coach's job to get his team ready to play, and there have been few, if any, who did that as well as Tom Landry.

For evidence, check Landry's record in season openers. Dallas won every season opener between 1965 and 1981, a string of 17 consecutive years. The Cowboys lost their season opener in 1982, then won the next four, making it 21 of 22 seasons that Dallas started the season with a 1-0 record. Clearly, when Tom Landry brought a team out of training camp, it was not merely ready to play; it was ready to win.

Landry, widely respected as one of the great strategists in NFL history, had a record of 270-178-6 in 29 years as head coach. In the 20 years between 1966 and 1985, he brought his team home either first or second 18 times. During that 20-year period, Dallas failed to qualify for postseason playoffs just twice.

Landry was inducted into Pro Football's Hall of Fame in 1990.

1961

Cowboys win three of first four games but only one of last 10. Add two key rookies: defensive tackle Bob Lilly, running back Don Perkins.

Calvin Hill

1964

Cowboys draft Roger Staubach, who will not be available for five years because of service commitment, plus Mel Renfro, and Bob Hayes; endure last losing season until 1986.

1965

Dallas continues to stockpile talent, adds Craig Morton, Jethro Pugh, and Dan Reeves.

The First STAR

Victories were scarce and heroes were few in the early 1960s, but Don Perkins gave Dallas fans reason to cheer. Perkins was the Cowboys' leading rusher every year from 1961-1968 and his career total of 6,217 rushing yards ranks second only to Tony Dorsett in Cowboys history.

other teams, Dallas had sufficient depth on the roster so that collapse was avoided.

The Cowboys were best symbolized in those days by their head coach, Tom Landry. Always cool, always in control, always dressed as if he were on his way to a board of directors' meeting. Landry was unflappable on the sidelines, seldom showing the slightest emotion. He was, after all, the man who had programmed the computer. Emotion was an unnecessary frill. He calmly walked the sidelines, neatly printed game plan in hand, occasionally conferring by phone with assistants in the coaching booth...or perhaps the computer room. It was an image recognized all over America.

Landry's Cowboys used an offense designed to confuse opponents. They would change formations, shifting players this way and that, doing their best to befuddle defenses before the ball was snapped.

For the better part of a decade, they had the perfect quarterback for the job. On the heels of Don Meredith and Craig Morton, both good quarterbacks, came Roger Staubach, who was better. He seemed a product

A CHAMPION

Heisman Trophy winner. NFL passing champion. Super Bowl MVP. By the time Roger Staubach retired after the 1979 season, he had done it all. Pro football has seen few quarterbacks who compare with Staubach.

He established Dallas records of all sorts - he was the NFL's passing leader four times in a nine-year period - but the number that tells the Roger Staubach story best is .737. That was his team's winning percentage in games he started; a record of 116-41-1.

Master of the fourth-quarter rally, Staubach had a dazzling record in his nine years as a starter: eight playoff appearances, five conference championships and four Super Bowls, including victories in Super Bowls VI and XII.

Staubach's career statistics: 1,685 completions, 22,700 yards, 153 touchdown passes, completion percentage of .570, and 2,264 rushing yards.

1966		1969	1971
Cowboys have 10-3-1 record, lose NFL Championship Game to Green Bay 34-27.	 Lee Roy Jordan	A changing of the guard: Don Meredith and Don Perkins retire, Roger Staubach and Calvin Hill arrive.	Cowboys move into Texas Stadium, Staubach moves in as starting quarterback, Dallas wins Super Bowl VI over Miami 24-3.

of the Dallas computer, programmed to win. Roger the Dodger was legendary for his narrow escapes, for his ability to snatch victory from near defeat at the last possible moment. In his nine years as the Cowboys' starting quarterback, Staubach engineered 23 come-from-behind victories in the fourth quarter, 14 of those in the final two minutes of the game.

The Dallas offense operated with speed and precision, as personified by running back Tony Dorsett, who was programmed to gain more than 1,000 yards season after season. Dorsett gained more than 1,000 yards in eight of his first nine years with Dallas, missing only in 1982, when the season was shortened to nine games by a players' strike. He averaged 83 yards per game that year, a pace that would have easily put him over 1,000 yards for a full season.

The Dallas receiver corps was swift and stylish, led by standouts such as Bob Hayes, Drew Pearson, and Tony Hill. Hayes was an Olympic sprinter whose speed terrorized opposing defenses; Pearson and Hill were clever, sure-handed wide receivers who combined to lead Dallas in catches for nine years.

The offensive line was what offensive lines are expected to be...mostly anonymous, but

Too Tall

His name was Ed Jones, but he rarely was called that. He was known simply as "Too Tall."

A remarkable athlete, the 6-foot 9-inch defensive end played 224 games in 15 years for Dallas, consistently ranking as one of best at his position. Jones, a first-round draft pick in 1974, has a unique footnote to his career: he retired before the 1979 season to pursue a professional boxing career. A far better football player than boxer, he returned to the Cowboys in 1980.

Bob Lilly

DOOMSDAY MEN

One of them was known as "Manster," because he was said to be half-man, half-monster. The other was called "Mr. Cowboy," a nickname that's self-explanatory.

Bob (Mr. Cowboy) Lilly and Randy (Manster) White were two of the all-time greats at defensive tackle. Lilly, the first draft choice in Dallas history, played for the Cowboys from 1961-1974 and was the keystone of the heralded Doomsday Defense. An all-pro selection seven times, Lilly missed only one game in his 14-year career.

White, a first-round pick in 1975, was an eight-time all-pro as the main man in Doomsday II. He retired in 1988.

Lilly is in the Pro Football Hall of Fame; White is a shoo-in to join him.

Randy White

A Perfect 10

A defensive back with sizzling speed and remarkable tenacity, Mel Renfro was named to the Pro Bowl in each of his first 10 years in the NFL. A second-round draft pick in 1964, Renfro played 14 years for the Cowboys and is the club's career leader in interceptions (52) and kickoff return average (26.4).

1974

A changing of the guard: Bob Lilly retires after season, Ed (Too Tall) Jones is first draft pick, Danny White is drafted on third round.

1975

Cowboys draft Randy White.

Harvey Martin

151

T.D.

Tony Dorsett was, quite simply, the Dallas running game from 1977 through 1986. A speedster with remarkable durability, Dorsett led Dallas in rushing 10 consecutive years, rolling up 12,036 yards. He played for Denver in 1988 before retiring with a career total of 12,739 yards, second highest in NFL history. Dorsett had eight 1,000-yard seasons in Dallas, four of those for more than 1,300 yards. His 72 rushing touchdowns exceeded by 30 the previous club record set by Don Perkins.

highly effective.

Cowboys defenders were anything but anonymous, answering to the chilling nickname of Doomsday Defense. What could be more intimidating? Defensive linemen such as Bob Lilly, Randy White, Ed (Too Tall) Jones, and Harvey Martin were among the best known at their positions. They played in a Landry creation called the "Flex," a scheme no other team could effectively emulate.

If the Dallas offense won with finesse and trickery, the Dallas defense won with quickness and strength.

Perhaps most discouraging to Dallas opponents was that the Cowboys never seemed to run out of replacement parts. When running back Don Perkins wore down, the computer found a splendid replacement in Calvin Hill, who was in turn replaced by Dorsett. At quarterback, Meredith was followed by Morton who was followed by Staubach who was followed by Danny White...and it was that way at every position, for two full decades.

The Cowboys were tough to compete with, even on the sidelines, where their cheerleading squad gained national prominence. The Dallas Cowboys cheerleaders featured precise timing,

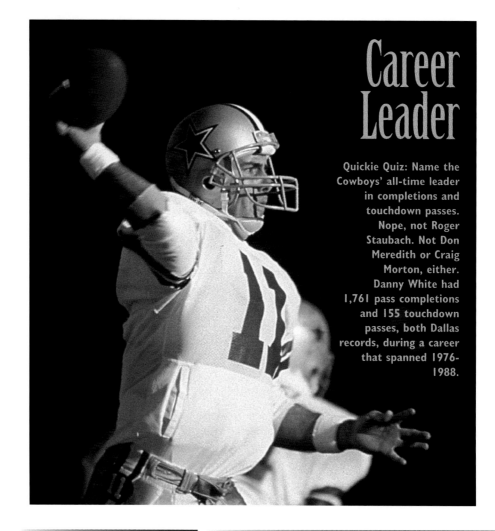

Career Leader

Quickie Quiz: Name the Cowboys' all-time leader in completions and touchdown passes. Nope, not Roger Staubach. Not Don Meredith or Craig Morton, either. Danny White had 1,761 pass completions and 155 touchdown passes, both Dallas records, during a career that spanned 1976-1988.

1977

Dallas trades four draft picks to Seattle for chance to draft Tony Dorsett, wins Super Bowl XII 27-10 over Denver.

1980

Roger Staubach retires.

Michael Irvin

precise choreography, and beauty.

And TV didn't miss a single play or a single cheer. Recognizing the Cowboys' appeal, the networks featured Dallas at every opportunity. Landry, Staubach, and the cheerleaders were weekly visitors in living rooms throughout the country.

They were, indeed, America's Team.

But not even the Cowboys could perpetuate success. When other teams began to scout as thoroughly as the Cowboys, replacement parts for Dallas became harder to find. There was a little slippage at one position, a little more at another and, finally, Dallas had a losing season - a 7-9 record in 1986. It was the first sub-.500 season since a 5-8-1 finish in 1964.

Losing seasons followed in 1987 and 1988, and in 1989 the biggest change of all took place. The Cowboys were sold to Jerry Jones, who brought in a new coach, Jimmy Johnson, who had directed the University of Miami to a national championship. Tex Schramm resigned as general manager, and an era officially was over.

Johnson began a massive overhaul of the roster, bringing in new players, trying to create a new era of excellence. ⊘

A Reversal of FORTUNE

The Cowboys couldn't do anything right in their early years when victories were scarce.

There was, for example, the September 23, 1962, game against Pittsburgh when quarterback Eddie LeBaron exulted after Frank Clarke raced the length of the field with what appeared to be a 99-yard touchdown reception.

But the celebration was short-lived. A Dallas lineman was called for offensive holding in the end zone, not only canceling the touchdown but giving Pittsburgh a safety.

The final score: Pittsburgh 30, Dallas 28.

Bullet Bob

He was not the leading receiver in Dallas history, but Bob Hayes certainly was the most feared. A sprinter with world-class speed, Hayes caught 365 passes in his Cowboys career (1965-1974) and had a spectacular 20-yard average per catch. The most impressive statistic of Hayes's career: he averaged a touchdown every 5.1 receptions.

DANDY DON

Quarterback Don Meredith suffered with the Cowboys through their early years and triumphed with them during the last three years of his career (1966-68).

A fine passer and tenacious competitor, Meredith retired with 17,199 passing yards and 135 touchdowns.

1984

After 25 years as Cowboys owner, the Murchison family sells team to partnership headed by H.R. (Bum) Bright.

Troy Aikman

1989

A changing of the guard: Bright sells team to Jerry Jones, who hires Jimmy Johnson; Schramm resigns and Randy White retires.

153

Denver BRONCOS

YEAR	■ WINS ■ LOSSES □ TIES	RECORD	PLACE	COACH
American Football League				
1960		4-9-1	4th	Frank Filchock
1961		3-11	3rd	Frank Filchock
1962		7-7	2nd	Jack Faulkner
1963		2-11-1	4th	Jack Faulkner
1964		2-11-1	4th	J. Faulkner, M. Speedie [1]
1965		4-10	4th	Mac Speedie
1966		4-10	4th	M. Speedie, R. Malavasi [2]
1967		3-11	4th	Lou Saban
1968		5-9	4th	Lou Saban
1969		5-8-1	4th	Lou Saban
National Football League				
1970		5-8-1	4th	Lou Saban
1971		4-9-1	4th	L. Saban, J. Smith [3]
1972		5-9	3rd	John Ralston
1973		7-5-2	2nd	John Ralston
1974		7-6-1	2nd	John Ralston
1975		6-8	2nd	John Ralston
1976		9-5	2nd	John Ralston
1977		12-2	1st	Red Miller
1978		10-6	1st	Red Miller
1979		10-6	2nd	Red Miller
1980		8-8	4th	Red Miller
1981		10-6	2nd	Dan Reeves
1982		2-7	12th	Dan Reeves
1983		9-7	3rd	Dan Reeves
1984		13-3	1st	Dan Reeves
1985		11-5	2nd	Dan Reeves
1986		11-5	1st	Dan Reeves
1987		10-4-1	1st	Dan Reeves
1988		8-8	2nd	Dan Reeves
1989		11-5	1st	Dan Reeves
1990		5-11	5th	Dan Reeves
1991		12-4	1st	Dan Reeves

1 — Jack Faulkner (4 games), Mac Speedie (10 games)
2 — Mac Speedie (2 games), Ray Malavasi (12 games)
3 — Lou Saban (9 games), Jerry Smith (5 games)

The Denver Broncos were the laughingstock of pro football in 1960-61, and they never could be sure why. Was it because of how they played or how they looked?

They won a total of only seven games in two years, finishing last and next-to-last in their division, dressed in outfits that could be described charitably as "distinctive."

As a cost-saving measure, the Broncos wore hand-me-down uniforms from the defunct Copper Bowl All-Star game, uniforms despised by Broncos players and ridiculed by opponents.

But survival wasn't easy for the eight teams of the fledgling American Football League, and the story of the Broncos illustrates those early struggles.

It also provides a remarkable contrast to the modern Denver

The Ones That Got Away

Denver fans can only wonder how quickly their Broncos would have become a powerhouse if the club had enjoyed better success in signing draft choices.

Denver's first-round pick in 1962, as an AFL team, was defensive tackle Merlin Olsen. In 1965, the Broncos selected linebacker Dick Butkus. Olsen opted for the Los Angeles Rams and Butkus for the Chicago Bears of the rival National Football League; both went on to Hall of Fame careers.

Two other notables who got away in the 1964 draft: tackle Bob Brown and wide receiver Bob Hayes, also standouts in the NFL.

1960

DENVER BRONCOS

Turning Points

Denver is awarded one of eight American Football League franchises; Broncos post 4-9-1 record under coach Frank Filchock.

Broncos, a highly successful franchise as beloved by its fans as any in professional football.

With the exception of two replacement games in the 1987 strike season, every Denver home game since 1970 has been a sellout. More than 75,000 Broncomaniacs, resplendent in bright orange and royal blue, regularly pack Mile High Stadium.

What a change.

There was a time when the Broncos' colors weren't bright orange and royal blue, but yellow and dull brown. Instead of 75,000 fans there were 5,000.

The most celebrated event in the Broncos' early years was a bonfire, in which the players' socks were burned. It was orchestrated by head coach Jack Faulkner and attended by 8,000 cheering fans.

The Infamous Denver Sock

The Comeback
KING

John Elway earned a reputation as a master of the fourth-quarter comeback, but none of his late-game heroics came in a more important game than "The Drive" in 1986.

The Broncos were playing at Cleveland for the AFC Championship and trailing 20-13 after the Browns scored a touchdown with 5:43 to go. After Gene Lang covered the kickoff at the Denver 2-yard line, Elway took his team on a 98-yard march despite bitterly cold weather (wind chill of five degrees).

Elway had runs of 11 and 9 yards during that drive, plus pass completions of 22, 20, 14, and 12 yards. The rally was capped by a 5-yard scoring pass to Mike Jackson with 39 seconds left in regulation.

Denver won the championship 23-20 in overtime on a 33-yard field goal by Rich Karlis.

1962	1965		1967
New coach Jack Faulkner presides over ceremony to burn the vertically striped brown and yellow stockings from the original uniforms; 8,000 attend.	Gerald and Allan Phipps, owners of 42 percent of club, purchase remainder of Broncos, ending speculation that franchise might move.	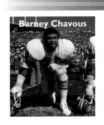 **Barney Chavous**	Running back Floyd Little is drafted.

Small, But Solid

At 5 feet 11 inches and 220 pounds, Tom Jackson wasn't the biggest linebacker in the NFL, but for many years, he was one of the best. Jackson played outside linebacker at Denver 14 seasons (1973-86), a club record, and was a three-time Pro Bowl selection. After retiring from pro football, he became a TV sports commentator.

The Broncos' outfits in those days included a brown helmet with a white stripe and white numbers on the side, a yellow jersey, brown pants, and vertically striped brown and yellow socks. If the rest of the uniform was merely bad, the socks were awful.

Fans had all but ignored the Broncos in their first two seasons. Only 5,861 attended a 1960 game against New York, and the last three home games of 1961 each drew fewer than 10,000 fans.

When Faulkner became the Broncos' coach in 1962, he was eager to change everything about those dismal seasons. He started with the socks, presiding over the sacrificial fire at an intrasquad scrimmage at Bears Stadium. A crowd of 8,000, more than had attended some of the games the previous season, attended the ceremony.

Attendance improved dramatically, from 74,000 in 1961 to 178,000 the next season (maybe it was the socks - but more than likely, it was the 6-1 start in a 7-7 season). Today, the Broncos draw more on a single Sunday than they did in the entire 1961 season.

GETTING THEIR KICKS IN DENVER

Jim Turner

Jim Turner came in a 1971 trade with the New York Jets; Rich Karlis emerged from a 1982 tryout that included 478 aspirants. Combined, they provided the Broncos with almost 1,400 points.

Turner was Denver's kicker from 1971-79, scoring 742 points. Karlis, who held the job from 1982-88, scored 655 points.

The Right Man for the Job

Dan Reeves was the youngest head coach in the NFL when he assumed the Broncos' reins at age 37 in 1981. He quickly dispelled any doubts about being ready for the job.

The Broncos posted a 10-6 record in Reeves's rookie season and won 10 or more games in seven of his first 11 years on the job, through the 1991 season.

1972
John Ralston becomes head coach; Broncos trade for quarterback Charley Johnson, draft tight end Riley Odoms.

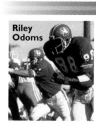

Riley Odoms

1973
Broncos have first winning season, posting 7-5-2 record.

1974
Linebacker Randy Gradishar is drafted.

It was easier to improve the team's appearance than its performance. Denver didn't have a winning season until 1973, its fourteenth year. Six coaches - Frank Filchock, Jack Faulkner, Mac Speedie, Ray Malavasi, Lou Saban, and Jerry Smith, came and went without a winning season. John Ralston arrived in 1972, and in his second season the Broncos were winners, with a 7-5-2 record.

Denver suffered through many seasons of instability at quarterback, where injuries and unfulfilled potential were the rule, not the exception.

Frank Tripucka was the original Denver quarterback, but he quit after two games in 1963. George Herring, George Shaw, Mickey Slaughter, Don Breaux, John McCormick, Max Chobian, Steve Tensi, Marlin Briscoe, Jim LeClair, Pete Liske, Tobin Rote, Al Pastrana, Steve Ramsey, and Don Horn all played quarterback for the Broncos during the first dozen years.

Denver finally showed improvement in 1972 after Ralston traded for veteran Charley Johnson, who shared the job with Ramsey for four seasons. The Broncos, who had finished

Little - A Big Contributor

Floyd Little, who broke many of Jim Brown's rushing records at Syracuse University, didn't enjoy quite the same success in professional football. The problem wasn't lack of ability; Little played behind some less talented offensive lines in Denver.

Nevertheless, he became the Broncos' all-time leading rusher, gaining 6,323 yards and scoring 43 touchdowns from 1967-1975. Little was virtually a one-man attack; the Broncos' best season during his career was 7-6-1 in 1974.

Safety First

The Broncos raised eyebrows when they drafted safety Steve Atwater in the first round in 1989, but the former Arkansas Razorback proved the choice was well warranted.

He established himself as one of the top defensive backs in the league and earned Pro Bowl berths in 1990 and 1991.

1977

Robert (Red) Miller becomes head coach, Broncos win first AFC championship but lose to Dallas 27-10 in Super Bowl XII.

Red Miller

1978

"Orange Crush" defense leads Broncos to another AFC West title, ousted in playoffs by eventual Super Bowl winner Pittsburgh.

1981

Dan Reeves becomes head coach.

157

Troubles at Quarterback

The Broncos encountered all sorts of problems in trying to fill the quarterback position in their early years. Two notable candidates were Jacky Lee and Steve Tensi. Lee was acquired in an unusual lend-lease arrangement with the Houston Oilers in 1964; the Broncos gave up defensive lineman Bud McFadin in exchange for two years of Lee's services. After that time, he was returned to Houston. Denver won only two games in 1964, and Lee seldom was used when the Broncos won four in 1965. Denver gave up two first round draft picks for Tensi in 1967, but injuries limited his playing time and his effectiveness until he retired in 1971.

higher than third only once in 13 years, were AFC West runners-up from 1973-76 with Johnson and Ramsey calling signals.

The biggest step forward, though, came after the Broncos acquired veteran quarterback Craig Morton from the Giants in 1977.

Morton, head coach Robert (Red) Miller, and the "Orange Crush" defense all arrived in 1977, and they promptly took the Broncos to their first AFC Western Division title and the Super Bowl. Only a 27-10 loss to Dallas in Super Bowl XII spoiled the celebration.

A changing of the guard in 1981 brought a new owner (Edgar Kaiser, Jr.), a new coach (Dan Reeves) and continued success. Except for the strike-shortened season of 1982 and a surprising stumble in 1990, the Broncos did not have a losing record between 1976 and 1992.

Reeves and quarterback John Elway, obtained in a 1983 trade with the Baltimore Colts, steered the Broncos to division titles in 1984, 1986, 1987, 1989, and 1991. Three times in a four-year period (1986-89), the Broncos were the AFC champions. Each time, they beat

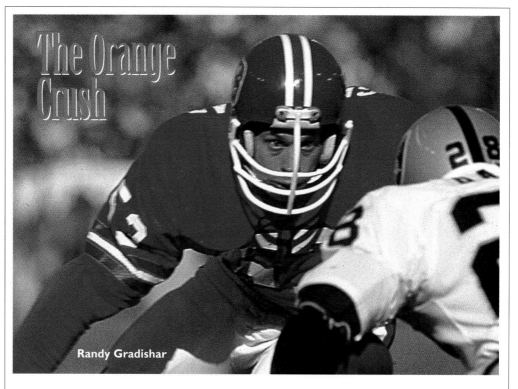

The Orange Crush

Randy Gradishar

Denver won back-to-back AFC West championships in 1977-78 largely on the strength of an exceptional defense popularly known as "The Orange Crush."

Randy Gradishar, a linebacker who played in seven Pro Bowl games, was the best known of the Denver defenders, but the unit included several other standouts, including four who joined Gradishar in the 1979 Pro Bowl game - linebacker Tom Jackson, end Lyle Alzado, and defensive backs Louis Wright and Bill Thompson. Other outstanding performers in the unit included nose tackle Rubin Carter and end Barney Chavous.

1983

Denver trades for quarterback John Elway.

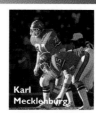

Karl Mecklenburg

1986

Broncos go 11-5, win AFC Championship at Cleveland in game highlighted by "The Drive," lose Super Bowl XXI to New York Giants 39-20.

Cleveland in the AFC title game and were beaten soundly in the Super Bowl.

Elway, a charismatic leader, was the central figure in Denver's success. A strong-armed passer with a flair for the dramatic comeback, he quickly established his place among the NFL's top quarterbacks.

The Denver attack under Elway emphasized the deep pass - often at the end of improvised scrambles - and the electrifying Broncos' quarterback was annually among the league leaders in passing yardage, if not completion percentage. His ability as a runner added another weapon; for seven consecutive years (1985-91), he passed for more than 3,000 yards and ran for more than 200 yards each season. It was evidence not only of his talent but also his durability; no other NFL quarterback eclipsed those standards more than three consecutive years.

If Denver fans were frustrated at the team's failures in four Super Bowl games, they could take solace in the fact that through 1991 only the Cowboys, Redskins, and Dolphins had appeared in more Super Bowl games. ⌀

He Caught On Quickly

Lionel Taylor got a late start on the 1960 season—he joined the Broncos after the first two games. But he quickly made up for lost time and led the AFL with 92 catches in only 12 games.

Taylor, a wide receiver whose sure hands were his greatest asset, led the AFL in receptions five times in the league's first six years. His best season was 1961, when he became the first pro player to catch 100 passes in a season.

Taylor caught 543 passes in seven seasons at Denver, gaining 6,872 yards and scoring 44 touchdowns.

Rushing Record Holder

Otis Armstrong was the main man in Denver's ground attack from 1973-1980, leading the team in rushing four times. Armstrong's best year was 1974, when he rushed for 1,407 yards, a club record that still stands.

Armstrong's Broncos career produced 4,453 rushing yards and 25 touchdowns.

Dan Reeves   John Elway

1987

Broncos repeat as division champions, beat Cleveland in AFC title game, lose Super Bowl XXII 42-10 to Washington.

1989

Denver takes another AFC West title, beats Cleveland for conference championship, loses Super Bowl XXIV 55-10 to San Francisco.

Detroit LIONS

YEAR	RECORD	PLACE	COACH
Portsmouth Spartans			
1930	5-6-3	8th	Hal Griffen
1931	11-3	2nd	George Clark
1932	6-2-4	3rd	George Clark
1933	6-5	2nd	George Clark
Detroit Lions			
1934	10-3	2nd	George Clark
1935	7-3-2	1st	George Clark
1936	8-4	3rd	George Clark
1937	7-4	2nd	Earl (Dutch) Clark
1938	7-4	2nd	Earl (Dutch) Clark
1939	6-5	3rd	Gus Henderson
1940	5-5-1	3rd	George Clark
1941	4-6-1	3rd	Bill Edwards
1942	0-11	5th	B. Edwards, J. Karcis [1]
1943	3-6-1	3rd	Gus Dorais
1944	6-3-1	2nd	Gus Dorais
1945	7-3	2nd	Gus Dorais
1946	1-10	5th	Gus Dorais
1947	3-9	5th	Gus Dorais
1948	2-10	5th	Alvin McMillin
1949	4-8	4th	Alvin McMillin
1950	6-6	4th	Alvin McMillin
1951	7-4-1	2nd	Buddy Parker
1952	9-3	1st	Buddy Parker
1953	10-2	1st	Buddy Parker
1954	9-2-1	1st	Buddy Parker
1955	3-9	6th	Buddy Parker
1956	9-3	2nd	Buddy Parker
1957	8-4	1st	George Wilson
1958	4-7-1	5th	George Wilson
1959	3-8-1	5th	George Wilson
1960	7-5	2nd	George Wilson
1961	8-5-1	2nd	George Wilson
1962	11-3	2nd	George Wilson
1963	5-8-1	4th	George Wilson
1964	7-5-2	4th	George Wilson
1965	6-7-1	6th	Harry Gilmer
1966	4-9-1	6th	Harry Gilmer
1967	5-7-2	3rd	Joe Schmidt
1968	4-8-2	4th	Joe Schmidt
1969	9-4-1	2nd	Joe Schmidt
1970	10-4	2nd	Joe Schmidt
1971	7-6-1	2nd	Joe Schmidt
1972	8-5-1	2nd	Joe Schmidt
1973	6-7-1	2nd	Don McCafferty
1974	7-7	2nd	Rick Forzano
1975	7-7	2nd	Rick Forzano
1976	6-8	3rd	R. Forzano, T. Hudspeth [2]
1977	6-8	3rd	Tommy Hudspeth
1978	7-9	3rd	Monte Clark
1979	2-14	5th	Monte Clark
1980	9-7	2nd	Monte Clark
1981	8-8	2nd	Monte Clark
1982	4-5	8th	Monte Clark
1983	9-7	1st	Monte Clark
1984	4-11-1	4th	Monte Clark
1985	7-9	4th	Darryl Rogers
1986	5-11	3rd	Darryl Rogers
1987	4-11	5th	Darryl Rogers
1988	4-12	4th	D. Rogers, W. Fontes [3]
1989	7-9	3rd	Wayne Fontes
1990	6-10	3rd	Wayne Fontes
1991	12-4	1st	Wayne Fontes

Legend: WINS / LOSSES / TIES

1 — Bill Edwards (3 games), John Karcis (8 games)
2 — Rick Forzano (4 games), Tommy Hudspeth (8 games)
3 — Darryl Rogers (11 games), Wayne Fontes (5 games)

It was a tragedy that stunned the Detroit Lions. Shocked them, broke their hearts. And inspired them to the most victories that any Lions team ever had in a season.

Thumbs Up.

Mike Utley, 25, the team's starting right guard, suffered a terrible injury in Detroit's eleventh game of 1991. His spinal cord was damaged. He was paralyzed from the chest down.

As medical personnel carried him from the field on a stretcher

Detroit Spartans?

When George Richards bought the NFL's Portsmouth (Ohio) Spartans in 1934, he moved them to Detroit and renamed the team. Since Detroit already had the Tigers, Richards decided he would add the Lions. The team had a roaring start, going 10-3 in 1934, and didn't sustain a losing season until 1941, when World War II began playing havoc with NFL rosters.

1934

DETROIT LIONS
Turning Points

George Richards buys Portsmouth Spartans of the NFL, moves team to Detroit and renames it Lions.

and the Silverdome crowd watched in fearful silence, Utley's right hand moved. The movement was slight, but the signal was clear.

Thumbs Up.

In the weeks ahead, Thumbs Up became the rallying cry of the Lions, a tribute to a fallen teammate whose future would hold challenges more difficult than any he faced on a football field.

Inspired by Mike Utley's spirit in the face of terrible adversity, the Lions rallied and became a stronger team, a more unified team. They drew inspiration from his courage.

Little was expected of the Lions in 1991. The team had staggered through seven consecutive losing seasons and began the campaign by being embarrassed 45-0 by Washington. After 10 games, Detroit had a ho-hum 6-4 record and seemed headed for another mediocre finish.

But the Lions won the game in which Utley was injured, beating the Rams and breaking a

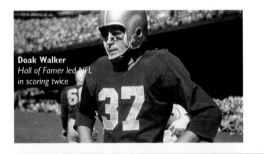

Doak Walker
Hall of Famer led NFL in scoring twice

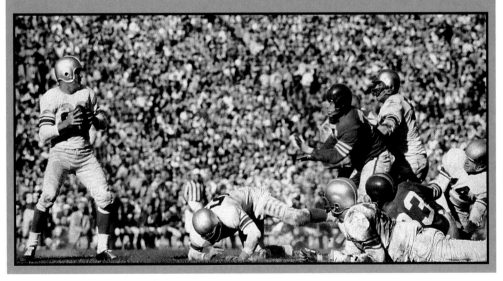

THE GENERAL *of* DETROIT

The legend of Bobby Layne claims he was a hard-partying, fast-living, devil-may-care tough guy whose attitude about life was symbolized by his refusal to wear a face mask when nearly everyone around him did.

The legend is mostly fact, but it obscures the reality that Bobby Layne was a great quarterback. He spent nine years with the Lions (1950-58), and got his team into the NFL championship game four times, three of those resulting in league titles for Detroit.

The Lions were, without a doubt, Layne's team. He was the general and everybody knew it. If they didn't, he let them know in unmistakable terms.

Layne, whose career was capped by induction into the Hall of Fame, provided the Lions with 15,710 yards passing, 118 touchdowns and, most important, three NFL championships.

Tragedy in Detroit

The Detroit Lions have suffered more than their share of tragedies, losses much more important than football scores.

In addition to the career-ending spinal injury to right guard Mike Utley in 1991, Detroit lost two members of the Lion family between the 1991 and 1992 seasons. Assistant coach Len Fontes died of a heart attack and starting left guard Eric Andolsek was killed when hit by a truck that veered off the road near his Louisiana home.

Wide receiver Chuck Hughes died of a heart attack on the field at Tiger Stadium during a 1971 game against the Bears. And head coach Don McCafferty suffered a fatal heart attack in July, 1974.

1935

Lions beat New York Giants 26-7 to win NFL championship.

Jack Christensen
Hall of Fame defensive back

1950

Lions trade for quarterback Bobby Layne, draft running back Doak Walker and end Leon Hart.

1951

Buddy Parker becomes head coach, directs Lions to three first place finishes in next four years.

A Football First

George Richards, the man who converted the Portsmouth Spartans into the Detroit Lions, was a radio station owner. It was appropriate, then, that he should be the first to recognize the value of broadcasting pro football games. Richards assembled a network of 94 stations to carry the 1934 Thanksgiving Day game between the Bears and Lions.

two-game losing streak. Then they beat the Vikings. Then the Bears. Then the Jets, Packers, and Bills, and by the end of the season the Lions had a 12-4 record, the most regular-season victories in their 61-year history.

Thumbs Up.

The Lions' brightest chapters were written in the early 1950s, when Detroit played for the NFL title three consecutive years (1952-54), winning back-to-back championships in 1952 and 1953. The heroes were quarterback Bobby Layne, halfback Doak Walker, linebacker Joe Schmidt, and defensive backs Jack Christensen and Yale Lary, all now in the Hall of Fame. There were other heroes, including tackle Lou Creekmur, defensive back Don Doll, running back Bob Hoernschemeyer, end Cloyce Box, and guard Les Bingaman, who was listed at 335 pounds, the heaviest player of his era.

Those Detroit teams were coached by Buddy Parker, who posted a remarkable record of three first-place finishes and two seconds in a six-year span, then abruptly resigned two days

The Mightiest Lion

The Lions have had many great football players, but perhaps none better than Joe Schmidt, who came to Detroit as a lightly regarded seventh round draft pick in 1953.

A 6-foot, 222-pound center at the University of Pittsburgh, Schmidt became one of the NFL's most dominant middle linebackers of his time (1953-65), earning All-Pro honors nine years and playing in nine Pro Bowls. He was a key factor in the Lions' NFL championship teams in 1953 and 1957. Team captain for nine years, Schmidt was honored as Detroit's MVP four times, more than anyone else in team history.

After retiring as a player, Schmidt coached the Lions for six seasons that included four second-place finishes. His coaching record was 43-34-7.

1952	1953	1957
Detroit drafts defensive backs Yale Lary and Jim David; beats Cleveland 17-7 for NFL championship.	Lions beat Cleveland 17-16 for NFL title; draft linebacker Joe Schmidt, who becomes best linebacker in Detroit history.	Buddy Parker quits as coach before season opens, George Wilson coaches Lions to NFL title, 59-14 win over Browns.

Yale Lary

before the 1957 season opener. The Lions had a fine year despite losing Parker, finishing first with an 8-4 record. They beat the 49ers 31-27 in a playoff game, then thrashed Cleveland 59-14 in the NFL Championship Game.

That was the last time the Lions would finish first until they won the NFC Central Division title in 1983.

Detroit went through a frustrating string of near-misses from 1969 to 1975, finishing second for seven consecutive years under three different coaches. Those were years when Minnesota was a powerhouse, and the Lions were destined to continually chase the Vikings.

Except for the decade of the Fifties, when they won championships, the Lions often have fielded teams that were good, but not great.

While there have been few playoff seasons for Detroit fans, there has been a wealth of outstanding players, in part because of the Lions' propensity for acquiring Heisman Trophy winners.

THE LAST 0~0 GAME

The last time a National Football League game ended in a scoreless tie was in 1943, when the Lions and Giants played 60 minutes to a 0-0 deadlock.

HIGH-STEPPING LIONS

Billy Sims and Barry Sanders, two of pro football's most electrifying runners of recent years, both came to Detroit by way of Oklahoma. Both were Heisman Trophy winners, Sims at Oklahoma in 1978 and Sanders at Oklahoma State in 1988. Each lived up to the standard of excellence expected of him.

Sims set the Detroit rushing record of 5,106 yards despite having his career cut short by a severe knee injury; he played only 62 NFL games in five years.

Sanders, the Lions' first pick in 1989, carried for 4,322 yards and 43 touchdowns in his first three seasons.

Barry Sanders

Billy Sims

1964
William Clay Ford becomes sole owner of Lions.

1967
Lions have two NFL Rookies of Year: running back Mel Farr, defensive back Lem Barney.

Lem Barney

Mel Farr

1975
Pontiac Silverdome becomes Lions' new home field.

Detroit has drafted eight Heisman winners, including Frank Sinkwich (1942), Doak Walker (1948), Leon Hart (1949), Howard (Hopalong) Cassady (1955), Steve Owens (1969), Billy Sims (1978), Barry Sanders (1988), and Andre Ware (1989).

Walker earned a berth in the Pro Football Hall of Fame, one of 13 Lions so honored. The NFL's Rookie of the Year in 1950, Walker led the league in scoring both in 1950 and 1955. Other Lions in the Hall include quarterbacks Earl (Dutch) Clark and Bobby Layne, fullback John Henry Johnson, halfbacks Bill Dudley, Ollie Matson and Hugh McElhenny, linebacker Joe Schmidt, linebacker/center Alex Wojciechowicz, and defensive backs Lem Barney, Jack Christensen, Dick (Night Train) Lane, and Yale Lary.

Dudley, Johnson, Matson, and McElhenny won entry to the Hall after having their best years elsewhere, leaving nine Hall of Famers whose best years were

Night Train

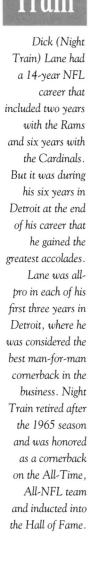

Dick (Night Train) Lane had a 14-year NFL career that included two years with the Rams and six years with the Cardinals. But it was during his six years in Detroit at the end of his career that he gained the greatest accolades. Lane was all-pro in each of his first three years in Detroit, where he was considered the best man-for-man cornerback in the business. Night Train retired after the 1965 season and was honored as a cornerback on the All-Time, All-NFL team and inducted into the Hall of Fame.

Byron (Whizzer) White

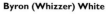

WHIZZER

Long before he became a Supreme Court Justice, Byron (Whizzer) White was a Detroit Lion. After graduating from the University of Colorado, White joined the Steelers, who had drafted him, and led the NFL in rushing as a rookie. Then, he went to England as a Rhodes Scholar. The Lions bought White's NFL rights, and he joined Detroit for the 1940 season after finishing his studies at Oxford. White had a terrific year, leading the NFL in rushing for the second time with 514 yards, then joined the Army before the 1942 season.

1980
Lions draft Billy Sims, who becomes team's all-time rushing leader.

Chris Spielman
Lions' superstar at linebacker

Doug English
Defensive tackle, four-time Pro Bowl selection

1983
Lions' 9-7 record is best in NFC Central, Detroit finishes in first place for first time in 26 years.

164

with Detroit. It's remarkable that four of the nine were defensive backs.

But the Lions were known for fierce defense during their championship years, and Christensen and Lary were key members of the famed "Chris's Crew" that also included Jim David and Bob Smith. Christensen made all-pro six consecutive years (1952-57), led the league in punt returns four times and in interceptions twice. Lary, a four-time all-pro safety, was a three-time NFL leader in punting, finishing his career with an average of 44.3 yards.

Lane, who previously played for the Los Angeles Rams and Chicago Cardinals, was with Detroit 1960-65, making all-pro his first three years.

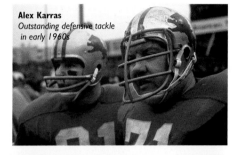

Alex Karras
Outstanding defensive tackle in early 1960s

Barney, voted into the Hall in 1992, was a Lion from 1967 through 1977. Recognized as one of the best of his time, Barney played in seven Pro Bowls. On a team with such a rich history of greatness in the secondary, Barney stands second in career interceptions with 56, behind only Dick LeBeau. ⌀

	1988	1989	1991
	Wayne Fontes becomes head coach, replacing Darryl Rogers after eleventh game of season.	*First-round draft choice is Barry Sanders, who immediately establishes himself as one of NFL's best runners.*	*Lions post 12-4 record for NFC Central title, win first postseason game in 34 years.*

Wayne Fontes

165

Green Bay
PACKERS

SIDELINES

YEAR	■ WINS □ LOSSES □ TIES	RECORD	PLACE	COACH
1921		3-2-1	6th	Earl (Curly) Lambeau
1922		4-3-3	7th	Earl (Curly) Lambeau
1923		7-2-1	3rd	Earl (Curly) Lambeau
1924		7-4	6th	Earl (Curly) Lambeau
1925		8-5	9th	Earl (Curly) Lambeau
1926		7-3-3	5th	Earl (Curly) Lambeau
1927		7-2-1	2nd	Earl (Curly) Lambeau
1928		6-4-3	4th	Earl (Curly) Lambeau
1929		12-0-1	1st	Earl (Curly) Lambeau
1930		10-3-1	1st	Earl (Curly) Lambeau
1931		12-2	1st	Earl (Curly) Lambeau
1932		10-3-1	2nd	Earl (Curly) Lambeau
1933		5-7-1	3rd	Earl (Curly) Lambeau
1934		7-6	3rd	Earl (Curly) Lambeau
1935		8-4	2nd	Earl (Curly) Lambeau
1936		10-1-1	1st	Earl (Curly) Lambeau
1937		7-4	2nd	Earl (Curly) Lambeau
1938		8-3	1st	Earl (Curly) Lambeau
1939		9-2	1st	Earl (Curly) Lambeau
1940		6-4-1	2nd	Earl (Curly) Lambeau
1941		10-1	2nd	Earl (Curly) Lambeau
1942		8-2-1	2nd	Earl (Curly) Lambeau
1943		7-2-1	2nd	Earl (Curly) Lambeau
1944		8-2	1st	Earl (Curly) Lambeau
1945		6-4	3rd	Earl (Curly) Lambeau
1946		6-5	3rd	Earl (Curly) Lambeau
1947		6-5-1	3rd	Earl (Curly) Lambeau
1948		3-9	4th	Earl (Curly) Lambeau
1949		2-10	5th	Earl (Curly) Lambeau
1950		3-9	5th	Gene Ronzani
1951		3-9	5th	Gene Ronzani
1952		6-6	4th	Gene Ronzani
1953		2-9-1	6th	Ronzani, Devore & McLean [1]
1954		4-8	5th	Lisle Blackburn
1955		6-6	3rd	Lisle Blackburn
1956		4-8	5th	Lisle Blackburn
1957		3-9	6th	Lisle Blackburn
1958		1-10-1	6th	Ray McLean
1959		7-5	3rd	Vince Lombardi
1960		8-4	1st	Vince Lombardi
1961		11-3	1st	Vince Lombardi
1962		13-1	1st	Vince Lombardi
1963		11-2-1	2nd	Vince Lombardi
1964		8-5-1	2nd	Vince Lombardi
1965		10-3-1	1st	Vince Lombardi
1966		12-2	1st	Vince Lombardi
1967		9-4-1	1st	Vince Lombardi
1968		6-7-1	3rd	Phil Bengtson
1969		8-6	3rd	Phil Bengtson
1970		6-8	4th	Phil Bengtson
1971		4-8-2	4th	Dan Devine
1972		10-4	1st	Dan Devine
1973		5-7-2	3rd	Dan Devine
1974		6-8	3rd	Dan Devine
1975		4-10	4th	Bart Starr
1976		5-9	4th	Bart Starr
1977		4-10	4th	Bart Starr
1978		8-7-1	2nd	Bart Starr
1979		5-11	4th	Bart Starr
1980		5-10-1	5th	Bart Starr
1981		8-8	3rd	Bart Starr
1982		5-3-1	3rd	Bart Starr
1983		8-8	2nd	Bart Starr
1984		8-8	2nd	Forrest Gregg
1985		8-8	2nd	Forrest Gregg
1986		4-12	4th	Forrest Gregg
1987		5-9-1	3rd	Forrest Gregg
1988		4-12	5th	Lindy Infante
1989		10-6	2nd	Lindy Infante
1990		6-10	4th	Lindy Infante
1991		4-12	4th	Lindy Infante

1 — Gene Ronzani (10 games),
Hugh Devore & Ray McLean (co-coaches) (2 games)

s Bart Starr leaned forward to take the snap, the sports world froze in place. The Green Bay Packers had the ball at the Dallas 1-yard line, with no timeouts remaining and only 16 seconds left to play in the 1967 NFL Championship Game. This was the "Ice Bowl," a war fought on the frozen Wisconsin tundra at 13 degrees below zero, and it had come down to a single play.

Dallas protected a 17-14 lead.

What Is A Packer?

The NFL is filled with teams bearing fierce nicknames: Bears, Lions, Seahawks, Rams, Vikings, Broncos, and Giants.

But what in the world is a Packer?

In the Green Bay of 1919, a packer was an employee of the Indian Packing Company. Solicited for support, the meat-packing company provided the start-up football team with jerseys and a field for practices. In exchange, Green Bay got a team called: The Packers.

1921

GREEN BAY PACKERS
Turning Points

J.E. Clair of the Acme Packing Company is granted a franchise, the Green Bay Packers join the APFA, the NFL's predecessor.

This play would decide the championship; it became a frozen moment in football lore.

Starr, who had run the quarterback sneak just once in 12 years, ran it again, following guard Jerry Kramer's block. Touchdown, Green Bay. Championship...again.

The Packers in those days were coached by the legendary Vince Lombardi, who made certain his team understood that losing was not an acceptable option.

"Winning isn't everything, it's the only thing," he said.

No obstacle was acceptable for Lombardi. Not injury. Not fatigue. Not 13 below zero.

Lombardi had an incomparable will to win; he demanded victory of himself and of those around him. He was a tough guy, a screamer, a drill sergeant. He accepted nothing less than success. Lombardi was a winner as a football coach.

He drove a good football team to greatness; in nine years in Green Bay, from 1959-1967, his Packers won six conference or division titles, five NFL championships, and two Super Bowls. The Super Bowl trophy is named after Lombardi.

After losing their first championship game under Lombardi in 1960, the Packers were told they would never be permitted to lose another. In the five championship games that followed,

THE STARR OF THE TEAM

The headlines were usually reserved for Paul Hornung and Jim Taylor, Ray Nitschke and Willie Davis - but quarterback Bart Starr was perhaps the brightest star of the Green Bay Packers who dominated pro football in the 1960s.

He was neither flamboyant nor flashy. His passing style was efficient, not gaudy. His performance left a defense in tatters, but he did it quietly.

Starr was the NFL's leading passer three times (1962, 1964, 1966), and the MVP in Super Bowls I and II. He quarterbacked the Packers to nine victories in 10 playoff games. Starr, who played in four Pro Bowls, passed for 24,718 yards and 152 touchdowns in a club-record 16-year career.

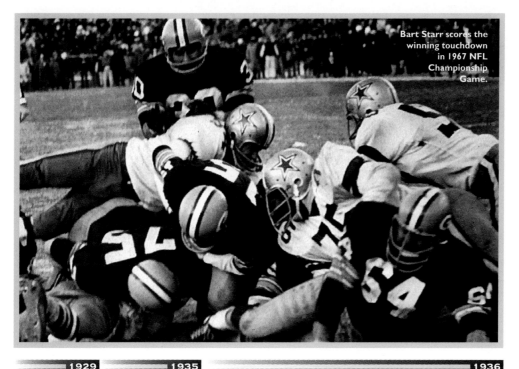

Bart Starr scores the winning touchdown in 1967 NFL Championship Game.

1929	1935		1936
Packers sign halfback John Blood (McNally), tackle Cal Hubbard, and guard Mike Michalske, all future Hall of Famers; win first NFL championship with 12-0-1 record.	Green Bay signs end Don Hutson, greatest pass receiver of pro football's early era.	 Boyd Dowler	Packers win first NFL title under a postseason playoff system, beat Boston Redskins 21-6 in championship game.

Pass Rusher Supreme

Willie Davis didn't attract much attention from pro football scouts while at Grambling College. In fact, the Cleveland Browns drafted him in 1956 on the fifteenth round. A 1960 trade sent him to Green Bay, where he played for 10 years and became one of the premier defensive ends. Davis, a tremendous pass rusher, had remarkable durability, playing in 162 consecutive games for the Packers. He played in five Pro Bowls and was inducted into the Pro Football Hall of Fame.

they were unbeaten.

Turning around a franchise that hadn't had a winning season in 11 years required every bit of Lombardi's indomitable will.

There had been another Packers coach with a similar will to win - Earl (Curly) Lambeau, who played a critical role in Green Bay's pro football history. He coached the Packers to seven first-place finishes in 29 years. Lombardi notched six in nine years. It was the combined efforts of Lambeau and Lombardi that put Green Bay on the pro football map, despite imposing odds.

The NFL is a company of giants, a league that includes the largest cities in America - New York, Los Angeles, Chicago, Philadelphia, Dallas, Houston, Detroit...and Green Bay, Wisconsin.

What is Green Bay, a city of only 90,000, doing in this company?

Little Green Bay has handled itself quite well against the big boys. In fact, there have been many years when little Green Bay was more than the big boys could handle.

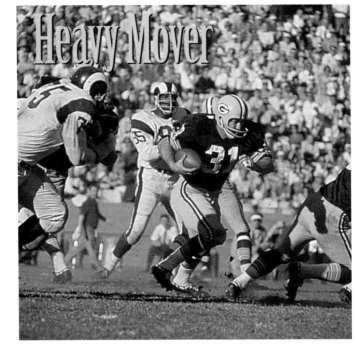

Heavy Mover

Most bulldozers are much larger, but Jim Taylor did quite nicely at 6 feet and 216 pounds. That's small for a fullback by today's standards, but no power runner was more feared than Taylor during his nine years (1958-1966) with Green Bay. He believed it was the ball carrier's role to deliver the hit rather than absorb it, and Taylor made a habit of running straight for defensive players.

A member of the Pro Football Hall of Fame, Taylor rushed for more than 1,000 yards five consecutive years (1960-64), and is the Packers' all-time leading rusher with 8,207 yards. He averaged 4.5 yards per carry in his nine-year career with Green Bay, an excellent average for a runner who gained much of his yardage between the tackles.

In A Class By Himself

There was no doubt who was the NFL's best pass receiver in the 1935-1945 era because the same man led the league in receptions eight times and in scoring five times.

Don Hutson was in a class by himself.

A 6-foot 1-inch sprinter from Alabama, Hutson had 488 receptions when he retired. The second-best total in the NFL record book at that time was 190. Hutson's best year was 1942, when he became the first receiver to exceed 1,000 yards in a season, gaining 1,211. He caught 74 passes that year, 47 more than his closest competitor. Hutson caught 17 touchdown passes in 1942, a record unbroken until 1984, when Miami's Mark Clayton caught 18.

1939
After losing title previous year 23-17 to Giants, Packers blank Giants 27-0 in NFL Championship Game.

1950
Earl (Curly) Lambeau, the only head coach the Packers have had, resigns; his career record: 212-106-21.

1956
Green Bay drafts tackle Forrest Gregg and quarterback Bart Starr, both future Hall of Famers.

Bart Starr

The Green Bay Packers have won more championships (11) than any other team in NFL history, and they are almost as old at the NFL itself, having kicked off in 1921.

One of the Packers' golden eras occurred in the early years; Green Bay had five NFL titles within an 11-year period (1929-1939).

But Green Bay also had a period of domination in the modern era; the name Packers was synonymous with football success in the 1960s, when the team won five league championships in a span of seven years.

In both the 1930s and 1960s, the key to Green Bay's success was that the Packers had an extraordinary head coach guiding the team, first Lambeau, then Lombardi. Both earned berths in the Pro Football Hall of Fame.

Mike Holmgren, who took the reins in 1992, is the eleventh head coach in Packers history. Of the previous 10, only Lambeau and Lombardi compiled winning records.

Lambeau coached the Packers from 1921-1949, and racked up a record of 212-106-21.

The Golden Boy

They called him "The Golden Boy," a Heisman Trophy winner at Notre Dame and the first pick in the 1957 pro football draft.

But Paul Hornung didn't become a star until Vince Lombardi became the Packers' coach in 1959. Then, the 220-pounder's career began to flourish.

A versatile performer who had been shuffled between quarterback and fullback during his rookie season, Hornung was permanently assigned to halfback by Lombardi.

Hornung, also the Packers' kicker, led the NFL in scoring for three consecutive seasons, beginning in 1959. It was in 1960 that he scored 176 points, a record that still stands.

A two-time Pro Bowl selection, Hornung retired after the 1966 season. He scored 760 points (62 touchdowns, 66 field goals, 190 extra points), rushed for 3,711 yards, caught passes for 1,480 yards and passed for 383 yards.

Paul Hornung runs Green Bay's famed power sweep.

1957	1958	1959
Packers get new home field, City Stadium (later renamed Lambeau Field).	Extremely strong draft brings fullback Jim Taylor, linebacker Ray Nitschke, both future Hall of Famers, plus standout guard Jerry Kramer.	Vince Lombardi becomes general manager and head coach.

Lynn Dickey

A Sharpe Performer

Sterling Sharpe, the Packers' first-round selection in 1988, quickly established himself as one of the NFL's premier wide receivers. He caught 212 passes from 1988-1990, tying Tom Fears's record for catches in the first three seasons in the league. Sharpe, Green Bay's leading receiver each of his first four seasons, posted his best numbers in 1989, when he set club records for receptions (90) and receiving yardage (1,423).

Lombardi's tenure was shorter - only nine years - but his impact on professional football was at least as profound. Lombardi's Packers had a record of 98-30-4.

Lambeau and Lombardi both are revered in Green Bay. The Packers' stadium, Lambeau Field, is named for the man who founded the team.

Without Lambeau, there might not have been a beginning for pro football in Green Bay. Along with George Calhoun, Lambeau decided in 1919 to start a football team. Lambeau worked for the Indian Packing Company, and he asked his employer to fund the team. He was given jerseys and the use of a practice field.

The opponents on those early schedules were teams from the Wisconsin and Michigan towns of Menomonee, Marinette, Sheboygan, Ispheming, and Oshkosh, and the Packers won almost effortlessly. Later, when Green Bay was given a franchise in the NFL, the opponents became challenging and victories more difficult, but Green Bay continued to win.

Lambeau brought home three championships in three years, 1929-1931, three more in

Ray Nitschke

Mr. Mean in the Middle

A vicious hitter with a nasty mean streak, Ray Nitschke was exactly the player Vince Lombardi wanted at middle linebacker. A 6-foot 3-inch 235-pounder, Nitschke was "The Enforcer" on the vaunted Green Bay defenses of the 1960s.
Nitschke, who played 15 seasons for the Packers, was named the middle linebacker on the All-Time All-Pro team selected by the Hall of Fame in 1969. He retired in 1972, and was inducted into the Pro Football Hall of Fame in 1978.

Green Bay's Deep Threat

The Packers struggled from 1981-85, four times posting 8-8 records, but there was no denying their talent at wide receiver.
James Lofton, an outstanding deep threat, enjoyed four 1,000-yard receiving years during that time. The club leader in receptions eight times in his nine-year (1978-1986) Green Bay career, Lofton finished as the Packers' all-time leader in receptions (530) and receiving yardage (9,656).

1961
Packers win first NFL championship since 1944, beat New York Giants 37-0.

John Brockington

1966
Green Bay wins fourth NFL championship of 1960s, 34-27 over Dallas, qualifies for Super Bowl I, a 35-10 victory over Kansas City.

1967
Packers win third consecutive NFL championship, beating Dallas in famed "Ice Bowl" game 21-17, defeat Oakland 33-14 in Super Bowl II.

1936, 1939, and 1944. He did it with an impressive collection of future Hall of Famers - halfback Johnny Blood (McNally), tackle Cal Hubbard, guard Mike Michalske, quarterback Arnie Herber, fullback Clarke Hinkle, halfback Tony Canadeo, and end Don Hutson.

After Lambeau left the Packers in 1949, Green Bay didn't have another winning season until Lombardi took charge in 1959. Like Lambeau, he had a wealth of Hall-of-Fame candidates in the lineup. In addition to quarterback Starr, the Lombardi Packers had fullback Jim Taylor, halfback Paul Hornung, center Jim Ringo, tackle Forrest Gregg, defensive end Willie Davis, linebacker Ray Nitschke, and defensive backs Herb Adderley and Willie Wood, each of whom is now in the Pro Football Hall of Fame.

Since Lombardi's resignation as coach after the 1967 season, the Packers have had only one first-place finish.

Lambeau and Lombardi transformed little Green Bay into David in the face of NFL Goliaths. ✐

Ball Hawk

Excellent vision normally is essential to a professional athlete, but Green Bay's Bobby Dillon became an excellent defensive back despite being blind in one eye.

Dillon was Green Bay's leader in pass interceptions seven consecutive years (1952-58), and holds the club record for interceptions in a career (52).

The Coach - Vince Lombardi

1968
Vince Lombardi resigns as head coach with record of 98-30-4.

1972
Packers win only division title in post-Lombardi era, post 10-4 record under coach Dan Devine.

Willie Wood

171

Houston OILERS

YEAR	WINS	LOSSES	TIES	RECORD	PLACE	COACH
American Football League						
1960				10-4	1st	Lou Rymkus
1961				10-3-1	1st	L. Rymkus, W. Lemm [1]
1962				11-3	1st	Frank (Pop) Ivy
1963				6-8	3rd	Frank (Pop) Ivy
1964				4-10	4th	Sammy Baugh
1965				4-10	4th	Hugh Taylor
1966				3-11	4th	Wally Lemm
1967				9-4-1	1st	Wally Lemm
1968				7-7	2nd	Wally Lemm
1969				6-6-2	2nd	Wally Lemm
National Football League						
1970				3-10-1	4th	Wally Lemm
1971				4-9-1	3rd	Ed Hughes
1972				1-13	4th	Bill Peterson
1973				1-13	4th	B. Peterson, S. Gillman [2]
1974				7-7	3rd	Sid Gillman
1975				10-4	3rd	O. A. (Bum) Phillips
1976				5-9	4th	O. A. (Bum) Phillips
1977				8-6	2nd	O. A. (Bum) Phillips
1978				10-6	2nd	O. A. (Bum) Phillips
1979				11-5	2nd	O. A. (Bum) Phillips
1980				11-5	2nd	O. A. (Bum) Phillips
1981				7-9	3rd	Ed Biles
1982				1-8	13th	Ed Biles
1983				2-14	4th	E. Biles, C. Studley [3]
1984				3-13	4th	Hugh Campbell
1985				5-11	4th	H. Campbell, J. Glanville [4]
1986				5-11	4th	Jerry Glanville
1987				9-6	2nd	Jerry Glanville
1988				10-6	3rd	Jerry Glanville
1989				9-7	2nd	Jerry Glanville
1990				9-7	2nd	Jack Pardee
1991				11-5	1st	Jack Pardee

1 — Lou Rymkus (5 games), Wally Lemm (9 games)
2 — Bill Peterson (5 games), Sid Gillman (9 games)
3 — Ed Biles (6 games), Chuck Studley (10 games)
4 — Hugh Campbell (14 games), Jerry Glanville (2 games)

They were quarterbacks that NFL teams didn't want. One was released by the Chicago Bears, his pro football career apparently over at age 32. The other was by-passed after finishing college, and had to prove himself in the Canadian Football League before NFL teams took an interest.

And, yes, they shared one other similarity. Both led the Houston Oilers in glorious chapters of their history.

First was George Blanda, the Oilers' quarterback in the initial American Football League season.

The second was Warren Moon, who signed with the Oilers after several years in Canada.

Both men lifted the Houston Oilers to championships, and that's not easy to do. Check the record. Between the time Blanda last led the Oilers to a division

A Texas Treasure

Just how seriously do they take their football heroes in Texas? Here's a clue: The Texas State Legislature has assigned only four people the designation "Texas Legend." The four - Davy Crockett, Sam Houston, Stephen F. Austin, and Earl Campbell.

1960

HOUSTON OILERS

Turning Points

Houston Oilers become one of American Football League's original teams; George Blanda comes out of retirement to lead team to 10-4 record and AFL championship.

championship - 1962 - and the time that Moon did it - 1991 - three decades elapsed. In between, a multitude of quarterbacks failed to hoist Houston to the top.

During that span, Houston finished first in its division only in 1967, and that was on the strength of a defense that gave up only 18 touchdowns the entire season. The Houston offense in 1967 consisted primarily of powerful fullback Hoyle Granger running between the tackles; the Oilers' passing game, with Pete Beathard at quarterback, averaged fewer than 100 yards per game.

Between Blanda's departure (1966) and Moon's arrival (1984), the Oilers employed a variety of quarterbacks - Jacky Lee, Don Trull, Charley Johnson, Dan Pastorini, Gifford Nielsen, Ken Stabler, Archie Manning, and Oliver Luck, among others - who were unable to produce a division winner.

That makes Blanda's and Moon's accomplishments so much more impressive.

Blanda was Houston's quarterback when the team was started in 1960. The Oilers had to

Defensive Ace

Ray Childress, a 6-foot 6-inch, 275-pound strongman, was the third player selected in the 1985 draft. He lived up to the high expectations, establishing himself as one of the NFL's premier defensive linemen in the late 1980s and early 1990s.

Quarterback George Blanda and coach Wally Lemm

A Star, By George

Only one Oilers defender was selected to the All-Time AFL Team: linebacker George Webster.

A first-round draft pick in 1967 out of Michigan State, Webster played with Houston until being traded in 1972. The hard-hitting defensive star was selected to play in three AFL All-Star Games.

1961

Despite not starting in first five games, Blanda throws 36 touchdown passes, a pro football record, and leads Oilers to second AFL championship.

Charley Hennigan

1967

Houston releases Blanda, Charley Hennigan. Defensive unit allows only 18 touchdowns, Oilers vault from last place to first in AFL Eastern Division.

1968

Astrodome becomes pro football's first domed stadium. Safety Jim Norton, last of original Oilers, retires; Houston drafts linebacker George Webster.

173

bring him out of mothballs...he had been released by the Chicago Bears after the 1958 season. Actually, he was merely getting his second wind. Blanda had spent 10 years in Chicago, but only two of those as a starting quarterback. His primary duties in Chicago were kicking field goals and extra points.

A chance to play quarterback in the American Football League interested Blanda, and he proved to be the class of the new league. Within three years he gave the Oilers 8,553 passing yards, 87 touchdown passes, 31 regular season victories, three championship game appearances, and two league titles. Blanda quarterbacked the Oilers to AFL Championship Game victories over the Chargers in 1960 and 1961. He almost made it three in a row, but the Oilers lost the 1962 title game to the Dallas Texans in overtime.

Houston's success came in spite of the fact that the Oilers were in a constant state of turmoil - three different head coaches in three seasons.

The early AFL was noted for wide-open offenses and free scoring, and Blanda epitomized the style. He threw 36 touchdown passes in 1961 - a pro football record at the time - and an

Haywood Jeffires

100
CATCH MEN

Only five receivers in NFL history have posted 100 or more receptions in a season, and two of them were Houston Oilers. Charley Hennigan caught 101 passes (1,561 yards) in 1964; Haywood Jeffires caught 100 (1,181 yards) in 1991.

The Earl of Houston

Earl Campbell certainly knew how to make an entrance. A 235-pounder with awesome power and surprising speed, he burst onto the NFL scene in 1978 by leading the league in rushing with 1,450 yards. That earned him unanimous selection as rookie of the year and most valuable player honors from UPI and The Sporting News.

Just to show he was no one-year wonder, Campbell led the NFL in rushing again in 1979 - 1,697 yards - and earned NFL most valuable player honors from AP.

And finally, just in case anybody hadn't gotten the message yet, Campbell retained the rushing title in 1980, running for 1,934 yards. Campbell is the only player besides Jim Brown to lead the NFL in rushing his first three years in the league.

Campbell played for the Oilers 6 1/2 years and finished his career with 1 1/2 years at New Orleans. He gained 9,407 yards in his eight-year NFL career, and was inducted into the Pro Football Hall of Fame in 1991, his first year of eligibility.

1971	**1975**	**1978**
Rookie quarterback Dan Pastorini wins starting job.	O.A. (Bum) Phillips becomes head coach, Oilers win 10 games, highest victory total in 13 years.	Houston drafts Earl Campbell, he wins most valuable player honors in 1978 and 1979.

Ken Burrough

incredible 42 interceptions the next year. Those 42 interceptions remain an NFL season record; he also holds the career record for interceptions (277).

Blanda used the classic dropback style, and his favorite receivers were Charley Hennigan and Bill Groman, a pair whose success was even more surprising than the recycled quarterback's. The year before they began playing for the Oilers, Groman was a student at Heidelberg University and Hennigan was a high school teacher. Groman caught 72 passes in 1960 for 1,473 yards and 12 touchdowns; Hennigan stayed with Houston as long as Blanda did - seven years - and caught 410 passes for 6,823 yards and 51 touchdowns. All were club records, and Hennigan's reception and touchdown marks stood until 1991.

Blanda was tireless - he led the AFL in pass attempts each year from 1963-65 - but the Oilers were in a downward spiral, winning only 17 games in his final four years with the team.

In 1967, Blanda went to Oakland to begin a nine-year stint as a miracle worker.

Blanda had only modest success before coming to Houston - he led the NFL with 169 completions in 1953 - but Warren Moon arrived in Texas amid fanfare and high expectations.

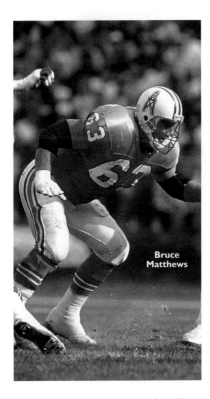

Bruce Matthews

THE ROYAL GUARDS

Bruce Matthews and Mike Munchak were considered the NFL's premier guard tandem in the late 1980s. That changed in 1991, when Matthews was moved to center. Then they became known as perhaps the most powerful center-guard combination in the league. Munchak was the eighth player chosen in the 1982 draft; Matthews was selected ninth in 1983.

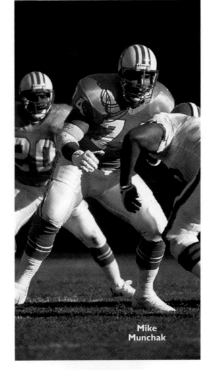

Mike Munchak

65

No member of the Oilers played as long as Elvin Bethea - 210 games in 16 years - and few played as well. A terrific pass rusher from his defensive end position, Bethea played in eight Pro Bowls.
At the end of his Oilers career (1968-1983), Bethea was honored by having his number 65 retired.

1980

In all-out attempt to win title, Bum Phillips trades for veteran quarterback Ken Stabler; Oilers lose in first round of playoffs and Phillips is fired.

Ernest Givins

1983

Defensive end Elvin Bethea retires after outstanding 16-year career.

1984

Warren Moon leaves Canadian Football League, becomes Oilers quarterback.

Before joining the Oilers, Moon had an exceptional career with the Edmonton Eskimos of the Canadian Football League. In six seasons he passed for 21,228 yards and 144 touchdowns, as Edmonton won the league championship five times. Moon was the CFL's player of the year in 1983.

Moon passed for more than 10,500 yards in his last two seasons in Canada, and there were high hopes in Houston that he could be the catalyst to an Oilers turnaround.

He was, although not immediately, for it was a woeful team he joined (3-22 the two years before his arrival). But after a 3-13 season, followed by two 5-11 years, Moon's Oilers went 9-6 in 1987, the team's first winning season in seven years. That began a string of successful seasons for Houston and produced an AFC Central Division championship in 1991, the Oilers' first division title in 24 years.

Moon not only made the Oilers successful, but he also made them entertaining. Since 1990, Houston's offensive scheme has been the Run-and-Shoot, with an emphasis on quarter-

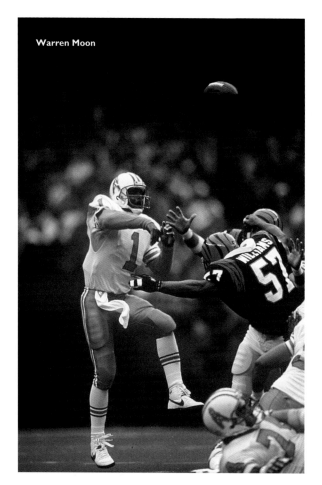

Warren Moon

A Day to Remember

Billy Cannon was the subject of a celebrated tug of war between the Oilers and Los Angeles Rams in 1959, when the NFL and AFL were battling over star players.

Cannon signed with both teams, but was awarded to the Oilers in a court fight. The LSU graduate had the game of a lifetime on December 10, 1961, against the New York Titans at the Polo Grounds, when he scored five touchdowns and accounted for 331 yards from scrimmage. The running back carried 25 times for 216 yards and caught five passes for 115 yards.

Cannon led the Oilers in rushing their first two years, but injuries reduced his effectiveness in 1962 and 1963. He was traded to the Raiders after the 1963 season.

Jerry Glanville

1985

Defensive coordinator Jerry Glanville is promoted to head coach two games before end of season.

1987

Oilers qualify for playoffs for first time since 1980.

back rollouts and quick passes.

The Oilers supplied Moon with a collection of nimble wide receivers who could quickly find the open spots in opposing defenses. Ernest Givins, Drew Hill, and Haywood Jeffires were excellent targets, and in 1991 they combined for 260 catches. Jeffires had 100, Hill 90, and Givins 70.

The Run-and-Shoot was ideal for Moon, and it helped make stars of his receiver corps. Hill, for example, averaged 63 receptions per year in his first five seasons in Houston. Then the Oilers switched to the Run-and-Shoot in 1990, and Hill caught 74 and 90 passes in the next two years. Hill signed with the Falcons in 1992, leaving Houston after catching a club-record 480 passes.

No NFL quarterback had ever thrown as often (655 attempts) as Moon did in 1991. And no NFL quarterback had ever completed so many passes (404) in a season. Moon connected on 61.7 percent of his throws - not bad for an "old man" of 35. ✐

What A Bum!

The Houston Oilers employed 14 head coaches from 1960-1992, and the man with the greatest longevity also was the most colorful...O.A. (Bum) Phillips, who served six seasons.

Phillips coached the Oilers during the Earl Campbell era, but it was the Oilers' misfortune to be in the same division as the Pittsburgh Steelers, who were en route to four Super Bowl titles in a six-year span.

After four consecutive second-place finishes, Phillips was released on December 31, 1980, after the team had been eliminated from the playoffs after posting an 11-5 regular season record. His record: 59-38-0. After Phillips was dismissed, Houston did not have a winning record again for seven years.

Houston's IRON MAN

Robert Brazile, who holds the Houston record for consecutive starts (147), was one of the NFL's most respected linebackers during his career (1975-1984).

A ferocious hitter with outstanding speed, Brazile earned all-pro honors in only his second year in the league and was named to the Pro Bowl squad seven times.

White Shoes

Billy (White Shoes) Johnson drew attention to himself with a wobbly-legged dance in the end zone, igniting a wave of showboating that eventually resulted in league restrictions.

Johnson would have been noticed even without the theatrics. He was a fine kick returner. In 1974, he tied the NFL record for touchdowns on kick returns - one on a kickoff and three on punt returns.

1990
Jack Pardee becomes Houston's head coach.

1991
Oilers win first division championship since 1967.

Indianapolis COLTS

YEAR ■ WINS □ LOSSES ■ TIES	RECORD	PLACE	COACH
Baltimore Colts			
All-America Football Conference			
1947	2-11-1	4th	Cecil Isbell
1948	7-7	1st	Cecil Isbell
1949	1-11	7th	C. Isbell, Walt Driskill [1]
National Football League			
1950	1-11	7th	Clem Crowe
1951 Franchise Dissolved			
1953	3-9	5th	Keith Molesworth
1954	3-9	6th	Weeb Ewbank
1955	5-6-1	4th	Weeb Ewbank
1956	5-7	4th	Weeb Ewbank
1957	7-5	3rd	Weeb Ewbank
1958	9-3	1st	Weeb Ewbank
1959	9-3	1st	Weeb Ewbank
1960	6-6	4th	Weeb Ewbank
1961	8-6	3rd	Weeb Ewbank
1962	7-7	4th	Weeb Ewbank
1963	8-6	3rd	Don Shula
1964	12-2	1st	Don Shula
1965	10-3-1	2nd	Don Shula
1966	9-5	2nd	Don Shula
1967	11-1-2	2nd	Don Shula
1968	13-1	1st	Don Shula
1969	8-5-1	2nd	Don Shula
1970	11-2-1	1st	Don McCafferty
1971	10-4	2nd	Don McCafferty
1972	5-9	3rd	McCafferty, Sandusky [2]
1973	4-10	4th	Howard Schnellenberger
1974	2-12	5th	Schnellenberger, Thomas [3]
1975	10-4	1st	Ted Marchibroda
1976	11-3	1st	Ted Marchibroda
1977	10-4	1st	Ted Marchibroda
1978	5-11	5th	Ted Marchibroda
1979	5-11	5th	Ted Marchibroda
1980	7-9	4th	Mike McCormack
1981	2-14	4th	Mike McCormack
1982	0-8-1	14th	Frank Kush
1983	7-9	4th	Frank Kush
Indianapolis Colts			
1984	4-12	4th	F. Kush, H. Hunter [4]
1985	5-11	4th	Rod Dowhower
1986	3-13	5th	R. Dowhower, R. Meyer [5]
1987	9-6	1st	Ron Meyer
1988	9-7	2nd	Ron Meyer
1989	8-8	2nd	Ron Meyer
1990	7-9	3rd	Ron Meyer
1991	1-15	5th	R. Meyer, R. Venturi [6]

1 — Cecil Isbell (4 games), Walt Driskill (8 games)
2 — Don McCafferty (5 games), John Sandusky (9 games)
3 — Howard Schnellenberger (3 games), Joe Thomas (11 games)
4 — Frank Kush (15 games), Hal Hunter (1 game)
5 — Rod Dowhower (13 games), Ron Meyer (3 games)
6 — Ron Meyer (5 games), Rick Venturi (11 games)

After the Baltimore Colts defeated the New York Giants in the NFL Championship Game on December 28, 1958, *Sports Illustrated* headlined its coverage, "The Best Football Game Ever Played."

Since then, the contest has been immortalized as, "The Greatest Game Ever Played."

But was it, really?

Does the game deserve its place in history or, has legend surpassed fact?

A Moving Experience

The Colts came to life in 1947, when the bankrupt Miami Seahawks franchise of the All-America Football Conference was transferred to Baltimore and renamed.

When the AAFC disbanded, the club was absorbed into the National Football League in 1950, but the franchise folded after only one season.

In 1953, the Dallas Texans relocated to Baltimore and were renamed the Colts. The team played in Baltimore until owner Robert Irsay shifted the franchise to Indianapolis in 1984.

1947

INDIANAPOLIS COLTS
Turning Points

Miami Seahawks of All-America Football Conference move to Baltimore, are renamed Colts.

In the more than three decades that have passed, there have been better games. Some have been better played, others have been equally suspenseful.

But no game was more important to the growth and popularity of the National Football League.

Pro football was played in only 12 cities in 1958, and average attendance was 41,000. The sport was not the national phenomenon it is today, with average attendance exceeding 61,000 and games telecast by four national networks featuring 28 NFL teams across the country.

The huge popularity of the game today can be traced to that last Sunday in December, 1958.

It was not the first nationally televised league championship game. The Dumont network began televising NFL title games coast-to-coast in 1951. But it was the first championship game decided in "sudden death" overtime.

It was a matchup of two colorful teams. The Giants were known for their intimidating defense, and the Colts were armed with quarterback Johnny Unitas, who had led the league in passing for two years.

Alan Ameche scores the winning touchdown in "The Greatest Game Ever Played"

Lydell Mitchell

The Workhorse

The Colts have had some celebrated running backs - Alan Ameche, Lenny Moore, Tom Matte, and Eric Dickerson - but none produced as many rushing yards for the club as Lydell Mitchell.

A second-round pick in 1972 out of Penn State, where he was a backfield mate of Franco Harris, Mitchell was the Colts' workhorse for six years. He was the team leader in both rushing yardage and pass receptions four consecutive years (1974-77). The Colts' all-time leading rusher had 5,487 yards, and caught 298 passes for 2,523 yards.

Everything Was Wrong Except the Results

He wasn't big, strong, or fast. His eyes were bad and one leg was shorter than the other. He had a bad back. And despite all that, Raymond Berry earned a place in the Pro Football Hall of Fame.

One of the amazing success stories in pro football history, Berry was a twentieth-round draft pick in 1955. Combining great hands with a penchant for hard work, he overcame his physical limitations and became an extraordinary pass receiver. He ran routes with precision and caught virtually every ball within reach.

Berry's 631 receptions were an NFL record when he retired in 1967. He gained 9,275 yards and scored 48 touchdowns in his 13-year career (1955-1967).

1950	1953	1954	1956
After 1-11 season, Colts franchise folded.	Dallas Texans club moves to Baltimore, is renamed Colts.	Weeb Ewbank becomes head coach.	Colts draft running back Lenny Moore, sign free-agent quarterback Johnny Unitas.

Mike Curtis

179

The underdog Colts jumped to a 14-3 lead and threatened to blow the game open when the vaunted Giants defense, led by Andy Robustelli, Roosevelt Grier, Jim Katcavage, and Sam Huff, stopped Baltimore with a goal-line stand.

Quarterback Charlie Conerly rallied the Giants to a pair of second-half touchdowns and a 17-14 lead, and New York seemed to have the game wrapped up when Baltimore got the ball on its 14-yard line with two minutes to go.

Primarily on the strength of passes from Unitas to Raymond Berry, the Colts drove to the New York 13 with 30 seconds remaining, setting up a 20-yard Steve Myrha field goal that tied the game 17-17 and forced an overtime.

On Baltimore's first possession of overtime, Unitas again dissected the New York defense and drove the Colts 80 yards. Alan Ameche delivered the winning score with a 1-yard run after 8 minutes 15 seconds of overtime.

The game details were dramatic, but equally important to the future of pro football were the colorful players, especially Unitas.

His was the ideal story to captivate a national audience.

Gino Marchetti wasn't really a giant; he merely played like one. The prototype pass rusher, Marchetti was the best of his time. The Pro Football Hall of Fame Selection Committee in 1969 honored Marchetti as the best defensive end in the NFL's first 50 years. Marchetti played for the Colts 1953-1964, then came out of retirement to play again in 1966. The 6-foot 4-inch, 245-pounder played in 10 Pro Bowls in 11 years, missing only the 1958 game, when he was sidelined with a broken leg.

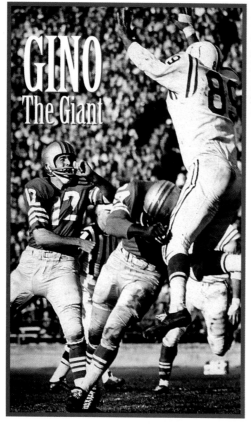

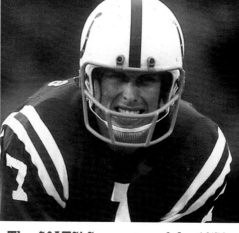

The COLTS' Superstar of the 1970s

Bert Jones had the misfortune of following in the footsteps of Johnny Unitas, perhaps the greatest quarterback in NFL history. Jones was drafted in 1973, the year Unitas was traded, and Colts fans made the inevitable comparisons throughout his career.

Actually, Jones was one of the NFL's brightest stars in the 1970s. Miami coach Don Shula described him as "the best there is around," when Jones was leader of Colts teams that won three consecutive AFC East titles from 1975-77.

The LSU product played for the Colts nine years, several of those cut short by a recurring shoulder problem. He passed for more than 3,000 yards in three seasons and is second only to Unitas in club records with 1,382 completions, 17,663 yards passing and 122 touchdown passes.

Jones played in the 1977 Pro Bowl; his father, Dub, a halfback for the Cleveland Browns, played in the 1952 Pro Bowl.

◢1958	◢1959	◢1963	◢1967
Colts win Western Conference title with 9-3 record, beat New York Giants 23-17 in overtime to win NFL championship.	Another 9-3 record, another victory (31-16) over Giants in NFL Championship Game.	Don Shula becomes head coach.	Despite 11-1-2 record, Colts fail to qualify for Conference championship game.

Unitas was a Horatio Alger - the guy who comes from nowhere to be the hero. Cut by the Pittsburgh Steelers in 1955, he had refused to give up his dream, playing a season for the semipro Bloomfield Rams at $6 per game. He could make time stand still as he rallied his team to last-minute, come-from-behind victories. He was fearless in the face of a pass rush. The tougher the situation, the better he played.

Unitas, nicknamed "The Man with the Golden Arm," was the right hero, in the right place, at the right time.

That championship game drew a larger television audience than any previous sports event, and Unitas mesmerized the country with a dramatic performance in a pressure-packed game.

Others - Roger Staubach, Joe Montana, John Elway - would later become masters of last minute heroics. But Unitas did it first, and he did it when the country was still discovering professional football.

Unitas led the NFL in touchdown passes in 1957, then again for the next three years. He led the league in passing yardage four times, and set the NFL record that may be the most difficult to break - touchdown passes in 47 consecutive games.

THE
Sack Pack

After winning only six games in two years, the Colts came roaring back as contenders in 1975, and a key factor in the resurgence was the work of The Sack Pack. Because the defensive line had been a weakness, the Colts used four premium picks in the 1973 and 1974 drafts to select ends Fred Cook and John Dutton, and tackles Mike Barnes and Joe Ehrmann. Dutton and Ehrmann were first-round picks; Barnes and Cook were second-rounders.

The Sack Pack collected a club-record 59 sacks in 1975 and helped lead Baltimore to three consecutive division titles.

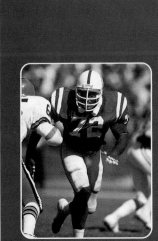

Fred Cook

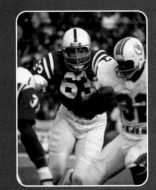

Mike Barnes

Joe Ehrmann

John Dutton

The Bodyguard

It was Jim Parker's job to ensure that no harm befell Johnny Unitas. The 275-pound tackle carried out his responsibilities splendidly - so well, in fact, that in 1973 he became the first player inducted into the Pro Football Hall of Fame based strictly on his performance as an offensive lineman.

1969	1970	1972
Colts stunned 16-7 by Jets in Super Bowl III.	Don Shula resigns, Don McCafferty becomes head coach; Colts post 11-2-1 regular-season record, win Super Bowl V 16-13.	Robert Irsay acquires franchise from Carroll Rosenbloom in trade for Los Angeles Rams; Joe Thomas becomes general manager.

Ted
Marchibroda

One In Ten

*Only one of the 10
head coaches the
Colts employed
between mid-1972
and 1991 had a
winning record. He
was Ted
Marchibroda, who
produced a 41-36
record and three
AFC East cham-
pionships from
1975-79.
Marchibroda's
1975 Colts were the
first NFL team to go
from last place in
one season to the
division cham-
pionship the next
year.
He returned to
the Colts in 1992,
after a 12-year
absence, to take
over a team that had
been 1-15 the
previous season.*

A clever play caller and daring passer with excellent receivers, Unitas became a legendary figure. The cool confident look, the out-of-date crewcut, and the black high-top shoes became widely recognized Unitas trademarks.

When he retired after the 1973 season, Unitas held NFL records for pass attempts (5,186), completions (2,830), touchdown passes (290), passing yardage (40,239), and 300-yard games (26).

He established himself as the passer against whom all others would be compared.

Unitas was the central figure in the 1958 championship game, but six other participants for the Colts would later join him in the Pro Football Hall of Fame - Berry, flanker Lenny Moore, offensive tackle Jim Parker, defensive linemen Gino Marchetti and Art Donovan, and coach Weeb Ewbank.

The Giants had their own squad of future Hall of Famers, including offensive tackle Roosevelt Brown, running back Frank Gifford, linebacker Sam Huff, and safety Emlen Tunnell.

The game had heroes, drama, tension, a last-minute rally, a sudden death championship - everything a Hollywood script writer would have included.

Perhaps it was the greatest game ever played. Perhaps not. But it surely was the most important pro football game ever played.

Johnny Unitas

1973

*Johnny Unitas is traded
to San Diego, Bert Jones
is drafted.*

1975

*Ted Marchibroda
becomes head coach,
Colts become first team
in NFL history to go from
last place to division
championship in one
year.*

Roger
Carr

1983

*Colts draft quarterback
John Elway, trade him to
Denver.*

Weeb
Ewbank

The title in 1958 was the first of several great chapters in the Colts' success story. They repeated as NFL champions in 1959, beating the Giants 31-16 in the title game.

The Colts won the NFL championship again in 1968 and took a 15-1 record into Super Bowl III, where they were upset by the Joe Namath-led New York Jets 16-7. But two years later the Colts were back, this time taking the championship with a 16-13 victory over Dallas in Super Bowl V.

Age and injuries took a toll on the Colts, but Ted Marchibroda engineered one of the great turnarounds in league history in 1975. Taking over as coach after a 2-14 record, he led the Colts to the AFC Eastern Division title, the first of three consecutive division championships.

Those Colts teams were quarterbacked by Bert Jones, an exciting strong-armed passer, and an aggressive defensive line nicknamed "The Sack Pack" (Mike Barnes, Fred Cook, John Dutton, and Joe Ehrmann).

After winning the 1979 division title, the Colts suffered a series of losing seasons. The franchise moved to Indianapolis in 1984, and in 1987 won another division title when a midseason trade for running back Eric Dickerson sparked coach Ron Meyer's team to a first-place finish. ✐

The Brain Trust

Has any team ever had better coaches, back-to-back, than Weeb Ewbank and Don Shula? Ewbank is one of only a dozen coaches enshrined in the Pro Football Hall of Fame. Shula is sure to join him after he retires.

Ewbank coached Baltimore from 1954-1962, leading the Colts to NFL championships in 1958 and 1959. Shula coached the Colts for the next seven years, directing them to a conference championship in 1964 and the NFL championship in 1968, after which they lost Super Bowl III to the New York Jets.

The Jets were coached by Ewbank. Shula moved to Miami in 1970, where he enjoyed four more Super Bowl appearances and two victories of his own.

The Man Could Do It All

There have been better pass receivers and better runners, but no one combined the two skills as well as Lenny Moore. The only man in pro football who gained more than 5,000 yards rushing and pass receiving, Moore played both running back and flanker during his 12 years with the Colts (1956-1967). His 6,039 receiving yards are second only to Raymond Berry in Colts records; his 5,174 rushing yards put him behind only Lydell Mitchell.

Lenny Moore

MR. TIGHT END

When John Mackey entered the Pro Football Hall of Fame in 1992, he became only the second tight end to be inducted. Mike Ditka, who played for Chicago, Philadelphia, and Dallas, is the other.

Mackey was an outstanding athlete, a 6-foot 3-inch, 225-pound powerhouse who resembled a runaway train after making receptions. Mackey played for the Colts from 1963-1971, catching 320 passes for an average of 16 yards per reception.

1984
Franchise is moved to Indianapolis.

1987
Colts trade for running back Eric Dickerson.

Jeff George

1992
Ted Marchibroda, last coach to lead Colts into playoffs (1975-77), returns as head coach.

YEAR	WINS	LOSSES	TIES	RECORD	PLACE	COACH
Dallas Texans						
American Football League						
1960				8-6	2nd	Hank Stram
1961				6-8	2nd	Hank Stram
1962				11-3	1st	Hank Stram
Kansas City Chiefs						
1963				5-7-2	3rd	Hank Stram
1964				7-7	2nd	Hank Stram
1965				7-5-2	3rd	Hank Stram
1966				11-2-1	1st	Hank Stram
1967				9-5	2nd	Hank Stram
1968				12-2	2nd	Hank Stram
1969				11-3	2nd	Hank Stram
National Football League						
1970				7-5-2	2nd	Hank Stram
1971				10-3-1	1st	Hank Stram
1972				8-6	2nd	Hank Stram
1973				7-5-2	3rd	Hank Stram
1974				5-9	3rd	Hank Stram
1975				5-9	3rd	Paul Wiggin
1976				5-9	4th	Paul Wiggin
1977				2-12	5th	P. Wiggin, T. Bettis [1]
1978				4-12	5th	Marv Levy
1979				7-9	5th	Marv Levy
1980				8-8	3rd	Marv Levy
1981				9-7	3rd	Marv Levy
1982				3-6	11th	Marv Levy
1983				6-10	5th	John Mackovic
1984				8-8	4th	John Mackovic
1985				6-10	5th	John Mackovic
1986				10-6	2nd	John Mackovic
1987				4-11	5th	Frank Gansz
1988				4-11-1	5th	Frank Gansz
1989				8-7-1	2nd	Marty Schottenheimer
1990				11-5	2nd	Marty Schottenheimer
1991				10-6	2nd	Marty Schottenheimer

[1] Paul Wiggin (7 games), Tom Bettis (7 games)

I t isn't difficult to start a sports league. The hard part is making it successful. Sports history books are filled with names of failed leagues, especially in professional football.

But Lamar Hunt provided the exception. Frustrated in efforts to buy a National Football League franchise, in 1959 Hunt founded a league of his own - the American Football League - and awarded a franchise to himself. He was 27 years old at the time.

More than three decades later, Lamar Hunt still owns that franchise - the Kansas City Chiefs - and the American Football League he started has been absorbed into the NFL.

Hunt was a wunderkind in the sports business world; not surprisingly, his team was one of the best in the AFL's 10-year existence. The president of the AFL, he was a

A Well-Chosen Name

The franchise originally was named the Dallas Texans, but when owner Lamar Hunt decided to move it to Kansas City, he obviously needed a new nickname.

Kansas City Mayor H. Roe Bartle was instrumental in selling Hunt on the virtues of Kansas City, promising to increase the seating capacity of Municipal Stadium and to triple season-ticket sales for the team.

In appreciation, Hunt gave his team a name similar to the nickname enjoyed by the mayor - "Chief."

1959

KANSAS CITY CHIEFS

Turning Points

Lamar Hunt organizes American Football League, acquires franchise in Dallas.

central figure in negotiations to effect the merger; his contribution to football was recognized when he was inducted into the Pro Football Hall of Fame in 1972.

Life was a struggle in the AFL's early days, and Hunt's team exemplified the troubles. He established his team in Dallas, his hometown, and named it the Dallas Texans. But the NFL's Cowboys also called Dallas home, and the city wasn't big enough to support both teams. After losing money, Hunt moved his team to Kansas City in 1963 and changed the nickname to Chiefs.

In addition to battling for fans, the AFL and NFL also fought for players. Hunt won a few and lost a few. He lost when both the Cowboys and Texans wanted quarterback Don Meredith from Southern Methodist University in Dallas in 1960. He lost to the Cowboys again the next year in a fight to get defensive tackle Bob Lilly from nearby Texas Christian. And he lost to the Chicago Bears in 1965 when he made his first draft pick running back Gale Sayers of Kansas. Both Lilly and Sayers went on to Hall of Fame careers in the NFL.

Otis Taylor

KC Catchers

Otis Taylor was among the elite pass receivers during his 11 years with the Chiefs (1965-1975), catching 410 passes for a club-record 7,306 yards and 57 touchdowns.

The year after Taylor retired, a new pass catching ace arrived - Henry Marshall. Marshall retired in 1987, surpassing one of Taylor's marks with a club-record 416 catches.

Hank Stram
Lamar Hunt

Fred Arbanas

1960	**1961**	**1962**
Dallas Texans begin play; Hank Stram is head coach.	Rich draft brings E.J. Holub, Jim Tyrer, Jerry Mays, and Fred Arbanas.	Texans sign Len Dawson, win AFL championship.

185

But there were victories, too. Signing Texas Tech linebacker E.J. Holub was a coup in 1961, and running back Mike Garrett of Southern California was a highly sought prize in the 1966 draft. Both Holub and Garrett are in the Chiefs' Hall of Fame.

While Hunt had to fight for talent to stock his roster, he had no problem finding the right coach. Hank Stram, who had been an assistant coach at the University of Miami, worked wonders with the team. The Chiefs won three league championships in 10 years, and no AFL team could match Kansas City's regular-season record of 87-48-5 in the decade.

Stram, a master of organization, took a scientific approach to football, an approach that required just the right quarterback. Stram found his man in Len Dawson, who had been a bench warmer at Pittsburgh and Cleveland in the NFL, attempting only 45 passes in five seasons. Dawson had been a star at Purdue when Stram was an assistant coach there, and Stram believed that Dawson simply hadn't found

SUNDAY BEST

In addition to being the only Kansas City Chiefs runner to lead the NFL in rushing, Christian Okoye has one of the most colorful nicknames: "The Nigerian Nightmare." The Nigerian-born 260-pounder was a second-round draft choice from Azusa Pacific in 1987 and immediately became the key man in the Chiefs' ground game. Okoye in Nigerian means "Sunday." Sunday's best, indeed.

Jan Stenerud

Fancy Footwork

Two of the most productive kickers in the history of pro football have played for the Kansas City Chiefs.

Jan Stenerud, the only kicking specialist voted into the Pro Football Hall of Fame, spent the first 13 of his 19 NFL seasons with Kansas City. Stenerud, pro football's second all-time scorer (1,699 points) behind only George Blanda, kicked 279 of his career 373 field goals for the Chiefs.

Stenerud was replaced in 1980 by Nick Lowery, who continued the tradition of spectacular kicking for Kansas City. Lowery topped the 100-point mark for an NFL-record ninth time in 1991. Through the 1991 season, Lowery had 284 field goals and 1,262 points.

1963

Franchise moves to Kansas City, is renamed Chiefs; drafts Bobby Bell, Ed Budde, and Buck Buchanan, all long-time superstars.

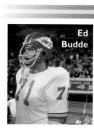

Ed Budde

1966

Chiefs win bidding war for Mike Garrett, who becomes mainstay of offense.

1967

Chiefs lose to Packers 35-10 in Super Bowl I.

the right team or the right opportunity. He was right. A pinpoint passer, Dawson would lead the AFL in completion percentage seven times.

The Dallas Texans were 14-14 with Cotton Davidson as their quarterback in 1960 and 1961. Dawson arrived the next season and immediately took Dallas to an 11-3 record and the AFL championship. Dawson led the AFL in passing in 1962 and was *The Sporting News* AFL player of the year.

The team had only two losing seasons in the 13 years that Stram and Dawson worked together. One of those, in 1963, provided a real oddity - the Chiefs outscored their opponents by 84 points, but had a record of 5-7-2. When Stram's Chiefs were good that year, they were very good indeed, winning by margins of 52, 21, 31, 32, and 48 points.

Not surprisingly - they were the most successful team in AFL history - the Chiefs emerged as AFL champions in 1966 and represented their league in the first AFL-NFL Championship Game, later known as Super Bowl I. Vince Lombardi's powerhouse Green Bay Packers

Len Dawson Hank Stram

The First Infantryman

Fans of the Dallas Texans and early Kansas City Chiefs thrilled to the work of Abner Haynes, the team's leading rusher four of its first five years.

Haynes was the AFL's leading ground gainer in its first season (1960), when he gained 875 yards. He was the main man in the Texans' attack, leading the team both in rushing and pass receptions (55 catches for 576 yards).

1970
Chiefs defeat Vikings 23-7 in Super Bowl IV.

1971
Chiefs, Dolphins play in NFL's longest game, Chiefs lose 27-24 after 82 minutes, 40 seconds.

1972
Team gets a new home: Arrowhead Stadium.

Bobby Bell

The Longest Game (At The Time)

When the Dallas Texans and Houston Oilers played for the AFL championship on December 23, 1962, it proved to be more than a normal championship game...much more. Neither quarterback - the Texans' Len Dawson nor the Oilers' George Blanda - could mount any great offensive attack, and at the end of the fourth quarter, the teams were tied 17-17. After a 15-minute overtime, the score remained 17-17. Finally, in the sixth period, rookie kicker Tommy Brooker connected on a 25-yard field goal to give Dallas a 20-17 victory. The winning points came 77 minutes, 54 seconds after the opening kickoff. At the time, it was pro football's longest game.

clobbered the AFL champs 35-10, but the Stram-Dawson team returned three years later to beat the Vikings 23-7 in Super Bowl IV. Dawson was the MVP in that game.

Kansas City's high-powered offense also featured standout running backs Abner Haynes, Ed Podolak, and Mike Garrett, and receivers Otis Taylor and Chris Burford. Taylor and Burford were dangerous deep threats; Taylor caught 57 touchdown passes, Burford 55. Garrett and Podolak were central to the Chiefs' success on offense. Stram emphasized a ball-control passing game, and the two running backs were excellent receivers. Podolak led Kansas City in rushing four years and in pass receptions three times. Garrett was the leading receiver twice and the leading rusher three times.

Dawson and kicker Jan Stenerud were the only players from the offensive unit who were selected to the Pro Football Hall of Fame. Three of the Chiefs' defensive players - linebackers Bobby Bell and Willie Lanier, and tackle Buck Buchanan - were also enshrined. That trio, along with end Jerry Mays, tackle Curley Culp, linebacker Jim Lynch, and backs Johnny

Deron Cherry

A History of Excellence

The Kansas City Chiefs have had a rich history of terrific talent at defensive back, a legacy started in 1960 by Johnny Robinson, who intercepted 57 passes in his 12-year career. The only Chiefs player with more interceptions was Emmitt Thomas, who picked off 58 between 1966-1978. And yet, Kansas City's best defensive back may have been Deron Cherry, a fixture on Pro Bowl teams throughout the 1980s. Cherry, who retired after the 1991 season, intercepted 50 passes. Other premier Chiefs defensive backs selected to play in the Pro Bowl have been Thomas, Albert Lewis, Kevin Ross, Lloyd Burruss, Gary Green, and Gary Barbaro.

Record Breaker

No one in pro football paid much attention to Stephone Paige when he graduated from Fresno State in 1983. But Kansas City gave the 6-foot, 2-inch free agent a tryout, and he blossomed into an excellent wide receiver.

Paige's best day came in 1985, when he gained 309 yards on 8 receptions, breaking an NFL record for reception yardage that had stood for 40 years.

Paige's record was erased four years later by Willie Anderson of the Rams, who totalled 336 reception yards in a game.

Buck Buchanan All-time great at defensive tackle

1974

Hank Stram is replaced despite only two losing seasons in 15 years.

1975

Len Dawson retires.

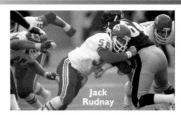

Jack Rudnay

Robinson and Emmitt Thomas, gave Stram's Chiefs one of the league's best defenses.

Stram coached the Texans/Chiefs for 15 years (1960-1974) and had only his second losing season in 1974, when the Chiefs stumbled to 5-9. Replaced by Paul Wiggin in 1975, Stram left with an overall record of 129-79-10.

Chiefs' fans who had become accustomed to success learned that winning wasn't as easy as Stram had made it seem. In the club's first 15 years, it had only two losing seasons. In the next 15 years, it had only three winning seasons.

The coaches who followed - Paul Wiggin, Tom Bettis, Marv Levy, John Mackovic, and Frank Gansz - each left with a losing record. None of Stram's successors managed back-to-back winning seasons until Marty Schottenheimer took over in 1989.

In his first three seasons, Schottenheimer directed the Chiefs to seasons of 8-7-1, 11-5, and 10-6, securing back-to-back playoff berths (1990-91) for the first time since 1968-69. ⊘

The Longest Game (Part II)

When the record for pro football's longest game was rewritten, the Chiefs were involved...again.

On Christmas Day (and night), 1971, the Chiefs and Miami Dolphins battled in a marathon in an AFC Divisional Playoff Game.

The score was tied 10-10 at halftime, 17-17 after three periods, and 24-24 at the end of the fourth quarter. Neither team scored in a 15-minute overtime, forcing the second overtime. Miami kicker Garo Yepremian decided the issue with a 37-yard field goal 82 minutes and 40 seconds after it had begun.

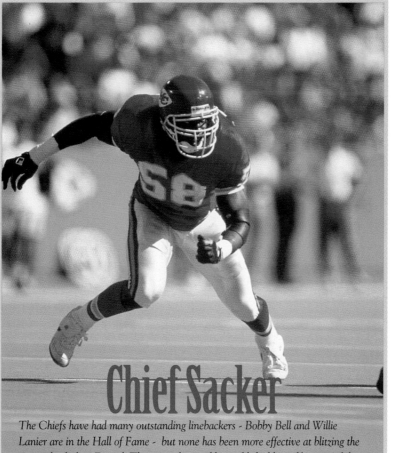

Chief Sacker

The Chiefs have had many outstanding linebackers - Bobby Bell and Willie Lanier are in the Hall of Fame - but none has been more effective at blitzing the quarterback than Derrick Thomas, who quickly established himself as one of the most feared pass rushers in the NFL.

A first round draft choice in 1989, Thomas racked up 43 1/2 sacks in his first three seasons, including a club-record 20 in 1990. He set an NFL single game record with seven sacks against Seattle in 1990.

1986

After getting first playoff berth in 15 years, Chiefs fire coach John Mackovic.

Marty Schottenheimer

1989

Marty Schottenheimer becomes head coach.

YEAR	■ WINS □ LOSSES □ TIES	RECORD	PLACE	COACH
Oakland Raiders				
American Football League				
1960		6-8	3rd	Eddie Erdelatz
1961		2-12	4th	E. Erdelatz, M. Feldman [1]
1962		1-13	4th	M. Feldman, R. Conkright [2]
1963		10-4	2nd	Al Davis
1964		5-7-2	3rd	Al Davis
1965		8-5-1	2nd	Al Davis
1966		8-5-1	2nd	John Rauch
1967		13-1	1st	John Rauch
1968		12-2	1st	John Rauch
1969		12-1-1	1st	John Madden
National Football League				
1970		8-4-2	1st	John Madden
1971		8-4-2	2nd	John Madden
1972		10-3-1	1st	John Madden
1973		9-4-1	1st	John Madden
1974		12-2	1st	John Madden
1975		11-3	1st	John Madden
1976		13-1	1st	John Madden
1977		11-3	2nd	John Madden
1978		9-7	2nd	John Madden
1979		9-7	4th	Tom Flores
1980		11-5	2nd	Tom Flores
1981		7-9	4th	Tom Flores
Los Angeles Raiders				
1982		8-1	1st	Tom Flores
1983		12-4	1st	Tom Flores
1984		11-5	3rd	Tom Flores
1985		12-4	1st	Tom Flores
1986		8-8	4th	Tom Flores
1987		5-10	4th	Tom Flores
1988		7-9	3rd	Mike Shanahan
1989		8-8	3rd	M. Shanahan, A. Shell [3]
1990		12-4	1st	Art Shell
1991		9-7	3rd	Art Shell

1 Eddie Erdelatz (2 games), Marty Feldman (12 games)
2 Marty Feldman (5 games), Red Conkright (9 games)
3 Mike Shanahan (4 games), Art Shell (12 games)

They have a reputation for being the bad boys of the NFL, tough guys in silver and black who intimidate opponents and win championships in the process.

But a closer look reveals that the Los Angeles Raiders may not be as bad as their reputation suggests.

"We have an image of being renegades and real bad guys," Tom Flores said in 1981, when he coached the Raiders to Super Bowl XV. "We wear black and that is associated with villains. But we're really not that bad. These players are pretty nice guys once you get to know them."

The Raiders have carried the "bad boy" tag for years, and they have had several players who fit the image. But the image probably has had little to do with the team's success.

"Blocking and tackling is what wins football games," explained

Oakland - A Late Entry

Oakland was one of the original eight AFL teams, but not by design. The franchise was awarded only after a previously invited Minneapolis group chose to accept a franchise in the NFL, leaving the AFL with only seven teams.

When Barron Hilton, owner of the Los Angeles Chargers, threatened to fold his franchise unless another team was placed on the West Coast, Oakland became the replacement site.

Hilton subsequently moved his AFL team from Los Angeles to San Diego in 1961; the Raiders moved from Oakland to Los Angeles in 1982.

1960

LOS ANGELES RAIDERS

Turning Points

Oakland is awarded AFL franchise, has 6-8 record in first season.

Vince Lombardi, who coached Green Bay to victories in Super Bowls I and II and who knew a thing or two about the subject.

Superior blocking and tackling, along with running, throwing, and catching, has made the Raiders successful. The "bad boy" image has done more to titillate fans than to intimidate opponents.

The Raiders have had success - 20 winning seasons in 21 years from 1965-1985 - but they did so by playing better football than their opponents. Certainly, the Raiders have had players who frustrated foes with distracting tactics, but the same is true of other teams.

Just as there have been limits to the reality of the Raiders' image, there have also been limits to the team's success.

The Miracle Worker

George Blanda, 43, assured his place as a football legend during a five week span in 1970, when he produced four victories and a tie, all in the final minutes of games.

⊘ October 25 - Blanda comes off bench in relief of Daryle Lamonica, throws touchdown passes of 19 and 43 yards to beat Steelers 31-14.

⊘ November 1 - Blanda's 48-yard field goal, with three seconds remaining, ties Kansas City 17-17.

⊘ November 8 - Blanda's 52-yard field goal, again with three seconds left, beats Cleveland 23-20.

⊘ November 15 - In relief of Lamonica, Blanda rallies Raiders to 24-19 victory over Denver with 20-yard touchdown pass.

⊘ November 22 - A 19-yard field goal with four seconds to play beats San Diego 20-17.

Blanda was selected by the Maxwell Club as the NFL's most valuable player in 1970.

Blanda, who played 26 seasons, is the all-time leading scorer with 2,002 points.

The Mad Bomber

Al Davis favored a wide-open, throw-it-deep offense, and Daryle Lamonica was ideal for the Raiders' attack.

Lamonica, nicknamed "The Mad Bomber," was Oakland's starting quarterback for six years (1967-1972), a span during which the Raiders finished first five times. Acquired in a trade from Buffalo for quarterback Tom Flores, Lamonica is second to Ken Stabler among Raiders in completions (1,138), yards (16,655) and touchdown passes (148).

1963	1966	1967
Al Davis, 33, becomes head coach and general manager of Raiders.	Raiders move into Oakland Coliseum after playing at Kezar Stadium, Candlestick Park, and Frank Youell Field their first six seasons.	In trade of quarterbacks, Raiders send Tom Flores to Buffalo for Daryle Lamonica; post 13-1 record, win AFL title.

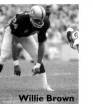

Willie Brown

Raider Rules

Two changes were written into NFL rules at least partially in response to tactics used by the Raiders. With only 10 seconds remaining in a 1978 game and the Raiders trailing San Diego 20-14, quarterback Ken Stabler fumbled the ball forward when hit at the Chargers' 24-yard line by Fred Dean. Running back Pete Banaszak fumbled the ball forward to Raiders tight end Dave Casper, who batted the ball toward the end zone, where he recovered the fumble for a touchdown that enabled the Raiders to win.

By the next season, a rule prohibited such advances of fumbles.

Several Raiders, most notably wide receiver Fred Biletnikoff and cornerback Lester Hayes, made liberal use of "stick-um," a glue-like substance applied to hands and arms that helped them hold on to the ball.

In 1981, the league outlawed "the use of adhesive or slippery substances on the body, equipment or uniform."

In the Raiders' first 32 years, they posted a regular-season record of 287-170-11, better than any other team in the same span. But they've had trouble extending their success into the postseason. No team has been frustrated more often in conference championship games. The Raiders have compiled a 4-8 record in 12 AFC or AFL championship games.

Of the four times the Raiders have advanced to the Super Bowl, they won three, beating Minnesota 32-14 in Super Bowl XI, Philadelphia 27-10 in Super Bowl XV, and Washington 38-9 in Super Bowl XVIII. Their only loss was a 33-14 setback to Lombardi's Green Bay Packers in Super Bowl II.

The three Super Bowl victories came within eight years, but when the Raiders came into existence in Oakland in 1960, they gave no indication of becoming a long-time powerhouse.

Fred Biletnikoff

RAIDERS' FREQUENT FLIERS

Fred Biletnikoff and Cliff Branch, a spectacular duo at wide receiver, combined for nearly 1,100 catches and more than 17,000 yards for the Raiders. Biletnikoff, whose greatest assets were precision routes and excellent hands, caught 589 passes for 8,974 yards and 76 touchdowns in a career spanning 1965-1978. Branch, a speedster, snared 501 passes for 8,685 yards and 67 touchdowns from 1972-1985. Biletnikoff gained more than 100 receiving yards in a game 21 times; Branch did it in 22 games. Biletnikoff is in the Pro Football Hall of Fame.

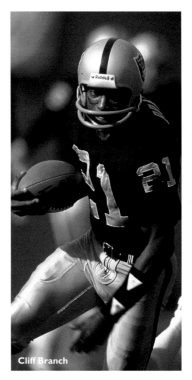

Cliff Branch

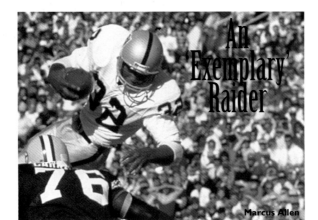

Marcus Allen

An 'Exemplary' Raider

Raiders players annually vote on the "Commitment to Excellence" award, which goes to the player who "best exemplifies the pride, poise, and spirit of the Raiders."

Only one player - running back Marcus Allen - won the award as many as four times. Among his other decorations are the Pro Football Writers' Most Valuable Player award (1985), Super Bowl MVP (XVIII), Heisman Trophy (1981), and five Pro Bowl selections.

Allen led the team in rushing seven consecutive years (1982-1988), including successive 1,000-yard seasons from 1983-85. During that time, the Raiders had a 35-13 regular-season record and won Super Bowl XVIII.

1969	1970		1973
John Madden becomes head coach.	George Blanda, at 43 the oldest player in pro football, passes Raiders to victories over Denver and Cleveland in relief role, provides winning points with field goals in three other games.	**Dave Casper**	Ken Stabler takes over as Raiders' starting quarterback.

Oakland's first team produced a mediocre 6-8 record and went downhill from there. The Raiders were 2-12 and 1-13 in the following seasons. In fact, the AFL had a special draft of veteran players to help bolster the weak Raiders.

Then, along came Al Davis, the man who would become synonymous with this franchise. He took the head-coaching position in 1963 and immediately drove the team to a 10-4 record, scoring more victories than Oakland had managed in its previous three seasons. His coaching success slowed - the Raiders were only 13-12-3 in the next two years - but by then, he had already pumped life into a shaky franchise.

From April 7 to July 25, 1966, Davis served as commissioner of the American Football League (the position was eliminated after the AFL and NFL reached

Bo

Before a hip injury prematurely ended his football career, the Raiders' Bo Jackson was one of the most scintillating runners in the NFL. He electrified fans with his breakaway potential, accounting for three of the four longest runs in Raiders history. His career rushing total of 2,782 yards included runs of 92, 91, and 88 yards.

Although his Raiders career was brief (1987-1990), Bo left his mark on club records: rushing yards in one game (221 against Seattle in 1987), yards per carry for a season (6.8 in 1987), and yards per carry for a career (5.4).

Ray Guy
Punter who averaged 42.4 yards (1973-1986)

ONE OF A KIND

The Raiders never have had another defensive lineman quite like Howie Long. A fierce competitor, the 270-pound defensive end has played in six Pro Bowl games.

Only two other Raiders defensive linemen, Otis Sistrunk and Greg Townsend, have earned Pro Bowl berths. Each was selected once.

1976	1979	1980
Raiders post 13-1 record, beat Minnesota 32-14 in Super Bowl XI.	John Madden retires, Tom Flores becomes head coach.	Raiders qualify for play-offs as wild card, win Super Bowl XV over Philadelphia 27-10.

Clem Daniels

193

merger agreement in June). Davis returned to run the Raiders franchise and demonstrated that he had few superiors in operating a professional football team.

One of Davis's fortes proved to be his selection of head coaches. Four of the men he hired - John Rauch, John Madden, Tom Flores, and Art Shell - won coach of the year honors. All but Shell delivered the team to the Super Bowl.

An even more important Davis knack has been identifying talented players ready to be discarded by other teams. The Raiders' lengthy success story is dotted with names of players acquired by trade or as free agents.

Quarterback-placekicker George Blanda, cornerback Willie Brown, and linebacker Ted Hendricks were three acquisitions by Davis who earned Hall-of-Fame recognition. Other

Double Zero

Jim Otto was one of the original Raiders, and perhaps the best. The 6-foot 2-inch, 255-pound Hall of Famer, who wore number 00, played 15 years for Oakland and was the AFL's All-Star center all 10 years of the league's existence. Otto started in 210 consecutive games for the Raiders. Dave Dalby and Don Mosebar, who followed in Otto's footsteps, were the only other regular starting centers in the team's first 32 years.

The Raiders' Biggest Winner

Before becoming a celebrated TV football analyst, John Madden had a remarkable career as head coach of the Raiders.

Madden became the Raiders' boss in 1969 at age 32 and, including the postseason, averaged more than 11 victories per season for 10 years. His career record: 112-39-7, with seven AFC Western Division titles and one Super Bowl victory. Tom Flores is second among Raiders coaches with 91 wins, John Rauch third with 35.

Madden retired after the 1978 season.

The Snake

The Raiders have had a sterling cast of characters, perhaps none more colorful than quarterback Ken (The Snake) Stabler. An outstanding left-handed passer, Stabler was the starting signal-caller from 1973-79, leading the team to four first-place finishes, two seconds and a fourth.

Although the Raiders' roster has included several outstanding quarterbacks, The Snake holds club records for passing yardage (19,078), attempts (2,481), and touchdown passes (150). He was named to the Pro Football Writers' all-pro team in 1974 and selected for the Pro Bowl four times.

Todd Christensen

1981	1982
A 7-9 record marks first losing season in 17 years.	Raiders move to Los Angeles, draft running back Marcus Allen.

notable success stories after joining the Raiders involved quarterbacks Daryle Lamonica and Jim Plunkett, tight end Todd Christensen, and defensive lineman Lyle Alzado.

During three decades of Raiders' success, coaches changed and players changed, but Davis was a constant.

He has manipulated the roster and the coaching staff masterfully, almost always pushing the right buttons and pulling the right levers to keep his team among the best in the league.

From the time Davis joined the organization in 1963 through 1991 - 29 seasons - the Raiders have had only four losing seasons.

Davis was inducted into the Pro Football Hall of Fame in 1992. ✐

Gene Upshaw

DYNAMIC DUO

It's doubtful that professional football ever has seen a better left-side combination on the offensive line than guard Gene Upshaw and tackle Art Shell, who played side-by-side for 13 years. Both are enshrined in the Pro Football Hall of Fame.

Shell, a 285-pounder, was a Pro Bowl pick eight times, more than any other Raider. Upshaw played in six Pro Bowls and one AFL All-Star Game. Shell was with the Raiders from 1968-1982, Upshaw 1967-1982.

Al Davis

Art Shell

1983

Raiders defeat Washington 38-9 in Super Bowl XVIII for third NFL championship in eight seasons.

Jim Plunkett

1989

Art Shell becomes head coach.

Los Angeles
RAMS

SIDELINES

YEAR ■ WINS □ LOSSES □ TIES	RECORD	PLACE	COACH
Cleveland Rams			
1937	1-10	5th	Hugo Bezdek
1938	4-7	4th	H. Bezdek, A. Lewis [1]
1939	5-5-1	4th	Dutch Clark
1940	5-5-1	4th	Dutch Clark
1941	2-9	5th	Dutch Clark
1942	5-6	3rd	Dutch Clark
1943 Suspended Operations			
1944	4-6	4th	Aldo Donelli
1945	9-1	1st	Adam Walsh
Los Angeles Rams			
1946	6-4-1	2nd	Adam Walsh
1947	6-6	4th	Bob Snyder
1948	6-5-1	3rd	Clark Shaughnessy
1949	8-2-2	1st	Clark Shaughnessy
1950	9-3	1st	Joe Stydahar
1951	8-4	1st	Joe Stydahar
1952	9-3	2nd	J. Stydahar, H. Pool [2]
1953	8-3-1	3rd	Hampton Pool
1954	6-5-1	4th	Hampton Pool
1955	8-3-1	1st	Sid Gillman
1956	4-8	5th	Sid Gillman
1957	6-6	4th	Sid Gillman
1958	8-4	2nd	Sid Gillman
1959	2-10	6th	Sid Gillman
1960	4-7-1	6th	Bob Waterfield
1961	4-10	6th	Bob Waterfield
1962	1-12-1	7th	B. Waterfield, H. Svare [3]
1963	5-9	6th	Harland Svare
1964	5-7-2	5th	Harland Svare
1965	4-10	7th	Harland Svare
1966	8-6	3rd	George Allen
1967	11-1-2	1st	George Allen
1968	10-3-1	2nd	George Allen
1969	11-3	1st	George Allen
1970	9-4-1	2nd	George Allen
1971	8-5-1	2nd	Tommy Prothro
1972	6-7-1	3rd	Tommy Prothro
1973	12-2	1st	Chuck Knox
1974	10-4	1st	Chuck Knox
1975	12-2	1st	Chuck Knox
1976	10-3-1	1st	Chuck Knox
1977	10-4	1st	Chuck Knox
1978	12-4	1st	Ray Malavasi
1979	9-7	1st	Ray Malavasi
1980	11-5	2nd	Ray Malavasi
1981	6-10	3rd	Ray Malavasi
1982	2-7	4th	Ray Malavasi
1983	9-7	2nd	John Robinson
1984	10-6	2nd	John Robinson
1985	11-5	1st	John Robinson
1986	10-6	2nd	John Robinson
1987	6-9	3rd	John Robinson
1988	10-6	2nd	John Robinson
1989	11-5	2nd	John Robinson
1990	5-11	3rd	John Robinson
1991	3-13	4th	John Robinson

1 — Hugo Bezdek (3 games), Art Lewis (8 games)
2 — Joe Stydahar (1 game), Hampton Pool (11 games)
3 — Bob Waterfield (8 games), Harland Svare (6 games)

They started life in Cleveland, but this always has been a Hollywood-type team. The Rams have, indeed, been a team worthy of the entertainment capital of the world.

Glamour names at glamour positions. Bob Waterfield. Norm Van Brocklin. Elroy (Crazylegs) Hirsch. Tom Fears. Dick Bass. (Deacon) Dan Towler. Roman Gabriel. Eric Dickerson. Guys who could light up the scoreboard in a flash, and do it with flair.

Few franchises have been as colorful or successful as the Rams. The color has come from the

The Championship Years

The Rams have won the National Football League championship twice. The first time was in 1945, when they were the Cleveland Rams. They brought the championship to Los Angeles in 1951.

1937

LOS ANGELES RAMS

Turning Points

The NFL awards a franchise to a syndicate headed by Homer Marshman. The team is based in Cleveland, Ohio, and is named the Rams.

headliners, the superstar scorers, and defenders. Jon Arnett. Lawrence McCutcheon. Henry Ellard. Jack Snow. Harold Jackson. Merlin Olsen. David (Deacon) Jones. Jack Youngblood. Jack Reynolds. Eddie Meador. Nolan Cromwell. Dick (Night Train) Lane. Marquee names in a marquee town.

The success is measured by the numbers. Since the Rams first made the playoffs in 1945, only two teams - the Browns and the Giants - have made as many trips to the playoffs as L.A.'s 22.

In the past 25 years, the Rams have finished first or second 19 times. That's success.

And yet, there has been frustration. Despite being contenders year after year, coming close...so close...so often, the Rams have won only two NFL championships - one in 1945 and the other in 1951. In their only Super Bowl appearance - Super Bowl XIV - they were beaten by the Pittsburgh Steelers.

Although often frustrated in their quest for the NFL's ultimate prize, the Rams certainly have been entertaining.

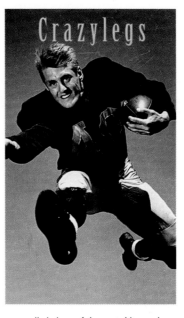

Crazylegs

Sensational Start, Sensational Career

Bob Waterfield truly had a storybook career.

He was a standout at UCLA and was drafted by the Cleveland Rams in 1945. As a rookie quarterback, he took the Rams to a first-place finish with a 9-1 record.

In the league championship game against the Redskins, Waterfield threw touchdown passes of 37 and 44 yards for both Rams' touchdowns. And, he kicked an extra point.

Waterfield was the NFL passing leader in 1946 and 1951, when the Rams won their only other league championship. He retired after the 1952 season with career totals of 97 touchdown passes, 13 touchdown runs, and 11,849 passing yards. A true triple threat, he also intercepted 20 passes and averaged 42.4 yards on 315 punts.

Not surprisingly, Waterfield is a member of the Pro Football Hall of Fame.

Oh, yes. One other thing. Bob Waterfield was married to Jane Russell, one of the most glamorous actresses in Hollywood history.

Some guys have it all.

He had one of the great nicknames in NFL history - Crazylegs - and has a place in the NFL record book as one of the greatest pass catchers of all time.

Elroy Hirsch, nicknamed Crazylegs because of a unique running style that made his legs appear to fly in several directions simultaneously, will always be remembered as one of the finest deep receivers in pro football history. He was inducted into the Pro Football Hall of Fame in 1968 and was honored as the flanker on the all-pro team for the NFL's first 50 years, which was chosen in 1969. Hirsch's statistics, including three years in the AAFC: 387 receptions, 7,029 yards, 60 touchdowns, 18.2 yards per catch.

1941	**1945**	**1946**
Daniel Reeves becomes the youngest sports franchise owner at age 29 when he and Fred Levy, Jr., buy the Rams for $100,000.	Rookie quarterback Bob Waterfield leads the Rams to their first winning season (9-1). In the 15-14 championship game win, he throws two touchdown passes and kicks the decisive extra point.	Dan Reeves wins league approval to move the Rams, and the Los Angeles era begins.

Elroy (Crazylegs) Hirsch

197

74

Many, many super-stars have worn the Rams' uniform, but only one player has been accorded the honor of having his number retired. Merlin Olsen, number 74, is considered by many to have been the finest defensive lineman of all time. In a career that spanned 15 seasons (1962-1976) he was honored as an all-pro six times and played in the Pro Bowl 14 consecutive years.

Although not officially retired by the club, three other jersey numbers are not issued. They were worn by Bob Waterfield (7), Elroy Hirsch (40), and Jack Youngblood (85).

The franchise was born in 1937, originally awarded to Cleveland. It was in 1946 that owner Dan Reeves, in search of bluer waters, left the shores of Lake Erie and took his team west. The Rams' last season in Cleveland was a great one - they went 9-1 in the regular season and won the league championship in 1945.

Reeves encountered opposition to the move. Commercial airline travel was still years away from "shrinking" the U.S., and other club owners weren't eager to subject their teams to cross-country train trips for a single game. Reeves's persistence opened a great new world to the National Football League.

Reeves insisted that his organization scout more thoroughly than any other team, and the result was a bounty of players whose names and skills fit beautifully at the L.A. Coliseum. One was quarterback Bob Waterfield, an All-America at UCLA before being drafted and playing one season with the Cleveland Rams. He brought quite a resume for his homecoming - NFL Most Valuable Player in 1945, a superstar on the league's championship team. But Waterfield

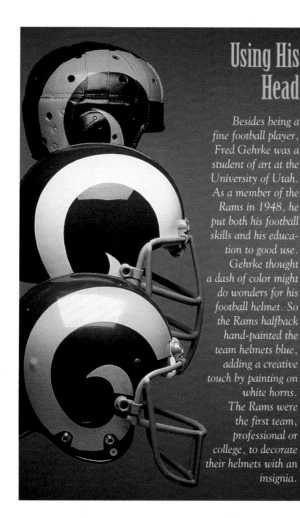

Using His Head

Besides being a fine football player, Fred Gehrke was a student of art at the University of Utah. As a member of the Rams in 1948, he put both his football skills and his education to good use. Gehrke thought a dash of color might do wonders for his football helmet. So the Rams halfback hand-painted the team helmets blue, adding a creative touch by painting on white horns. The Rams were the first team, professional or college, to decorate their helmets with an insignia.

Norm Van Brocklin

1951

The Rams win their first NFL championship in Los Angeles, beating the Cleveland Browns 24-17 in the title game on a 73-yard fourth quarter pass from Norm Van Brocklin to Tom Fears.

1952

After four years of sharing quarterback duties, Van Brocklin leads the NFL in passing; Waterfield retires.

wasn't a one-man show. In 1949, the Rams added Norm Van Brocklin, forming the greatest one-two punch at quarterback in NFL history. With those two passing to Elroy (Crazylegs) Hirsch and Tom Fears, receivers with spectacular skills, and the trio of (Deacon) Dan Towler, Tank Younger, and Dick Hoerner forming the mighty "Bull Elephant" backfield, the Rams were awesome. They won three consecutive Western Division titles from 1949-1951.

No NFL franchise is immune to ups and downs, but L.A.'s down cycles have been remarkably brief. Only once since moving to Los Angeles have the Rams endured sub-.500 seasons more than two consecutive years. Sid Gillman became head coach and rallied the Rams in the mid 1950s, George Allen did it in the 1960s, Chuck Knox had a remarkable record in the 1970s, John Robinson revived the Rams in the 1980s, and Knox returned for another term in 1992.

The Rams' owners found the right coaches, and the coaches got the right players.

In a style that befits their hometown, the Rams have always done things in a big way.

Consider, for example, their record in trading. If it was a big deal, a really big deal, chances

How Did They Let Him Get Away?

After six consecutive winning seasons, the Rams fell to a 6-7-1 record in 1972. The sub-.500 season prompted a coaching change, with Tommy Prothro moving out and Chuck Knox moving in.

And that started the most incredible stretch in Rams' history. Knox promptly took the Rams to five consecutive first-place finishes, posting a regular-season record of 54-15-1. Knox resigned after the 1977 season, shuffling off to Buffalo.

Minus Knox, the Rams were first for two more seasons, but then had only one first-place finish over the next 11 years. In hopes of returning to their previous greatness, the Rams hired Knox to come back as their head coach for the 1992 season.

Roman Gabriel
Superb in the '60s, his 22,223 yards passing and 154 TDs are Rams records.

1958	1962	1966	1972
Van Brocklin is traded to Philadelphia and the Rams go into a seven-season slump, failing to post a winning record again until 1966.	The Rams hit the jackpot in the draft, selecting quarterback Roman Gabriel from North Carolina and defensive tackle Merlin Olsen from Utah State.	George Allen is hired as head coach and the Rams immediately reverse their direction. After seven consecutive losing seasons, they post six straight winning years.	Robert Irsay pays $19 million to the Reeves estate for the Rams, then swaps franchises with Carroll Rosenbloom, owner of the Baltimore Colts.

are the Rams were involved. In fact, four of the five biggest player trades in NFL history have involved Los Angeles.

There was the 1987 three-way deal among the Rams, Colts, and Bills that involved 10 players and draft picks. The Rams sent Eric Dickerson to the Colts and acquired running backs Greg Bell and Owen Gill plus three first-round and three second-round draft picks, while the Bills acquired Cornelius Bennett from the Colts.

In 1959, the Rams were in another 10-man deal, a celebrated swap with the Cardinals in which they got running back Ollie Matson for eight players and a draft choice.

L.A. swung a 12-man trade with the Dallas Texans in 1952, getting the rights to linebacker Les Richter for 11 players, including running back Dick Hoerner, a member of the "Bull Elephant" backfield.

The Fearsome Foursome

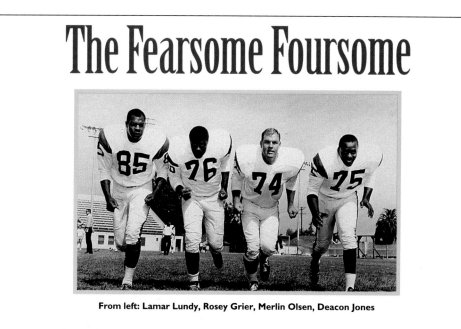

From left: Lamar Lundy, Rosey Grier, Merlin Olsen, Deacon Jones

Hollywood hype mills have spawned more than a fair share of puffery, but all the superlatives heaped on The Fearsome Foursome were well deserved. For four years - 1963-1966 - the quartet of Lamar Lundy, Merlin Olsen, Rosey Grier, and David (Deacon) Jones terrorized opponents and established itself as one of the best units of all time.
Curiously, the Rams had only one winning season in those four years.

Coaching: By the Numbers

The Rams have employed 17 head coaches, three of whom led the team to victory more than 70 percent of the time.

Coach	Years	W	L	T	Pct.
Adam Walsh	1945-46	16	5	1	.750
Chuck Knox	1973-77	57	20	1	.737
George Allen	1966-70	49	19	4	.708

1973

Chuck Knox becomes head coach of the Rams and ignites the most successful era in team history, resulting in seven consecutive first place finishes.

1979

Carroll Rosenbloom dies. His widow, Georgia, becomes majority owner of the Rams. Team wins NFC title, loses Super Bowl XIV 31-19 to Steelers

1983

John Robinson begins a nine-year term as head coach. The Rams select Eric Dickerson in the draft.

Henry Ellard

A bigger trade yet was the 1971 exchange with the Redskins - a 15-man deal. The Rams acquired linebacker Marlin McKeever and seven draft picks in exchange for an eight-man package that included linebackers Maxie Baughan, Jack Pardee, and Myron Pottios and defensive lineman Diron Talbert as ex-Rams coach George Allen instituted his "future is now" philosophy in Washington.

But even that wasn't the biggest swap in Rams history. In 1972, Chicagoan Robert Irsay bought the Rams from the Reeves estate for $19 million, and promptly traded the entire franchise - players, coaches, footballs, shoulder pads, socks, shoes, and everything else - to Carroll Rosenbloom for the entire Baltimore Colts franchise.

When they do things in L.A., they do them in a big way. Marquee names in a marquee town. That's entertainment. ✐

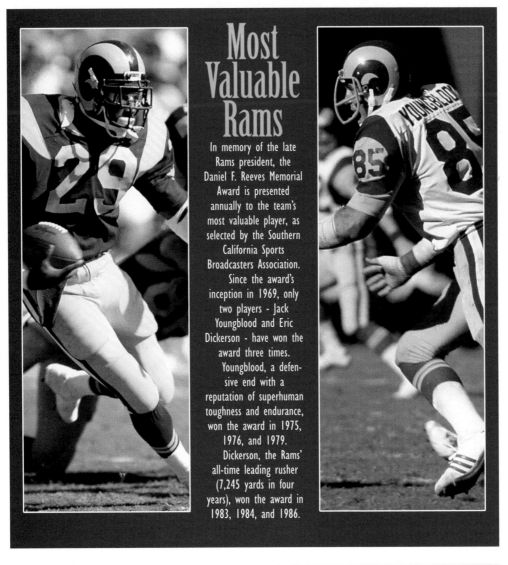

Most Valuable Rams

In memory of the late Rams president, the Daniel F. Reeves Memorial Award is presented annually to the team's most valuable player, as selected by the Southern California Sports Broadcasters Association. Since the award's inception in 1969, only two players - Jack Youngblood and Eric Dickerson - have won the award three times. Youngblood, a defensive end with a reputation of superhuman toughness and endurance, won the award in 1975, 1976, and 1979. Dickerson, the Rams' all-time leading rusher (7,245 yards in four years), won the award in 1983, 1984, and 1986.

1986

The Rams trade two players and three draft choices (two first rounders) to the Houston Oilers for rookie quarterback Jim Everett.

Jim Everett

1992

After 14 years in Buffalo and Seattle, Chuck Knox returns to coach the Rams.

Miami DOLPHINS

YEAR	■ WINS	■ LOSSES	☐ TIES		RECORD	PLACE	COACH
American Football League							
1966					3-11	5th	George Wilson
1967					4-10	3rd	George Wilson
1968					5-8-1	3rd	George Wilson
1969					3-10-1	5th	George Wilson
National Football League							
1970					10-4	2nd	Don Shula
1971					10-3-1	1st	Don Shula
1972					14-0	1st	Don Shula
1973					12-2	1st	Don Shula
1974					11-3	1st	Don Shula
1975					10-4	2nd	Don Shula
1976					6-8	3rd	Don Shula
1977					10-4	2nd	Don Shula
1978					11-5	2nd	Don Shula
1979					10-6	1st	Don Shula
1980					8-8	3rd	Don Shula
1981					11-4-1	1st	Don Shula
1982					7-2	2nd	Don Shula
1983					12-4	1st	Don Shula
1984					14-2	1st	Don Shula
1985					12-4	1st	Don Shula
1986					8-8	3rd	Don Shula
1987					8-7	2nd	Don Shula
1988					6-10	5th	Don Shula
1989					8-8	3rd	Don Shula
1990					12-4	2nd	Don Shula
1991					8-8	3rd	Don Shula

illions of words have been uttered in praise of Don Shula, but it was said best by Bum Phillips, who coached against him: "Shula can take his'n and beat your'n, or he can take your'n and beat his'n."

The homespun philosophy pinpoints the key to Shula's long-term coaching success. The man has adapted. He has produced championship teams from a variety of ingredients.

Some Shula teams featured a powerful ground game. Others were awesome through the air. Some teams overcame weaknesses in the defensive line, others in the secondary or at linebacker. Shula's teams compensated for weaknesses and capitalized on strengths.

Shula started the 1992 season with a record of 306-145-6, only 19

A Real Bargain

When Don Shula left the Colts to become head coach of the Dolphins, Commissioner Pete Rozelle ordered Miami to give the Colts a first-round draft choice in 1971 as compensation.

Giving up a premium pick was a stiff penalty for a young team that had never had a winning season, but Shula proved to be the biggest bargain in Dolphins' history.

1965

MIAMI DOLPHINS

Turning Points

Joe Robbie is awarded American Football League expansion franchise for Miami.

victories behind George Halas's all-time record.

The Dolphins' coach has achieved everything in the NFL - great winning percentage, division titles, Super Bowl championships, a 17-0 season - but perhaps his most remarkable achievement has been his ability to remain at the pinnacle of his profession.

Shula's coaching career began with a seven-year (1963-1969) term at Baltimore, where his teams won more than 71 percent of their regular-season games and finished either first or second in six of seven years. Since moving to Miami in 1970, he has produced nine AFC Eastern Division champions, five AFC champions, and two Super Bowl winners. Through 1991, his Dolphins had won 67 percent of their regular-season games. In 14 of his 22 seasons in Miami, the Dolphins have won 10 or more games.

Shula has been so successful that he has been taken for granted. He has not won a coach of the year award from a major publication or news organization since 1972. Coach of the year awards usually go to coaches who spur their teams to unexpected success. With Shula, success is expected.

THE PERFECT SEASON

The Miami Dolphins in 1972:

Date	Opponent	Score	Record
Sept. 17	at Kansas City	20-10	1-0
Sept. 24	Houston	34-13	2-0
Oct. 1	at Minnesota	16-14	3-0
Oct. 8	at New York Jets	27-17	4-0
Oct. 15	San Diego	24-10	5-0
Oct. 22	Buffalo	24-23	6-0
Oct. 29	at Baltimore	23-0	7-0
Nov. 5	at Buffalo	30-16	8-0
Nov. 12	New England	52-0	9-0
Nov. 19	New York Jets	28-24	10-0
Nov. 27	St. Louis	31-10	11-0
Dec. 3	at New England	37-21	12-0
Dec. 10	at New York Giants	23-13	13-0
Dec. 16	Baltimore	16-0	14-0
American Conference Playoff			
Dec. 24	Cleveland	20-14	15-0
American Conference Championship			
Dec. 31	at Pittsburgh	21-17	16-0
Super Bowl VII (at Los Angeles)			
Jan. 14	Washington	14-7	**17-0**

1966

George Wilson becomes first head coach of Dolphins, team has 3-11 record.

1967

Quarterback Bob Griese is Miami's first-round draft pick.

Dick Anderson

1968

Dolphins make fullback Larry Csonka their first draft pick.

In 29 years as an NFL head coach, he has endured only two losing seasons.

The Dolphins began winning from the time Shula arrived in 1970. Never winners of more than five games in previous seasons, Shula's Dolphins posted a 10-4 record in his initial season, and won 10 or more games in nine of his first 10 years.

The Dolphins hadn't won often before Shula arrived, but they had stockpiled talent. When Shula became coach, the Miami roster already included three future Hall of Fame members - running back Larry Csonka, quarterback Bob Griese, and wide receiver Paul Warfield - plus others who would become perennial standouts: safety Dick Anderson, linebacker Nick Buoniconti, tackle Norm Evans, guard Larry Little, running backs Jim Kiick and Eugene (Mercury) Morris, defensive tackle Manny Fernandez, defensive end Bill Stanfill, and wide receiver Howard Twilley.

Shula knew precisely how to handle the talent. Although his first Miami game was a loss, it was followed by four consecutive wins, and the Dolphins were en route to their first playoff berth.

The Mercurial Mr. Morris

Larry Csonka was Mr. Inside, but Eugene (Mercury) Morris was Miami's Mr. Outside. The well-nicknamed running back played for Miami seven years (1969-1975), and his 3,877 yards are second to Csonka's club-record 6,737.

Morris is one of only two NFL players with a career average of more than 5 yards per carry. Cleveland's Jim Brown averaged 5.22, Morris 5.14.

Sky King

For many years in the NFL, there was a theory that a young quarterback needed several seasons to learn his craft. Dan Marino destroyed that myth in 1983. He served notice in his rookie season that his career would be special. He passed for 2,210 yards, but the eye-catching statistics were his touchdowns-to-interceptions ratio: 20 touchdowns, only 6 interceptions. Obviously, the kid didn't get rattled. In his second season, Marino shattered NFL records for yardage and touchdowns, passing for 5,084 yards and 48 touchdowns. The previous best for touchdown passes had been 36, by Hall of Famers George Blanda and Y.A. Tittle. Entering the 1992 season, Marino's total of 35,386 passing yards was fourth in NFL history, behind only Fran Tarkenton, Dan Fouts, and Johnny Unitas. Only Tarkenton and Unitas had more touchdown passes than Marino's 266. After only nine seasons, Marino was already in the company of quarterbacks who had taken 18 years to set the records.

1969	1970	1971
Miami continues to stockpile talent, trades for linebacker Nick Buoniconti and guard Larry Little, drafts running back Mercury Morris.	Don Shula becomes head coach; Dolphins have first winning season with 10-4 record, lose first playoff game to Oakland.	10-3-1 record brings first AFC East title; Miami wins AFC Championship Game 21-0 over Baltimore, loses Super Bowl VI 24-3 to Dallas.

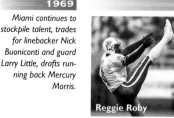

Reggie Roby

The next season they won their first division title.

And then came 1972. Perfection. No team in NFL history had gone unbeaten and untied throughout the entire season. But the 1972 Dolphins won 14 regular-season contests and three playoff games, including a 14-7 triumph over Washington in Super Bowl VII. When Shula left the Los Angeles Memorial Coliseum, he took with him the NFL's first 17-0 season.

It was a team with no weaknesses. Csonka and Kiick were outstanding power runners, Morris was a fearsome breakaway artist, Warfield the deep threat, Twilley the sure-handed guy who ran the short routes, and Griese the superb field general who made it all work. Even when Griese was sidelined by injuries that year, backup Earl Morrall was unflappable. The offensive linemen - Langer, Little, Evans, Bob Kuechenberg, and Wayne Moore - had been released by other clubs, but they jelled as a unit.

The defense, devoid of marquee names, became famous as the "No-Name Defense." They yielded the fewest points in the league and were anonymous no more. The Miami defense sent four players to the Pro Bowl game: Scott, Anderson, Buoniconti and Stanfill. The

Mark Duper   Mark Clayton

THE MARKS BROTHERS

The "Marks Brothers," a pair of 5-foot 9-inch wide receivers, have been an exceptional pair of targets for Dan Marino's passes.

Mark Clayton and Mark Duper had a combined total of 974 catches, 16,131 yards, and 130 touchdowns entering the 1992 season. Duper had played in 130 games, Clayton in 129.

Duper, a second-round pick from Northwestern Louisiana State in 1982, had 467 receptions, 8,107 yards, and 52 touchdowns.

Clayton, an eighth-round pick from Louisville in 1983, had 507 catches, 8,024 yards, and 78 touchdowns.

NUMBER 12 WAS NUMBER 1

The Dolphins have honored only one player by retiring his number. It's doubtful anyone else could wear number 12 as well as quarterback Bob Griese did.

An outstanding field general, Griese was exactly the quarterback Don Shula needed for the Miami offense. He was an expert at attacking a defense, and willing to utilize the entire Dolphins' arsenal.

Because of his reliance on Miami's ground game, Griese was underrated as a passer, but he threw for 25,092 yards and 192 touchdowns in his 14-year career.

Griese, who played in six Pro Bowl games, was inducted into the Pro Football Hall of Fame in 1990.

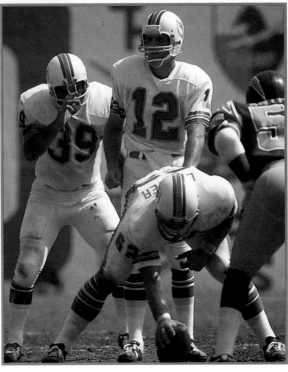

A Perfect 5-for-5

It was more than coincidence that Paul Warfield's teams had a losing record only once in the 13 years he played in the NFL.

The Hall of Fame wide receiver played with Miami only five years, but they were five great ones. Warfield was invited to the Pro Bowl in each of his five seasons in Miami (1970-74).

Because he had only a short stay, several Dolphins have bettered his 3,355 receiving yards, but he still holds the club record for average per catch (21.5 yards).

Warfield signed with the World Football League in 1975.

1972	1973		1975
Dolphins complete 17-0 season with 14-7 victory over Washington in Super Bowl VII.	Miami season-ticket sales hit 74,961; Dolphins go 12-2, win Super Bowl VIII over Minnesota 24-7.		Larry Csonka, Jim Kiick, and Paul Warfield sign with World Football League.

Offense: Where The Stars Are

The Dolphins have been best known for their heroes on the offensive unit. Entering the 1992 season, Miami had received Pro Bowl invitations for 71 players on offense, but only 30 on defense. The Dolphins most frequently selected to the Pro Bowl: quarterbacks Bob Griese and Dan Marino, guard Bob Kuechenberg, and center Jim Langer, with six each; offensive stars Mark Clayton, Larry Csonka, Dwight Stephenson and Paul Warfield, and defenders Bob Baumhower, John Offerdahl and Jake Scott, selected five times each.

Dolphins' offense sent five players: Evans, Little, Morris, Csonka, and Warfield.

As if to prove their perfect performance was no fluke, the Dolphins repeated as champions the next year - and almost had another perfect season. Their only losses in 17 games were by scores of 12-7 to Oakland and 16-3 to Baltimore. The Dolphins won Super Bowl VIII 24-7 over Minnesota.

The Dolphins had to cope with roster changes. Csonka, Kiick and Warfield went to the World Football League in 1975. Players retired and others were sidelined by injury, but it didn't prevent the Dolphins from winning. Shula always seemed to have enough replacement parts - a few new, unexpected heroes - to complete the puzzle.

A prime example was at quarterback, where Griese sustained a series of disabling injuries. Shula located temporary replacements like Earl Morrall or Don Strock, and Miami continued to win. When he needed someone to bridge the end of the Griese era and the start of the Dan Marino era, he found David Woodley, an eighth-round draft pick from LSU. Woodley

THE KILLER B'S

The Dolphins have led the NFL in defense only twice. The first time was in 1972, when the famed "No-Name Defense" helped Miami to a 17-0 record and a victory in Super Bowl VII.

The other time was in 1982, when "The Killer B's" were the buzz of the NFL. Miami's starting defense included six players whose surname started with the same letter: linemen Doug Betters, Bob Baumhower and Kim Bokamper, linebacker Bob Brudzinski, and safeties Glen and Lyle Blackwood. Among the Dolphin reserves on defense were linebacker Charles Bowser and nose tackle Richard Bishop.

The "Killer B's" helped Miami get to Super Bowl XVII, but the Dolphins were beaten by Washington 27-17.

MIAMI'S SCORING ACE

The film clip of Garo Yepremian that has been shown most often is of his clumsy fumble as he attempted to pass after a botched field-goal attempt in Super Bowl VII.

But Yepremian wasn't paid to be a passer. His specialty was kicking, and he did it well, providing the Dolphins with a club-record 830 points on 165 field goals and 335 extra points in his nine-year stint (1970-78) with the team.

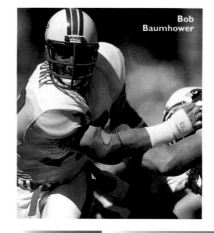

Bob Baumhower

1981
Bob Griese and Larry Little retire.

1982
Miami posts 7-2 record in strike-shortened season, wins AFC tournament, loses Super Bowl XVII to Washington 27-17.

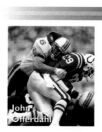
John Offerdahl

1983
Miami drafts quarterback Dan Marino.

guided the Dolphins to first-place and second-place finishes during his three years as Miami's starter, highlighted by an appearance in Super Bowl XVII.

And then, in 1983, Shula got lucky in the draft when 26 teams bypassed Marino. Miami selected wide receiver Mark Clayton in the eighth round that year, to go with Mark Duper, a second-round pick from 1982. The Dolphins began writing another great chapter in their history.

Shula's offense during the Csonka-Griese era focused primarily on the ground game; Miami was among the top four teams in rushing every year from 1970-75. With the arrival of Marino and the Marks Brothers, Miami's air attack became the most potent in the NFL; the Dolphins ranked in the top five in passing offense every year from 1984-1991.

Shula recognized that "the way we did it in the old days" wasn't always what was best for the new era, so he adjusted.

That's been the Don Shula way...able to win with whatever talent was available. ⌀

The Money Man

Don Shula referred to Nat Moore as "our money man," and the fleet wide receiver paid big dividends. Moore was on the receiving end of more Bob Griese passes than any other Dolphin. A 5-foot 9-inch speedster, he played for Miami 13 years (1974-1986) and caught a club-record 510 passes for 7,547 yards and 74 touchdowns.

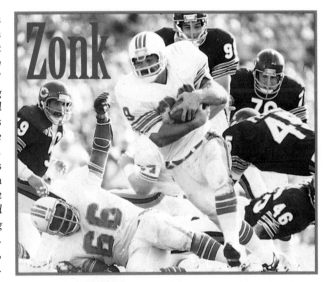

Don Shula referred to him as "a modern day Bronko Nagurski," and fans from the modern era responded, "Wow, that Nagurski guy must have been really something."
Larry Csonka was an awe-inspiring power runner, a punishing 235-pound fullback who was the heart of Miami's offense when the Dolphins played in three consecutive Super Bowls. Csonka gained more than 1,000 yards in each of those years and finished with 6,737 yards and 53 touchdowns in eight seasons with Miami. He also played three years for the Giants, gaining 1,344 yards. Csonka, the MVP in Super Bowl VIII, is in the Pro Football Hall of Fame.

Rock Solid

Was there ever a more dependable short-yardage play than Larry Csonka up the middle behind center Jim Langer and guards Bob Kuechenberg and Larry Little?

The trio played a key role in Miami's success; Little came to Miami in 1969, Langer and Kuechenberg arrived the next year. Langer, claimed on waivers from the Cleveland Browns, became a six-time Pro Bowler for the Dolphins and was inducted into the Hall of Fame. Kuechenberg also earned six trips to the Pro Bowl, Little four.

Kuechenberg played for Miami a club-record 15 years, Little 12, and Langer 10.

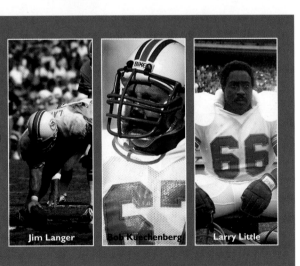

Jim Langer   Bob Kuechenberg   Larry Little

1984

Dolphins win 14 of 16 in regular season, defeat Pittsburgh for AFC championship, lose Super Bowl XIX to San Francisco 38-16.

Jake Scott

1987

Dolphins move into Joe Robbie Stadium, the first stadium built entirely with private funds.

Minnesota VIKINGS

YEAR	■ WINS ▭ LOSSES ▭ TIES	RECORD	PLACE	COACH
1961		3-11	7th	Norm Van Brocklin
1962		2-11-1	6th	Norm Van Brocklin
1963		5-8-1	4th	Norm Van Brocklin
1964		8-5-1	2nd	Norm Van Brocklin
1965		7-7	5th	Norm Van Brocklin
1966		4-9-1	6th	Norm Van Brocklin
1967		3-8-3	4th	Bud Grant
1968		8-6	1st	Bud Grant
1969		12-2	1st	Bud Grant
1970		12-2	1st	Bud Grant
1971		11-3	1st	Bud Grant
1972		7-7	3rd	Bud Grant
1973		12-2	1st	Bud Grant
1974		10-4	1st	Bud Grant
1975		12-2	1st	Bud Grant
1976		11-2-1	1st	Bud Grant
1977		9-5	1st	Bud Grant
1978		8-7-1	1st	Bud Grant
1979		7-9	3rd	Bud Grant
1980		9-7	1st	Bud Grant
1981		7-9	4th	Bud Grant
1982		5-4	4th	Bud Grant
1983		8-8	4th	Bud Grant
1984		3-13	5th	Les Steckel
1985		7-9	3rd	Bud Grant
1986		9-7	2nd	Jerry Burns
1987		8-7	2nd	Jerry Burns
1988		11-5	2nd	Jerry Burns
1989		10-6	1st	Jerry Burns
1990		6-10	5th	Jerry Burns
1991		8-8	3rd	Jerry Burns

A novelty song on the rock 'n roll charts about a "one-eyed, one-horned, flying purple people eater," a silly ditty that came and went quickly, provided the inspiration for a nickname that long will have a niche in pro football annals.

"The Purple People Eaters" was the tag applied to the Minnesota Vikings' defensive line of the 1970s, one of the best of all time.

The Vikings were an NFL powerhouse during that era, winning 10 division titles in 11 years (1968-1978), and the team's greatest asset was its defensive front wall.

The Vikings appeared in Super Bowls IV, VIII, IX, and XI, only to suffer defeat each time. An

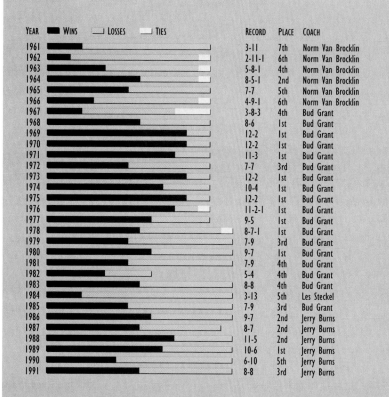

GRANT THE GREAT

He was an excellent athlete, playing professional basketball for the Minneapolis Lakers and football for the Philadelphia Eagles, but it is for his coaching that Bud Grant is remembered best.

His Winnipeg teams won five Grey Cup championships in the Canadian Football League before Grant came south to Minnesota. His first team had a 3-8-3 record in 1967, but then the Vikings won division championships in 11 of the next 13 years.

Grant compiled a record of 168-108-5 in 18 years at Minnesota.

1960

MINNESOTA VIKINGS
Turning Points

NFL grants franchise to Minneapolis-St. Paul area, to be known as Minnesota Vikings. Norm Van Brocklin is head coach.

unexpected offensive collapse - the Vikings' offense scored a total of four touchdowns in four Super Bowls - denied Minnesota a championship, but it didn't diminish the team's accomplishments. The Vikings, led by the Purple People Eaters, built a solid reputation for excellence.

Ends Carl Eller and Jim Marshall, plus tackles Gary Larsen and Alan Page, provided a furious pass rush, but they may have been even better against the run.

Minnesota gave up only two touchdowns on the ground in 1971, equaling an NFL record. In 1969 and 1970, the Vikings yielded only four rushing touchdowns each season. In both 1970 and 1971, Minnesota surrendered an average of one touchdown per game. A solid linebacker corps of Jeff Siemon, Roy Winston (later replaced by Matt Blair), and Wally Hilgenberg played a key role, but the focus was deservedly on the dominating front four.

Two of the Purple People Eaters were first-round Minnesota draft picks, two others were acquired from other teams. Marshall joined the Vikings in a 1961 trade with Cleveland, and

Vikings' First Choice

Tommy Mason, an outstanding broken-field runner from Tulane, was the Vikings' first draft choice and their first all-pro. He led Minnesota in rushing in 1962 and 1963 and played in the Pro Bowl for three consecutive years, beginning in 1962.

Mason played for Minnesota six years before being traded to the Rams.

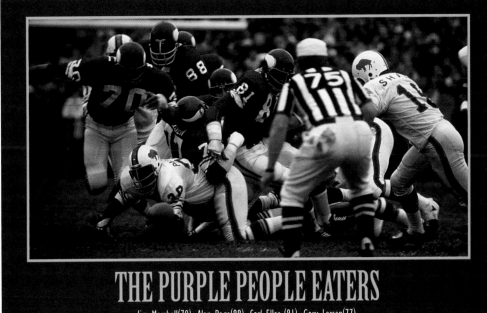

THE PURPLE PEOPLE EATERS

Jim Marshall(70), Alan Page(88), Carl Eller (81), Gary Larsen(77).

The Big Bomber

Tommy Kramer, Minnesota's quarterback from 1977-1989, could produce aerial fireworks as well as almost anyone in the league. He passed for more than 300 yards in a game 19 times, including four games of more than 400 yards. His single-game best was 490 yards against the Redskins in 1986.

Kramer is second only to Fran Tarkenton in most Vikings passing statistics. His career numbers: 2,011 completions, 24,775 yards, and 159 touchdown passes.

1961
First draft brings running back Tommy Mason and quarterback Fran Tarkenton. Vikings win first game, 37-13 over Chicago; post 3-11 record.

Fran Tarkenton

Norm Van Brocklin

1964
Jim Finks becomes general manager; Vikings' first round draft pick is defensive end Carl Eller.

Larsen came from the Rams in 1965. Eller was a first-round draft pick in 1964, and Page in 1967.

In 1968, only their second season as a unit, the Purple People Eaters led Minnesota to its first division championship, and started the remarkable run of 10 titles in 11 years. After age took its toll on the line, Minnesota slipped, winning only two division titles in the next 13 years.

Larsen retired and was replaced by Doug Sutherland in 1975. Eller and Page departed in 1978, Page claimed on waivers by Chicago in midseason and Eller traded to Seattle before the 1979 season. Marshall retired in 1979, after spending an NFL-record 19 seasons with the same club.

All of the Purple People Eaters were tall, 6 feet 4 inches to 6-6, but they weren't especially big. Marshall was the lightest at 230 pounds, Larsen the heaviest at 255. They relied on quickness and finesse rather than heft.

Page, one of the best defensive linemen of his era, was singled out for the most honors. He played in nine consecutive Pro Bowls (1968-1976), was named to all-pro teams six times and was named MVP by the *Associated Press* in 1971. He was elected to the

No-Passing Zone

Safety Paul Krause had a remarkable 16-year career as a ballhawk, intercepting an NFL-record 81 passes. Krause played for Washington four years before arriving in Minnesota in 1968; 53 of his interceptions came during his years with the Vikings. He earned Pro Bowl berths six times in his 12 years with Minnesota.

A Different Style Of Attack

Joe Kapp's style of playing quarterback was anything but typical.

"Most quarterbacks look for somewhere to run out of bounds. Mine looks for someone to run into," coach Bud Grant said of Kapp.

A rugged battler who specialized in passes that wobbled but somehow found their target, Kapp had a brief, but colorful stay in Minnesota.

He arrived in 1967 after playing in the Canadian Football League, quarterbacked the Vikings to two division titles in three years and Super Bowl IV, and was sold to the Patriots after a salary squabble before the 1970 season.

His most memorable performance came on September 28, 1969, when he threw 7 touchdown passes and gained 449 yards in a 52-14 victory over the Colts.

Minnesota's Best Offensive LINEMEN

Mick Tingelhoff was an unheralded free agent who asked the Vikings for a tryout in 1962. Ron Yary was the first pick in the 1968 draft.

Although they arrived in Minnesota with different credentials, they became the two most celebrated offensive linemen in Vikings history.

Tingelhoff was Minnesota's center for 17 years, and a six-time Pro Bowl selection.

Yary, a tackle, earned seven trips to the Pro Bowl in a 15-year career.

Ron Yary

Mick Tingelhoff

Jim Marshall

1967	1968	1969
Van Brocklin is replaced by Bud Grant; Tarkenton is traded to Giants; Joe Kapp is signed as free agent from CFL; draft brings Alan Page, Gene Washington, Clint Jones, Bobby Bryant, John Beasley and Bob Grim.	Vikings win first division championship.	Vikings go 12-2 in regular season, lose Super Bowl IV to Kansas City 23-7.

Pro Football Hall of Fame in 1988.

Eller was named to six Pro Bowls, and Larsen and Marshall were chosen for two each. In 1969, all four Vikings linemen played in the Pro Bowl, the only time any team's entire line has earned that honor. Eller had 130 sacks for the Vikings, Marshall 127, Page 108.

Coach Bud Grant, who arrived in 1967, orchestrated a sensational turnaround in the Vikings' fortunes. Minnesota had only one winning season before Grant arrived after a stint in the Canadian Football League. After a 3-8-3 start, he led the Vikings to 11 division titles in 13 years.

Grant's offense featured quarterback Fran Tarkenton and running back Chuck Foreman; the deep strike potential was provided by John Gilliam, who preceded Ahmad Rashad and Sammy White as a standout wide receiver. Although the Vikings were shut down in Super Bowl games, they rolled up impressive yardage and big scores during the regular season.

Tarkenton was a torment to opponents, a gifted scrambler who exhausted defenders while searching for open receivers. An unequaled escape artist and remarkably durable, he passed for

A Welcome Change Of Scenery

A change of scenery was just what Chris Doleman needed to help him fulfill the promise that made him a first-round draft pick in 1985.

Doleman labored for two undistinguished seasons as a linebacker, but blossomed into a star after moving to defensive end in 1987. He was a standout at the new position and played in four consecutive Pro Bowls. Doleman led the NFL with 21 sacks in 1989, just one short of Mark Gastineau's league record.

An Unusual Combination

Not many NFL players are graduates of Brown University, and even fewer have degrees in civil engineering.

But Steve Jordan not only has an engineering degree from the Ivy League school, he also has a trophy case full of football awards. Among the NFL's premier tight ends, Jordan earned his sixth consecutive Pro Bowl invitation in 1991. In his first 10 years with the Vikings, Jordan caught a club-record 411 passes for 5,348 yards and 25 touchdowns.

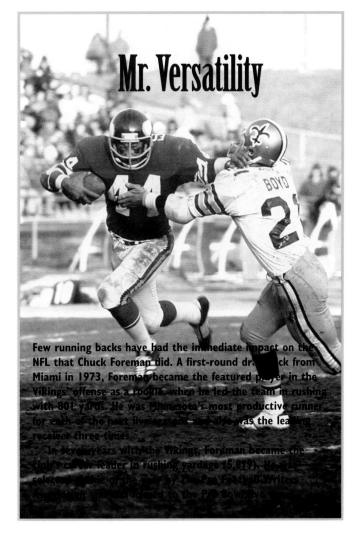

Mr. Versatility

Few running backs have had the immediate impact on the NFL that Chuck Foreman did. A first-round draft pick from Miami in 1973, Foreman became the featured player in the Vikings' offense as a rookie, when he led the team in rushing with 801 yards. He was Minnesota's most productive runner for each of the next five seasons and also was the leading receiver three times.

In seven years with the Vikings, Foreman became the club's career leader in rushing yardage (5,879). He was selected Rookie of the Year by the Pro Football Writers and was invited to the Pro Bowl.

1970
Salary dispute results in Kapp being sold to Patriots.

1972
Tarkenton re-acquired in trade with Giants.

1973
Vikings draft Chuck Foreman in first round; post 12-2 record, lose Super Bowl VIII to Miami 24-7.

Minnesota's Point Man

Fred Cox was the

Vikings' kicker for

15 seasons (1963-

1977), scoring a

club-record 1,365

points on 282 field

goals and 519

PATs.

an NFL-record 47,003 yards in 18 seasons to surpass the standard set by legendary Johnny Unitas.

Foreman was the other key in Minnesota's best years. A strong runner with great agility, he provided the Vikings with superb rushing and pass catching.

Along with receivers Gilliam, White, and Rashad, Tarkenton and Foreman propelled a Minnesota team that would be remembered as one of the NFL's dynasties if it had not stumbled in its Super Bowl opportunities.

Tarkenton quarterbacked the Vikings in their last three Super Bowls, but Joe Kapp called signals in Super Bowl IV. A charismatic leader who always seemed able to get the maximum from his talent, Kapp was better known for his results than his style and grace. But as in later Super Bowls, the results were disappointing in a 23-7 loss to Kansas City. The Vikings gained only 67 yards and two first downs by rushing in that game.

Time and age separated the Vikings' stalwarts in the late 1970s. Tarkenton retired in 1978. Foreman left in 1979 and played one more season, for New England. Grant retired in 1983,

Bud Grant

Jeff Siemon

1974
Minnesota wins NFC Central with 10-4 record, loses Super Bowl IX to Pittsburgh 16-6.

1976
Vikings win eighth division title in nine years, lose fourth Super Bowl in eight years, 32-14 to Oakland.

1978
Purple People Eaters broken up: Carl Eller is benched, Alan Page waived.

1979
Vikings have first losing season since 1967. End of an era: Tarkenton, Mick Tingelhoff and Jim Marshall retire, Eller traded to Seattle.

came back for one season in 1985, and then an era ended.

Jerry Burns, for many years regarded as one of the top offensive coaches in the league, became the Vikings' head coach in 1986 and did well under difficult circumstances.

Grant's act would have been hard for anyone to follow, yet Burns led Minnesota through a transitional period with only one losing season in six years. The Vikings developed new stars on offense - quarterbacks Wade Wilson and Rich Gannon, running back Darrin Nelson, tight end Steve Jordan and wide receivers Anthony and Cris Carter on offense, plus defensive standouts in end Chris Doleman, tackle Keith Millard, linebacker Scott Studwell, and safety Joey Browner.

The Vikings won a division title in 1989 and were runners-up three times under Burns, who retired after the 1991 season with a record of 55-46.

Dennis Green, who had coached previously at Northwestern University and Stanford, replaced Burns in 1992. ⌀

The Scramblin' Man

Fran Tarkenton was renowned as a scrambling quarterback, darting from sideline to sideline in search of an open receiver.

But he was also an excellent quarterback with remarkable durability. He played 18 seasons, writing his name into the NFL record book as pro football's all-time passing-yardage leader with 47,003 yards. Dan Fouts is second with 43,040.

Tarkenton began his career with Minnesota as a third-round draft choice in 1961, was traded to the Giants in 1967, then was swapped back to Minnesota in 1972. He retired after the 1978 season.

Tarkenton is the NFL career leader in pass attempts (6,467), completions (3,686), touchdown passes (342) and times sacked (483).

His record-setting performance earned him selection to the Pro Football Hall of Fame.

1983	**1985**		**1989**	**1992**
Grant retires after team finishes 8-8.	Grant returns to coach Vikings to 7-9 record, retires again.	Anthony Carter	Jerry Burns becomes only coach besides Grant to lead Vikings to division championship.	Burns retires after six seasons and 55-46 record; Dennis Green becomes Minnesota's fifth head coach.

SIDELINES

YEAR	■ WINS ■ LOSSES ☐ TIES	RECORD	PLACE	COACH
Boston Patriots				
American Football League				
1960		5-9	4th	Lou Saban
1961		9-4-1	2nd	L. Saban, M. Holovak [1]
1962		9-4-1	2nd	Mike Holovak
1963		7-6-1	1st	Mike Holovak
1964		10-3-1	2nd	Mike Holovak
1965		4-8-2	3rd	Mike Holovak
1966		8-4-2	2nd	Mike Holovak
1967		3-10-1	5th	Mike Holovak
1968		4-10	4th	Mike Holovak
1969		4-10	3rd	Clive Rush
National Football League				
1970		2-12	5th	C. Rush, J. Mazur [2]
New England Patriots				
1971		6-8	3rd	John Mazur
1972		3-11	5th	J. Mazur, P. Bengtson [3]
1973		5-9	3rd	Chuck Fairbanks
1974		7-7	3rd	Chuck Fairbanks
1975		3-11	4th	Chuck Fairbanks
1976		11-3	2nd	Chuck Fairbanks
1977		9-5	3rd	Chuck Fairbanks
1978		11-5	1st	C. Fairbanks, Erhardt & Bullough [4]
1979		9-7	2nd	Ron Erhardt
1980		10-6	2nd	Ron Erhardt
1981		2-14	5th	Ron Erhardt
1982		5-4	7th	Ron Meyer
1983		8-8	2nd	Ron Meyer
1984		9-7	2nd	R. Meyer, R. Berry [5]
1985		11-5	3rd	Raymond Berry
1986		11-5	1st	Raymond Berry
1987		8-7	2nd	Raymond Berry
1988		9-7	3rd	Raymond Berry
1989		5-11	4th	Raymond Berry
1990		1-15	5th	Rod Rust
1991		6-10	4th	Dick MacPherson

1 – Lou Saban (5 games), Mike Holovak (9 games)
2 – Clive Rush (7 games), John Mazur (7 games)
3 – John Mazur (9 games), Phil Bengtson (5 games)
4 – Chuck Fairbanks (15 games),
 Ron Erhardt & Hank Bullough (co-coaches) (1 game)
5 – Ron Meyer (8 games), Raymond Berry (8 games)

For the New England Patriots, the Cinderella story just hasn't worked out the way it does in the fairy tale.

The Patriots have tried to live the Cinderella saga three times, each at least 10 years apart, but they just haven't been able to get the Super Bowl slipper to fit.

Their most recent Cinderella episode came in 1985, when they tried to win the Super Bowl the most difficult way possible - by qualifying as a wild-card team and winning three consecutive playoff games to advance to Super Bowl XX.

In 1976, the Patriots vaulted from a 3-11 record in 1975 to 11-3, one of the most dramatic turnarounds in history, only to have their quest for the Super Bowl cut short.

And in their first decade, the 1963 Patriots found themselves playing for the AFL championship despite a 7-6-1 record.

Oh, Give Me a Home...

The Boston Patriots had trouble finding a permanent home, playing games at Boston University Field, Fenway Park, Harvard Stadium, and Boston College Alumni Stadium in their first decade.

Construction of Schaefer Stadium (later renamed Sullivan Stadium and now called Foxboro Stadium) in Foxboro, Mass., finally provided the club with a home of its own in 1971.

That's when the Patriots changed the team name to reflect a more regional appeal.

1959

NEW ENGLAND PATRIOTS
Turning Points

One of eight original American Football League franchises is granted to group of 10 New England business-men headed by William H. Sullivan, Jr.

They fell short in each bid, but the Patriots have shown a flair for being championship contenders when it was least expected.

The 1985 Patriots provided an especially dramatic chapter, making a strong run at the NFL championship with a series of stunning upsets.

The club had fallen into a pattern of mediocrity...not too good, not too bad...beginning in 1982, when the Patriots went 5-4. The next season, they were 8-8. In 1984, the team was 5-3 when coach Ron Meyer was replaced by Raymond Berry. The change in coaches brought no dramatic change in results; the Patriots were 4-4 under Berry.

The pattern seemed set, but in 1985, New England improved sharply, posting an 11-5 record that qualified for the second of two AFC wild-card berths.

That was good news and bad news. The good news was a trip to the playoffs. The bad news was that the second wild-card team played every game on the road, a very difficult assignment.

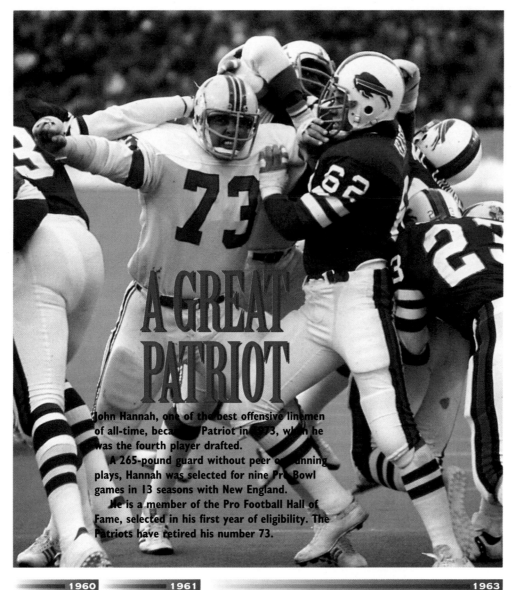

A GREAT PATRIOT

John Hannah, one of the best offensive linemen of all-time, became a Patriot in 1973, when he was the fourth player drafted.

A 265-pound guard without peer on running plays, Hannah was selected for nine Pro Bowl games in 13 seasons with New England.

He is a member of the Pro Football Hall of Fame, selected in his first year of eligibility. The Patriots have retired his number 73.

AT THE CENTER OF THE ACTION

For 11 years, the Patriots paid center Bill Lenkaitis to drill holes through opposing defenses, creating running room for New England ball carriers.

More recently, his focus has been on a different type of drill. Lenkaitis is the club's dentist.

The Penn State graduate was the Patriots' center from 1971-1981, part of an offensive line that included guard John Hannah and tackle Leon Gray, and was one of the best in the league.

1960	1961	1963
Boston Patriots, coached by Lou Saban, register 5-9 record in first season.	Saban is replaced after five games by Mike Holovak; team goes 7-1-1 under new coach for season record of 9-4-1.	Boston ties Buffalo for first place with 7-6-1 record, wins playoff, loses AFL Championship Game 51-10 to San Diego.

Babe Parilli

Sam Bam

Sam (Bam) Cunningham was among the top running backs in the 1970s, when he was the key to the New England offense. The Patriots' rushing leader six times, Cunningham holds the club yardage record of 5,453. Sam is the older brother of Eagles quarterback Randall Cunningham.

Two wild-card teams had previously reached the Super Bowl, the Cowboys in 1975 and the Raiders in 1980, but neither had to win three road games before getting to the Super Bowl.

The Patriots began their bid at New York, where they beat the Jets 26-14, despite getting only one touchdown from the offensive unit. Tony Franklin kicked four field goals, linebacker Johnny Rembert ran 15 yards for a touchdown with a recovered fumble, and that was enough to move to the next playoff round.

The second stop was Los Angeles, where safety Jim Bowman recovered a fumbled kickoff in the Raiders' end zone for the touchdown that gave New England a 27-20 victory and a shot at the AFC championship in Miami.

That appeared to be an impossible mission - the Patriots had lost 18 consecutive games in the Orange Bowl. But they saved their best for that day, routing the Dolphins 31-14 to earn a spot opposite Chicago in Super Bowl XX.

A 'Find' in the Fifth Round

The Patriots drafted three quarterbacks in the first round - Jack Concannon (1964), Jim Plunkett (1971), and Tony Eason (1983) - and traded first-round draft choices for other quarterbacks - Joe Kapp and Tom Owen.
But no quarterback served New England as long, or as well, as Steve Grogan, a fifth-round selection in 1975. He played 16 years for the Patriots and led the team in passing 11 times.
Grogan, who retired after the 1990 season, had 1,879 completions for 26,886 yards and 182 touchdowns, all club records. An outstanding scrambler, he also had 2,164 rushing yards and scored 35 touchdowns.

1965	1971		1973	
Patriots draft fullback Jim Nance on nineteenth round; he becomes club's all-time rushing leader.	*Club changes name to New England Patriots, moves to Schaefer Stadium in Foxboro, Mass.; drafts quarterback Jim Plunkett in first round.*		*Chuck Fairbanks becomes Patriots' coach; team drafts fullback Sam Cunningham, guard John Hannah, and wide receiver Darryl Stingley.*	

That's when New England ran out of magic. The Bears had a 17-1 record and had shut out the Giants and Rams en route to the Super Bowl. There would be no more miracles from the upstarts in this one; the Bears won 46-10.

The Patriots had another "come out of nowhere" season nine years earlier. The 1975 Patriots were weak, losing their last six games in a 3-11 season. They were outscored by 100 points.

But they were a different team in 1976, as the defense had 50 takeaways, the offense was second in the league in scoring, and the team pounded out an 11-3 record.

The Patriots suffered a heartbreaking 24-21 loss to the Raiders in the divisional playoff game when Oakland quarterback Ken Stabler scored a touchdown with 10 seconds remaining. New England was guilty of a key personal foul penalty on a third down play in the Raiders' winning drive.

The first Cinderella effort, in 1963, didn't have such a dramatic ending. The Patriots' 7-6-1

A Late-Round Bargain

Jim Nance came to New England as a nineteenth (next-to-last) round draft pick from Syracuse in 1965, a fullback with a reputation of problems keeping his weight under control.

But he became an outstanding player, piling up 5,323 rushing yards in a seven-year Patriots career. Only Sam Cunningham (5,453) had more yardage. Nance holds the Patriots' record of 45 rushing touchdowns.

Fleet Feet

The Patriots have had no other wide receiver quite like Stanley Morgan. In fact,

they haven't had two receivers whose combined statistics were the equal of Morgan's.

The speedster from Tennessee, a first-round pick in 1977, played for New England

13 years and piled up 10,352 receiving yards, more than the next two Patriots combined.

1975

New England drafts tight end Russ Francis in first round, quarterback Steve Grogan in fifth.

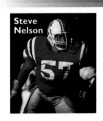

Steve Nelson

1978

Before the last game, Fairbanks announces plans to quit at season's end. AFC East champions, Patriots lose in first round of playoffs.

1983

Patriots draft quarterback Tony Eason in first round.

The (Un)Masked Marvel

Forget all the advances in technology, space age plastics, and such. Jesse Richardson preferred things the old-fashioned way. A defensive tackle, Richardson played for the Patriots from 1962-64, a time when facemasks were standard equipment. But the veteran, who had played for the Philadelphia Eagles from 1953-1961, got special permission from American Football League Commissioner Joe Foss to play without a face mask. The 6-foot 2-inch, 270-pounder suffered a broken nose several times, but retired without having lost any teeth...a remarkable achievement.

record tied Buffalo for first place in the AFL Eastern Division; New England beat Buffalo 26-8 in a playoff, then got bounced 51-10 in the AFL Championship Game by a superior San Diego team.

That 1963 division title was one of only three the Patriots have won. Another came in 1978 and the most recent was in 1986.

The 1978 season ended with some bizarre circumstances. Using a powerful ground game that featured fullback Sam Cunningham behind an excellent offensive line headed by John Hannah and Leon Gray, New England had an 11-4 record and was a strong Super Bowl possibility. But in the hours before the last game of the season, coach Chuck Fairbanks announced his intention to quit the team after the season to become head coach at the University of Colorado.

Shocked by the news, the Patriots lost the season finale 23-3 to Miami, then were eliminated from the playoffs the following week 31-14 by Houston.

Fairbanks's stunning exit wasn't the only unusual coaching change in Patriots' history. In

A Change for the Better

Gino Cappelletti played well in Boston's secondary in 1960, leading the team with four interceptions. But head coach Lou Saban saw untapped potential in the rookie from Minnesota, and he made a change in the last game of the year, playing Cappelletti at wide receiver.

He caught only one pass for 28 yards that day, but it was the start of a great career. He played 11 years for the Patriots, catching 292 passes, including 42 for touchdowns.

He was even better as a kicker, and accounted for 1,130 points as a kicker and receiver. Cappelletti led the AFL in scoring five times in seven seasons (1960-66). The Patriots have retired his number 20.

Russ Francis
"All-Universe" tight end caught 207 passes in eight seasons

1984	**1985**	**1986**
Raymond Berry replaces Ron Meyer as head coach at midseason.	Patriots qualify as wild card for postseason play-offs with 11-5 record, win road games at New York, Los Angeles, and Miami; lose Super Bowl XX 46-10 to Chicago.	John Hannah retires.

1972, when New England was struggling with a 2-7 record, coach John Mazur resigned. That wasn't surprising. But the choice of replacement was - Phil Bengtson, a former Packers head coach, who was working as a scout for San Diego. Bengtson, on loan from the Chargers, coached the last five games of the season, then returned to San Diego.

In 1984, the Berry-for-Meyer change occurred after Meyer fired defensive coordinator Rod Rust without general manager Patrick Sullivan's permission. Sullivan then replaced Meyer with Berry, and rehired Rust. The next year, Berry led the Patriots to the Super Bowl, and in 1986 he took them to an AFC East title.

New England slipped to 5-11 in 1989 and 1-15 in 1990 before hiring Dick MacPherson from the University of Syracuse. The Patriots responded well to MacPherson's enthusiastic leadership, rallying to a 6-10 season in 1991. ⊘

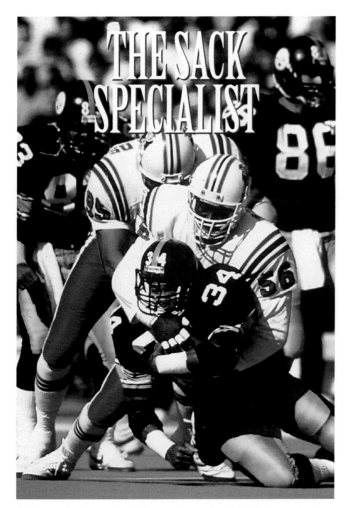

Andre Tippett has been a nightmare for opposing quarterbacks. A linebacker equally adept at rushing the passer or dropping back into coverage, he had accounted for a club-record 84 1/2 sacks at the end of the 1991 season. A second-round draft pick out of Iowa in 1982, Tippett was a Pro Bowl linebacker five times in 10 years.

Only shoulder injury kept him from even more all-star game invitations.

HE ANSWERED THE CALL

When the Boston Patriots assembled their first squad in 1960, they drew players from a variety of sources. Ed (Butch) Songin was working as a Boston-area probation officer when he responded to a call for tryouts. The 36-year old Songin, who had played in the Canadian Football League, became the Patriots' first quarterback, passing for 3,905 yards and 36 touchdowns in two seasons.

HAYNES: The Label of Quality

Mike Haynes, a cornerback gifted with great speed and pass coverage skills, was the Patriots' first-round draft pick in 1976, the fifth player chosen.

He played for New England from 1976-1982, intercepting 28 passes and earning six Pro Bowl invitations. Haynes also was an excellent punt returner, averaging 10.4 yards.

1988	**1991**	**1992**
Victor Kiam becomes majority owner of Patriots.	Dick MacPherson becomes head coach.	Group headed by James B. Orthwein purchases Patriots.

YEAR	■ WINS □ LOSSES □ TIES	RECORD	PLACE	COACH
1967		3-11	4th	Tom Fears
1968		4-9-1	3rd	Tom Fears
1969		5-9	3rd	Tom Fears
1970		2-11-1	4th	T. Fears, J.D. Roberts [1]
1971		4-8-2	4th	J.D. Roberts
1972		2-11-1	4th	J.D. Roberts
1973		5-9	3rd	John North
1974		5-9	3rd	John North
1975		2-12	4th	J. North, E. Hefferle [2]
1976		4-10	4th	Hank Stram
1977		3-11	4th	Hank Stram
1978		7-9	3rd	Dick Nolan
1979		8-8	2nd	Dick Nolan
1980		1-15	4th	D. Nolan, D. Stanfel [3]
1981		4-12	4th	O.A. (Bum) Phillips
1982		4-5	9th	O.A. (Bum) Phillips
1983		8-8	3rd	O.A. (Bum) Phillips
1984		7-9	3rd	O.A. (Bum) Phillips
1985		5-11	3rd	B. Phillips, W. Phillips [4]
1986		7-9	4th	Jim Mora
1987		12-3	2nd	Jim Mora
1988		10-6	3rd	Jim Mora
1989		9-7	3rd	Jim Mora
1990		8-8	2nd	Jim Mora
1991		11-5	1st	Jim Mora

1 — Tom Fears (7 games), J.D. Roberts (7 games)
2 — John North (6 games), Ernie Hefferle (8 games)
3 — Dick Nolan (12 games), Dick Stanfel (4 games)
4 — Bum Phillips (12 games), Wade Phillips (4 games)

For two decades, "The Big Easy" was more than a nickname for New Orleans. It also referred to the city's football team. From 1967 through 1987, the Saints failed to have a winning season.

They employed nine head coaches, several general managers, and hundreds of players to little avail. The high-water marks were .500 seasons in 1979 and 1983.

The nadir arrived in 1980, when the Saints lost 15 of 16 games. Some fans, feigning embarrassment, wore paper bags over their heads at games. Others stopped attending; home atten-

WhoDat?

Long-suffering Saints' fans were eager to see their team have a winning season, and when they thought they were witnessing progress, they responded with enthusiasm.

Bum Phillips, who made the Houston Oilers a perennial contender in the 1970s, led the Saints to a 4-5 record in 1982 and 8-8 the following year. That was heady stuff by New Orleans standards, and fans were thrilled.

Attendance for home games soared to an average of 66,235 in 1983, an increase of 15,000 per game over the previous season. Saints' home games offered a party atmosphere, and the Superdome rocked to the rhythmic chant, "Who dat? Who dat? Who dat say dey gonna beat dem Saints? Who dat?"

Years later, the Saints' fan club continues to be called "The Who Dat Club."

	1966
NEW ORLEANS SAINTS	NFL awards franchise to New Orleans on All Saints Day.
Turning Points	

dance fell by nearly 110,000 from the previous year. The average home attendance, 48,227, was the second-lowest in club history.

A turnaround started in 1986, the twentieth year of the team's existence. The key events:

- Tom Benson, the club's new owner, hired Jim Finks as general manager.
- Finks recruited Jim Mora to coach the Saints.

Finks, who played a major role in building strong teams at Minnesota and Chicago, had an impressive resume. And Mora had distinguished himself as a coach who won championships in the United States Football League.

Finks and Mora were a formidable team. In 1986, their first season together, New Orleans had a 7-9 record. The next year, the Saints were 12-3 - the first winning season in 21 tries - and Benson's victory dance on the sidelines became a regular occurrence.

New Orleans followed with seasons of 10-6 and 9-7, then won its first division champ-

RECORD BREAKER

Tom Dempsey was an unlikely hero for the New Orleans Saints. Born without a right hand and no toes on his right foot, Dempsey nevertheless had a memorable career as a kicker for the Saints. He set an NFL record in 1970 when he kicked a 63-yard field goal against the Detroit Lions.

Dempsey's kick came as time expired and gave the Saints a 19-17 victory. It was one of only two victories for New Orleans that season.

Dempsey, who was with New Orleans two years (1969-1970), was successful on 40 of 75 field goal attempts.

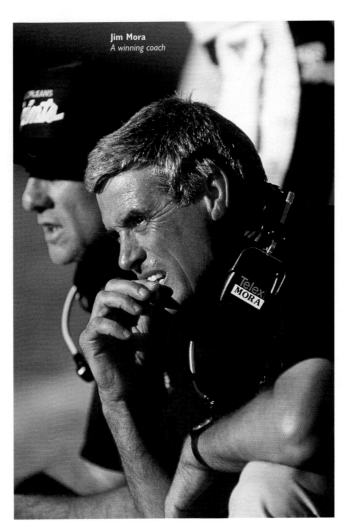

Jim Mora
A winning coach

1967

With Tom Fears as head coach, Saints have 3-11 record in first season.

1970

Tom Dempsey kicks NFL record 63-yard field goal.

A Sign of Things to Come

It happened in the Saints' initial season, and it was a portent of the frustrations the team would encounter for two decades.

In a game at Philadelphia on November 19, 1967, quarterback Billy Kilmer threw a pass to Walter Roberts that turned into the longest gain in Saints' history - 96 yards - but it wasn't a touchdown.

Kilmer was the Saints' quarterback for four seasons, passing for 7,490 yards and 47 touchdowns, before being traded to coach George Allen's "Over The Hill Gang" in Washington.

ionship with an 11-5 record in 1991.

A no-nonsense coach whose approach reflected his background as a Marine captain, Mora whipped the Saints into winning shape. His imprint was unmistakable.

Mora had coached the Philadelphia/Baltimore franchise of the USFL, posting a 48-13-1 mark and winning two league championships in three years. His teams were known for solid defense, and an offense that made few mistakes.

He brought a similar style to New Orleans. He also took in-depth knowledge of USFL personnel. Some of the players who played major roles in the Saints' surge - quarterback Bobby Hebert and linebackers Vaughan Johnson and Sam Mills - came from the failed league.

Johnson and Mills joined Rickey Jackson and Pat Swilling to form a linebacker corps that soon was among the best. Each of the four earned at least three Pro Bowl selections.

Hebert, a fiery field leader, worked Mora's ball-control passing game well, completing a

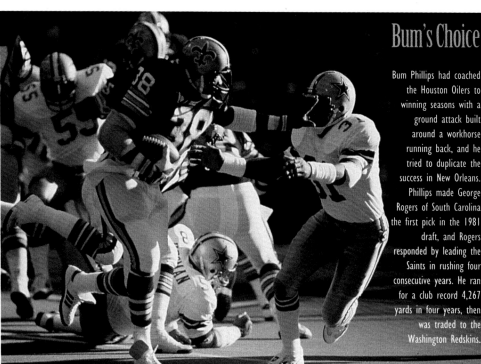

Bum's Choice

Bum Phillips had coached the Houston Oilers to winning seasons with a ground attack built around a workhorse running back, and he tried to duplicate the success in New Orleans. Phillips made George Rogers of South Carolina the first pick in the 1981 draft, and Rogers responded by leading the Saints in rushing four consecutive years. He ran for a club record 4,267 yards in four years, then was traded to the Washington Redskins.

Retired Numbers

The Saints began life in 1967 with two future Hall of Famers in their lineup, having acquired fullback Jim Taylor from Green Bay and defensive end Doug Atkins from Chicago in the expansion draft.
Taylor played only one season before retiring; he was the Saints' leading rusher in 1967, gaining 390 yards on 130 carries. Atkins played three seasons.
Taylor's 31 and Atkins's 81 are the only two numbers retired by the Saints.

1971	**1975**	**1976**
New Orleans drafts Mississippi quarterback Archie Manning.	*Saints move into Superdome.*	*Hank Stram becomes head coach, Saints have 4-10 record.*

club-record 62.9 percent of his passes in 1989.

The Saints earned three playoff berths in Mora's first six years but were winless in postseason games.

New Orleans had been a perennial doormat before Finks and Mora took over; the Saints had a cumulative record of 83-187-5 over 20 years.

They began with a cast of veterans who had seen better years. In the expansion draft of 1967, New Orleans selected running back Jim Taylor, defensive end Doug Atkins, quarterback Billy Kilmer, and defensive tackles Earl Leggett and Lou Cordileone.

"You need some old heads to settle the youngsters," explained coach Tom Fears. Over the course of the next three years, all but Kilmer retired.

Morten Andersen's career in professional football didn't start quite the way he would have liked - he sprained his ankle on the opening kickoff of the opening game in 1982.

Andersen finished his rookie season with only two field goals and six extra points, but his performance improved dramatically the next season, when he produced 91 points. After 1991, his tenth season with the Saints, Andersen held club records for scoring (965 points), field goals (217), and extra points (285). His field goal accuracy (.772) is one of the best in the history of the game.

Saints' Scoring ACE

1978	1979	1981
Quarterback Archie Manning is UPI National Conference player of year, MVP on team with 7-9 record.	Saints have 8-8 record under coach Dick Nolan, only non-losing record in franchise's first 16 years.	O.A. (Bum) Phillips is hired as head coach.

223

A Fast Start

John Gilliam got the Saints off on the right foot when he returned the opening kickoff in their first game 94 yards for a touchdown. Despite Gilliam's heroics, the Saints lost to the Rams 27-13. Gilliam returned 31 kickoffs for New Orleans, but his first was the only one for a touchdown.

The new expansion team started respectably, with records of 3-11, 4-9-1, and 5-9, but then progress stopped. The Saints simply didn't do a good job of replenishing the roster.

A critical area of failure was the first round of the draft. Because of their poor record each year, the Saints always were among the first in line at the annual draft. But they repeatedly traded away their first pick - in 1967, 1968, and 1969 - and they also dealt away second-round picks from 1968-1972.

The coach's office had a revolving door. Fears was fired after seven games of his fourth season and was followed by J.D. Roberts, John North, Ernie Hefferle, Hank Stram, Dick Nolan, Dick Stanfel, Bum Phillips, and Wade Phillips in the next 15 years. Only Bum Phillips managed to hold the job for at least three full seasons.

Except for quarterback Archie Manning, wide receiver Danny Abramowicz, and running

Saint Archie

Even when there was little else for Saints' fans to cheer, there was quarterback Archie Manning. New Orleans's first draft choice in 1971 made quite a debut, scoring the winning touchdown on the final play of the season opener to give the Saints a 24-20 victory over the Rams.

The next year, Manning accounted for 20 of the Saints' 26 touchdowns. In 1978, even though New Orleans had another losing record, Manning was honored by UPI as the NFC's player of the year.

Manning, an All-America at nearby Ole Miss, played 11 seasons for the Saints and holds most of the club's passing records. He had 1,849 completions for 21,734 yards and 115 touchdowns.

Thunder & Lightning

Coach Hank Stram made running backs Chuck Muncie and Tony Galbreath the Saints' first two draft picks in 1976, and promptly designated them his "Thunder and Lightning" attack.

Muncie led the Saints in rushing, and Galbreath led in pass receptions in 1976 and 1977. They played together in New Orleans for a little more than four years. Muncie had 3,386 rushing yards and 1,086 receiving yards; Galbreath ran for 2,865 yards and caught 284 passes for 2,221 yards.

1982
Saints trade Archie Manning to Houston Oilers for tackle Leon Gray.

1984
New Orleans trades first-round draft picks in 1984 and 1985 to acquire quarterback Richard Todd and running back Earl Campbell.

1985
Tom Benson buys Saints.

backs Chuck Muncie and George Rogers, the Saints had few standouts on offense in their first two decades. Only two offensive linemen have been selected to play in the Pro Bowl - guards Jake Kupp (1969) and Brad Edelman (1987).

When Finks arrived in New Orleans, the Saints stopped dealing away first-and second-round draft picks. The only exception in his first seven years on the job occurred in 1990, when Finks traded first-and third-round picks in the 1991 draft and a conditional second-rounder in 1992 to acquire quarterback Steve Walsh from Dallas. That trade was motivated by Hebert's season-long holdout.

The new emphasis on building through sound drafting helped end the long drought in New Orleans. ⌀

ALL-STAR LINEBACKERS

When the Saints arrived as a contender, it was largely on the strength of solid defense, and the linebacker corps was the heart of the unit.

The quartet of Rickey Jackson, Vaughan Johnson, Sam Mills, and Pat Swilling was outstanding as a group, and each linebacker earned individual honors. Johnson, Mills, and Swilling were starters in the 1992 Pro Bowl, the third appearance for each. Jackson played in four consecutive Pro Bowls from 1984-87.

Jackson was a second-round draft pick out of Pittsburgh in 1981; Swilling, a third-rounder out of Georgia Tech in 1986. Johnson was taken on the first round of the USFL supplemental draft in 1984, and Mills was signed in 1986 as a free agent after playing in the USFL.

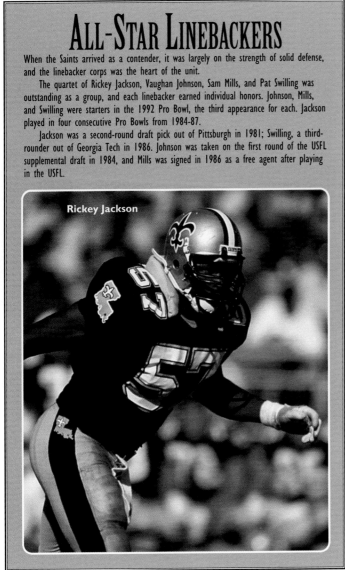

Rickey Jackson

The Last Shall Be First

Danny Abramowicz wasn't the last player taken by New Orleans in the 1967 draft, but he was close. The wide receiver from Xavier (Ohio) was picked in the seventeenth - and last - round. The Saints also had two other picks in that round.

Those other seventeenth-rounders, Billy Bob Stewart and Jimmy Walker, didn't make the team, but Abramowicz wrote his name into the New Orleans record book, leading the Saints in receptions each of the club's first five years. He played six and a half years for New Orleans, with 309 receptions for 4,875 yards and 37 touchdowns.

1986

Jim Finks becomes general manager, hires Jim Mora as head coach.

1987

In twenty-first season, Saints finally have winning record, posting 12-3 mark

1991

New Orleans wins first NFC Western Division championship with 11-5 record.

New York GIANTS

YEAR	■ WINS ■ LOSSES □ TIES	RECORD	PLACE	COACH
1925		8-4	4th	Robert Folwell
1926		8-4-1	6th	Joseph Alexander
1927		11-1-1	1st	Earl Potteiger
1928		4-7-2	6th	Earl Potteiger
1929		13-1-1	2nd	LeRoy Andrews
1930		13-4	2nd	L. Andrews, B. Friedman [1]
1931		7-6-1	5th	Steve Owen
1932		4-6-2	5th	Steve Owen
1933		11-3	1st	Steve Owen
1934		8-5	1st	Steve Owen
1935		9-3	1st	Steve Owen
1936		5-6-1	3rd	Steve Owen
1937		6-3-2	2nd	Steve Owen
1938		8-2-1	1st	Steve Owen
1939		9-1-1	1st	Steve Owen
1940		6-4-1	3rd	Steve Owen
1941		8-3	1st	Steve Owen
1942		5-5-1	3rd	Steve Owen
1943		6-3-1	2nd	Steve Owen
1944		8-1-1	1st	Steve Owen
1945		3-6-1	3rd	Steve Owen
1946		7-3-1	1st	Steve Owen
1947		2-8-2	5th	Steve Owen
1948		4-8	3rd	Steve Owen
1949		6-6	3rd	Steve Owen
1950		10-2	2nd	Steve Owen
1951		9-2-1	2nd	Steve Owen
1952		7-5	2nd	Steve Owen
1953		3-9	5th	Steve Owen
1954		7-5	3rd	Jim Lee Howell
1955		6-5-1	3rd	Jim Lee Howell
1956		8-3-1	1st	Jim Lee Howell
1957		7-5	2nd	Jim Lee Howell
1958		9-3	1st	Jim Lee Howell
1959		10-2	1st	Jim Lee Howell
1960		6-4-2	3rd	Jim Lee Howell
1961		10-3-1	1st	Allie Sherman
1962		12-2	1st	Allie Sherman
1963		11-3	1st	Allie Sherman
1964		2-10-2	7th	Allie Sherman
1965		7-7	2nd	Allie Sherman
1966		1-12-1	8th	Allie Sherman
1967		7-7	2nd	Allie Sherman
1968		7-7	2nd	Allie Sherman
1969		6-8	2nd	Alex Webster
1970		9-5	2nd	Alex Webster
1971		4-10	5th	Alex Webster
1972		8-6	3rd	Alex Webster
1973		2-11-1	5th	Alex Webster
1974		2-12	5th	Bill Arnsparger
1975		5-9	4th	Bill Arnsparger
1976		3-11	5th	B. Arnsparger, J. McVay [2]
1977		5-9	5th	John McVay
1978		6-10	5th	John McVay
1979		6-10	4th	Ray Perkins
1980		4-12	5th	Ray Perkins
1981		9-7	3rd	Ray Perkins
1982		4-5	10th	Ray Perkins
1983		3-12-1	5th	Bill Parcells
1984		9-7	2nd	Bill Parcells
1985		10-6	2nd	Bill Parcells
1986		14-2	1st	Bill Parcells
1987		6-9	5th	Bill Parcells
1988		10-6	2nd	Bill Parcells
1989		12-4	1st	Bill Parcells
1990		13-3	1st	Bill Parcells
1991		8-8	4th	Ray Handley

1 — LeRoy Andrews (15 games), Benny Friedman (2 games)

2 — Bill Arnsparger (7 games), John McVay (7 games)

DEE-fense...DEE-fense...DEE-fense.

From the Bronx to Brooklyn, from Manhattan to The Meadowlands, the chant reverberates each time the New York Giants play.

The storied franchise, now in its eighth decade, has a legacy of excellence on defense. There have been great passers and runners, stars at every position on offense. But, above all, the New York

BEWARE OF GIANTS WEARING SNEAKERS

Two of the New York Giants' NFL championships can be attributed, at least in part, to the shoes they wore...basketball shoes.

On a frigid day in December, 1934, the Giants and Bears were skidding around on the icy Polo Grounds field, neither team able to gain traction. Before the game, a Giants' equipment manager had hurried to nearby Manhattan College and returned to the stadium loaded down with basketball shoes. The Giants changed to the basketball shoes at halftime, and went on to score 27 points in the final quarter to win the championship 30-13 over the slip-sliding Bears.

In 1956, the Giants played the Bears (again) for the championship (again) on an icy field (again). This time it was Giants defensive end Andy Robustelli, owner of a sporting goods store, who supplied his teammates with sneakers. The underdog Giants won the championship 47-7.

1925

NEW YORK GIANTS

Turning Points

Tim Mara purchases an NFL franchise for New York City for $500.

Giants have been synonymous with defense.

It was in 1960 that CBS presented a 30-minute documentary entitled, "The Violent World of Sam Huff." The Giants' middle linebacker was wired for sound in an exhibition game against the Bears, and the cameras zoomed in for close-ups of the action. The show was televised in prime time to a nation just fully awakening to professional football. The country heard the collisions and almost felt the impact as armored 230-pounders slammed into each other at high speed...dramatic stuff.

This was before the era of slow motion replays and tight camera closeups; the documentary showed sports fans something new.

It was fitting that the New York Giants were selected to be "stars" of a show that glorified defense as played in the National Football League.

For 23 years - 1931-1953 - the Giants were coached by Steve Owen, who believed football games were won on defense. He was a tackle on the 1927 Giants, winners of the NFL championship with an 11-1-1 record that included 10 shutouts. When Owen became head coach four years later, he built his team around the defense.

Jim Thorpe

Jim Thorpe, a legendary name in American sports, played professional football for seven teams. One was the Giants, who signed him for the 1925 season, their first.

Thorpe, a gold medal winner in the 1912 Olympics, had already played 11 pro football years. Although he was past his prime, the halfback still helped the Giants to an 8-4 record.

A Giant Pioneer

Steve Owen earned a berth in the Pro Football Hall of Fame with 23 years at the helm of the New York Giants, a span in which the team won eight divisional championships and two NFL titles. His contract consisted only of a handshake with the owner.

A coach who emphasized power offense and strong defense, Owen was the innovator who introduced the concept of two-platoon football. He also devised the "umbrella defense," which Tom Landry later adapted to the 4-3-4 alignment that became the standard.

Owen's career record was 153-108-17; he was replaced after the 1953 season.

Sam Huff
Hall of Fame Middle Linebacker

Andy Robustelli and Jim Katcavage

1927	**1930**
Giants have 11-1-1 record, win first league championship.	Club ownership is turned over to Jack and Wellington Mara, sons of the founder.

Super Safety

When Steve Owen designed his famous "umbrella defense" to stop the aerial attack of the Cleveland Browns, he had the perfect player for the safety position. Emlen Tunnell, a rookie free agent signed in 1948, had great speed, good hands, and ballhawk instincts. He became a superb safety, earning nine trips to the Pro Bowl (eight with the Giants), and winning induction into the Pro Football Hall of Fame. When he retired in 1961, Tunnell held the league interception record with 79.

Owen coached the Giants to three consecutive division titles from 1933-35, won three in a four-year span from 1938-1941, and won two in three years again from 1944-46, giving New York eight Eastern Division titles in 14 years. The club won NFL championships in 1934 and 1938.

When the NFL absorbed the Cleveland Browns from the All-America Football Conference in 1950, the Browns overwhelmed everyone...except the Giants. Cleveland lost only twice that season, both times to New York. Owen devised the "umbrella defense," a 6-1-4 or 5-1-5 alignment that held the explosive Browns' offense to only 21 points in three games, including Cleveland's 8-3 playoff victory for the division title.

The Browns and Giants battled at the top of the standings for several years, and each club developed new headliners. For the Cleveland offense, it was running back Jim Brown, the NFL rushing champ eight times in nine years (1957-1965). For the New York defense, it was Huff, linemen Andy Robustelli, Jim Katcavage, Roosevelt Grier, and Dick Modzelewski, and backs Emlen Tunnell, Jim Patton, Linden Crow and Erich Barnes. Huff, Robustelli, and Tunnell all have earned selection to the Pro Football Hall of Fame. Not surprisingly, Brown had more trouble against the Giants than against any other team.

Tom Landry, who played defensive back in Owen's "umbrella defense," became an assistant coach in the late 1950s. Landry altered the "umbrella" to a 4-3-4, an alignment that became standard for every team in the league. The 4-3-4 provided additional strength in the line and at the wings to harness Brown.

He Came, He Conquered, He Left

The best way for a coach to assure job security is to win. But Bill Parcells had a relatively brief eight-year career despite being very successful.

Parcells became the Giants' boss in 1983, taking over a club that had only one winning season the previous 10 years, and quickly turned it into one of pro football's best.

The Giants were 3-12-1 in Parcells's rookie season, then finished either first or second in the NFC East in six of the next seven years. Parcells posted a record of 85-52-1, coached two Super Bowl winners, and retired in 1991.

The most dominant defensive player of the 1980s, Lawrence Taylor was elected to the Pro Bowl in each of his first 10 years in the NFL (1981-1990).

An outside linebacker who entered the 1992 season as the NFL's all-time leader in sacks (121 1/2), he was the second player chosen in the 1981 draft. He was a unanimous selection to the All-Pro Team of the 1980s.

1931

Steve Owen becomes head coach; Giants sign center-linebacker Mel Hein.

1934

In famous "Sneakers" game, Giants wear basketball shoes to gain traction on icy field and beat Bears 30-13 for NFL title.

Jim Patton

The New York defense was loaded with all-stars, but the primary focus was on two key players: Brown and Huff - the league's best runner, and the man assigned to shadow him.

Huff didn't discourage the "violent world" image. "We try to hurt everybody," he said. "We hit each other as hard as we can. This is a man's game."

Sports fans loved the macho, "tough guy" talk, and the popularity of defensive specialists increased as never before.

Owen was replaced after the 1953 season, but his New York successors continued the tradition. First Jim Lee Howell and then Allie Sherman coached the Giants; each won three division titles. The Giants finished first in six of eight seasons (1956-1963), and the reputation of their vaunted defense continued to grow.

Both Howell and Sherman had great success during the regular season, but the Giants lost five of six NFL Championship Games, beating only the Chicago Bears 47-7 in 1956. There were near-misses: an overtime 23-17 loss to the Colts in 1958 in "The Greatest Game Ever Played," 16-7 to Green Bay in 1962, and 14-10 to the Bears in 1963.

After the 1963 title game, age and injuries took a toll, and New York slipped in the standings.

The Giants were last in the division six times in eight years (1971-78) when Tim and Wellington Mara, the team's owners, made the first in a series of acquisitions that would return the Giants to powerhouse status.

In 1979, the Maras hired George Young as general manager. His first draft pick was a

Roosevelt Brown

THE TWO ROOSEVELTS

New York City, home of many Roosevelts, gained two more in the 1950s, when Roosevelt Brown and Roosevelt Grier were standouts for the Giants.

Brown, an offensive tackle out of Morgan State, was among the best of his era, winning selection to the Pro Bowl nine times in his 13-year career. The 255-pounder was inducted into the Pro Football Hall of Fame in 1975.

Grier, a defensive tackle out of Penn State, accompanied Brown to the Pro Bowl in 1957 and 1960. He was traded in 1963 to the Los Angeles Rams, where he played four seasons as a member of the "Fearsome Foursome" before retiring.

The Giffer:
A GIANT HERO

Frank Gifford was practically the entire Giants' offense when New York was winning division championships in the late 1950s. He led the club in rushing four consecutive years (1956-59), and doubled as the leading receiver five years (1955-59).

Gifford is fourth on the Giants' all-time rushing list with 3,609 yards, and is second with 367 pass receptions. He still has the best career rushing average (4.3 yards) and owns the Giants' record for total touchdowns with 78.

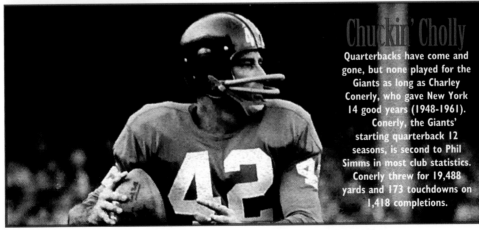

Chuckin' Cholly

Quarterbacks have come and gone, but none played for the Giants as long as Charley Conerly, who gave New York 14 good years (1948-1961). Conerly, the Giants' starting quarterback 12 seasons, is second to Phil Simms in most club statistics. Conerly threw for 19,488 yards and 173 touchdowns on 1,418 completions.

1938	1953	1956
Another NFL championship for New York; Giants beat Green Bay 23-17 for title.	*Jim Lee Howell succeeds Steve Owen after 23 years as head coach; Owen had a 153-108-17 record.*	*Giants draft linebacker Sam Huff, trade for defensive end Andy Robustelli; both go on to Hall of Fame careers. New York routs Bears 47-7 to win NFL title.*

Joe Morrison

229

controversial but great one - little-known quarterback Phil Simms out of Morehead State. Two years later, Young drafted linebacker Lawrence Taylor out of North Carolina. And in 1983, he added the last essential ingredient, head coach Bill Parcells.

Simms became a Pro Bowl quarterback and Super Bowl MVP, and Parcells was lauded as coach of the year, but it was Taylor who personified the "new" Giants, just as Tunnell, Huff and Robustelli had personified the Giants of an earlier time.

As other Giants before him, Taylor changed the way pro football defenses played. A 245-pounder with sensational speed, Taylor blitzed quarterbacks as no linebacker ever had, and offenses were forced into major adjustments to protect quarterbacks.

A Pro Bowl player his first 10 years in the NFL, Taylor was widely regarded as the greatest outside linebacker of all time.

With Taylor the centerpiece of a superb defensive unit that included linebackers Harry Carson and Carl Banks, linemen Jim Burt and Leonard Marshall, the Giants became football's best team again. They won Super Bowl XXI 39-20 over Denver, and took Super Bowl XXIV from Buffalo 20-19.

When the Giants were winning championships, there were many great performers on offense.

NOT TOO OLD

When the Giants acquired Y.A. Tittle from the San Francisco 49ers in a 1961 trade, he was already 34 years old and faced with proving he wasn't over the hill. He proved much more than that.

Tittle was the *United Press International* NFL player of the year in 1962, and led the league in passing in 1963. He took the Giants to three consecutive Conference championships. Tittle, a six-time Pro Bowl selection, retired in 1964 after throwing for 33,070 yards, including 4,731 in the AAFC, and 242 touchdowns (30 in the AAFC). He was inducted into the Hall of Fame in 1971.

Giants' All-Time Passing Leader

The Giants' first-round selection of Phil Simms in 1979 was greeted with a torrent of criticism and second-guessing. The Giants seemed to need help on defense more than offense, and who was this guy out of Morehead State, anyway? Simms showed 'em. After 12 seasons, his name is atop most of the Giants' passing records. Going into the 1992 season, Simms was number one in completions (2,246), passing yards (29,512), and touchdown passes (179). His best game was Super Bowl XXI, when he completed 22 of 25 passes for 268 yards and 3 touchdowns to spark the Giants to a 39-20 victory over Denver.

1961	1979	1981
Allie Sherman becomes head coach; New York gets quarterback Y.A. Tittle in trade.	George Young becomes general manager, quarterback Phil Simms is first round draft pick.	Giants draft linebacker Lawrence Taylor.

Pete Gogolak

Center Mel Hein and halfbacks Tuffy Leemans and Ed Danowski were heroes in the 1930s, quarterback Charley Conerly, halfbacks Frank Gifford and Kyle Rote, fullback Alex Webster, tackle Roosevelt Brown and center Ray Wietecha were offensive stars of the 1950s.

Brown, Gifford, quarterback Y.A. Tittle, and wide receiver Del Shofner were Pro Bowlers when the Giants won championships in the early 1960s.

Beginning in 1976, the Giants went nine years without sending an offensive player to the Pro Bowl, a drought broken by Simms and running back Joe Morris in 1985. Morris (who was succeeded by Ottis Anderson) and Simms rewrote the New York records for rushing and passing, adding balance that made the Giants almost impossible to beat.

Few teams did. The 1986 Giants were 17-2, in 1990 they were 16-3. Success at the Super Bowl level demands excellence on both offense and defense.

New York's offense carried its share of the load, but the Super Bowl Giants were generally recognized as teams that won with defense.

That perception wasn't surprising. Since the 1920s, the New York Giants have been synonymous with defensive excellence. ⊘

The Little Giant

At 5-feet 7-inches, Joe Morris was hardly a giant. But he was, without question, a Giant.

Morris, a 195-pound speedster who played for New York from 1982-88, is the club's all-time leading rusher with 5,296 yards. He also holds club marks for yards (1,516) and rushing touchdowns (21) in a season.

1983	**1986**	**1990**	**1991**
Bill Parcells becomes head coach, will lead Giants to three division titles and two Super Bowl victories in eight years.	Giants go 14-2, take NFC East title, win Super Bowl XXI 39-20 over Denver.	New York goes 13-3 to win another NFC East title, beats Buffalo Bills 20-19 in Super Bowl XXV.	Bill Parcells resigns, Ray Handley becomes head coach.

Harry Carson

SIDELINES

YEAR WINS LOSSES TIES	RECORD	PLACE	COACH
New York Titans			
American Football League			
1960	7-7	2nd	Sammy Baugh
1961	7-7	3rd	Sammy Baugh
1962	5-9	4th	Clyde (Bulldog) Turner
New York Jets			
1963	5-8-1	4th	Weeb Ewbank
1964	5-8-1	3rd	Weeb Ewbank
1965	5-8-1	2nd	Weeb Ewbank
1966	6-6-2	3rd	Weeb Ewbank
1967	8-5-1	2nd	Weeb Ewbank
1968	11-3	1st	Weeb Ewbank
1969	10-4	1st	Weeb Ewbank
National Football League			
1970	4-10	3rd	Weeb Ewbank
1971	6-8	4th	Weeb Ewbank
1972	7-7	2nd	Weeb Ewbank
1973	4-10	5th	Weeb Ewbank
1974	7-7	4th	Charley Winner
1975	3-11	5th	C. Winner, K. Shipp [1]
1976	3-11	4th	L. Holtz, M. Holovak [2]
1977	3-11	4th	Walt Michaels
1978	8-8	3rd	Walt Michaels
1979	8-8	3rd	Walt Michaels
1980	4-12	5th	Walt Michaels
1981	10-5-1	2nd	Walt Michaels
1982	6-3	6th	Walt Michaels
1983	7-9	5th	Joe Walton
1984	7-9	3rd	Joe Walton
1985	11-5	2nd	Joe Walton
1986	10-6	2nd	Joe Walton
1987	6-9	5th	Joe Walton
1988	8-7-1	4th	Joe Walton
1989	4-12	5th	Joe Walton
1990	6-10	4th	Bruce Coslet
1991	8-8	2nd	Bruce Coslet

1 — Charley Winner (9 games), Ken Shipp (5 games)

2 — Lou Holtz (13 games), Mike Holovak (1 games)

T he quote in the headlines came directly from Joe Namath: "We're going to win on Sunday. I guarantee you."

But there was another, less-publicized comment that may have been equally important. It was what Jets head coach Weeb Ewbank said quietly to his team as it prepared for Super Bowl III: "The whole world is against us. They're laughing at you."

Indeed, the sports world was laughing. Not only at the brash promise by the quarterback of a 17-point underdog, but also at the team and the league he represented.

Neither Namath nor the Jets were taken seriously until January 12, 1969, when they outplayed the NFL champion Baltimore Colts. Inspired by wounded pride, the Jets scored a resounding 16-7 victory, one of the great upsets in history.

Tiny Titans

New York is the largest city in the United States, but very few of its residents had an interest in the American Football League or its brand of football in the early 1960s.

The Titans, as they were named, averaged fewer than 5,200 fans per game in 1962, when the league office was forced to assume the club's operating costs.

By the next season, the franchise belonged to a five-man syndicate comprised of Sonny Werblin, Leon Hess, Philip Iselin, Townsend Martin, and Donald Lillis. The club also had a new head coach (Weeb Ewbank), and a new name (Jets).

1959

NEW YORK JETS

Turning Points

New York is awarded charter franchise in American Football League; team is named Titans, Sammy Baugh is head coach.

That's when the sports world stopped laughing at the American Football League.

The Jets played not only for a title, but also for respect. They were a team that had won 12 of 15 games, and yet, they were ridiculed.

But AFL champions (Kansas City and Oakland) had been hammered 68-24 by Green Bay in the first two Super Bowl games, and the league was regarded as vastly inferior to the NFL.

And Namath didn't command the respect his talent warranted because his football ability was obscured by his off-field image. He was "Broadway Joe" Namath, the bon vivant of The Big Apple.

He was a playboy with long hair and Fu Manchu mustache, whose Manhattan bachelor pad was celebrated in national magazines. As much publicity was devoted to his off-field playmates as to his Jets teammates.

And, for those who were counting, he had thrown 72 interceptions in the previous three

The list of pro football's greatest coaches includes the names Halas, Brown,
Lombardi, and Shula, but the coaches' corner in the Pro Football Hall of Fame
also has a special place for Weeb Ewbank.
The Jets' coach from 1963-1973, Ewbank had a modest record of 73-78-6 in
New York. But he is renowned for directing the Jets to their historic 16-7 victory over
Baltimore in Super Bowl III - the first time an American Football League
team won a Super Bowl game.
Ewbank is the only coach to take teams to championships in both the AFL and
NFL. His Baltimore Colts won the NFL title in 1958 and 1959.

1960
New York signs wide receiver Don Maynard, posts 7-7 inaugural season record.

1962
Titans average fewer than 5,200 per home game, AFL takes over costs of operating franchise.

1963
Five-man syndicate takes ownership of club; gets new name (Jets), and new head coach (Weeb Ewbank).

1964
Jets move to Shea Stadium, draft fullback Matt Snell.

233

seasons. Just another pitcher, with a tendency to be high and wild, from the pass-happy AFL. The only difference was his arrogance.

In a breach of pregame protocol, Namath publicly belittled the opposition. He said Colts quarterback Earl Morrall, who had thrown for 2,909 yards and 26 touchdowns that season, was inferior to several AFL passers.

Super Bowl III did nothing to temper Namath's reputation as an arrogant playboy, but it generated respect for his ability and his league. Morrall threw three interceptions and completed only six passes; Namath completed 17 of 28 for 206 yards. The Jets' defense took the ball away five times, and the offense, with Namath calling most of the plays at the line, played power football, using 43 running plays to control the clock.

The Jets were clearly the better team that day, and Namath's celebrity status was magnified. He became the biggest name in

JETS ON THE GROUND

Only two Jets running backs have ever been invited to play in the Pro Bowl. One is John Riggins, who parlayed good years with the Jets and great years with the Redskins into a Hall of Fame berth. He played in one Pro Bowl as a Jet.

Running back Freeman McNeil, a first-round draft choice in 1981, immediately made his presence felt. He led the Jets in rushing his first eight seasons. A three-time Pro Bowl selection, he stands atop the club's rushing records; he had 7,904 yards after the 1991 season. His best year was 1985, when he had 1,331 yards.

A pair of outstanding running backs - Emerson Boozer and Matt Snell - preceded Riggins and McNeil with the Jets; both were invited to play in the AFL All-Star Game.

Freeman McNeil

1965
Quarterback Joe Namath wins rookie-of-the-year awards although Jets post 5-8-1 record.

1968
Jets have 11-3 record, win first AFL title, defeat Baltimore 16-7 in Super Bowl III.

Jerome Barkum

1969
New York repeats as AFC Eastern Division champion, loses divisional playoff game to Kansas City 13-6.

team sports. He was featured in television commercials, hawking perfume, pantyhose, popcorn machines, hamburger cookers, and shaving cream.

A strong-armed passer with an extremely quick release, Namath played 12 years for the Jets (1965-1976) and one year for the Los Angeles Rams, completing 1,886 passes for 27,663 yards and 173 touchdowns. He also threw 220 interceptions.

Namath was selected for the AFL All-Star Game four times and the Pro Bowl once. In 1985, he was inducted into the Pro Football Hall of Fame.

He came to the Jets as a first-round draft pick in 1965, and New York tried to find successors in the same way. The Jets drafted Richard Todd of Alabama, Namath's alma mater, in the first round in 1976. They selected Ken O'Brien from the University of California-Davis in the first round in 1983. Both Todd and O'Brien had some great days and good years, but neither brought a championship to New York.

No Ordinary Joe

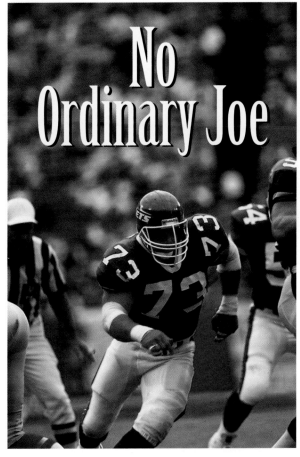

One of the most talented defensive linemen in Jets history, Joe Klecko was a huge favorite with New York fans. He could play any line position - tackle, end, or nose tackle - and play it well.

Klecko, who was a bargain as a sixth-round draft pick out of Temple in 1977, played in four Pro Bowl games, earning selection at three different positions. He played for the Jets from 1977-1987 and recorded 77 1/2 sacks, second only to Mark Gastineau.

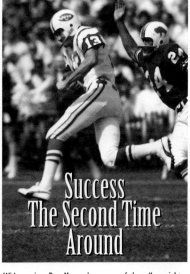

Success The Second Time Around

Wide receiver Don Maynard was one of those "overnight success" stories who took several years to succeed.

A ninth-round draft choice of the New York Giants in 1957, Maynard was a fringe player for one NFL season (1958), before trying the Canadian Football League.

He returned to New York in 1960, signed with the Jets, and went on to a Hall of Fame career. Maynard played for the Jets 13 seasons before closing out his career with the St. Louis Cardinals. When he retired he held the NFL record for receptions with 633. He gained 11,834 yards, averaging an outstanding 18.7 yards per catch, and scored 88 touchdowns.

Art Monk, Steve Largent, and others have passed him on the all-time reception list, but Maynard still holds the record for most games with 100 or more yards pass receiving (50).

Maynard, who wore number 13, is the only Jets player besides Joe Namath whose number has been retired.

No Sad Sack Here

For Mark Gastineau, rushing the passer was an art; he racked up 107 1/2 sacks in his 10 seasons with the Jets. A favorite of New York fans, he also was one of the most controversial players in the game. Gastineau was flamboyant, launching into a celebration dance near the fallen quarterback after each sack, a tactic that infuriated opponents who felt he was trying to embarrass them.

Gastineau, a little-known second-round draft pick from East Central Oklahoma in 1979, set the NFL single-season sack record of 22 in 1984. He also had 20 sacks in 1981 and 19 in 1983. He played in five consecutive Pro Bowls, beginning with the 1981 season, but in none of those seasons did his teammates select him as the most valuable player on the team.

1974	1976		1977
Weeb Ewbank retires with 73-78-6 record, Charley Winner becomes head coach.	*New York drafts quarterback Richard Todd, Joe Namath plays his last game for Jets.*	 **Emerson Boozer**	*Walt Michaels becomes head coach; Jets draft Marvin Powell, Wesley Walker, Joe Klecko.*

Big Foot in the Big City

When kicker Pat Leahy ended an 18-year career with the Jets after the 1991 season, he was the third-leading scorer in NFL history, producing 1,470 points with 304 field goals and 558 extra points. Only George Blanda and Jan Stenerud scored more.

Namath, who led the Jets to only one Super Bowl appearance, was hampered by bad knees and frequently surrounded by a mediocre team. The Jets had only three winning seasons during his 12 years with the club.

In the Jets' first 32 seasons, they have produced eight winning records, eight break-even seasons, and 16 losing records. During that time, they made seven playoff appearances, but Namath took the Jets to their only division titles, in 1968 and 1969.

The Jets have had many outstanding individual performers. Wide receiver Don Maynard is in the Pro Football Hall of Fame, and Wesley Walker and Al Toon have been outstanding modern-era wide receivers. Running backs Matt Snell, Emerson Boozer, John Riggins, and Freeman McNeil each represented the club in all-star games.

Joe Namath

Deep Threat

Wesley Walker became the NFL's most dangerous deep threat as soon as he joined the Jets in 1977. He led the league with an average of 21.1 yards per catch, earning rookie-of-the-year honors. He got better with experience, averaging 24.4 yards the next season and 24.7 the year after.

Walker, who led the club in receiving yardage six times, finished his Jets career with 438 receptions for 8,306 yards, at the time second only to Don Maynard in club records.

1981
Jets draft Freeman McNeil, who will become club's all-time leading rusher; post 10-5-1 record, best since 1969.

1984
Jets move home games to The Meadowlands.

Randy Rasmussen

1982
Jets have 6-3 record in strike-shortened season, win playoff games against Bengals and Raiders, lose AFC Championship Game to Miami 14-0.

The Jets have had fewer defensive standouts, but two notable exceptions were defensive linemen Mark Gastineau and Joe Klecko.

Gastineau played for New York from 1979-1988 and was the most flamboyant pass rusher in the league, providing a signature "sack dance" each time he got to the quarterback. Gastineau racked up 107 1/2 sacks for the Jets.

Klecko was a talented and versatile defensive lineman, in different years playing end, tackle, and nose tackle. Among Jets, he is second to Gastineau in career sacks with 77 1/2.

Of the 10 head coaches in Jets history, only Weeb Ewbank, Joe Walton, Walt Michaels, and Bruce Coslet logged more than two seasons. Ewbank served 11 seasons (1963-1973), Walton 7 seasons (1983-89), and Michaels 6 seasons (1977-1982). Coslet entered his third season in 1992. ✐

Hard Mark to Reach

The Jets have employed 10 head coaches since 1960, and none has a winning record.

Sammy Baugh had a 14-14 record over the club's first two seasons. Joe Walton was 54-59-1, Walt Michaels 41-49-1, and Weeb Ewbank 73-78-6.

Bruce Coslet, who took over in 1990, owned a 14-19 mark after his first two seasons.

Richard Todd

HIGH-FLYING JETS

Richard Todd and Ken O'Brien were New York's starting quarterbacks in 13 of the first 15 years of the post-Namath era, each piling up impressive passing totals.

Todd, a 1976 first-round draft pick from Alabama, had 18,241 yards and 110 touchdowns before being traded to New Orleans in 1984.

O'Brien, a 1983 first-round choice from California-Davis, had 23,744 yards and 119 touchdowns after the 1991 season.

Ken O'Brien

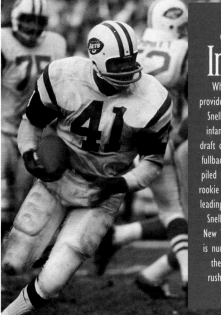

Joe's Infantry

While Joe Namath provided the bombs, Matt Snell was New York's infantry. A first-round draft choice in 1964, the fullback from Ohio State piled up 948 yards as a rookie and was the club's leading rusher five times. Snell, who played for New York nine seasons, is number three among the team's all-time rushing leaders, with 4,285 yards.

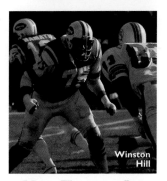

Winston Hill

MOST HONORED JET

Quickie Quiz: Name the Jets player invited to the most league all-star games.

The honor belongs to Winston Hill, a mammoth offensive tackle who played in four AFL All-Star Games and four Pro Bowls from 1964-1973.

Hill, a 275-pounder from Texas Southern, played 14 seasons for the Jets.

1986

Al Toon

With Joe Walton as head coach, Jets have 10-6 record, win first round playoff over Kansas City, lose divisional playoff at Cleveland 23-20 in double overtime.

1990

Bruce Coslet becomes Jets' tenth head coach.

YEAR ■ Wins □ Losses □ Ties	RECORD	PLACE	COACH
1933	3-5-1	4th	Lud Wray
1934	4-7	3rd	Lud Wray
1935	2-9	5th	Lud Wray
1936	1-11	5th	Bert Bell
1937	2-8-1	5th	Bert Bell
1938	5-6	4th	Bert Bell
1939	1-9-1	4th	Bert Bell
1940	1-10	5th	Bert Bell
1941	2-8-1	4th	Greasy Neale
1942	2-9	5th	Greasy Neale
Combined with Pittsburgh Steelers			
1943	5-4-1	3rd	G. Neale & W. Kiesling [1]
Resumed Traditional Operations			
1944	7-1-2	2nd	Greasy Neale
1945	7-3	2nd	Greasy Neale
1946	6-5	2nd	Greasy Neale
1947	8-4	1st	Greasy Neale
1948	9-2-1	1st	Greasy Neale
1949	11-1	1st	Greasy Neale
1950	6-6	3rd	Greasy Neale
1951	4-8	5th	B. McMillin, W. Millner [2]
1952	7-5	2nd	Jim Trimble
1953	7-4-1	2nd	Jim Trimble
1954	7-4-1	2nd	Jim Trimble
1955	4-7-1	4th	Jim Trimble
1956	3-8-1	6th	Hugh Devore
1957	4-8	5th	Hugh Devore
1958	2-9-1	5th	Buck Shaw
1959	7-5	2nd	Buck Shaw
1960	10-2	1st	Buck Shaw
1961	10-4	2nd	Nick Skorich
1962	3-10-1	7th	Nick Skorich
1963	2-10-2	7th	Nick Skorich
1964	6-8	3rd	Joe Kuharich
1965	5-9	5th	Joe Kuharich
1966	9-5	2nd	Joe Kuharich
1967	6-7-1	2nd	Joe Kuharich
1968	2-12	4th	Joe Kuharich
1969	4-9-1	4th	Jerry Williams
1970	3-10-1	4th	Jerry Williams
1971	6-7-1	3rd	J. Williams, E. Khayat [3]
1972	2-11-1	5th	Ed Khayat
1973	5-8-1	3rd	Mike McCormack
1974	7-7	4th	Mike McCormack
1975	4-10	5th	Mike McCormack
1976	4-10	4th	Dick Vermeil
1977	5-9	4th	Dick Vermeil
1978	9-7	2nd	Dick Vermeil
1979	11-5	2nd	Dick Vermeil
1980	12-4	1st	Dick Vermeil
1981	10-6	2nd	Dick Vermeil
1982	3-6	13th	Dick Vermeil
1983	5-11	4th	Marion Campbell
1984	6-9-1	5th	Marion Campbell
1985	7-9	4th	M. Campbell, F. Bruney [4]
1986	5-10-1	4th	Buddy Ryan
1987	7-8	4th	Buddy Ryan
1988	10-6	1st	Buddy Ryan
1989	11-5	2nd	Buddy Ryan
1990	10-6	2nd	Buddy Ryan
1991	10-6	3rd	Rich Kotite

1 — Greasy Neale & Walt Kiesling (co-coaches)
2 — Bo McMillin (2 games), Wayne Millner (10 games)
3 — Jerry Williams (3 games), Ed Khayat (11 games)
4 — Marion Campbell (15 games), Fred Bruney (1 game)

The NFL of the 1990s is a story of great success - packed stadiums, luxury boxes, big player contracts, the spotlight of national TV.

But it wasn't always that way, and the Philadelphia Eagles exemplify the transformation of the NFL.

When the Eagles play a home game today, 66,000 zealots jam Veterans Stadium in south Philadelphia. Thousands more

Steelers+ Eagles= Steagles

When the armed services found the NFL to be a ready supply of able-bodied men during World War II, many rosters were depleted. Two hard-hit teams, the Steelers and Eagles, combined rosters for the 1943 season. Officially known as Pitt-Phil, the team was popularly known as The Steagles.

The record: 5-4-1, Philadelphia's first winning season in its 11-year existence.

1933

PHILADELPHIA EAGLES

Turning Points

Bert Bell and Lud Wray buy NFL franchise for $2,500, with stipulation Bell and Wray pay 25 percent of debts owed by defunct Frankford Yellow Jackets. Team becomes Philadelphia Eagles.

would be there if they could get tickets.

It wasn't always that way.

When the Eagles played the Brooklyn Dodgers at 100,000-seat Philadelphia Municipal Stadium in 1939, they performed in front of about 99,000 empty seats and a scattering of spectators.

Bert Bell and Lud Wray bought the franchise in 1933, for $2,500. Today's franchise is valued at many millions, if it could be had at any price.

It wasn't always that way. The Eagles have been bought and sold seven times, most recently in 1985. Like an orphan, they have shuffled from home to home in Philadelphia, going from the Baker Bowl to Municipal Stadium to Shibe Park (later Connie Mack Stadium) to Franklin Field to Veterans Stadium.

In the days when pro football was not a lucrative proposition, Bert Bell not only bought

Runnin' Randall

Eagles quarterback Randall Cunningham, among the most exciting players of his time, not only did what was expected from a quarterback in his first four seasons (1987-1990), he also did what wasn't expected. In addition to passing for 13,460 yards, he was the team's leading rusher each season with totals of 505, 624, 621, and 942 yards.

Pete Retzlaff

1939

The Eagles make Heisman Trophy winner Davey O'Brien first draft pick. As a rookie quarterback, he sets NFL passing record with 1,324 yards.

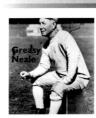

Greasy Neale

1941

New Yorker Alexis Thompson becomes owner of Eagles; Earl (Greasy) Neale is hired as head coach. Neale turns doormat franchise into perennial contender.

the franchise but he absorbed years of financial losses. He suffered through lean years as coach, general manager, promoter, ticket seller, financial officer, and probably chief cook and bottle washer. Through the formative years...through the war years...he endowed the Eagles with a resilience that has served the franchise well.

Bell sold the Eagles in 1941 and became partners with pal Art Rooney in ownership of the Steelers. In 1946, the other owners drafted Bell to be commissioner of the NFL. He died of a heart attack while attending a Steelers-Eagles game in 1959.

During the years when Bell was nurturing the NFL to powerhouse status, the Eagles grew wings of their own, becoming one of the league's cornerstone franchises.

Like every team, Philadelphia had ups and downs, with the ups usually tied to successful coaching changes. Earl (Greasy) Neale became head coach in 1941, and the Eagles finished first or second for six consecutive years from 1944-49, capped by three consecutive first-place

AIR MAIL: L.A. to Philly

Three of Philadelphia's great quarterbacks came from the same source - the Los Angeles Rams. Three times, the Eagles have traded with L.A. to acquire a premier passer - Norm Van Brocklin, Roman Gabriel, and Ron Jaworski.

Van Brocklin, obtained in 1958, took the Eagles to the NFL championship in 1960. Gabriel, acquired in 1973, led the league in passing and was the comeback player of the year. And Jaworski, who came in a 1977 deal, quarterbacked Philadelphia to Super Bowl XV in 1981. Van Brocklin and Gabriel each led the team in passing three times; Jaworski was the starting quarterback for almost 10 years.

Bert Bell

Ron Jaworski

1944

Rookie Steve Van Buren takes over as Eagles' halfback; launches career that culminates in Hall of Fame.

Bobby Walston

1948

Eagles win first NFL championship, beating Chicago Cardinals 7-0 in blinding snowstorm.

finishes. But after the next-to-last game of the 1950 season, Neale got in a fistfight with owner James Clark. Not surprisingly, that proved to be Neale's next-to-last game.

Buck Shaw's arrival in 1958 led to a second-place finish in 1959 and an NFL championship in 1960. Dick Vermeil became coach in 1976 and two years later helped the team break a string of 11 non-winning seasons before piloting the Eagles to the Super Bowl in 1980. More recently, flamboyant Buddy Ryan helped the Eagles break a six-year skein of losing seasons and claim an NFC East flag in 1988.

Neale, Shaw, Vermeil, and Ryan provided the motivation and leadership, and a stellar cast of characters provided the heroics.

The key players under Neale's tutelage were halfback Steve Van Buren, quarterback Tommy Thompson, end Pete Pihos, defensive lineman Bucko Kilroy, and linebacker Alex Wojciechowicz.

Neale's teams won the NFL title in both 1948 and 1949, proving to be foul weather birds

The Last of the
IRONMEN

It was the day that one legend stopped another. And then, stopped himself.

The NFL championship game of 1960 stands as the only blemish on Vince Lombardi's record in championship games. His Packers were beaten by Philadelphia 17-13.

Chuck Bednarik played a major role in the outcome. With just 17 seconds remaining and Green Bay on the Eagles' 22, Hall of Fame Packer fullback Jim Taylor caught a screen pass and headed for the end zone and the world championship. But Bednarik nailed him at the 9-yard line, then lay on him the final few seconds as the clock ran out.

Time ran out on a special chapter of pro football history that day, too. Bednarik was football's last 60-minute man, a superstar on both offense (center) and defense (linebacker). Bednarik, age 35 then, played two more years for the Eagles, but not as a two-way performer.

He retired after 14 years; no one ever played longer for Philadelphia. Honored as the center on pro football's all-time team, he is a member of the Hall of Fame.

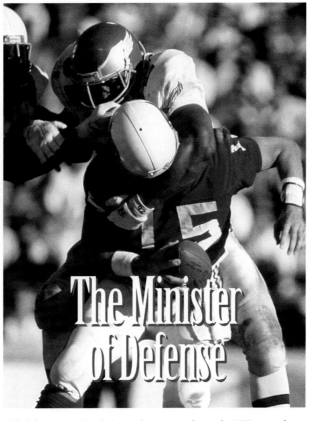

The Minister of Defense

Of all the outstanding defensive linemen to play in the NFL, none has been better at rushing the passer than Reggie White.

A licensed Baptist minister with the NFL nickname "Minister of Defense," White has been nothing short of sensational from the day he began his NFL career in 1985.

A 285-pounder with incredible drive and quickness, White has been a near-unanimous all-pro choice every year. Through his first seven years in the NFL, he had played in 105 games and recorded 110 sacks - the only player with a career average of more than a sack per game.

1949

Eagles draft future Hall of Famer and legendary iron man Chuck Bednarik; win another NFL title, 14-0 over Rams.

Bob Brown

1958

Buck Shaw becomes new Eagles coach; team acquires quarterback Norm Van Brocklin from Rams.

1960

Van Brocklin and Bednarik lead Eagles to first NFL title in 11 years; Van Brocklin and Shaw retire after season.

Little Big Man

Philadelphia's first draft pick in 1939 was quarterback Davey O'Brien, the Heisman Trophy winner from TCU. O'Brien had the big trophy, but he didn't have much size - he was only 5-7, 150 pounds. Despite his slight stature, O'Brien set an NFL record for passing yardage in his rookie season (1,324 yards). His most celebrated game came in his second season, when he hooked up with another TCU alumnus, Sammy Baugh, in a wild passing duel. O'Brien completed 33 of 60 passes, but the Eagles still lost, 13-6. In fact, Philly won only one game in each of O'Brien's two seasons at the helm. Following the 1940 season, O'Brien quit football for an even more hazardous profession. He became an FBI agent.

in both championship games. On the day of the 1948 title game against the Cardinals, a blinding snowstorm buried the city of Philadelphia. When Van Buren awoke and saw the snow, he assumed the game would be postponed, and went back to sleep. Only a phone call from a frantic Neale and a trolley car ride to the stadium got him to Shibe Park on time; he scored the game's only touchdown with a 5-yard run in the fourth quarter.

The next year's championship game was in Los Angeles, and everyone knows it never rains in southern California. But it poured on the day of the game, and Van Buren, accustomed to soakings on the Eastern seaboard, danced past the flustered Rams for 196 yards on 31 carries in a 14-0 victory.

Shaw's stalwarts were veteran quarterback Norm Van Brocklin and a superstar receiver corps of Pete Retzlaff, Tommy McDonald, and Bobby Walston, plus a defense anchored by Chuck Bednarik.

THE EAGLE INFANTRY

Steve Van Buren and Wilbert Montgomery stand at the top of the list as the Eagles' all-time leading rushers. Montgomery, who played from 1977 through 1984, rolled for 6,538 yards and 45 touchdowns. His 1979 total of 1,512 yards is a club record. Van Buren, a 200-pounder who combined blazing speed with outstanding power, was football's finest runner in the late 1940s, when he led the league in rushing four times. At his best in NFL championship games, he scored the only touchdown in the 1948 contest and gained 196 yards on 31 carries in the 1949 title game. Van Buren retired after the 1951 season with 5,860 rushing yards and 69 touchdowns. He is in the Hall of Fame.

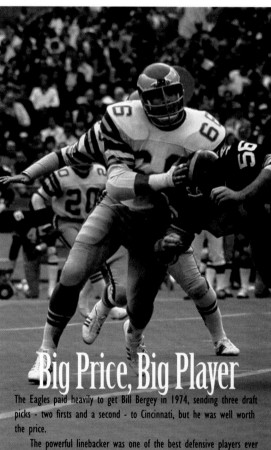

Big Price, Big Player

The Eagles paid heavily to get Bill Bergey in 1974, sending three draft picks - two firsts and a second - to Cincinnati, but he was well worth the price.

The powerful linebacker was one of the best defensive players ever to wear the Philadelphia uniform; he earned selection to four Pro Bowls and was a key on the Eagles' 1980 NFC championship team. A knee injury forced him into retirement after Super Bowl XV.

1971
Eagles leave Franklin Field for modern home - Veterans Stadium.

1974
Middle linebacker Bill Bergey comes to Philadelphia in trade with Cincinnati, gives team all-pro force on defense.

1976
Dick Vermeil is hired to coach Eagles and begins turnaround that will lead team to first winning season in 11 years in 1978.

Vermeil rallied the Eagles in the late 1970s on the running of Wilbert Montgomery and the passing combination of Ron Jaworski to Harold Carmichael, a trio that still stands as Philly's all-time yardage leaders in rushing, passing and receiving.

The Eagles soared again when owner Norman Braman hired Ryan. Offensive heroics came from quarterback Randall Cunningham, receivers Keith Jackson, and Mike Quick, and pass rusher extraordinaire Reggie White led a revitalized defense.

Despite its early struggles, the Philly franchise has enjoyed its years of glory and provided a pathway to the Hall of Fame for a variety of superstars...Bell, Neale, Van Buren, Bednarik, Wojciechowicz, Pihos, and Van Brocklin. Other Hall of Famers who contributed to the Eagles' success but had their greatest years with other teams were Bill Hewitt, Ollie Matson, Jim Ringo, Sonny Jurgensen, and Mike Ditka. ⬚

A Remarkable Catch(er)

Pete Pihos had one of the most remark-able careers of any Eagles player. He led the team in pass receiving his first five seasons (1947-1951), then was switched to defense in 1952. His replacement, Bud Grant (yes, that Bud Grant) led the team in pass receiving in 1952 while Pihos merely made all-pro as a defensive end.

When Grant went to the Canadian Football League in 1953, Pihos went back to his former position and led the Eagles in receptions for the next three seasons, then retired.

Pihos, who caught 373 passes for 5,619 yards and 61 touchdowns, is in the Hall of Fame.

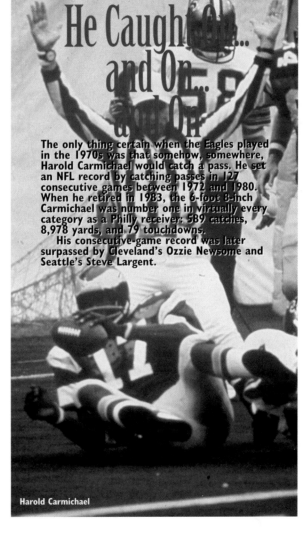

He Caught On... and On... and On

The only thing certain when the Eagles played in the 1970s was that somehow, somewhere, Harold Carmichael would catch a pass. He set an NFL record by catching passes in 127 consecutive games between 1972 and 1980. When he retired in 1983, the 6-foot 8-inch Carmichael was number one in virtually every category as a Philly receiver: 589 catches, 8,978 yards, and 79 touchdowns.

His consecutive-game record was later surpassed by Cleveland's Ozzie Newsome and Seattle's Steve Largent.

Harold Carmichael

1980	1984	1985	1986
Quarterback Ron Jaworski and wide receiver Harold Carmichael take Eagles to first division title since 1960 and first Super Bowl appearance.	Eagles select defensive end Reggie White in sup-plemental draft, he will become NFL's premier pass rusher.	Eagles draft quarter-back Randall Cunningham of UNLV in second round; he will become NFL's most electrifying offensive player.	Controversial Buddy Ryan becomes head coach; he will lead Eagles to another era of excellence.

Mike Quick

Phoenix
CARDINALS

SIDELINES

YEAR ▰ WINS ▱ LOSSES ▱ TIES	RECORD	PLACE	COACH
Chicago Cardinals			
1920	6-2-2	4th	Paddy Driscoll
1921	3-3-2	8th	Paddy Driscoll
1922	8-3	3rd	Paddy Driscoll
1923	8-4	6th	Arnie Horween
1924	5-4-1	9th	Arnie Horween
1925	11-2-1	1st	Norm Barry
1926	5-6-1	10th	Norm Barry
1927	3-7-1	9th	Guy Chamberlin
1928	1-5	9th	Fred Gillies
1929	6-6-1	4th	Dewey Scanlon
1930	5-6-2	7th	Ernie Nevers
1931	5-4	4th	L. Andrews, E. Nevers [1]
1932	2-6-2	6th	Jack Chevigny
1933	1-9-1	5th	Paul Schissler
1934	5-6	4th	Paul Schissler
1935	6-4-2	3rd	Milan Creighton
1936	3-8-1	4th	Milan Creighton
1937	5-5-1	4th	Milan Creighton
1938	2-9	5th	Milan Creighton
1939	1-10	5th	Ernie Nevers
1940	2-7-2	5th	Jimmy Conzelman
1941	3-7-1	4th	Jimmy Conzelman
1942	3-8	4th	Jimmy Conzelman
1943	0-10	4th	Phil Handler
Combined with Pittsburgh Steelers			
1944	0-10	5th	Phil Handler & Walt Kiesling
Resumed Traditional Operations			
1945	1-9	5th	Phil Handler
1946	6-5	3rd	Jimmy Conzelman
1947	9-3	1st	Jimmy Conzelman
1948	11-1	1st	Jimmy Conzelman
1949	6-5-1	3rd	P. Handler, B. Parker [2]
1950	5-7	5th	Curly Lambeau
1951	3-9	6th	Lambeau, Handler & Isbell [3]
1952	4-8	5th	Joe Kuharich
1953	1-10-1	6th	Joe Stydahar
1954	2-10	6th	Joe Stydahar
1955	4-7-1	4th	Ray Richards
1956	7-5	2nd	Ray Richards
1957	3-9	6th	Ray Richards
1958	2-9-1	5th	Frank (Pop) Ivy
1959	2-10	6th	Frank (Pop) Ivy
St. Louis Cardinals			
1960	6-5-1	4th	Frank (Pop) Ivy
1961	7-7	4th	Frank (Pop) Ivy
1962	4-9-1	6th	Wally Lemm
1963	9-5	3rd	Wally Lemm
1964	9-3-2	2nd	Wally Lemm
1965	5-9	5th	Wally Lemm
1966	8-5-1	4th	Charley Winner
1967	6-7-1	3rd	Charley Winner
1968	9-4-1	2nd	Charley Winner
1969	4-9-1	3rd	Charley Winner
1970	8-5-1	3rd	Charley Winner
1971	4-9-1	4th	Bob Hollway
1972	4-9-1	4th	Bob Hollway
1973	4-9-1	4th	Don Coryell
1974	10-4	1st	Don Coryell
1975	11-3	1st	Don Coryell
1976	10-4	3rd	Don Coryell
1977	7-7	3rd	Don Coryell
1978	6-10	4th	Bud Wilkinson
1979	5-11	5th	B. Wilkinson, L. Wilson [4]
1980	5-11	4th	Jim Hanifan
1981	7-9	5th	Jim Hanifan
1982	5-4	6th	Jim Hanifan
1983	8-7-1	3rd	Jim Hanifan
1984	9-7	3rd	Jim Hanifan
1985	5-11	5th	Jim Hanifan
1986	4-11-1	5th	Gene Stallings
1987	7-8	3rd	Gene Stallings
Phoenix Cardinals			
1988	7-9	4th	Gene Stallings
1989	5-11	4th	G. Stallings, H. Kuhlmann [5]
1990	5-11	5th	Joe Bugel
1991	4-12	5th	Joe Bugel

1 — LeRoy Andrews (1 game), Ernie Nevers (8 games)
2 — Phil Handler (6 games), Buddy Parker (6 games)
3 — Curly Lambeau (10 games), Phil Handler & Cecil Isbell (2 games)
4 — Bud Wilkinson (13 games), Larry Wilson (3 games)
5 — Gene Stallings (11 games), Hank Kuhlmann (5 games)

C harles Bidwill had a dream, and his pursuit of that dream is one of the remarkable chapters in NFL history.

Bidwill was vice president of the Chicago Bears, a club owned by his friend, George Halas. But he wanted more. He dreamed of having his own team, one that would be the best in the National Football League.

When Bidwill was offered the Chicago Cardinals franchise in

What If It Had Been Ecru Or Chartreuse?

The Cardinals did not get their nickname from the brilliantly colored redbird. Actually, the 1898 Morgan Street Athletic Club, called the Morgan Street Normals because it played on Normal Field, was offered a bargain on some old University of Chicago football uniforms. The jerseys, once maroon, had faded, and team organizer Chris O'Brien described the color as cardinal. The Morgan Street Normals then became Morgan Street Cardinals, which became the Racine Cardinals, which became the Chicago Cardinals in 1920.

The Cardinals moved to St. Louis in 1960 and to Phoenix in 1988. Fans can be eternally grateful the color of those jerseys wasn't ecru, puce, lavender, or chartreuse.

1920

PHOENIX CARDINALS

Turning Points

Chicago Cardinals are one of 14 charter franchises in the American Professional Football Conference, (later the National Football League); player-coach John (Paddy) Driscoll leads team to 6-2-2 record.

1933 for $50,000, he jumped at the opportunity.

That was a record price for a professional football team, but Bidwill was eager to build a champion that would be the talk of Chicago and the entire country...a team that would be better even than Halas's Bears.

The club Bidwill bought was mediocre on the field and had little fan support. While the crosstown Bears lost only one game in 1932, the Cardinals won only two.

In Bidwill's first year as owner, the team struggled through a 1-9-1 season. He overhauled the roster, and the Cardinals improved to 5-6 in 1934 and 6-4-2 the following year. But the Bears were the more popular team, and Bidwill continued to lose money.

He absorbed losses and continued to build, only to watch in frustration as the Cardinals continued to struggle, finishing near the bottom of the division.

Many of the Cardinals' top players were called to service in World War II; the team was winless in 1943 and 1944, and won only one game in 1945.

Still, Bidwill persisted. He had drafted some outstanding prospects who had gone to the military, and he was confident that when they returned, his team would prosper.

A Friend Indeed

George Halas, part-owner of the Chicago Bears, wanted to buy out his partner, Dutch Sternaman, in 1932, but he was a little short on cash.

So Halas went to his friend, Charles Bidwill, Sr., and borrowed $5,000 that helped close the deal. A year later, Bidwill bought the Cardinals franchise for $50,000 from Chicago dentist David Jones.

The franchise has belonged to the Bidwill family since.

THE 'OTHER' O.J.

Football fans had enjoyed the exploits of a sensational running back named O.J. in the 1970s, but when St. Louis tabbed another O.J. in the first round of the 1979 draft, he met with a "show me" attitude.

Show them he did. Ottis (O.J.) Anderson had a spectacular debut, rushing for 193 yards against the Cowboys. He continued to roll, setting an NFL rookie rushing record of 1,605 yards, a mark later topped by George Rogers and Eric Dickerson.

Anderson led St. Louis in rushing six consecutive seasons and gained more than 1,000 yards each season except strike-shortened 1982.

The club's all-time rushing leader with 7,999 yards, Anderson was traded to the Giants in 1986.

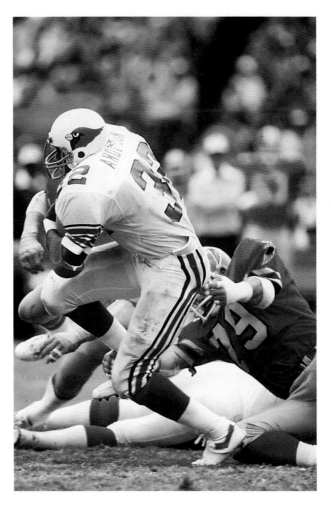

1929	1933	1946	1947
Cardinals acquire full-back Ernie Nevers, a future Hall of Famer, who scores 40 points in 40-6 Thanksgiving Day victory over crosstown rival Bears.	Charles W. Bidwill, Sr., buys franchise for $50,000.	Jimmy Conzelman becomes coach, team adds fullback Pat Harder to second-year quarter-back Paul Christman and halfback Marshall Goldberg in outstanding backfield.	Rookie halfback Charley Trippi completes "Dream Backfield"; Cardinals go 9-3, win NFL Championship Game 28-21 over Philadelphia.

He was right.

First came the 1945 signing of quarterback Paul Christman, a second-round draft pick in 1941. Then came the return of Marshall (Biggie) Goldberg, a halfback chosen on the second round in 1939. Goldberg had played well for two years, and was now returning. The 1946 draft added fullback Pat Harder, giving Chicago its best assembly of talent in history. The Cardinals went 6-5, winning more games in a single season than in the previous four combined.

But the best was yet to come. In 1947, the Cardinals signed All-America halfback Charlie Trippi, a player hotly pursued by baseball's New York Yankees. But Bidwill won the bidding war, and declared, "This will complete my Dream Backfield."

Indeed, it did. The 1947 Cardinals were the best in the league, posting a 9-3 record and winning the NFL Championship Game 28-21 over the Philadelphia Eagles. It was the first Cardinals championship since their unofficial title of 1925, when they finished with the best record before there was a championship game.

Unfortunately, Charles Bidwill didn't see his dream of a championship come true. He had assembled his "Dream Backfield" and built a great team, but he died of pneumonia before the

They Had to Have
HART

Undrafted after finishing his career at Southern Illinois University, Jim Hart got a free-agent tryout from the St. Louis Cardinals in 1966. Coach Charley Winner liked the kid's potential and decided to keep him as a long-term development project. But "long-term" proved short. Starting quarterback Charley Johnson was called into the service four days before the 1967 season opener, leaving the job to Hart. The young quarterback took the team to a 6-7-1 record and was its leading passer 13 times in 15 seasons (1967-1981). He was at the helm when the Cardinals won back-to-back NFC Eastern Division championships in 1974-75. Hart played 18 years for the Cardinals and owns club records for passing yardage (34,639), completions (2,590), and touchdown passes (209).

1948
Cardinals repeat as Western Division champions, lose NFL title game 7-0 to Eagles.

1952
Chicago drafts running back and Olympic sprinter Ollie Matson, a future Hall of Famer.

1960
Franchise is transferred to St. Louis.

Bobby Joe Conrad

1947 season started.

Charles's widow, Violet, ran the team for the next 15 years. After her death in 1962, sons Bill, and Charles, Jr., took control. Bill became sole owner in 1972, and continues to be team president.

The success of 1947 continued into the next season, when the Cardinals had an 11-1 record - best in franchise history - but lost the NFL Championship Game to the Eagles 7-0 in a game played in a Philadelphia blizzard.

Coach Jimmy Conzelman retired after that game, and the Cardinals began to slip. They were 6-5-1 in 1949, then had losing records nine of the next 10 years.

The franchise was shifted to St. Louis in 1960, where coach Wally Lemm made the Cardinals contenders again. Going 9-5 in 1963 and 9-3-2 in 1964, the Cardinals were a wonderfully entertaining team. Charley Johnson led the NFL in pass completions (223) and yardage (3,045) in 1964, throwing to wide receivers Sonny Randle, Billy Gambrell, and Bobby Joe Conrad, and tight end Jackie Smith. Running backs Bill Triplett and Joe Childress both finished among the league's top 10 rushers.

A ONE-MAN GANG

When Chicago drafted Ollie Matson in the first round in 1952, it was with high hopes that the Olympic sprint bronze medalist could make champions of the Cardinals.

It didn't happen. In fact, the Cardinals had only one winning season during Matson's career (1952-58), but it wasn't because the future Hall of Famer didn't do his share.

Matson made all-pro on defense as a rookie, went into the Army for one year, then returned to Chicago and made all-pro four consecutive years (1954-57) on offense.

A 220-pounder with superior speed, Matson was an electrifying breakaway threat, but he was virtually the club's only weapon. Matson led the Cardinals in rushing five years, averaging 4.4 yards per carry, and also handled kickoff and punt return duties. He still holds the club record of 35.5 yards per kickoff return, set in 1958. The speedster had kickoff returns of 100, 101, and 105 yards.

Unable to win with a one-man army in the lineup, the Cardinals traded Matson to the Rams in 1959 for eight players and a draft choice.

The Scoring Department

When Dr. David Jones bought the Chicago Cardinals in 1929, he was eager to sign a drawing card to rival the popularity of the crosstown Bears.

He found his man in Ernie Nevers, a fullback who had starred earlier for the Duluth Eskimos. Nevers delivered, especially against the Bears. On Thanksgiving Day, 1929, he scored all the Cardinals' points against the Bears in a 40-6 triumph. Nevers ran for six touchdowns and kicked four extra points. The following week, he again scored all the Cardinals' points in a 19-0 victory over Dayton.

Although Nevers played professional football only five years, he was selected to the Hall of Fame.

Loser Leave Town?

An official Cardinals' publication from an earlier era tells the following story:

"It was 1920, and a team known as the Chicago Tigers was battling the Cardinals for supremacy in Chicago. [Team owner] Chris O'Brien challenged the Tigers, with the stakes to be the loser's franchise as a professional team. The Cardinals' John (Paddy) Driscoll ran 40 yards for the game's only touchdown in a 6-3 victory for the Big Red, and the Cardinals were the only team in town."

A good story, albeit untrue. The Tigers did go out of business, only because the Cardinals' victory helped make them the more popular team in town, causing the Tigers' attendance to drop.

1965	**1966**
Cardinals draft Alabama quarterback Joe Namath; he signs with New York Jets of rival American Football League.	*St. Louis signs free agent rookie quarterback Jim Hart, who will play for Cardinals next 18 seasons.*

Charley Johnson

OH, NO! NO JOE

Pro football fans can only wonder what might have been...
Both the St. Louis Cardinals of the NFL and the New York Jets of the AFL drafted Alabama quarterback Joe Namath in 1965.
The Jets won the bidding war with a $400,000 contract that made Namath the highest-paid player in sports. But if the Cardinals had won the bidding:
◊ Would he have been Riverboat Joe instead of Broadway Joe?
◊ Would the Cardinals' offensive line have given him better protection and a longer career than he had in New York?
◊ Would the Baltimore Colts have won Super Bowl III ("We're going to win...I'll guarantee you.")?
◊ Would the presence of a future Hall of Fame quarterback have made the Cardinals a championship team?

The Cleveland Browns edged the Cardinals out of the 1964 Eastern Conference championship by the thinnest of margins: Cleveland had a 10-3-1 record; St. Louis was 9-3-2.

St. Louis lost the Century Division title to Cleveland by the same margin four years later: Cleveland was 10-4, St. Louis 9-4-1.

One year after becoming head coach, Don Coryell broke the Cardinals' championship drought with division titles in 1974 and 1975. Coryell's offense was among the most feared in the league as St. Louis went 10-4, 11-3, and 10-4 in three consecutive seasons (1974-76).

Coryell taught a wide-open offense, with long passes to speedy receivers, and he had the right cast of players. Quarterback Jim Hart was at the peak of his 19-year career. Terry Metcalf was among the top players in the conference in rushing, receiving, and punt returns, and led the NFL in kickoff returns in 1974. Speedy Mel Gray and Ike Harris were dangerous deep receivers, and fullback Jim Otis became only the second player in club history to rush for more than 1,000 yards, with 1,076 in 1975.

Their way was paved by an outstanding offensive line which included center Tom Banks, guards Conrad Dobler and Bob Young, and tackle Dan Dierdorf - all Pro Bowl players.

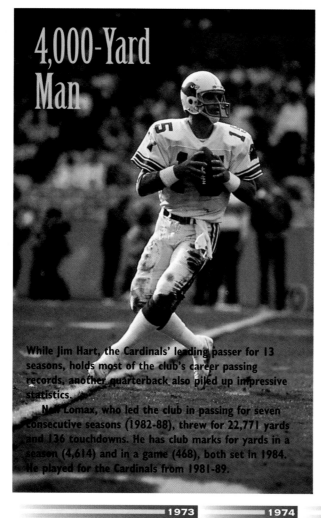

4,000-Yard Man

While Jim Hart, the Cardinals' leading passer for 13 seasons, holds most of the club's career passing records, another quarterback also piled up impressive statistics.

Neil Lomax, who led the club in passing for seven consecutive seasons (1982-88), threw for 22,771 yards and 136 touchdowns. He has club marks for yards in a season (4,614) and in a game (468), both set in 1984. He played for the Cardinals from 1981-89.

GREEN LOOKED GREAT IN CARDINAL RED

The Cardinals have had many outstanding receivers, but perhaps none better than Roy Green. A fourth-round draft pick out of Henderson State in 1979, originally projected as a defensive back, Green played 12 seasons for the Cardinals. He set club career records for receptions (522), receiving yards (8,496) and touchdown catches (66). Green also holds the Cardinals' record of 106 yards on a kickoff return.

1973	1974	1977
Don Coryell becomes head coach.	*Cardinals go 10-4, win first division title since 1948.*	*Cardinals are 7-7, first time in four years without winning record; Coryell resigns.*

Don Coryell

Those NFC East titles in the mid-1970s were especially impressive because they came in the era when Tom Landry's Dallas Cowboys and George Allen's Washington Redskins were perennial powerhouses.

But lack of a strong defense hurt St. Louis in the playoffs in both 1974 and 1975, and the Cardinals lost divisional playoff games, 30-14 to Minnesota and 35-23 to Los Angeles.

St. Louis was 10-4 in 1976, the year of the "Cardiac Cardinals," winning eight of 10 games by seven points or less, several with dramatic, come-from-behind efforts. But 10-4 only tied the Cardinals with Washington, which qualified for the playoffs by tie-breaker. (Dallas won the division.)

Coryell resigned after the Cardinals went 7-7 in 1977. Jim Hanifan engineered the club's next near-miss, a 9-7 record in 1984 that tied New York and Dallas for second place, but the Giants squeezed into the playoffs on a tie-breaker.

The franchise was moved to Phoenix in 1988, and coach Joe Bugel was hired in 1990 to move the Cardinals up the NFC East ladder again. ✐

He Changed the Game

The safety blitz is common today, but when Larry Wilson decked New York Giants quarterback Charley Conerly in a 1961 game, it was an NFL first.

Under the tutelage of defensive coach Chuck Drulis, Wilson charged at the quarterback from a variety of spots, changing forever the way offenses set blocking assignments.

Wilson, who was legendary for his toughness, played for the Cardinals from 1960-72, earning eight Pro Bowl invitations.

He also was a runner-up at safety on the NFL's All-Time All-Pro team and was inducted into the Pro Football Hall of Fame in 1978.

Conrad Dobler

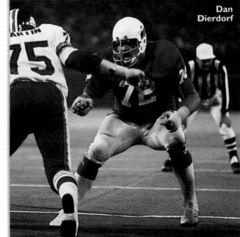

Dan Dierdorf

All-Star Air Guard

When St. Louis coach Don Coryell unleashed his vaunted air attack on the NFL in the mid-1970s, he furnished quarterback Jim Hart and his speedy corps of receivers with outstanding protection.

The Cardinals' offensive line included center Tom Banks, guards Conrad Dobler and Bob Young, and tackle Dan Dierdorf, all Pro Bowlers. Dierdorf earned five consecutive (1974-78) Pro Bowl invitations, Banks went four consecutive years (1975-78), Dobler was honored three times (1975-77) and Young twice (1978-79).

1979

St. Louis drafts running back Ottis Anderson, who becomes leading rusher in club history.

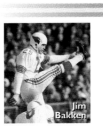

Jim Bakken

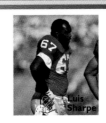

Luis Sharpe

1988

Franchise is moved to Phoenix.

YEAR ■ WINS □ LOSSES □ TIES	RECORD	PLACE	COACH
Pittsburgh Pirates			
1933	3-6-2	5th	Jap Douds
1934	2-10	5th	Luby DiMelio
1935	4-8	3rd	Joe Bach
1936	6-6	2nd	Joe Bach
1937	4-7	3rd	John Blood
1938	2-9	5th	John Blood
1939	1-9-1	4th	J. Blood, W. Kiesling [1]
1940	2-7-2	4th	Walt Kiesling
Pittsburgh Steelers			
1941	1-9-1	5th	Bell, Donelli, Kiesling [2]
1942	7-4	2nd	Walt Kiesling
Combined with Philadelphia Eagles			
1943	5-4-1	3rd	W. Kiesling & G. Neale [3]
Combined with Chicago Cardinals			
1944	0-10	5th	W. Kiesling & P. Handler [4]
Resumed Traditional Operations			
1945	2-8	5th	Jim Leonard
1946	5-5-1	3rd	Jock Sutherland
1947	8-4	2nd	Jock Sutherland
1948	4-8	3rd	John Michelosen
1949	6-5-1	2nd	John Michelosen
1950	6-6	3rd	John Michelosen
1951	4-7-1	4th	John Michelosen
1952	5-7	4th	Joe Bach
1953	6-6	4th	Joe Bach
1954	5-7	4th	Walt Kiesling
1955	4-8	6th	Walt Kiesling
1956	5-7	4th	Walt Kiesling
1957	6-6	3rd	Buddy Parker
1958	7-4-1	3rd	Buddy Parker
1959	6-5-1	4th	Buddy Parker
1960	5-6-1	5th	Buddy Parker
1961	6-8	5th	Buddy Parker
1962	9-5	2nd	Buddy Parker
1963	7-4-3	4th	Buddy Parker
1964	5-9	6th	Buddy Parker
1965	2-12	7th	Mike Nixon
1966	5-8-1	6th	Bill Austin
1967	4-9-1	4th	Bill Austin
1968	2-11-1	4th	Bill Austin
1969	1-13	4th	Chuck Noll
1970	5-9	3rd	Chuck Noll
1971	6-8	2nd	Chuck Noll
1972	11-3	1st	Chuck Noll
1973	10-4	2nd	Chuck Noll
1974	10-3-1	1st	Chuck Noll
1975	12-2	1st	Chuck Noll
1976	10-4	1st	Chuck Noll
1977	9-5	1st	Chuck Noll
1978	14-2	1st	Chuck Noll
1979	12-4	1st	Chuck Noll
1980	9-7	3rd	Chuck Noll
1981	8-8	2nd	Chuck Noll
1982	6-3	4th	Chuck Noll
1983	10-6	1st	Chuck Noll
1984	9-7	1st	Chuck Noll
1985	7-9	3rd	Chuck Noll
1986	6-10	3rd	Chuck Noll
1987	8-7	3rd	Chuck Noll
1988	5-11	4th	Chuck Noll
1989	9-7	2nd	Chuck Noll
1990	9-7	3rd	Chuck Noll
1991	7-9	2nd	Chuck Noll

1 — John Blood (3 games), Walt Kiesling (8 games)
2 — Bert Bell (2 games), Aldo Donelli (5 games), Walt Kiesling (4 games)
3 — Walt Kiesling & Greasy Neale (co-coaches)
4 — Walt Kiesling & Phil Handler (co-coaches)

As commissioner of the National Football League, Pete Rozelle had a responsibility to be neutral. He ran the league evenhandedly ...no rooting for one team over another.

On one occasion, though, Rozelle couldn't resist. He permitted himself a bit of cheering.

"I am not ashamed to admit that I had tears of joy in my eyes when I presented the Super Bowl trophy to Art Rooney," the former

What's In A Name?

At first, they were the Pirates, named after the city's baseball team. But that got people confused, so Art Rooney renamed the team Steelers in 1941.

Military demands in World War II sapped the rosters of many NFL teams, and in 1943 Rooney combined his Steelers with the Philadelphia Eagles. They were known as the "Steagles."

In 1944 Rooney found a new partner, combining his team with the Chicago Cardinals. The team was officially known as Card-Pitt, but a record of 0-10 earned the nickname "Carpets." The team was outscored 328-108.

"That was the worst team ever put together," said Rooney, who had occasion to see more than his share of bad ones.

1933

PITTSBURGH STEELERS

Turning Points

Art Rooney buys NFL franchise for $2,500.

commissioner said. "No man ever deserved it more."

Rooney's Pittsburgh Steelers won the ninth Super Bowl by beating Minnesota 16-6.

No one who knew the Art Rooney story could resist feeling moved.

Success was a long time in coming for the Steelers' owner. And no one was more deserving of his reward.

Even Rooney's extraordinary patience was not his most endearing feature; that was his remarkable grace under conditions that would overwhelm most others.

Rooney owned the Steelers 40 years before they ever finished in first place. Forty years of trying. Forty years of frustration. Forty years of suffering with some of the worst teams in NFL history.

Rooney founded the Pittsburgh franchise (then known as the Pirates) in 1933, and it took his team 10 years to record its first winning season. In the first 25 years, Rooney's team had only four winning seasons and never finished higher than second place.

But through it all, Rooney was gracious and kind. He was beloved by the people of Pittsburgh, who knew him as the common man's man.

Art Rooney

The Good Hands People

They were bookends for almost a decade…the best pair of bookends in pro football. Lynn Swann and John Stallworth came to Pittsburgh in the 1974 draft, Swann in the first round from Southern California and Stallworth in the fourth round from Alabama A&M.

The wonderfully gifted wide receivers were spectacular targets for Terry Bradshaw. Swann, who retired after the 1982 season, caught 336 passes for 5,462 yards and 51 touchdowns. Stallworth played until 1987, catching 537 passes for 8,723 yards and 63 touchdowns.

Ernie Stautner

1940	1941	1942
Rooney sells Steelers to New Yorker Alexis Thompson.	Rooney buys Eagles, trades franchises with Thompson.	Rookie Bill Dudley leads Steelers to first winning season (7-4).

It wasn't that Rooney enjoyed losing, or lacked competitive fire. Undefeated as an amateur boxer, and a signee of the Boston Red Sox, Rooney was fiercely competitive. He was, in fact, a speculative investor and a horse player. He started the Steelers with $2,500 won at the racetrack.

"The Chief," as he was known, loved to win. It's just that he recognized that winning wasn't everything.

During the team's first nine seasons, there were only 25 victories, an average of fewer than three per year. There were two years with just one victory, two others with two victories.

Rooney tried almost everything to improve the team. He changed coaches. He changed players. He changed the team's nickname from Pirates to Steelers. He tried changing owners, selling the team to Alexis Thompson after the 1940 season. But he immediately regretted the decision, and within months bought the Philadelphia Eagles and promptly traded his way back into Pittsburgh, swapping the Eagles franchise for the Steelers. He tried combining operations with the Eagles in 1943 and with the Cardinals in 1944. He brought back coach Joe Bach for a second term after a 16-year absence. He brought back coach Walt Kiesling for a second term and

A WINNER

He was maligned because he was a big kid from a small school. A big reputation and, at first, a small performance. He had a strong arm and, it was suggested, a weak mind. The infamous putdown was that he couldn't spell cat even if you gave him the "c" and "t" for starters. Terry Bradshaw spent 14 years in the NFL, and for most of that time his critics were choking on their words. Twice an all-pro selection, twice a Super Bowl MVP, four-time Super Bowl winner and, eventually, a Hall of Famer.
Bradshaw completed 2,025 passes for 27,989 yards and 212 touchdowns. He was superb in playoff games and had postseason statistics of 30 touchdown passes and 3,833 yards.

He Could DO IT ALL

Bill Dudley broke into the NFL in a big way, leading the league in rushing (696 yards) as a rookie in 1942.

He spent the next two and a half years as a bomber pilot in the Army Air Corps, but when he returned to pro football, he made up for lost time. In 1946 Dudley led the NFL in rushing, punt returns, and interceptions, and also led Pittsburgh in scoring, passing, punting, and kickoff returns.

Accomplishing all that did not come without a price for the 5-foot 10-inch, 170-pound back. Dudley injured his ribs, and when Steelers coach Jock Sutherland forced him to play hurt, Dudley became enraged and demanded a trade. The Steelers reluctantly traded Dudley to Detroit.

1946
Legendary University of Pittsburgh coach Jock Sutherland is hired to lead Steelers.

Bobby Layne

1955
QB Johnny Unitas released in training camp; Unitas goes on to Hall of Fame career in Baltimore.

Buddy Dial

1957
Buddy Parker becomes head coach; perennial losers have only two losing seasons in next seven years.

then for a third term. Nothing seemed to work.

When success finally came, it came in a big way. Consistent has-beens in the 1930s, 1940s, 1950s, and 1960s, the Steelers became pro football's most dominant team in the 1970s.

The masterstroke came in 1969, when Rooney hired Chuck Noll to be head coach. Not only did Rooney hire Noll, but he allowed him time to get the job done. The Steelers posted a miserable 1-13 record in Noll's rookie year, and had losing seasons the next two years, too. But the patient Rooney stayed with Noll. The new coach had made a commitment to building through the draft, and a series of good selections enabled the team to accumulate remarkable talent.

The first great picks were two little-known defensive linemen from small schools, Joe Greene from North Texas State and L.C. Greenwood from Arkansas AM&N (now called Arkansas-Pine Bluff) in 1969. The next year Pittsburgh went to small southern schools again and got quarterback Terry Bradshaw (Louisiana Tech) and cornerback Mel Blount (Southern). Linebacker Jack Ham came in 1971, fullback Franco Harris in 1972, and wide receivers Lynn Swann and John Stallworth, linebacker Jack Lambert, and center Mike Webster in 1974.

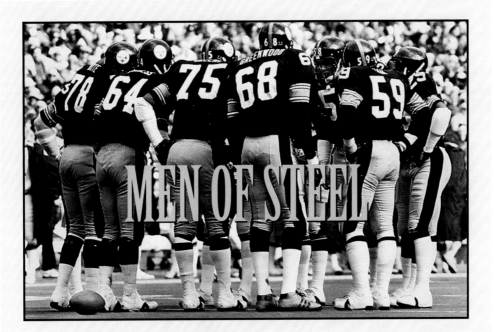

MEN OF STEEL

The best of all time…there can be no higher praise.

In an era when the draft effectively had equalized talent, the Steel Curtain put together an incredible performance on defense in 1976.

In a stretch of eight games, the Steelers had five shutouts and gave up only 22 points. That's fewer than three points per game. Sixteen of those points came in one game against the Houston Oilers. Besides that Houston game, the Steel Curtain yielded only three points apiece to Miami and Cincinnati, and shut out the Giants, Chargers, Chiefs, Bucs and Oilers. At one point, the Steelers had a streak of 22 consecutive quarters - 5 1/2 games - without giving up a touchdown.

Despite its excellence, that 1976 team was not a Super Bowl winner. The Steelers lost the AFC title game to Oakland 24-7.

Too What?

Too small…that's what some scouts said about Jack Lambert. At 6 feet 4 inches, 218 pounds, he was thought to be too skinny to be an NFL middle linebacker. Scouts feared his body wouldn't hold up to the pounding.

But Pittsburgh had no doubt, taking the Kent State product on the second round in 1974. Lambert rewarded that faith by missing only six games in his first 10 seasons.

When Lambert retired and headed for the Hall of Fame, his resume included: AP defensive rookie of the year in 1974, nine Pro Bowl selections, seven all-pro selections, and AP defensive player of the year in 1976.

1962
Steelers win nine games, highest total in 30-year history.

1969
Chuck Noll becomes head coach; Joe Greene is top draft pick.

1970
Steelers shift to AFC, move to Three Rivers Stadium, draft Terry Bradshaw.

Mr. Consistency

Franco Harris…
Mr. Consistency.
He was Pittsburgh's
leading rusher for 12
consecutive seasons,
and when he retired
after 13 years and
12,120 yards, he
owned or shared 24
NFL records.
The 6-foot 2-
inch, 225-pound
fullback from Penn
State left with all
the awards,
including 1972
rookie of the year
honors, nine Pro
Bowl selections, all-
pro, Super Bowl IX
MVP, and later,
induction into the
Hall of Fame.

Those were the players who provided Pittsburgh with one of the most glorious decades in any sport.

In their fortieth year of trying, the Steelers finally claimed a division championship in 1972, when they won a franchise-record 11 games. After going 39 years without ever winning more than nine games in a year, Pittsburgh won 10 or more regular-season games for five consecutive years and seven of eight.

Noll's team lost the AFC Championship Game to Miami in 1972 and a wild-card game to Oakland in 1973, but the next two seasons resulted in Super Bowl championships, 16-6 over the Vikings in Super Bowl IX and 21-17 over the Cowboys in Super Bowl X. After stumbling in the playoffs each of the next two years, the Steelers thundered to two more Super Bowl victories, 35-31 over Dallas in Super Bowl XIII and 31-19 over the Rams in Super Bowl XIV.

The Steelers of the 1970s enjoyed a truly remarkable reign. They won the AFC Central title seven of eight years and carried away four Super Bowl trophies in six years.

Such domination demands superb talent on both offense and defense, and the Steelers

Chuck Noll

A Four-Trophy Man

When Chuck Noll retired in 1991 after 23 years as the Steelers' head coach, he had a career record of 209-156-1, fifth on the all-time victory chart.

That's impressive. But eliminate the first few and last few years, and you get a clear view of just how dominant Noll's teams were.

The Steelers were 12-30 in Noll's first three seasons and 51-60 in his last seven years. In between, Pittsburgh was 130-58 in regular-season games, with 10 AFC Central titles in 13 years.

Noll retired as the only coach with four Super Bowl victories.

1972

Steelers draft Franco Harris, win first division title in 40 years.

Jack Ham

Rocky Bleier

1974-79

Pittsburgh wins Super Bowls IX, X, XIII, XIV in six-year span.

had both. They were best known for their Steel Curtain defense, perhaps the finest unit ever. It had no weaknesses and many superstars, including defensive linemen Greene and Greenwood, linebackers Ham, Lambert, and Andy Russell, and defensive backs Blount and Donnie Shell. Lesser-known defensive starters like Mike Wagner, J.T. Thomas, and Dwight White might have been stars on other teams.

The offensive unit was no less awesome. The pitch-catch combination of Bradshaw to Stallworth and Swann was destructive from long distances, and running back Franco Harris was machine-like in his consistency. Center Mike Webster anchored a solid line. The Steelers of the 1970s had no weaknesses.

Pittsburgh began to slip in 1980, a gradual decline. The Steelers finished first in their division in both 1983 and 1984, but these were clearly not the Steelers of a previous decade.

Art Rooney died at age 87 in 1988. He had suffered through decades of miserable teams, and he had savored the thrill of seeing his Steelers become the very best. He did both with unequaled dignity and grace. His son, Dan, has run the organization since. *⊘*

Franco Harris

Immaculate Reception

In the waning moments of Pittsburgh's 1972 playoff game with Oakland, the Steelers were down 7-6. Only 22 seconds remained and Pittsburgh was down to its last play - fourth-and-10 from the Pittsburgh 40.

Terry Bradshaw heaved a pass downfield, intended for John (Frenchy) Fuqua. Raiders safety Jack Tatum and the ball arrived at the same time. The ball ricocheted off Tatum, or Fuqua, or both, and back toward the line of scrimmage, right into the hands of Franco Harris. The rookie running back caught the ball in full stride and sprinted into the end zone for the winning touchdown. The miracle finish has been known as "The Immaculate Reception."

In that, the fortieth year of their existence, the Pittsburgh Steelers finally had their first postseason victory. But owner Art Rooney didn't see the winning play. He had already left the owner's box and started toward the locker room to console his players.

Joe Greene

Small Town Guys, Big Time Results

One popular theory on how to build a winning team is to start with the defensive line. The theory worked for the Steelers.

Joe Greene was the fourth player taken in the 1969 draft, when the Steelers faced a massive rebuilding job. A Pittsburgh newspaper greeted the selection of the defensive tackle from little North Texas State with a headline that read: "Joe Who?"

L.C. Greenwood, who attended Arkansas AM&N (now called Arkansas-Pine Bluff), got even less attention. He was drafted in the tenth round. Despite his lack of advance billing, Greenwood left the Steelers 12 years later with a team-record 73 1/2 sacks.

Greene, whom Chuck Noll called, "The best I've ever seen," was the *Associated Press* Defensive MVP in 1974, an all-pro selection eight consecutive years - and played in 10 Pro Bowls.

Greene was a tackle, Greenwood an end. They arrived together in 1969, left together in 1981.

L. C. Greenwood

1985
Steelers suffer first losing season in 14 years.

1991
Chuck Noll retires.

John Stallworth

San Diego

CHARGERS

SIDELINES

YEAR	■ WINS ◻ LOSSES ◻ TIES	RECORD	PLACE	COACH
Los Angeles Chargers				
American Football League				
1960		10-4	1st	Sid Gillman
San Diego Chargers				
1961		12-2	1st	Sid Gillman
1962		4-10	3rd	Sid Gillman
1963		11-3	1st	Sid Gillman
1964		8-5-1	1st	Sid Gillman
1965		9-2-3	1st	Sid Gillman
1966		7-6-1	3rd	Sid Gillman
1967		8-5-1	3rd	Sid Gillman
1968		9-5	3rd	Sid Gillman
1969		8-6	3rd	S. Gillman, C. Waller [1]
National Football League				
1970		5-6-3	3rd	Charlie Waller
1971		6-8	3rd	S. Gillman, H. Svare [2]
1972		4-9-1	4th	Harland Svare
1973		2-11-1	4th	H. Svare, R. Waller [3]
1974		5-9	4th	Tommy Prothro
1975		2-12	4th	Tommy Prothro
1976		6-8	3rd	Tommy Prothro
1977		7-7	3rd	Tommy Prothro
1978		9-7	4th	T. Prothro, D. Coryell [4]
1979		12-4	1st	Don Coryell
1980		11-5	1st	Don Coryell
1981		10-6	1st	Don Coryell
1982		6-3	5th	Don Coryell
1983		6-10	4th	Don Coryell
1984		7-9	5th	Don Coryell
1985		8-8	4th	Don Coryell
1986		4-12	5th	D. Coryell, A. Saunders [5]
1987		8-7	3rd	Al Saunders
1988		6-10	4th	Al Saunders
1989		6-10	5th	Dan Henning
1990		6-10	4th	Dan Henning
1991		4-12	5th	Dan Henning

1 — Sid Gillman (9 games), Charlie Waller (5 games)
2 — Sid Gillman (10 games), Harland Svare (4 games)
3 — Harland Svare (8 games), Ron Waller (6 games)
4 — Tommy Prothro (4 games), Don Coryell (12 games)
5 — Don Coryell (8 games), Al Saunders (8 games)

Most NFL teams subscribe to a similar formula for success: (1) a dependable defense, (2) a ground game that controls the clock, and, (3) a passing attack that prevents foes from overcrowding the line of scrimmage.

The formula has worked for numerous Super Bowl champions.

And then there's San Diego's way.

No, the Chargers never have played in the Super Bowl - in their first 32 years, they've won but one league title and had only 15 winning seasons - but the Chargers have been fun to watch. If there were standings to reflect entertainment quotient, the Chargers would be a perennial contender.

Two of the reasons are Sid Gillman and Don Coryell.

Gillman is a football mastermind, one of the most innovative offensive strategists the game has known. He coached the Chargers

What's In A Name?

There are differing accounts of why "Chargers" was chosen as the winning entry in the franchise's name-the-team contest. The oft-repeated version is that owner Barron Hilton, also owner of the Hilton hotel chain, wanted to help publicize his new Carte Blanche charge card. Another is that Hilton was thinking of a hard-charging steed as the team's mascot, while a third version is that he envisioned a team gifted with a lightning bolt charge.

1959

SAN DIEGO CHARGERS

Turning Points

Los Angeles Chargers, founded by Barron Hilton, are one of AFL's original franchises.

in their first decade (1960-69 and again in 1971), unveiling an unprecedented aerial circus. Coryell, who coached the Chargers 1978-1986, was cut from the same cloth.

Gillman had been coach of the Los Angeles Rams for five seasons (1955-59), when his quarterbacks were Norm Van Brocklin, a Hall of Fame passer, and Bill Wade. When he became coach of the Chargers in 1960, Gillman already was a master at designing a passing offense.

Other AFL teams simply weren't prepared to cope with Gillman's expertise. Talent on most early AFL clubs, especially in the secondary, was thin.

Gillman exploited weaknesses. His offensive schemes put intense pressure on opposing secondaries, and even good ones withered under the Chargers' attack. Gillman's offense, which exploited the shortcomings of man-for-man coverage, was a major factor in the development of zone defenses.

Under Gillman, the Chargers won the Western Division title five times in the AFL's first six years - with three different quarterbacks.

Jack Kemp was the starter in 1960-61, Tobin Rote was the quarterback on the 1963 championship team, and John Hadl led the Chargers to division titles in 1964-65. Kemp had been released by the Steelers, Giants, and 49ers of the NFL before getting an opportunity with the new league. Rote had been a journeyman quarterback at Detroit and Green Bay. Hadl was in only

Don Coryell

Sid Gillman

Pro Bowl Defender

Big Louie Kelcher, a 285-pound strongman who played defensive tackle for San Diego for nine years (1975-1983), was one of the most popular Chargers.

Although he lacked the speed to be a great pass rusher, Kelcher was dominant in the center of the line. He played in the Pro Bowl three times, twice as a starter.

1960	**1961**		**1962**	**1964**
With Sid Gillman as coach and Jack Kemp at quarterback, Chargers win AFC Western Division title.	Club moves to San Diego, drafts three key defensive players: linemen Ernie Ladd and Earl Faison, and linebacker Chuck Allen.	John Hadl	Chargers draft quarterback John Hadl and wide receiver Lance Alworth.	Veteran quarterback Tobin Rote suffers sore arm; Hadl becomes third quarterback in five years to take Chargers to AFC Western Conference title.

his third season when he led the Chargers to the division title in 1964. He held the starting job until 1973, when Dan Fouts took over.

Gillman provided his quarterbacks with outstanding pass receivers, none better than Lance Alworth.

A running back at the University of Arkansas, the 185-pound Alworth was moved to flanker in his rookie season (1962). It was a change that resulted in a Hall of Fame career. An acrobatic receiver with outstanding speed and exceptional hands, Alworth was the leading pass catcher in the AFL three times and played in the last seven AFL All-Star Games (1964-1970).

But Gillman believed that a passing attack had to have multiple weapons, and Chargers quarterbacks had a variety of targets. Gary Garrison was a star wide receiver for 11 years, earning a spot in three Pro Bowls and one AFL All-Star Game. Don Norton, on the original

Chargers' Best Blocker

Offensive tackle Ron Mix, a first-round selection by the NFL's Baltimore Colts in 1960, was one of the big prizes claimed by the rival American Football League in that year. The 6-foot 4-inch, 255-pounder from Southern California was widely regarded as the best offensive lineman in the AFL's 10-year history.

A TREND-SETTER

Few players can claim to have redefined the position they played, but Kellen Winslow did.

NFL tight ends had been blockers first, receivers second, before Winslow joined the Chargers as a first-round draft pick in 1979. With his exceptional combination of speed, quickness, and great hands, he became an outstanding deep threat in the "Air Coryell" passing attack. Winslow's 541 career catches are second only to Charlie Joiner's 586 in Chargers history.

1965
Chargers win fifth division title in six years, but last of any kind until 1979.

1966
Eugene Klein heads group that buys Chargers.

Gary Garrison

1971
Sid Gillman, after brief comeback, resigns as head coach.

Chargers roster, was selected for two AFL All-Star Games. Three different tight ends - Dave Kocourek, Willie Frazier, and Jacque MacKinnon - represented the Chargers in the AFL All-Star Game in the 1960s, as did running backs Keith Lincoln, Paul Lowe, and Dickie Post.

An array of stars performed for the Chargers, but it was Gillman's offensive scheme that elevated many players to all-star status.

The Chargers had only one losing season in the decade of the 1960s, but won the AFL championship only once in five tries. The axiom that defense wins league championships held true, even in the AFL, and the Chargers simply didn't have enough.

Gillman resigned as head coach because of poor health during the 1969 season, returned in 1971, but quit before the end of the season.

The Coryell era began with the fifth game of the 1978 season. San Diego had gone eight

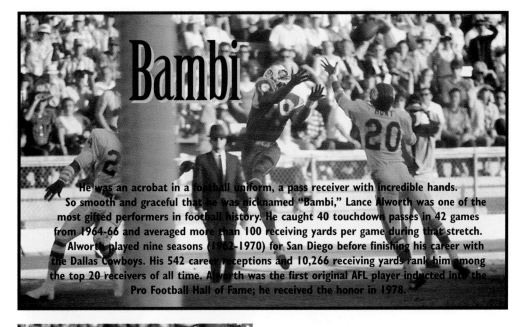

Bambi

He was an acrobat in a football uniform, a pass receiver with incredible hands. So smooth and graceful that he was nicknamed "Bambi," Lance Alworth was one of the most gifted performers in football history. He caught 40 touchdown passes in 42 games from 1964-66 and averaged more than 100 receiving yards per game during that stretch. Alworth played nine seasons (1962-1970) for San Diego before finishing his career with the Dallas Cowboys. His 542 career receptions and 10,266 receiving yards rank him among the top 20 receivers of all time. Alworth was the first original AFL player inducted into the Pro Football Hall of Fame; he received the honor in 1978.

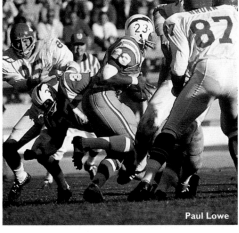

Paul Lowe

Lincoln & Lowe:
RUSHING LEADERS

One of them was a highly regarded second-round draft pick; the other had to phone the coach to request a free-agent tryout.

Together, Keith Lincoln and Paul Lowe were an extraordinary pair of running backs, stars in the years when the Chargers finished first five times in six seasons.

Lincoln, drafted out of Washington State, played for the Chargers from 1961-66 and 1968, and averaged 4.7 yards per carry. The only Chargers runner with a better average was Lowe, who averaged 4.9 yards per carry from 1960-68.

Lincoln starred in the only league championship game San Diego has won, a 51-10 victory over the Boston Patriots in 1963, when he accounted for 349 yards (206 rushing, 123 receiving, 20 passing).

Lowe is San Diego's all-time leading rusher with 4,963 yards.

1973	**1976**		**1978**
Chargers acquire two quarterbacks, trading for John Unitas and drafting Dan Fouts.	San Diego obtains wide receiver Charlie Joiner in trade with Cincinnati.		Don Coryell becomes head coach, wide receiver John Jefferson is first-round draft choice.

John Jefferson

years without a winning record when Coryell replaced Tommy Prothro. The Chargers rallied to win eight of 12 games in Coryell's first season, then won the AFC Western Division title the next three years.

The new-found success, as in the Gillman era, was a result of a magnificent passing game. "Air Coryell," as the Chargers' aerial fireworks were called, was built around quarterback Dan Fouts.

One of the great passers in football history, Fouts played 15 years for the Chargers (1973-1987), and made San Diego's offense the best in the NFL five times in a six-year span from 1980-85.

Like Chargers quarterbacks in the 1960s, Fouts had a gifted stable of receivers that included Charlie Joiner, John Jefferson, Wes Chandler, Lionel James, and Kellen Winslow.

Joiner set a Chargers' record over his 11 seasons with 586 receptions. Chandler and Jefferson were among the most feared deep threats of their time, James was a dangerous

BIG CAT

Ernie (Big Cat) Ladd was one of the more colorful players in the early years of the American Football League. A 6-foot 9-inch, 310-pound defensive tackle, Ladd was a fifteenth-round draft pick in 1961 who became a four-time starter in the AFL All-Star Game for San Diego. He played for the Chargers from 1961-65 before moving on to Houston and Kansas City. After eight seasons in pro football, he became a professional wrestler.

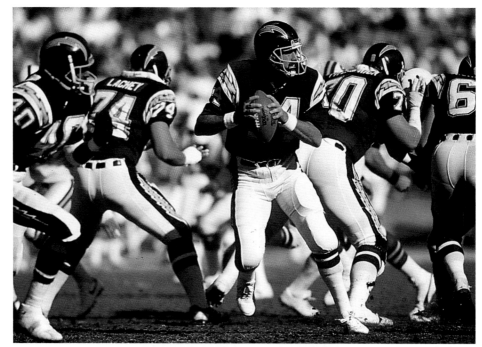

ONE OF A KIND

San Diego has had a galaxy of offensive stars, but only quarterback Dan Fouts's number 14 has been retired.
In his 15-year Chargers career (1973-1987), Fouts passed for 43,040 yards. No other quarterback ever passed for so many yards for one team. Only Fran Tarkenton, who compiled 47,003 passing yards for the Minnesota Vikings and New York Giants, threw for more.
Fouts, who played in six Pro Bowls, was unflinching in the pocket, frequently absorbing a hard hit while making a big completion. He had an NFL-record 51 games with 300 passing yards, and piled up career totals of 3,297 completions and 254 touchdown passes.

1979
Tight end Kellen Winslow is first-round draft pick.

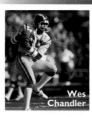
Wes Chandler

1984
Alex Spanos becomes club owner.

Rolf Benirschke

1986
Don Coryell resigns at midseason.

receiver out of the backfield, and Winslow was a 250-pound wide receiver disguised as a tight end. Together, they provided San Diego an unmatched arsenal.

But while Coryell's offense was the best, his defensive units were mediocre at best and, at worst, near the bottom of the league.

There were many similarities between the Chargers of the Gillman and Coryell eras. Both were head coaches who were offensive geniuses, and both fielded wonderfully entertaining teams. They had superb quarterbacks, exceptional receivers, terrific runners, and mediocre defensive units.

One other similarity: Gillman's Chargers won AFL Western Conference titles five times, but had a 1-4 record in AFL Championship Games; Coryell's teams played for the AFC championship twice and lost both times.

Offense entertains, defense wins championships. ⊘

Iron Man, Soft Hands

The San Diego Chargers had faster wide receivers, but none with better hands or more durability than Charlie Joiner.

When Joiner retired after the 1986 season, he was the NFL's all-time leading receiver, with 750 catches. His 239 games played at wide receiver is a record at the position. Joiner's NFL career spanned 18 seasons, the first seven at Houston and Cincinnati, and the last 11 at San Diego.

Russ Washington

SAN DIEGO BODYGUARDS

Doug Wilkerson

Russ Washington was the fourth player chosen in the 1968 draft; Doug Wilkerson, selected by Houston, was the first offensive lineman picked in 1970. They combined to provide the Chargers with one of the most solid offensive front walls in professional football.

Washington, a tackle, played in five Pro Bowls. He played 15 seasons for San Diego, a club longevity mark shared with Dan Fouts. Wilkerson, a guard, spent one season with the Oilers before joining San Diego in 1971. He played in three Pro Bowls during his 14 seasons with the Chargers.

1988	**1990**	**1992**
Dan Fouts retires.	Bobby Beathard becomes general manager.	Bobby Ross becomes the Chargers' ninth head coach.

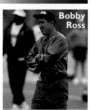

Bobby Ross

San Francisco 49ERS

SIDELINES

YEAR	WINS	LOSSES	TIES	RECORD	PLACE	COACH
All-America Football Conference						
1946				9-5	2nd	Buck Shaw
1947				8-4-2	2nd	Buck Shaw
1948				12-2	2nd	Buck Shaw
1949				9-3	2nd	Buck Shaw
National Football League						
1950				3-9	5th	Buck Shaw
1951				7-4-1	2nd	Buck Shaw
1952				7-5	3rd	Buck Shaw
1953				9-3	2nd	Buck Shaw
1954				7-4-1	3rd	Buck Shaw
1955				4-8	5th	Norman Strader
1956				5-6-1	3rd	Frankie Albert
1957				8-4	2nd	Frankie Albert
1958				6-6	4th	Frankie Albert
1959				7-5	3rd	Howard (Red) Hickey
1960				7-5	2nd	Howard (Red) Hickey
1961				7-6-1	5th	Howard (Red) Hickey
1962				6-8	5th	Howard (Red) Hickey
1963				2-12	7th	H. Hickey, J. Christiansen [1]
1964				4-10	7th	Jack Christiansen
1965				7-6-1	4th	Jack Christiansen
1966				6-6-2	4th	Jack Christiansen
1967				7-7	3rd	Jack Christiansen
1968				7-6-1	3rd	Dick Nolan
1969				4-8-2	4th	Dick Nolan
1970				10-3-1	1st	Dick Nolan
1971				9-5	1st	Dick Nolan
1972				8-5-1	1st	Dick Nolan
1973				5-9	4th	Dick Nolan
1974				6-8	2nd	Dick Nolan
1975				5-9	2nd	Dick Nolan
1976				8-6	2nd	Monte Clark
1977				5-9	3rd	Ken Meyer
1978				2-14	4th	P. McCulley, F. O'Connor [2]
1979				2-14	4th	Bill Walsh
1980				6-10	3rd	Bill Walsh
1981				13-3	1st	Bill Walsh
1982				3-6	11th	Bill Walsh
1983				10-6	1st	Bill Walsh
1984				15-1	1st	Bill Walsh
1985				10-6	2nd	Bill Walsh
1986				10-5-1	1st	Bill Walsh
1987				13-2	1st	Bill Walsh
1988				10-6	1st	Bill Walsh
1989				14-2	1st	George Seifert
1990				14-2	1st	George Seifert
1991				10-6	3rd	George Seifert

1 — Howard (Red) Hickey (3 games), Jack Christiansen (11 games)   2 — Pete McCulley (9 games), Fred O'Connor (7 games)

wo different drives - one on January 10, 1982, the other on January 22, 1989 - epitomize the San Francisco 49ers, the NFL team of the 1980s.

Other teams had dominated in other decades. The Chicago Bears in the 1940s, the Green Bay Packers in the 1960s, the Pittsburgh Steelers in the 1970s. The Monsters of the Midway. The Pack. The Steel Curtain. Always, it was a rock-hard team from a rock-hard place.

The Team Of The '80s

San Francisco had won only three division or conference championships in club history, but when the decade of the 1980s arrived, the 49ers were suddenly transformed into a powerhouse.

The 49ers won the NFC Western Division title seven times in 10 years (1980-89). They failed only in 1980, when the juggernaut was still under construction; 1982, when the season was shortened to nine games by a strike, and 1985, when their 10-6 record was one game behind the Los Angeles Rams.

San Francisco won Super Bowls at the end of the 1981, 1984, 1988 and 1989 seasons.

1946

SAN FRANCISCO 49ERS

Turning Points

Tony Morabito, partner in lumber firm, is awarded San Francisco franchise in All-America Football Conference. Named 49ers, team finishes second to Cleveland for the first of four times.

The San Francisco 49ers of the 1980s were a different type of team from a different type of town. They played good defense, but not Steel Curtain, paralyzing stuff. They ran the ball well, but not with down-your-throat, Packer power.

The 49ers of coach Bill Walsh and quarterback Joe Montana were surgeons with scalpels. They dissected the opposition before it realized it was on the operating table.

The drive that began a dynasty came in the 1981 NFC Championship Game against Dallas. The Cowboys owned a 27-21 lead with less than five minutes to play. San Francisco had the ball on its own 11-yard line, but it had Montana, and that was enough. He drove his team the length of the field and, on third down from the Dallas 6, with less than a minute remaining, threw The Pass to Dwight Clark, who made The Catch. San Francisco won 28-27, and followed with a 26-21 victory over Cincinnati in Super Bowl XVI.

The Catch(er)

Dwight Clark earned a place in NFL history when he made "The Catch" that gave San Francisco a victory in the 1981 NFL Championship Game over Dallas, but he was more than a one-day wonder.

Clark owned most of the club's receiving records until Jerry Rice came along. A wide receiver taken on the tenth round of the 1979 draft, Clark enjoyed an outstanding nine-year career at San Francisco. He finished with 6,750 receiving yards; only Rice and Roger Craig had more receptions than Clark's 506.

1950

49ers are one of three AAFC teams absorbed into National Football League.

Y. A. Tittle

1951

San Francisco acquires quarterback Y.A. Tittle in dispersal draft of players after Baltimore franchise is dissolved.

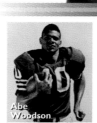

Abe Woodson

1952

Rookie running back Hugh McElhenny leads NFL with average of 7 yards per carry.

Drive II arrived in 1989, in Super Bowl XXIII, when the 49ers trailed Cincinnati 16-13, with just 3:20 left in regulation. Beginning at the San Francisco 8-yard line, Montana engineered another miracle: short passes to Roger Craig, John Frank, and Jerry Rice; a 17-yarder to Rice; a 13-yarder to Craig; a 27-yarder to Rice; an 8-yarder to Craig; a 10-yard touchdown pass to John Taylor. A 20-16 San Francisco victory.

The 49ers lost in the 1980s, but not often. They won four Super Bowls within nine years, compiling a league-best 117-51-1 record. They averaged almost 12 victories a season for 10 consecutive years. Only twice did the 49ers fail to win at least 10 games - in 1980, when they went 6-10, and 1982, when they were 3-6 in a strike-shortened season.

The only players who started in all four Super Bowl victories were Montana, defensive back Ronnie Lott and linebacker Keena Turner. Not even Walsh was around for the fourth

Alley-Oop

As a 6-foot 5-inch wide receiver with excellent jumping ability, rookie R.C. Owens gave San Francisco a unique weapon in 1957. Owens, who had been a collegiate basketball player, could reach passes that most defensive backs were helpless to stop, as the 49ers delighted fans with the "Alley-Oop" play. Owens would sprint to a corner of the end zone, where the quarterback would loft a high pass, allowing Owens to outjump defenders. The tactic attracted widespread attention, but it worked only a few times. Owens caught 27 passes his rookie season, only five for touchdowns.

Five-Star General

On a team laden with heroes, none of the other stars who made the 49ers the team of the 1980s were quite as brilliant as quarterback Joe Montana, perhaps the finest field general of all time.

Montana's numbers after the 1991 season were among the elite in NFL history: 2,914 completions, 34,998 passing yards, 242 touchdown passes.

But the numbers that tell the Montana story best are the ones that reveal an average of almost 12 victories per year over a 10-year period. Montana led his team to the playoffs eight times in a decade, winning seven NFC Western Division championships.

A master at engineering the come-from-behind victory, Montana took the 49ers to Super Bowl championships four times in nine years. Montana was the Super Bowl MVP three times.

A HAPPY ANNIVERSARY

It took San Francisco 25 years to win a championship of any kind, and the 49ers needed a tremendous season from quarterback John Brodie to finish with a 10-3-1 record, one game ahead of the Rams in the NFC West in 1970.

Brodie was the consensus NFL player of the year, leading the league in passing. He threw for 2,941 yards and 24 touchdowns on 223 completions.

During his 16-year career with the 49ers, Brodie passed for 31,548 yards and 214 touchdowns, marks later eclipsed by Joe Montana.

1954	1957	1960
Fullback John Henry Johnson comes to 49ers from Canadian Football League, joins with McElhenny, Tittle and Joe Perry to form "Million Dollar Backfield."	Rookie wide receiver R.C. Owens makes "Alley-Oop" pass one of NFL's most celebrated offensive weapons.	49ers unveil "Shotgun," a wide-open offensive style that becomes team's primary attack.

Charlie Krueger

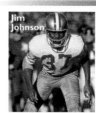

Jim Johnson

Super Bowl triumph. He resigned three days after winning Super Bowl XXIII; George Seifert coached San Francisco to a resounding 55-10 victory over Denver in Super Bowl XXIV.

Even when they lost, the 49ers didn't go down easily. In the 1983 NFC Championship Game, they rallied for 21 points in the fourth quarter to tie the game, only to lose 24-21 to Washington on a field goal in the last 40 seconds. Twice their march to the Super Bowl stalled at The Meadowlands, where they lost playoff games to the Giants in the 1985 and 1986 seasons.

Walsh, the offensive genius; Montana, the quarterback who wouldn't accept defeat; Rice, the most electrifying receiver of his time, and Lott, the bone-rattling defensive back with superior speed, all had a decade of excellence that will earn them berths in the Pro Football Hall of Fame. Others, like wide receivers Dwight Clark and Freddie Solomon, running backs

The Lion

No listing of pro football's greatest linemen is complete without Leo (The Lion) Nomellini, an extraordinary star who won all-pro honors twice on offense and four times on defense.

A 6-foot 3-inch, 285-pound strongman, Nomellini was the first player drafted by the 49ers after they joined the NFL in 1950, and he was a great choice. Nomellini played every game in his 14 year 49ers career, earning 10 Pro Bowl invitations. A Pro Football Hall of Famer, Nomellini was honored as the defensive tackle on the 50-year All-Time All-Pro team in 1969.

THE BEST EVER?

Professional football has been a haven for extraordinary athletes - big, fast, tough men who could do routinely what most others could only dream. In this elite company, Jerry Rice has stood as one of the most gifted of all time. With breathtaking speed, durability, and sure hands, Rice gained more than 1,000 yards on pass receptions in seven of his first eight years in the NFL. The only time he fell short was 1985, his rookie season, when he started only 4 of 16 games. He still managed to catch 49 passes for 927 yards. After the 1991 season, Rice owned the 49ers' records for touchdowns (97), receptions (526), and receiving yardage (9,072).

1970
49ers post 10-3-1 record and win NFC Western Division title, club's first championship.

Cedrick Hardman

1972
San Francisco is NFC West champion third consecutive year.

1973
Long-time heroes John Brodie and Charlie Krueger retire.

A Hard(y) Hitter

Although he weighed only 190 pounds, San Francisco linebacker Hardy Brown was one of the most feared hitters of his time (1951-56).

He perfected a tackling technique of driving his shoulder into the ball carrier's face, an especially dangerous tactic in the era before face masks were commonplace.

Brown was a reckless hitter, and his career was cut short by injuries.

Earl Cooper and Wendell Tyler, offensive linemen Randy Cross, Keith Fahnhorst and Guy McIntyre, defensive standouts such as Keena Turner, Fred Dean, Dwight Hicks, Carlton Williamson, and Michael Carter, earned Pro Bowl berths and other honors.

The success the 49ers brought to San Francisco ended four decades of frustration. It had begun in 1946, when, as a charter member of the All-America Football Conference, the 49ers finished second to Cleveland in the Western Division. Ditto 1947. And 1948. And 1949. No matter how well the 49ers played, the Browns played better.

After admission to the NFL in 1950, the 49ers endured two decades of mediocrity - albeit colorful mediocrity - before finally winning their first division title in 1970 under coach Dick Nolan. They won three consecutive division titles, but never could get past Dallas in the playoffs.

The 49ers had some exciting heroes. Quarterback Y.A. Tittle, running backs Hugh

Hugh McElhenny

A Lott of Great Plays

One of pro football's great defensive backs, Ronnie Lott had a spectacular 10-year career with the 49ers from 1981-1990 before joining the Los Angeles Raiders. A fierce hitter who was also exceptional at pass coverage, Lott was selected to play in the Pro Bowl nine times while with the 49ers. He is the 49ers' career leader in interceptions (51) and interceptions returned for touchdowns (5).

The King

The first time Hugh McElhenny carried the ball in an NFL game, he ran 42 yards for a touchdown. It was a sign of things to come. The running back known as "The King" was a unique talent, a superb broken field runner who could change speed and direction with incredible ease and abruptness.

McElhenny, with the 49ers from 1952-1960, was renowned for his darting runs from sideline to sideline, scattering defenders as he went. A first-round pick in 1952, he rushed for 684 yards as a rookie, averaging 7 yards per carry, and capped his first season by scoring two touchdowns in the Pro Bowl.

McElhenny, who later played for the Vikings, Giants and Lions, was voted into the Pro Football Hall of Fame in 1970.

Ronnie Lott

1977	1979		1981
Edward J. DeBartolo, Jr., becomes owner of 49ers.	Bill Walsh becomes head coach; quarterback Joe Montana and wide receiver Dwight Clark are drafted.	Ken Willard	Three rookie defensive backs - Ronnie Lott, Eric Wright, Carlton Williamson - become starters; 49ers surge to 13-3 record and win Super Bowl XVI over Cincinnati 26-21.

McElhenny, Joe (The Jet) Perry, and John Henry Johnson, receivers Gordy Soltau and Billy Wilson, linemen Leo Nomellini and Bob St. Clair, starred in the 1950s. The 1960s featured quarterback John Brodie, wide receiver Dave Parks, guard Howard Mudd, kick returner Abe Woodson, defensive tackle Charlie Krueger, and linebacker Matt Hazeltine. But the frustration continued. The 1970s featured defensive greats such as cornerback Jimmy Johnson, end Cedrick Hardman, and linebacker Dave Wilcox, but no championships.

Walsh and Montana, who arrived in San Francisco in 1979, helped the 49ers strike gold. Within a 10-year period, San Francisco won seven NFC Western Division titles, qualified for the playoffs eight times, and collected four Super Bowl trophies.

The 49ers of the 1980s were a unique collection of extraordinary players. Indeed, the NFL team of the decade. ◎

49ers' Special Numbers

San Francisco has retired the numbers of seven players, including quarterback John Brodie (12), running backs Joe Perry (34) and Hugh McElhenny (39), defensive back Jimmy Johnson (37), defensive tackles Charlie Krueger (70) and Leo Nomellini (73), and wide receiver Dwight Clark (87).

THE HUMAN JET

Joe (The Jet) Perry had one of the most appropriate nicknames in pro football. The most productive running back in 49ers history, Perry had 1,345 rushing yards for San Francisco in the All-America Football Conference, then added another 7,344 yards in 12 years after the 49ers joined the NFL.

A 200-pounder with exceptional quickness, Perry was the NFL rushing leader in 1953 and 1954, when he became the first player in history to rush for more than 1,000 yards two consecutive years. He was San Francisco's leading rusher a club-record eight times, including one in the AAFC.

Perry rushed for 8,378 yards in his NFL career, second only to Jim Brown when The Jet retired in 1963.

A second-round pick in the 1983 draft, Roger Craig was a great bargain. A running back equally adept at catching the ball and running with it, Craig earned a unique place in the NFL record book in 1985. He gained 1,050 rushing yards and 1,016 receiving yards, the only player to top the 1,000-yard mark in both categories in the same season.

Craig, who played for San Francisco from 1983-1990, is second in the 49ers' record book in both receptions (508) and rushing yardage (7,064), trailing only Jerry Rice and Joe Perry, respectively.

1983	1984		1988	1989
49ers build powerful running attack by drafting Roger Craig, trading for Wendell Tyler.	San Francisco wins 15 of 16 regular-season games, wins Super Bowl XIX over Miami 38-16.	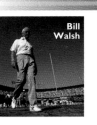 **Bill Walsh**	In Bill Walsh's final season as coach, 49ers have 10-6 record, win Super Bowl XXIII over Cincinnati 20-16.	George Seifert becomes head coach, 49ers win NFC West title with 14-2 record, beat Denver 55-10 in Super Bowl XXIV.

YEAR ■ WINS ■ LOSSES ☐ TIES	RECORD	PLACE	COACH
1976	2-12	5th	Jack Patera
1977	5-9	4th	Jack Patera
1978	9-7	3rd	Jack Patera
1979	9-7	3rd	Jack Patera
1980	4-12	5th	Jack Patera
1981	6-10	5th	Jack Patera
1982	4-5	10th	J. Patera, M. McCormack [1]
1983	9-7	2nd	Chuck Knox
1984	12-4	2nd	Chuck Knox
1985	8-8	3rd	Chuck Knox
1986	10-6	3rd	Chuck Knox
1987	9-6	2nd	Chuck Knox
1988	9-7	1st	Chuck Knox
1989	7-9	4th	Chuck Knox
1990	9-7	3rd	Chuck Knox
1991	7-9	4th	Chuck Knox

1 – Jack Patera (2 games), Mike McCormack (7 games)

When future expansion franchises are welcomed into the National Football League, they'll study the story of the Seattle Seahawks.

The Seahawks drew the blueprints for success.

No other franchise ever sprang to life as smoothly as Seattle.

It started with the stadium. Without an NFL team, without even the promise of one, a group of Seattle community and business leaders began construction of a 65,000-seat domed stadium.

The Kingdome proved to be a

Number 12: Someone Special

Seattle's Kingdome has the reputation of being the noisiest stadium in the NFL, and the team has recognized the value of the fans by retiring jersey No. 12, signifying the fans as Seattle's "Twelfth man."

SEATTLE SEAHAWKS
Turning Points

1972
Determined to land NFL franchise, Seattle begins construction of 65,000-seat Kingdome.

real-life field of dreams: "If you build it, they will come." Seattle built it, and the NFL came.

Seattle was awarded a franchise in 1974, to begin play in 1976. A season-ticket offering received phenomenal response - 24,000 requests the first day, and 59,000 sold in less than a month.

A "name-the-team" contest drew more than 20,000 responses with 1,700 different suggestions. Clearly, Washingtonians were eager for an NFL team. And the Seahawks didn't disappoint them.

The team staggered in its first season, with a 2-12 record - typical for an expansion team. But what happened after that was anything but typical. The Seahawks won five games in their second season and had a winning record, 9-7, the following year. No expansion team had ever done so well so quickly.

Why was Seattle so successful?

Much of the credit goes to John Thompson and Jack Patera, Seattle's first general manager

Down to the Wire

The Seahawks had a remarkable streak in 1990 - four consecutive games were decided on the last play.

The streak:

November 11 at Kansas City: Seahawks 17, Chiefs 16; Dave Kreig hits Paul Skansi with a 25-yard pass as time expires.

November 18 at Seattle: Vikings 24, Seahawks 21; Fuad Reveiz kicks decisive 24-yard field goal.

November 25 at San Diego: Seahawks 13, Chargers 10; Norm Johnson's 40-yard field goal decides overtime game.

December 2 at Seattle: Seahawks 13, Oilers 10; this time Johnson kicks a 42-yarder to end the overtime.

Warner: A Wonder

Curt Warner arrived with a big reputation - All-America at Penn State, the third pick in the entire draft - and he lived up to his billing.

Warner's rookie season was a great one - an AFC-leading 1,449 yards rushing, 14 touchdowns, Seahawks MVP, AFC player of the year.

But his second season lasted less than five minutes; he severely damaged a knee in the opening moments of the 1984 campaign. Warner came back in 1985 and led the team in rushing for the next five seasons. He retired after the 1989 season as Seattle's all-time leading rusher with 6,705 yards and 55 touchdowns.

1974

The NFL awards franchise to Seattle, with play to begin in 1976 season.

Jack Patera

What Might Have Been

Running back David Sims was unheralded as a rookie, coming from Georgia Tech in the seventh round of the draft. But in his second season (1978), the 6-foot 3-inch, 216-pounder got everybody's attention by leading the NFL with 15 touchdowns. The next year, however, his career ended after only 20 more carries; a knee injury forced him into retirement.

and head coach, respectively. Thompson assembled a capable staff that managed to evaluate and acquire player talent quickly. And Patera knew what to do with it.

From the beginning, the Seattle brain trust put a premium on defense. Patera had been Bud Grant's defensive chief of staff at Minnesota, and he put his imprint on the new team.

The first Seahawks draft choice was a defensive tackle, 270-pound Steve Niehaus from Notre Dame, and the second pick was Sammy Green, a linebacker from Florida. That established a pattern for the franchise.

The first two picks in the 1977 draft were offensive linemen, but the focus returned to defense in 1978 and beyond. Defensive backs Keith Simpson and Bob Jury and linebacker Keith Butler were Seattle's first three picks in 1978. Defensive tackle Manu Tuiasosopo and linebackers Joe Norman and Michael Jackson were the first three picks in 1979. Defensive ends Jacob Green and Terry Dion represented two of the first three picks in 1980. Safety Kenny Easley was the first-round pick in 1981. And defensive end Jeff Bryant was first in 1982.

Seahawk Ballhawks

Seattle's most celebrated defensive backs have been Dave Brown and Kenny Easley. Brown, a first-round draft choice whom the Steelers exposed in the 1976 expansion draft, is the Seahawks' all-time leading pass thief with 50 interceptions. Four times the Seahawks' defensive captain, Brown played in the 1984 Pro Bowl.

Easley, a first-round pick by Seattle in 1981, intercepted 32 passes before kidney failure forced his retirement after the 1987 season. He played in four Pro Bowls, three times as a starter. Easley was the NFL defensive player of the year in 1984.

Kenny Easley

THE SEAHAWKS' FIRST STAR

Free agent quarterback Jim Zorn, who had failed to win a job in tryouts with the Dallas Cowboys and Rams, found a starting job and a starring role with the Seattle Seahawks.

The left-handed passer was selected as Seattle's most valuable player in 1976 and 1978, and was the Seahawks' starting quarterback in the first seven years of the franchise. Although the Seahawks won only two games in their initial season, the 6-foot 2-inch, 200-pound Zorn set records for a first-year expansion team quarterback with 208 completions for 2,572 yards and 12 touchdowns.

John L. Williams

1977	1978
Seattle has 5-9 season, most victories ever for expansion team in second season.	Seahawks soar to 9-7 record, becoming first expansion team to have winning season in its third year.

In six of their first seven years, the Seahawks used their premium draft picks on defensive players, and the strategy paid dividends. There were two winning seasons within the first four years. By their ninth season, when the draft picks had matured, the Seahawks had a 12-4 record.

When the Seahawks finally broke the pattern and concentrated on offensive help, they did it in a big way. In the first draft under new coach Chuck Knox in 1983, Seattle used eight of nine picks on offensive help. The biggest prize was Curt Warner, a dazzling runner out of Penn State.

Warner was as good as publicized. He raced for a conference-leading 1,449 yards in his first season, earning AFC rookie of the year and player of the year honors. The Seahawks surged to their first playoff berth, then defeated Denver in the Kingdome and Miami on the road before losing to the Los Angeles Raiders in the AFC Championship Game.

Using the 1983 season as a take-off point, the Seahawks had only one losing season in the next eight years.

ONE OF A KIND

From the start, it was obvious that Steve Largent wasn't just another NFL receiver. In fact, the Houston Oilers didn't think he was any kind of NFL receiver...they released him in training camp.

Seattle gave Largent a tryout, perhaps intrigued that he ranked eighth academically at the University of Tulsa, where he majored in biology. More likely, though, they were intrigued that he caught 14 touchdown passes, the most in the nation, in both his junior and senior seasons.

Largent wasn't big (5-foot 11-inches, 184 pounds) or especially fast. But he could read a defense, run precise pass patterns, and he had great, great hands. In a career that spanned from 1976-1989, those hands caught more passes for more touchdowns and more yards than anyone else who had played professional football.

Largent's NFL records: 819 receptions, 100 touchdowns, 13,089 yards. He caught passes in 177 consecutive games, another league best.

He caught on quickly, snaring 54 passes as a rookie in 1976, and never looked back. Largent retired after the 1989 season.

1980

Defensive end Jacob Green is team's number one draft choice. He becomes one of NFL's finest pass rushers for more than a decade.

1982

Midway into third consecutive disappointing season, Jack Patera is fired, Mike McCormack finishes out season.

Brian Blades

He Wouldn't Stay Gone

Don Dufek was the kind of guy who just won't take "No" for an answer. He was released in training camp four times during his eight-year Seahawks career. But each time, Seattle had a change of heart, bringing him back. Today, he is remembered as one of the best special teams performers the team has had.

During the years when Patera was stockpiling defensive talent with high draft picks, the offense was getting great results from other teams' castoffs.

The club's first quarterback was Jim Zorn, an undrafted free agent out of Cal Poly (Pomona). He spent time in Cowboys and Rams camps, but couldn't win a job. After getting a chance in Seattle, the left-hander completed 1,593 passes for more than 20,000 yards and 107 touchdowns.

Zorn's favorite target was Steve Largent, a Houston Oilers reject. Largent had a remarkable rookie year, catching 56 passes in Seattle's first season. Then he caught 33, then 71, 66, 66, 75, 34, 72, 74, 79, 70, and 58, leading Seattle in pass receptions each of the first 12 years.

While Zorn and Largent were playing pitch and catch, Sherman Smith was doing the ground work. The ex-college quarterback led Seattle in rushing yardage each of the first four years, always averaging more than four yards per carry, until a knee injury ended his career.

AIR FORCE GENERAL

A free agent from Milton College, Dave Kreig arrived in Seattle without fanfare. But everybody knew him by the time he left in 1992. Kreig was the Seahawks' starting quarterback through most of the 1980s, passing for a team-record 2,096 completions, 26,132 yards and 195 touchdowns and leading Seattle to the playoffs four times. His streak of throwing a touchdown pass in 28 consecutive games, achieved 1983-85, is the third-longest in NFL history.

1983

Chuck Knox becomes head coach, Curt Warner is number one draft choice, Seahawks make postseason play-offs for first time.

Chuck Knox

1987

Steve Largent makes 751st career reception to become NFL's all-time leading receiver.

272

The 1982 season was Smith's last, 1983 was Warner's first. When Zorn's skills began to erode, free-agent quarterback Dave Kreig came out of practically nowhere (Milton College in Wisconsin) and didn't stop throwing until he had 2,096 completions, 26,132 yards and 195 touchdowns. He was a fixture in Seattle until the end of the 1991 season, when he left as a Plan B free agent.

From Smith to Warner, from Zorn to Kreig, plus the ever-present Largent, the Seattle offense was in good hands. Make that great hands.

Meanwhile, the stockpiling of defensive talent continued, and the Seahawks became a contender to be taken seriously year after year in the tough AFC West.

It's a blueprint that may be copied for many years to come. ⊘

Sack Man

The Seahawks drafted Jacob Green in the first round of the 1980 draft, expecting him to be the solution to their pass-rushing problems.

He didn't disappoint. The 6-foot 3-inch, 256-pound sometimes-end, sometimes-linebacker became one of the quickest, most intimidating pass rushers in the business, racking up 116 sacks in his first dozen years at Seattle.

He's The Boss

The Seahawks have had remarkable stability in the head coaching department. Jack Patera coached six-plus seasons and Chuck Knox was in charge for nine years. The only other head coach was Mike McCormack, who filled in for seven games after Patera was released in 1982.

Tom Flores, who had a highly successful nine-year term as the Raiders' head coach, took over the Seahawks in 1992. Flores' record with the Raiders was 85-53, with two Super Bowl victories.

Norm Johnson

1988

Seattle wins its first AFC Western Division championship.

1992

An era ends when Chuck Knox resigns; President/General Manager Tom Flores takes on additional duties of head coach.

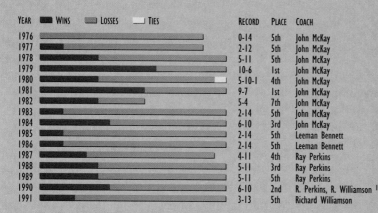

YEAR	WINS	LOSSES	TIES	RECORD	PLACE	COACH
1976				0-14	5th	John McKay
1977				2-12	5th	John McKay
1978				5-11	5th	John McKay
1979				10-6	1st	John McKay
1980				5-10-1	4th	John McKay
1981				9-7	1st	John McKay
1982				5-4	7th	John McKay
1983				2-14	5th	John McKay
1984				6-10	3rd	John McKay
1985				2-14	5th	Leeman Bennett
1986				2-14	5th	Leeman Bennett
1987				4-11	4th	Ray Perkins
1988				5-11	3rd	Ray Perkins
1989				5-11	5th	Ray Perkins
1990				6-10	2nd	R. Perkins, R. Williamson [1]
1991				3-13	5th	Richard Williamson

1 — Ray Perkins (13 games), Richard Williamson (3 games)

With the exception of two brief, shining moments, the Tampa Bay Buccaneers have been a study in frustration. In their first 16 years, they had only three winning seasons, and won less than 30 percent of their games.

Some of the most successful NFL franchises have gone through extended dry spells, but the disap-

Dubious Distinction

In the first 12 years of their existence, the Tampa Bay Buccaneers had the first pick in the NFL draft four times. Their selections: defensive end Lee Roy Selmon (1976), running back Ricky Bell (1977), running back Bo Jackson (1986), and quarterback Vinny Testaverde (1987).

Initially, Tampa Bay drafted first because it was an expansion team. The three other times, it earned the distinction by having the worst record the previous season. The only other teams with more than one chance at the first pick during that span were Buffalo and New England, with two apiece.

1974

TAMPA BAY BUCCANEERS

Turning Points

Tampa Bay is awarded an NFL franchise; Hugh Culverhouse is club owner.

pointment was doubled for Tampa Bay fans because the collapse came after it appeared the Buccaneers had cleared the toughest hurdles.

No franchise ever had a more difficult beginning - the Buccaneers lost their first 26 games, starting with the 1976 season, and failed to score a touchdown in 14 of them. Then, things began to improve.

First came modest success - five victories in 1978. By 1979 the Buccaneers' defense was manhandling opponents and Tampa Bay was writing a great rags-to-riches story. Last in the NFC Central Division in 1978, Tampa Bay exploded for a 10-6 record and the division championship in 1979. The Cincinnati Bengals were the only other expansion team in history to win a division title within their first four years.

Two years later, the Buccaneers were 9-7 and division champions again.

Two division titles in the first six years gave way to another playoff berth in the seventh year. Then the Buccaneers unexpectedly plunged to 2-14 in 1983. Recovery from that fall

BUCCANEERS' WINNER

Doug Williams was Tampa Bay's quarterback for five seasons, and led the team to its only three winning seasons in the first 16 years. A first-round pick in the 1978 draft, Williams was at the controls when Tampa Bay won NFC Central titles (1979 and 1981) and qualified for the playoffs in the strike-shortened 1982 season.

He jumped to the USFL in 1983, then returned to lead the Washington Redskins to victory in Super Bowl XXII, for which he was named Super Bowl MVP.

In five years at Tampa Bay, Williams completed 895 passes for 12,648 yards and 73 touchdowns.

Last-Second Heroics

The Buccaneers' 1982 season was one for the highlight reel.

After losing their first three games, they won five of the last six, each time pulling out victory in the final minutes. The narrow escapes came against Miami (23-17), New Orleans (13-10), Buffalo (24-23), Detroit (23-21) and Chicago (26-23). The game against the Bears was decided in overtime on a 33-yard field goal by Bill Capece, and qualified Tampa Bay for the playoffs.

1975
John McKay hired as Buccaneers coach; plans approved to increase Tampa Stadium to 72,000-seat capacity.

John McKay

1976
Buccaneers make Lee Roy Selmon first selection in draft; go 0-14 in first season.

1977
Losing streak ends after 26 games with 33-14 victory at New Orleans.

A Family Trait

Broderick Thomas, the sixth selection in the 1990 draft, had an outstanding second season. A linebacker from Nebraska, Thomas led the 1991 Buccaneers with 11 sacks and a club-record 174 tackles. It figures. His uncle is Chicago Bears superstar linebacker Mike Singletary.

proved slow and difficult; the next eight seasons produced eight losing records.

Owner Hugh Culverhouse seemed to make all the right moves after getting an NFL franchise. He hired highly regarded coach John McKay, who had won four national championships and made eight Rose Bowl appearances at the University of Southern California. McKay traded for a veteran quarterback - Steve Spurrier - and used the first pick in the draft to take Oklahoma's Lee Roy Selmon, a defensive lineman with sensational promise.

Spurrier was released after Tampa Bay's first season, but Selmon developed into the cornerstone of an outstanding defensive unit.

The second season was worse than the first on offense; Tampa's scoring fell from 125 points to a league-low 103. But the Buccaneers' defense served notice of better days ahead. After being battered for 412 points in 1976, Tampa Bay yielded only 223 the next season.

McKay stockpiled talent for his defensive unit. Along with Lee Roy and Dewey Selmon, he

A Rough Start

The first pick in the 1987 draft after winning the Heisman Trophy at the University of Miami, Vinny Testaverde encountered problems trying to ignite the sputtering Tampa Bay offense.

Testaverde was sacked 162 times and threw 96 interceptions in his first five seasons. During that time, he completed 920 of 1,802 pass attempts for 12,266 yards and 63 touchdowns.

Batman

No member of the Buccaneers played in more games (132) or made more tackles (851) than linebacker Richard (Batman) Wood.

The first three-time All-America at the University of Southern California, Wood was one of the original Tampa Bay players. He arrived by trade in 1976 after being a third-round draft pick by the Jets in 1975.

Wood was Tampa Bay's leading tackler four of the team's first five seasons.

1978
Buccaneers trade first overall pick in draft for tight end Jimmie Giles and seventeenth pick, take quarterback Doug Williams.

1979
Tampa Bay is NFC Central Division champion with 10-4 record; wins playoff game against Philadelphia 24-17, loses NFC Championship Game to Rams 9-0.

Steve Young

1981
Buccaneers bounce back from 5-10-1 season to 9-7 record and win NFC Central title second time in three years.

had talented safety Mark Cotney and linebackers Richard Wood and David Lewis. He traded for reinforcements - defensive linemen Wally Chambers, Randy Crowder, and David Pear, and cornerback Mike Washington.

By 1978 Tampa Bay was ranked fourth in the NFL on defense, and in 1979, no team was better. That defense, led by Lee Roy Selmon, powered Tampa to the NFC Central Division championship. The Buccaneers won their first playoff opportunity, 24-17 over Philadelphia, earning a berth in the NFC Championship Game. A Buccaneers trip to the Super Bowl was not to be, however; an outstanding defensive effort was squandered in a 9-0 loss to the Rams in the NFC title game.

The Buccaneers' attack, the weakest in the NFL for three years, climbed to fourteenth in 1979 as Doug Williams matured at quarterback and running back Ricky Bell delivered on the promise that had made him the first pick in the 1977 draft.

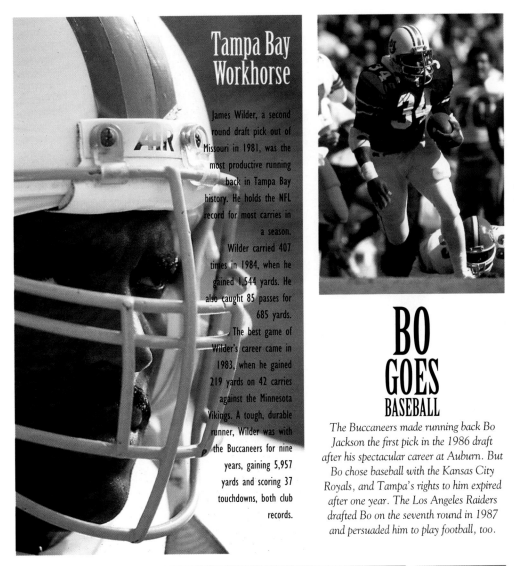

Tampa Bay Workhorse

James Wilder, a second round draft pick out of Missouri in 1981, was the most productive running back in Tampa Bay history. He holds the NFL record for most carries in a season. Wilder carried 407 times in 1984, when he gained 1,544 yards. He also caught 85 passes for 685 yards. The best game of Wilder's career came in 1983, when he gained 219 yards on 42 carries against the Minnesota Vikings. A tough, durable runner, Wilder was with the Buccaneers for nine years, gaining 5,957 yards and scoring 37 touchdowns, both club records.

BO GOES BASEBALL

The Buccaneers made running back Bo Jackson the first pick in the 1986 draft after his spectacular career at Auburn. But Bo chose baseball with the Kansas City Royals, and Tampa's rights to him expired after one year. The Los Angeles Raiders drafted Bo on the seventh round in 1987 and persuaded him to play football, too.

1983	1984
Williams leaves Tampa Bay for USFL.	McKay resigns with NFL career record 45-91-1.

Hugh Green

Injuries took a toll in 1980, and Tampa slipped to 5-10-1. But the Buccaneers were back the next year, winning the division title with a 9-7 record before losing a first-round playoff game to Dallas. In 1982, when they had a 5-4 record, the Buccaneers earned a playoff spot in a strike-shortened season.

That was to be a last glimpse of glory before fortunes reversed.

Tampa Bay suffered a serious loss when Williams bolted for the USFL after the 1982 season. Then came four years in which Tampa Bay failed to capitalize on the draft:

1983 - The Buccaneers' first-round pick was sent to Chicago in exchange for defensive lineman Booker Reese in 1982. The Bears used the pick to select wide receiver Willie Gault. Reese played for Tampa Bay for only three years, starting seven games.

1984 - The Buccaneers traded their first-round pick to Cincinnati for quarterback Jack Thompson, who stayed with Tampa Bay only two years.

A REUNION

Ricky Bell, a running back who was the main man in John McKay's offensive scheme at Southern California, rejoined his former college coach in 1977, when the Buccaneers made Bell the first pick in the draft.

The 212-pound tailback was Tampa Bay's leading rusher for the next four years; his best season was 1979, when he gained 1,263 yards. Bell and James Wilder are the only Buccaneers to rush for more than 1,000 yards in a season. Bell was traded to San Diego after the 1981 season.

Jimmie Giles

1985	**1986**	**1987**
Leeman Bennett is named head coach, Buccaneers have first of two consecutive 2-14 seasons.	Bo Jackson, Tampa Bay's first pick, chooses to play baseball instead.	Ray Perkins becomes head coach, quarterback Vinny Testaverde is first-round draft pick.

1985 - The Buccaneers used their first-round pick to select defensive end Ron Holmes. He played four seasons before being traded to Denver.

1986 - Tampa Bay's first pick was Bo Jackson, who opted to play professional baseball in the Kansas City Royals' organization.

Four premium draft choices brought no premium replacement parts for a roster that needed shoring up. The Buccaneers fell into a downward spiral that was difficult to reverse.

McKay resigned in 1984 after posting a record of 45-91-1. He was followed by Leeman Bennett (1985), Ray Perkins (1987), and Richard Williamson (1990), none of whom could engineer a winning season. In 1992 Tampa turned to Sam Wyche, who had taken the Cincinnati Bengals to Super Bowl XXIII and who had been described by three-time Super Bowl winner Bill Walsh as "the most brilliant coach in the NFL." ✐

The Best Buccaneer

The Buccaneers made their first venture into the NFL draft a great one, selecting defensive end Lee Roy Selmon from the University of Oklahoma with the first pick in 1976.

Selmon played for Tampa Bay nine years, leading the team in sacks eight times. He retired in 1984 with 78 1/2 sacks and six Pro Bowl selections. He was a unanimous selection as the NFL defensive player of the year in 1979, and his number (63) is the only one retired by the club.

One of Tampa Bay's second-round picks in 1976 was Lee Roy's brother, Dewey, who was a five-year starter at defensive tackle and linebacker.

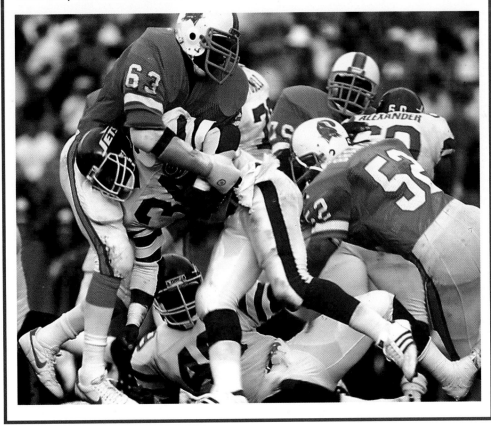

1990
Perkins is replaced by Richard Williamson.

Sam Wyche

1992
Sam Wyche becomes Tampa Bay's fifth head coach.

Washington REDSKINS

YEAR ■ WINS ☐ LOSSES ☐ TIES	RECORD	PLACE	COACH
Boston Braves			
1932	4-4-2	4th	Lud Wray
Boston Redskins			
1933	5-5-2	3rd	William Dietz
1934	6-6	2nd	William Dietz
1935	2-8-1	4th	Eddie Casey
1936	7-5	1st	Ray Flaherty
Washington Redskins			
1937	8-3	1st	Ray Flaherty
1938	6-3-2	2nd	Ray Flaherty
1939	8-2-1	2nd	Ray Flaherty
1940	9-2	1st	Ray Flaherty
1941	6-5	3rd	Ray Flaherty
1942	10-1	1st	Ray Flaherty
1943	6-3-1	1st	Arthur Bergman
1944	6-3-1	3rd	Dudley DeGroot
1945	8-2	1st	Dudley DeGroot
1946	5-5-1	3rd	Glen Edwards
1947	4-8	4th	Glen Edwards
1948	7-5	2nd	Glen Edwards
1949	4-7-1	4th	J. Welchel, H. Ball [1]
1950	3-9	6th	Herman Ball
1951	5-7	3rd	H. Ball, D. Todd [2]
1952	4-8	5th	Curly Lambeau
1953	6-5-1	3rd	Curly Lambeau
1954	3-9	5th	Joe Kuharich
1955	8-4	2nd	Joe Kuharich
1956	6-6	3rd	Joe Kuharich
1957	5-6-1	4th	Joe Kuharich
1958	4-7-1	4th	Joe Kuharich
1959	3-9	5th	Mike Nixon
1960	1-9-2	6th	Mike Nixon
1961	1-12-1	7th	Bill McPeak
1962	5-7-2	4th	Bill McPeak
1963	3-11	6th	Bill McPeak
1964	6-8	3rd	Bill McPeak
1965	6-8	4th	Bill McPeak
1966	7-7	5th	Otto Graham
1967	5-6-3	3rd	Otto Graham
1968	5-9	3rd	Otto Graham
1969	7-5-2	2nd	Vince Lombardi
1970	6-8	4th	Bill Austin
1971	9-4-1	2nd	George Allen
1972	11-3	1st	George Allen
1973	10-4	2nd	George Allen
1974	10-4	2nd	George Allen
1975	8-6	3rd	George Allen
1976	10-4	2nd	George Allen
1977	9-5	2nd	George Allen
1978	8-8	3rd	Jack Pardee
1979	10-6	3rd	Jack Pardee
1980	6-10	3rd	Jack Pardee
1981	8-8	4th	Joe Gibbs
1982	8-1	1st	Joe Gibbs
1983	14-2	1st	Joe Gibbs
1984	11-5	1st	Joe Gibbs
1985	10-6	3rd	Joe Gibbs
1986	12-4	2nd	Joe Gibbs
1987	11-4	1st	Joe Gibbs
1988	7-9	3rd	Joe Gibbs
1989	10-6	3rd	Joe Gibbs
1990	10-6	3rd	Joe Gibbs
1991	14-2	1st	Joe Gibbs

1 — John Welchel (7 games), Herman Ball (5 games)   2 — Herman Ball (3 games), Dick Todd (9 games)

The Washington Redskins had been winners...big winners at times...led by legendary coaches - Ray Flaherty, Curly Lambeau, Vince Lombardi, and George Allen.

Then, along came a guy with no previous head coaching experience, and he showed the Washington Redskins what success *really* means.

Joe Gibbs went to Washington in 1981 and built a machine that stamped out victories, and even

THE SHOWMAN

George Preston Marshall, owner of the Redskins from 1932 until his death in 1969, was a pioneer in packaging pro football games as entertainment events.

Among the Marshall innovations: the Redskins' marching band, a team fight song, halftime shows (marching bands, circus acts, fireworks), a radio network for his team's games, and local telecast of all Redskins games.

Important Marshall proposals that helped change the face of the pro football: split of NFL teams into two divisions, with a season-ending playoff for the championship, and a postseason all-star game. The former was implemented in 1933, the latter in 1939.

Marshall was recognized for his contributions by selection to the Pro Football Hall of Fame as a charter member in 1963.

1932

WASHINGTON REDSKINS

Turning Points

George P. Marshall heads group that is granted NFL franchise in Boston, team is called Braves.

championships, with remarkable consistency.

In his first 11 years as Redskins coach, Gibbs produced 130 victories, four NFC East Division champions, four Super Bowl teams, and three Super Bowl champions.

Not bad for a guy just starting out.

Although Gibbs had not previously been a head coach, his resume included impressive references.

He had been an assistant on the college staffs of Don Coryell (San Diego State), Bill Peterson (Florida State), and John McKay (University of Southern California), three successful coaches renowned for expertise on offense. Gibbs followed McKay and Coryell to the NFL, playing a key role in the design of the famed "Air Coryell" offense in San Diego.

When Jack Kent Cooke summoned him in 1981, the 40-year old Gibbs was ready.

It didn't appear that way initially; the Redskins lost their first five games under Gibbs before winning 8 of the last 11.

In his second season, Gibbs had a Super Bowl championship. The Redskins went 8-1 in the

SLINGIN' SAM

The Washington Redskins have retired only one uniform number - 33 - worn by Sammy Baugh.

The legendary quarterback, credited with changing the passing game, played for the Redskins from 1937-1952. He led the league in passing as a rookie, then repeated as the leader five more times in his career.

Baugh led the Redskins to their first title as a rookie, his first of six championship-game appearances. He retired after passing for 21,886 yards and 187 touchdowns.

Baugh's greatest season was 1943, when he led the NFL in passing (1,754 yards and 23 touchdowns), punting (45.9 yards), and interceptions (11). A superior punter, he set league records for a season (51.4 yards) and career (45.1).

Joe Gibbs

1933	**1937**		**1940**
Team name is changed to Redskins; Marshall buys out partners, becomes sole owner.	Franchise is moved to Washington; Redskins draft quarterback Sammy Baugh, win NFL Championship Game 28-21 over Bears.	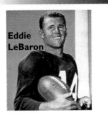 Eddie LeBaron	Redskins play Bears for NFL championship, get hammered 73-0.

The Right Move

Despite spending the first two years of his career as a running back, Charley Taylor became one of the NFL's greatest wide receivers. A first-round draft pick and United Press International rookie of the year in 1964, Taylor was moved to flanker by new Redskins coach Otto Graham in 1966. His 649 receptions were tops on the all-time list when he retired in 1977. Taylor played for Washington from 1964-1977 and caught 79 touchdown passes, a club record that still stands. He played in eight Pro Bowls and was selected for the Pro Football Hall of Fame.

strike-shortened 1982 season, then pounded out decisive victories in the playoffs: 31-7 over Detroit, 21-7 over Minnesota, 31-17 over Dallas, then 27-17 over Miami in Super Bowl XVII.

As if to prove it was no strike-induced fluke, the Redskins raced to the Super Bowl again in 1983, setting an NFL record for scoring.

Those years with Coryell, Peterson, and McKay paid off. Gibbs's team rolled up 541 points (an average of 33.8 per game) while going 14-2. The Redskins were held to fewer than 30 points only five times, and never scored fewer than 23.

Joe Theismann was the quarterback, John Riggins the running back, Art Monk and Charlie Brown the wide receivers, Don Warren the tight end, and "The Hogs" were the offensive linemen.

But the names would prove to be incidental.

Gibbs's teams continued to rack up victories, year after year, and it didn't seem to matter who the players were. Gibbs won Super Bowls with three different quarterbacks - Theismann, Doug Williams, and Mark Rypien. Jay Schroeder was the starter for two seasons; the Redskins won 12 games one year and 11 the next.

Sonny

His supporting cast was less than the best, and Christian (Sonny) Jurgensen appeared in only one playoff game in 11 years as a Redskin.

But there was never a doubt that the Washington quarterback was one of the best. When he retired in 1974, Jurgensen was the top-rated passer of all time.

Acquired from the Philadelphia Eagles in a preseason trade in 1964, Jurgensen led the NFL in passing in 1967 and 1969.

The career totals of the Hall of Famer: 2,433 completions, 32,224 yards, and 255 touchdown passes.

A WINNER, BY GEORGE

In a game designed for the young and the reckless, George Allen collected the geezers and wheezers, old-timers who knew how to play to win, and built them into one of the most colorful outfits in the league.

"The Over the Hill Gang" was assembled at the expense of youth. Preaching a "Future Is Now" philosophy, Allen never saw a draft choice he wasn't interested in trading.

Allen coached seven seasons (1971-77), producing an outstanding 69-35-1 record. Those were years when the Dallas Cowboys were a powerhouse, and Allen's Redskins won only one NFC Eastern Division crown.

1942
Sweet revenge: Redskins beat Bears 14-6 for NFL title.

Chris Hanburger

1964
Trades bring quarterback Sonny Jurgensen from Philadelphia Eagles, linebacker Sam Huff from New York Giants.

1969
Vince Lombardi becomes head coach, dies after only one season.

The running backs changed, too. From Joe Washington to Riggins to George Rogers to Kelvin Bryant to Gerald Riggs to Earnest Byner. Six different runners led the Redskins in rushing in 11 years.

And faces changed at wide receiver, too. Art Monk, Charlie Brown, Gary Clark, and Ricky Sanders each took a turn at leading the Redskins in receiving.

There were changes in the offensive line, changes in the defense, changes in the front office, changes everywhere except on the head coach's nameplate.

It wasn't always that easy in Washington.

Flaherty, coaching teams that featured the legendary Sammy Baugh at quarterback, won league championships in 1937 and 1942, and there were losses in NFL title games in 1943 and 1945. But then the Redskins fell into a prolonged swoon. From 1946-1971, Washington had 12 different coaches but only four winning seasons.

One of those 12 was Lombardi, who had gained acclaim during a nine-year stint at Green Bay. He took the Redskins to a 7-5-2 record in 1969, their first winning season in 14 years.

A REMARKABLE RECEIVER

After four years as an outstanding running back for the Cleveland Browns, Bobby Mitchell was traded to the Redskins and became an even better wide receiver.

In his first season at Washington, Mitchell caught a league-leading 72 passes for a club-record 1,384 yards. He was even better the next season, leading the NFL in receiving yards with 1,436.

Mitchell played for Washington from 1962-68, catching 393 passes for 6,491 yards. Overall, Mitchell caught 521 passes for 7,954 yards, the best in history when he retired after the 1968 season. He was inducted into the Pro Football Hall of Fame in 1983.

The Perfect Number One

Because a series of trades left the Redskins without a first-round draft choice for 11 consecutive years, the 1980 draft was a momentous event in Washington.

The Redskins celebrated the historic occasion by drafting a player who would have a historic career - wide receiver Art Monk, one of the all-time greats.

Pro football's record holder of 106 catches in a season (1984), Monk entered the 1992 season only 18 receptions behind Steve Largent's all-time record of 819.

An outstanding work ethic and great hands enabled Monk to record nine seasons with 50-plus catches in his first 12 years.

1971
George Allen becomes head coach; Redskins earn playoff berth for first time in 26 years.

1972
"Over The Hill Gang" goes 11-3, beats Packers and Cowboys in playoffs, loses Super Bowl VII to Dolphins 14-7.

Pat Fischer

1974
Jack Kent Cooke becomes majority owner of Redskins franchise.

283

Lombardi's Redskins career was tragically brief; he died of cancer before the 1970 season began.

The last of the 12 was George Allen, whose "Future Is Now" philosophy made the Redskins one of the NFL's most colorful teams of the 1970s.

Allen believed in building through trades, all but ignoring the draft. He traded draft picks so quickly they were hard to track. With Allen wheeling and dealing, Washington was without a first-round draft pick for 11 years. From 1972-76, the Redskins had no choices before the fifth round.

Prior to coaching his first game in Washington, Allen assembled the "Over The Hill Gang," importing veterans from rosters throughout the league: quarterback Billy Kilmer, receivers Roy Jefferson, Boyd Dowler, and Clifton McNeil, defensive linemen Diron Talbert, Verlon Biggs, and Ron McDole, linebackers Myron Pottios and Jack Pardee, and defensive backs Richie Petitbon and Speedy Duncan.

And that was just for starters. Allen continued to acquire veterans every year. Some had

The Redskins' Best Runner

It was said that John Riggins marched to a different drummer. But when he ran, he did it as most others wished they could.

A Mohawk haircut, toenails painted green, showing up shirtless for a press conference to announce a contract signing...only a few of the distinctions that branded Riggins as a "character."

His eccentric behavior aside, Riggins was an excellent running back. He ran for an NFL record 23 touchdowns in 1983 and totaled 104 in his career. Only Walter Payton and Jim Brown had more.

Riggins, who was inducted into the Hall of Fame in 1992, had his best years in 1983-84, when he rushed for 2,586 yards. He had 11,352 rushing yards in 14 seasons, sixth on the all-time list.

Joe Theismann

John Riggins

The Leader in Washington

Quickie Quiz: The Redskins' all-time leading passer in completions and yards was: (A) Hall of Famer Sammy Baugh, (B) Hall of Famer Sonny Jurgensen, or (C) Joe Theismann?

Answer: (C).

A Redskin from 1974-1985, Theismann had 2,044 completions for 25,206 yards, both club records. He was also an excellent scrambler, and his career rushing average of 5.1 yards is a Redskin record.

Mark Moseley

1980
Redskins draft wide receiver Art Monk of Syracuse in first round.

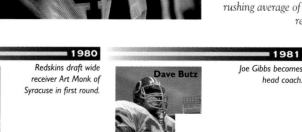

Dave Butz

1981
Joe Gibbs becomes head coach.

1982
Redskins go 8-1 in strike-shortened season, win Super Bowl XVII 27-17 over Dolphins, club's first championship in 40 years.

many good years left and were standouts in Washington, especially defensive back Ken Houston and defensive tackle Dave Butz.

Allen made the roster moves pay. In 1971, his first year, Washington was 9-4-1, its highest victory total since 1942. In his second season, he took his old timers to Super Bowl VII in Los Angeles, where they lost 14-7 to Miami in the Dolphins' perfect (17-0) season.

Washington, which had not qualified for postseason play since 1945, made the playoffs in each of Allen's first four years.

Those were strong Washington teams, quarterbacked by Kilmer and future Hall of Famer Sonny Jurgensen, but they won the NFC East Division only once, in 1972. Allen was in Washington seven years, producing one division title, five runners-up, and one third-place finish. He resigned after the 1977 season.

Four years later, Gibbs arrived, and the championships began to roll in. *⊘*

The Hogs

The "Hogs"?
"It's the guys with no finesse," explained R.C. Thielemann, a member of the famed offensive line. "They call us dirt bags, lunch-pail guys, blue-collar guys."

They also called them the best in the business. The Hogs, so named by offensive line coach Joe Bugel in 1982, changed several faces in the lineup, but never the name of the unit.

The original line included center Jeff Bostic, guards Russ Grimm and Mark May, and tackles Joe Jacoby and George Starke.

Weird Games Against Giants

The fierce rivalry between the Redskins and Giants has produced some memorable games; two of the most unusual were played in 1942 and 1966.

Washington's only loss of the 1942 season was 14-7 to the Giants, a game in which New York made no first downs, had only one yard rushing and completed only one pass. That pass completion was for a touchdown, however, and the Giants also scored on a pass interception.

The 1966 game was a 72-41 Washington victory despite the fact that the Giants had more total yardage, 389-344.

1983
Washington scores NFL record 541 points; Redskins win NFC East with 14-2 record, beat Rams and 49ers in play-offs, lose Super Bowl XVIII 38-9 to Raiders.

1987
Redskins go 11-4, win NFC East; beat Bears and Vikings in playoffs, win Super Bowl XXII over Broncos 42-10.

Gary Clark

1991
Redskins win Super Bowl XXVII 37-24 over Bills for third title in 10 years.

Mark Rypien

THE WRITERS

To provide the football fan with the ultimate insider's look behind the scenes of pro football, The Editor selected some of the most knowledgeable sports reporters throughout the U.S. Each of them is experienced in coverage of professional football; they average nearly 21 years as sports journalists.

THE PHOTOGRAPHERS

Title Spread: Michael Yada
Table of Contents: Vernon J. Biever, Herb Weitman, Paul Jasienski, Pete J. Groh, Pete J. Groh, Vernon J. Biever, Corky Trewin, NFL Photos, Al Messerschmidt, Michael Zagaris, Tom Guidera/J. Brough Schamp, NFL Photos
Last page: Louis Deluca

Legend:
t=top, *m*=middle, *b*=bottom
l=left, *lt*=left top, *lm*=left middle, *lb*=left bottom
r=right, *rt*=right top, *rm*=right middle, *rb*=right bottom

Tom Albert *165b*
Allen's Studio *133m, 277b*
Bill Amatucci *253, 254mb*
Fred Anderson *212t*
Charles Aquaviva *258rb*
Associated Press *52*
Morris Berman *230rm*
John Betancourt *158b, 283r*
John E. Biever *112, 120m, 131rb, 135b, 151lm, 170r, 209b, 210mb*
Vernon J. Biever *7m, 63, 132rl, 145lm, 161b, 163rb, 168b, 169b, 169m, 171rm, 171lm, 171t, 171m, 192lb, 216mb, 249lb, 254rb*
David Boss *12, 121rm, 135m, 149b, 152b, 162m, 181rb, 193rm, 195rb, 205rt, 207lm, 209b, 224m, 242rm, 257b, 261lm, 261rm, 282l, 285m*
Peter Brouillet *195m, 199l, 265m*
Tampa Bay Buccaneers *98*
Jim Chaffin *248m*
Kansas City Chiefs Football Club *44, 45, 48*
Color Master *165t*
Merv Corning *126m, 132mb, 212m, 247rm, 252lb, 263lb*
Fred Cornwell *156b*
Thomas J. Croke *49, 152m, 216m, 217rb, 219m*
Timothy A. Culek *37*
Bill Cummings *228lm, 231b*
Scott Cunningham *29r, 83, 123lb, 135mb, 266rm, 281r*
Jonathan Daniel *76lm*
Jay Dickman *222m*
Patrick Downs *192rm*
Rick Doyle *261rb*
Brian Drake *92, 146b, 218m, 260lb, 273b*
David Drapkin *140rb, 231lm, 285lb*
Malcolm W. Emmons *58, 72, 128b, 137m, 137b, 151b, 159m, 163lb, 173rt, 177m, 188mb, 191m, 195rt, 207b, 209m, 235m, 275m, 277r, 278m*
James F. Flores *25, 115, 157m, 194lt, 199r, 205rm, 259m, 259lb, 264lm*
L. D. Fullerton *138m*
George Gaadt *41*

George S. Garot *123mb*
George Gellatly *74r*
George Gojkovich *27, 35, 56, 139m, 140lb, 176b, 183b, 188b*
Pete J. Groh *13, 30l, 43rm, 51, 129b, 163rm, 175lm, 176lm*
Tom Guidera/J. Brough Schamp *107, 109*
Hall of Fame Photo *38, 167m, 239rb, 252rm, 265rt*
Ken Hardin *221b*
Andy Hayt *71, 257rm*
Skip Heine *187b*
Thearon Henderson *174t*
Walter Iooss, Jr. *53*
George Jardine *155r*
Paul Jasienski *33, 40, 61, 175b, 241m*
Allan Kaye *149rt*
Rick Kolodziej *99*
Al Kooistra *111, 237rt*
Larry Lambrecht *163lm*
Don Larson *182lt*
Laughead Photography *162b*
Tom Lehman *19*
Anos Love *173lm*
Ed Mahan *242rb, 243rm*
Tak Makita *236rm*
John McDonough *260m, 267mb, 270lm, 284l*
Rob McElroy *126t*
Perry McIntyre *122rm*
Al Messerschmidt *9, 16, 55, 66, 84, 85, 88, 95, 96, 102, 104, 120lt, 141m, 153b, 203m, 205lm, 206lm, 206b, 207t, 207rm, 223, 230mb, 237lb, 275b, 276m, 276b, 277l*
Peter Read Miller *181rm, 182b, 194lb, 260rb, 269m, 270rm, 270b*
Vic Milton *193lm*
Mike Moore *249rb*
Paul Moseley *149m*
Bill Mount *17, 145r*
NFL Films *281l*
NFL Photos *24, 60, 79, 94, 113, 117, 129t, 129m, 131lm, 132m, 133mb, 134b, 134r, 144b, 144t, 146m, 147m, 150lt, 151lm, 151rm, 155lm, 161m, 164m, 164rm, 167b, 168r, 168m, 170b, 170l, 171b, 174b, 179m, 179lm, 181rt, 183rt, 185m, 186b, 187m, 191b, 192lm, 192b, 197b, 198l, 210t, 211m, 221l, 222lb, 225r, 227lm, 229lm, 229mb, 235lm, 236lm, 239lb, 240rm, 241rm, 241rb, 243lm, 246b, 247m, 252rb, 254m, 255mb, 263rb, 264lb, 264lt, 278b, 281b, 282r, 282b, 283l*
Darryl Norenberg *120m, 121lm, 134m, 144rb, 150lb, 176rm, 183rm, 185t, 212b, 237lm, 258lt, 266rb*
Keith J. Randolph *213b*
Dick Raphael *234b, 272m, 284r*
Richard Raphael *164lb, 183lm, 193b, 217rm, 218lm, 230b, 283b*
John Reid III *147rb*
Robert Riger *227lb*

Frank Rippon *131mb, 143b, 145m, 161mb, 180lm, 198r, 240b, 266lm, 267lm*
George Robarge *195b, 201l*
Fred Roe *194m*
Bob Rosato *8, 10, 11, 93, 122mb, 123lm, 123rm, 159b, 175rm, 186l, 189m, 203b, 251m, 285rm*
George Rose *221r, 267rm*
David Ross *210r*
Ron Ross *147lb, 179lb, 180rm, 181lb, 236mb*
Daniel R. Rubin *227rm, 228b, 229rl, 237rm, 242lb, 251lb*
Manny Rubio *65, 90, 119m, 121mb, 122lm, 138b, 140m, 141b, 151r, 193rt, 201r, 216rb, 225l, 245m, 252lm*
Ross Russell *222rb*
John Sandhaus *128m, 217lb*
J. Brough Schamp/Tom Guidera *107, 109*
Alan Schwartz *87, 279m*
Robert B. Shaver *127b, 128l*
Owen C. Shaw *201b, 248rm, 271m*
Carl Skalak *139b, 186r, 191rt, 203lt, 255lm*
Bill Smith *246m, 255rt*
Robert L. Smith *125b, 126lm, 127m*
Chuck Solomon *235rt*
Jay Spencer *206rm*
Paul Spinelli *14, 36l, 80*
Brian Spurlock *116*
R. H. Stagg *108, 125l, 157b, 194rb, 248b, 255rm, 260lt*
Barry Staver *89*
Allan Dean Steele *189b, 279b*
Vic Stein *100, 197l, 197r, 200m*
Tim Steinberg *106*
Rick Stewart *258m*
Dave Stock *207m, 263m, 264m*
Stock Photo Finders *131rm*
George Tiedemann *229b*
Al Tielemans *165m*
Tony Tomsic *15, 20, 34l, 39rt, 110, 114, 126rm, 138r, 143m, 144m, 146t, 150m, 152lt, 153r, 156m, 158m, 164rb, 175rb, 181lm, 204b, 204rm, 210lb, 213m, 215m, 215mb, 235mb, 237lt, 264rb, 265mb, 284rb, 284lb*
Corky Trewin *73, 75rb, 76lt, 77, 269b, 271b, 272b, 273m*
Greg Trott *145b*
Jim Turner *39rb, 228rm, 234rm*
Ron Vesel *64*
Ralph Waclawicz *239m*
Ed Webber *28*
Herb Weitman *54, 153l, 182m, 188m, 233m, 247b, 249rm, 249lm, 249rt*
Lou Witt *18, 159rt, 173m, 173b, 174m, 185b, 233rb, 257lm*
Ron Wyatt *243b*
Michael Yada *200b, 259mb*
Michael Zagaris *67, 68, 97, 155b, 240m*
Jack Zehrt *86*
Joel Zwink *261t*

PUBLISHER
CADMUS MARKETING, INC.
Don Remley, *Vice President & General Manager*; Bruce Thomas, *Vice President*;
Mauri Whitehurst, *Financial Consultant*; David Watkins, *Controller*; Dave Moore, *Credit Management*

CADMUS COMMUNICATIONS, INC.
Wallace Stettinius, *Chairman*; Steve Gillispie, *Chief Executive Officer*; John Phillips, *Executive Vice President & Chief Operating Officer*; Dave Bosher, *Vice President & Chief Financial Officer*; Bruce Thomas, *Vice President, Secretary & General Counsel*

Project Management: Tri-Pro, Inc.:
Don Fish, *President*; Joe Drescher, *Sr. Vice President*.

Marketing Agent: Locker Room Communications, Inc.
John Magee, *Director of Sales*; Peter Bruch, *Sales*; Dan Norman, *Compilation*;
Sherri Bees, *Administration*; Karen Schilling, *Assistant Administration*

Publishing Consultants: James Causey, Don J. Beville.

SIDELINES MAJOR CONTRIBUTORS

Byrd Press
Cadmus
   Communications, Inc.
Cadmus Marketing, Inc.
Caterpillar
Citibank
Coca-Cola

Delta Airlines
Gatorade
Locker Room
   Communications, Inc.
Marriott Corporation
NFL Properties, Inc.
Shapiro and Olander

Starter
Swiss Army Brands
Trench Manufacturing
Tri-Pro, Inc.
Upper Deck
Wilson
Zenith Data Systems

SIDELINES CONTRIBUTORS

3M Company
Action Images
Advocate/Abacus
American Tag Co.
Apex One
Athletic Supply
Avis Rent-A-Car
Betras Plastics
The Bibb Co.
Canon USA
Chalkline
Chattem Consumer
Chicagoland Processing
Clarin Corp.
Classic Balloon Corp.
Classic Carolina Collections-
   Dramtree
Cliff Engle, Inc.
Clorox
Commemorative Sports
   Fragrances, Inc.
Custom Edge
Davis & Jones
Diana Home Fashions
Emerson Flag
Eyelevel

Fan Dome
Fantasy Marketing
F.S.C. Wallcoverings
Fuji
General Electric
Georgia Pacific
Glidden
Gold Medal
Good Stuff
Greenleaf
GTE Telephone
H&H Furniture
Hi-Tech Expressions
Irvings Sport Shops
JAG Manufacturing
John Baum
Laserform
Leaf, Inc.
Life Fitness
Mack Sports Ltd.
Micro Sports
Miller Brewing Co.
Mobil
New York Life
Ocean Spray
Oscar Mayer-Louis Rich

Owens Corning
Perceived Images
Peter David-
   The California Mint
Polygram
Proper Framework
R. A. Designs
Realistic Designs
Riddell
Russ Berrie
Russell Corp.
Schuessler Knitting Mills
Schneidereit Glass
S. C. Johnson
Sports Impressions
Sports Marketing USA
Sportpads
The Stadium Store
Ted Provenza
Textile Designs
Tombstone Pizza
Toon Art
Unbalanced Lines Inc.
US Graphics
VPC Packaging & Displays